Schildt's Windows Programming in C and C++

Schildt's Windows 95 Programming in C and C++

Herbert Schildt

Osborne **McGraw-Hill**

Berkeley New York St. Louis San Francisco Auckland Bogotá Hamburg London Madrid Mexico City
Milan Montreal New Delhi Panama City Paris São Paulo Singapore Sydney Tokyo Toronto

Osborne **McGraw-Hill**
2600 Tenth Street
Berkeley, California 94710
U.S.A.

For information on translations or book distributors outside of the U.S.A.,
please write to Osborne **McGraw-Hill** at the above address.

Schildt's Windows 95 Programming in C and C++

9-12-96-1932998

This book is based on information on Windows 95 made public by Microsoft
as of 2/6/95. Since this information was made public before the release of the
product, we encourage you to visit your local bookstore after the product is
released for updated books on Windows 95.

If you have a modem or access to the Internet, you can always get
up-to-the-minute information on Windows 95 direct from Microsoft on
WinNews:

On CompuServe:	GO WINNEWS
On the Internet:	ftp://ftp.microsoft.com/PerOpSys/Win_News/Chicago
	http://www.microsoft.com
On AOL:	keyword WINNEWS
On Prodigy:	jumpword WINNEWS
On GEnie:	WINNEWS file area on Windows RTC

You can also subscribe to Microsoft's WinNews electronic newsletter by
sending Internet e-mail to enews@microsoft.nwnet.com and putting the
words SUBSCRIBE WINNEWS in the text of the e-mail.

Publisher
Lawrence Levitsky

Acquisitions Editor
Jeffrey M. Pepper

Project Editor
Emily Rader

Copy Editor
Vivian Jaquette

Proofreader
Linda Medoff

Indexer
Sheryl Schildt

Computer Designer
Roberta Steele

Illustrator
Rhys Elliot

Quality Control Specialist
Joe Scuderi

Cover Design
Ted Mader Associates

Contents at a Glance

Table of Contents

Introduction

The first time I saw Windows 95 run, I felt that something important was about to take place in the world of computing. As soon as I began to use it, I knew that the face of computing was going to change. The version I saw was a beta release, code named *Chicago*. Even this early beta had about it the feel of genius, the hint of greatness, and the smell of success. I immediately knew that Windows 95 was more than just the next release of Windows. It was *the* operating system designed to take computing into the 21st century.

Windows 95 is arguably the most flexible and powerful operating system designed for general purpose use on a PC. It is also very complex. Despite its complexity, it is one of the most thoroughly thought-out operating systems in existence and is logically consistent from one subsystem to the next. Once you have mastered its essentials and created a reserve of reusable code fragments, it is a pleasure to work with. Without question, learning to program for Windows 95 is worth all the time and effort you expend.

One of the joys of writing about Windows 95 is that it provides a nearly limitless range of topics to discuss. As soon as I finished one chapter, the next chapter's topic would immediately suggest itself. However, this blessing can also be a curse—it is difficult to *stop* writing about this exciting system! There is so much to say about Windows 95 that the hardest part of the task of writing this book was deciding which topics would be included and which would have to wait for subsequent books. I made the selections according to the following criteria. All programming essentials are discussed. That is, those elements common to all Windows 95 applications are thoroughly examined. Conversion from Windows 3.1 to Windows 95 is covered. Since many programmers will be converting older Windows code to the new

Windows 95 system, it is important to include information on this procedure. Finally, several features unique to Windows 95 are highlighted. These include the new common controls, consoles, and thread-based multitasking.

Whether you are converting older Windows 3.1 programs, or writing Windows-style programs for the first time, this book will help you accomplish your goals. It contains all the information you need to begin writing Windows 95 programs. It also lays a firm foundation upon which you may build your knowledge of Windows 95 in those specialized areas that apply to your own programming situation. Finally, it contains special Windows 3.1 conversion notes, which help fast-track the conversion process.

Who Is This Book for?

This book is for any programmer who wants to learn to write programs for Windows 95. It ***does not*** assume that you have written Windows 3.1 programs. However, it does assume that you are an accomplished C or C++ programmer. If you are new to C/C++, I suggest that you first take some time to learn it, because many Windows 95 constructs make use of rather sophisticated programming techniques. Specifically, you should have no trouble using pointers, structures, or unions.

Although this book ***does not*** assume that you are familiar with the essentials of operating system theory, Windows 95 is sufficiently sophisticated that you will have an easier time learning to program for it if you have some background or experience with operating system basics.

One last point: If you have never written Windows-style programs before, be patient! They are much different from the type of programs that you have been writing. However, by the end of Chapter 4, the overall structure of a Windows 95 program should be clear and you will have no trouble creating Windows 95 programs.

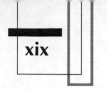

What Programming Tools You Will Need

The code in this book was written, compiled, and tested using Microsoft's Visual C++, version 2.0. You will need either this compiler or another C/C++ compiler that is designed to produce Windows 95-compatible object code.

H.S.
Mahomet, IL

Diskette Offer

There are many useful and interesting programs contained in this book. If you're like me, you probably would like to try them, but hate typing them into the computer. When I key in routines from a book, it always seems that I type something wrong and spend hours trying to get the program to work. This is especially true for Windows 95 programs, which tend to be long. For this reason, I am offering the source code on diskette for all the programs contained in this book for $24.95. Just fill in the order blank on the next page and mail it, along with your payment, to the address shown. Or, if you're in a hurry, just call (217) 586-4021 (the number of my consulting office) and place your order by telephone. You can also fax your order to (217) 586-4997. (VISA and MasterCard accepted.)

Please send me _____ copies, at $24.95 each, of the programs in *Schildt's Windows 95 Programming in C and C++* on an IBM-compatible diskette.

Foreign orders only: Checks must be drawn on a U.S bank. Please add $5.00 for shipping and handling.

_____
Name

_____
Address

_____ _____ _____
City   State   ZIP

_____
Telephone

Diskette size (check one): 5 1/4" _____   3 1/2"_____

Method of payment: Check_____   VISA_____   MC_____

Credit card number: _____

Expiration date: _____

Signature: _____

Send to:

   Herbert Schildt
   398 County Road 2500 N
   Mahomet, IL 61853

   Phone: (217) 586-4021
   Fax: (217) 586-4997

For Further Study

Schildt's Windows 95 Programming in C and C++ is just one of the many programming books written by Herbert Schildt. Here are some others that you will find of interest:

✦ To learn more about Windows, we recommend the *Osborne Windows Programming Series,* co-authored by Herbert Schildt. You will find it to be invaluable when trying to understand the complexities of Windows. The series titles are

> **Volume 1: Programming Fundamentals**
> **Volume 2: General Purpose API Functions**
> **Volume 3: Special Purpose API Functions**

✦ If you want to learn more about the C language, then the following titles will be of interest:

> **C: The Complete Reference**
> **The Annotated ANSI C Standard**
> **Teach Yourself C**

✦ To learn more about C++, you will find these books especially helpful:

> **C++: The Complete Reference**
> **Teach Yourself C++**
> **C++ From the Ground Up**

✦ Finally, here are some other books about C and C++ written by Herbert Schildt that you will find useful and interesting:

> **The Art of C**
> **The Craft of C**
> **Turbo C/C++: The Complete Reference**

When you need solid answers fast, turn to Herbert Schildt, the recognized authority on programming.

Chapter 1

Windows 95 Overview

This book is, first and foremost, a practical "how to" guide to Windows 95 programming. As such, it is not overly concerned with the theoretical aspects of Windows 95 except as they directly relate to writing programs. Instead, this book provides a hands-on approach that will have you writing Windows 95 applications as soon as possible.

The preceding paragraph notwithstanding, before you can become a Windows 95 programmer it is necessary that you understand in a general way how Windows 95 operates, what design concepts it embodies, and how it manages your computer. It is also important to understand how Windows 95 differs from its predecessors: DOS and Windows 3.1. Therefore, this chapter presents an overview of Windows 95 and discusses ways in which it relates to and differs from its forerunners.

If you have never written a Windows program before, then most of the information in this book will be new to you. Just be patient. If you proceed methodically, you will become an accomplished Windows 95 programmer by the time you finish this book. If you have programmed for Windows 3.1, then you will be able to advance more quickly, but be careful. There are some differences between Windows 95 and Windows 3.1 that will affect the way you write programs.

One more point: Windows 95 is a very large, complex programming environment. It cannot be fully described in one book. (Indeed, a full description would require several volumes!) This books covers those elements of Windows 95 programming that are common to all programs, that are frequently used, or that are important innovations unique to Windows 95. After you have completed this book, you will have sufficient understanding of Windows 95 programming to easily explore any of its other subsystems.

What Is Windows 95?

Windows 95 is part of the next generation of operating systems intended to operate PCs well into the next century. It was specifically designed to overcome several of the limitations imposed by its earlier incarnation: Windows 3.1. It also adds a substantial number of new features and provides a new and improved user interface.

Perhaps the single most important characteristic of Windows 95 is that it is a 32-bit operating system, as you will see when you progress through this book. By moving to a 32-bit implementation, Windows 95 has left behind many of the quirks and problems associated with the older 16-bit systems.

A primary design goal of Windows 95 was compatibility with both Windows 3.1 and with DOS—and the programs designed to run under them. That is, Windows 95 was designed to be compatible with the large base of existing PC applications. Toward this end, Windows 95 can run four types of programs: those written for DOS, those written for Windows 3.1, those written for Windows NT, and those written specifically for Windows 95. Windows 95 automatically creates the right environment for the type of program you run. For example, when you execute a DOS program, Windows 95 automatically creates a windowed command prompt in which the program runs.

Windows 95 Uses Thread-based Multitasking

As you almost certainly know, Windows 95 is a multitasking operating system. As such, it can run two or more programs concurrently. Of course, the programs share the CPU and do not, technically, run simultaneously; but because of the speed of the computer, they appear to. Windows 95 supports two forms of multitasking: process-based and thread-based. A *process* is a program that is executing. The fact that Windows 95 can multitask processes means that it can run more than one program at a time. Thus, Windows 95 supports the traditional, process-based multitasking with which you are probably familiar.

Windows 95's second form of multitasking is thread-based. A *thread* is a dispatchable unit of executable code. The name comes from the concept of a "thread of execution." All processes have at least one thread; a Windows 95 process may have several.

Since Windows 95 multitasks threads and each process can have more than one thread, this implies that it is possible for one process to have two or more pieces of itself executing simultaneously. As it turns out, this implication is correct. Therefore, when working with Windows 95, it is possible to multitask both programs and pieces of a single program. As you will see later in this book, this capability makes it possible to write very efficient programs.

The Windows 95 Call-based Interface

If you come from a DOS background, you know that you interface to DOS using various software interrupts. For example, the standard DOS interrupt is 0x21. While using a software interrupt to access DOS services is perfectly acceptable (given the limited scope of the DOS operating system), it is completely inadequate as a means of interfacing to a full-featured, multitasking operating system like Windows 95. Instead, Windows 95, like Windows 3.1 before it, uses a *call-based interface*.

The Windows 95 call-based interface uses a rich set of system-defined functions to access operating system features. Collectively, these functions are called the Application Programming Interface, or API for short. The API contains several hundred functions that your application program calls in order to communicate with Windows 95. These functions include all necessary operating system–related activities, such as memory allocation, outputting to the screen, creating windows, and the like.

Dynamic Link Libraries (DLLs)

Because the API consists of several hundred functions, you might be thinking that a large amount of code is linked into every program compiled for Windows 95, causing each program to contain much duplicate code.

However, this is not the case. Instead, the Windows 95 API functions are contained in *dynamic link libraries*, or DLLs for short, to which each program has access when executed. This section explains how dynamic linking works.

The Windows 95 API functions are stored in a relocatable format within a DLL. During the compilation phase, when your program calls an API function, the linker does not add the code for that function to the executable version of your program. Instead, it adds loading instructions for that function, such as what DLL it resides in and its name. When your program is executed, the necessary API routines are also loaded by the Windows 95 loader. In this way, each application program does not need to contain the actual API code. The API functions are added only when the application is loaded into memory for execution.

Dynamic linking has some very important benefits. First, since virtually all programs will use the API functions, DLLs prevent disk space from being wasted by the significant amount of duplicated object code that would be created if the API functions were actually added to each program's executable file on disk. Second, updates and enhancements to Windows 95 can be accomplished by changing the dynamic link library routines. Existing application programs do not need to be recompiled.

Windows 95 Versus Windows 3.1

While Windows 95 is the next step in the Windows product line, which began with the original release of Windows in 1985, it represents a major step forward in operating system design.The good news is that if you are familiar with Windows 3.1, you will have no trouble learning to use or program Windows 95. From the user's point of view, Windows 95 adds an improved interface and has moved toward a document-centered organization. Specifically, such fundamental items as the Program Manager and the File Manager have been replaced with the Start menu and the Explorer. However, if you can run Windows 3.1, you will feel at home with Windows 95. Things still work essentially the same way.

From the programmer's point of view, the more important good news is that you program for Windows 95 in much the same way that you did for Windows 3.1. Windows 95 preserves the name space of the original Windows API functions. The added functionality in Windows 95 generally comes from new functions. While there are some differences between Windows 3.1 and Windows 95, for the most part these differences are easy to accommodate. Also, old Windows 3.1 programs run fine under Windows 95, so you won't have to port all of your applications at once.

The following sections look at the differences between Windows 3.1 and Windows 95 in more detail.

Differences for the User

From the user's point of view, Windows 95 differs from Windows 3.1 in four major ways:

♦ The desktop interface has changed.

♦ The style of the window has been altered.

♦ New control elements are available to applications.

♦ DOS is not required to run it.

As mentioned, the Program Manager found in Windows 3.1 has been replaced by the Start menu. Furthermore, the desktop now contains a Task Bar. The Task Bar displays a list of all active tasks in the system and allows you to switch to a task by clicking on it. Most users will find the Start menu and Task Bar significant improvements over the Program Manager.

The appearance of windows under Windows 95 has been redesigned. To most users, the new look will seem more stylish and "snappy." One of the criticisms of Windows 3.1 was its rather "clunky" look. The look of Windows 95 has been updated for the better.

When you use Windows 95 applications, you will notice that several new control elements will appear quite frequently. Some of these are the toolbar, the spin control, the tree view, and the status bar. Windows 95 has defined several exciting, new *common controls* that any application may use. (You will learn how to handle several of these controls later in this book.) Using the new controls gives your application the modern look that will clearly identify it as a Windows 95 program.

As noted, Windows 95 does not require DOS. You probably know that Windows 3.1 was not a stand-alone operating system, but ran on top of DOS, which provided support for the file system. Windows 95 is a complete operating system, and DOS is no longer needed. However, Windows 95 still provides support for DOS programs. (In fact, some DOS programs run better under Windows 95 than they do under DOS!) Also, using Windows 95, you can have multiple "DOS" sessions.

Windows 95 also adds substantial functionality, including the ability to transparently run DOS programs. When you run a DOS program, a windowed command prompt interface is automatically created. Furthermore, this windowed command prompt is fully integrated into the overall Windows 95 graphical interface. Also, you can now execute Windows programs directly from the prompt. (Under Windows 3.1, you had to execute Windows programs from within Windows.)

Another new feature of Windows 95 is its support for long filenames. As you probably know, DOS and Windows 3.1 only allowed eight-character filenames followed by a three-character extension. Windows 95 allows filenames as long as 255 characters.

Windows 95 includes a number of accessories and administrative tools not supported by Windows 3.1. For example, Windows 95 supports portable computing, e-mail, pen-based computing, and remote computing. It also supports *"plug and play,"* a feature that allows the easy installation of new hardware components.

Differences for the Programmer

From the programmer's point of view, there are two main differences between Windows 3.1 and Windows 95. First, Windows 95 supports full 32-bit addressing and uses virtual memory. Windows 3.1 uses a 16-bit segmented addressing mode. For many application programs, this difference will have little effect. For others, the effect will be substantial. Frankly, while the transition may not be painless, you will find the Windows 95 32-bit memory model much easier to program for.

The second major difference concerns the way that multitasking is accomplished. Windows 3.1 uses a nonpreemptive approach to task switching. This means that a Windows 3.1 task must manually return control to the scheduler in order for another task to run. In other words, a Windows 3.1 program retains control of the CPU until it decides to give it up. Therefore, an ill-behaved program could monopolize the CPU. By contrast, Windows 95 uses preemptive, time-slice–based tasking. In this scheme, tasks are automatically preempted by Windows 95, and the CPU is then assigned to the next task (if one exists). Preemptive multitasking is generally the superior method, because it allows the operating system to fully control tasking and prevents one task from dominating the system. Most programmers view the move to preemptive multitasking as a step forward.

In addition to the two major changes just described, Windows 95 differs from Windows 3.1 in some other, less dramatic ways, which are described here.

Input Queues

Input queues hold messages, such as a keypress or mouse activity, until they can be sent to your program. In Windows 3.1, there is just one input queue for all tasks running in the system. However, Windows 95 supplies each thread with its own input queue. The advantage to each thread having its own queue is that no one process can reduce system performance by responding slowly to its messages.

Although multiple input queues are an important addition, this change has no direct impact on how you program for Windows 95.

Threads and Processes

Windows 3.1 only supports process-based multitasking. That is, the *process* is Windows 3.1's smallest dispatchable unit. As mentioned earlier, Windows 95 multitasks both threads and processes. While older Windows programs will run fine under Windows 95 without any changes, you may want to enhance them to take advantage of thread-based multitasking.

Consoles

In the past, text-based (i.e., nonwindowed) applications were fairly inconvenient to use from Windows. However, Windows 95 supports a special type of window called a *console*. A console window provides a standard text-based interface, command-prompt environment. However, aside from being text-based, a console acts and can be manipulated like other windows. The addition of the text-based console not only allows nonwindowed applications to run in a full Windows environment but also makes it more convenient for you to create short, throwaway utility programs. Perhaps more importantly, the inclusion of consoles in Windows 95 is a final acknowledgment that some text-based applications make sense, and now they can be managed as part of the overall Windows environment. In essence, the addition of console windows completes the Windows application environment.

Flat Addressing

Windows 95 applications have available to them 4 gigabytes of virtual memory in which to run! Further, this address space is *flat*. Unlike Windows 3.1, DOS, and other 8086-family operating systems, which use segmented memory, Windows 95 treats memory as though it were linear. And because it virtualizes memory, each application has as much memory as it could possibly (and reasonably) want. While the change to flat addressing is mostly transparent to the programmer, it does relieve much of the tedium and frustration of dealing with the old segmented approach.

Changes to Messages and Parameter Types

Because of Windows 95's shift to 32-bit addressing, some messages passed to a Windows 95 program will be organized differently than they are when passed to a Windows 3.1 program. Also, the parameter types used to declare a window function have changed because of the move to 32-bit addressing. The specific changes to the messages and parameters will be discussed later in this book, as they are used.

New Common Controls

Windows 3.1 supports several standard controls such as push buttons, check boxes, radio buttons, edit boxes, and the like. While Windows 95 includes support of these standard controls, it also defines several new ones. The new controls added by Windows 95 are called *common controls*. The common controls include such things as toolbars, tool tips, status bars, progress bars, track bars, and tree views (to name just a few). The new controls improve the user interface and give a "modern" look to applications that use them.

The NT Connection

You have probably heard about Windows NT. Perhaps you have even used it. Windows NT is Microsoft's high-end Windows-based operating system. Windows NT has much in common with Windows 95. Both support 32-bit, flat addressing. Both support thread-based multitasking. And both support the console-based interface. However, Windows 95 is *not* Windows NT. For example, Windows NT uses a special approach to operating system implementation based on the client/server model. Windows 95 does not. Windows NT supports a full security system; Windows 95 does not. While there is no doubt that much of the basic technology developed for use in Windows NT eventually found its way into Windows 95, the two versions are not identical.

What Software Is Needed

The code in this book was compiled using Microsoft's Visual C++ 2.0. By the time you read this book, you will probably be able to choose from several other compilers to create Windows 95 code. You should be able to compile the programs in this book using any Windows 95–compatible compiler. The examples in this book are written in standard C/C++ so that they can be compiled by any C/C++ compiler.

Conversion Notes

One of the first jobs you will likely face when programming for Windows 95 is the conversion of Windows 3.1 applications. To aid in this process, notes on Windows 3.1 conversion are included throughout the text. While conversion of Windows 3.1 applications to Windows 95 is not fundamentally difficult, several important differences will be highlighted.

Chapter 2

Windows 95 Programming Overview

This chapter introduces Windows 95 programming. It has two main purposes. First, it discusses how a program must interact with Windows 95 and what rules must be followed by every Windows 95 application. Second, it develops an application skeleton that will be used as a basis for the other Windows 95 programs developed in this book. As you will see, all Windows 95 programs share several common traits. It is these shared attributes that will be contained in the application skeleton.

As mentioned in Chapter 1, although they are similar in spirit, there are significant differences between Windows 3.1 and Windows 95. These differences will be discussed as they occur. Pay special attention to the differences if you will be porting older applications.

To begin, this chapter presents the Windows 95 programming perspective.

Note: If you already know how to write programs for Windows 3.1, then you are already familiar with many of the fundamental Windows programming concepts and techniques contained in this and the next few chapters. (In fact, Windows 3.1 and Windows 95 programs are, on the surface, almost identical.) However, you should at least skim through these chapters because there are differences between Windows 3.1 and Windows 95 that you need to understand.

Windows 95 Programming Perspective

The goal of Windows 95 (and Windows in general) is to enable a person who has basic familiarity with the system to sit down and run virtually any application without prior training. To accomplish this end, Windows provides a consistent interface to the user. In theory, if you can run one Windows-based program, you can run them all. Of course, in actuality, most useful programs will still require some sort of training in order to be used effectively, but at least this instruction can be restricted to *what* the program *does*, not *how* the user must *interact* with it. In fact, much of the code in a Windows application is there just to support the user interface.

Before continuing, it must be stated that not every program that runs under Windows 95 will necessarily present the user with a Windows-style interface. It is possible to write Windows programs that do not take advantage of the Windows interface elements. To create a Windows-style program, you must purposely do so using the techniques described in this book. Only those programs written to take advantage of Windows will look and feel like Windows programs. While you can override the basic Windows design philosophy, you had better have a good reason to do so, because the users of your programs will, most likely, be very disturbed. In general, any application programs you are writing for Windows 95 should utilize the normal Windows interface and conform to the standard Windows design practices.

Windows 95 is graphics-oriented, which means that it provides a Graphical User Interface (GUI). While graphics hardware and video modes are quite diverse, many of the differences are handled by Windows. This means that, for the most part, your program does not need to worry about what type of graphics hardware or video mode is being used. However, because of its graphical orientation, you as the programmer have added responsibility when creating Windows applications. As you will see, many chapters in this book are devoted to the correct management of the screen.

Let's look at a few of the more important features of Windows 95.

The Desktop Model

2

With few exceptions, the point of a window-based user interface is to provide the equivalent of a desktop on the screen. On a desk you might find several different pieces of paper, one on top of another, often with fragments of different pages visible beneath the top page. The equivalent of the desktop in Windows is the screen. The equivalents of pieces of paper are represented by windows on the screen. On a desk you may move pieces of paper about, maybe switching which piece of paper is on top or how much of another is exposed to view. Windows allows the same type of operations on its windows. By selecting a window, you can make it current, which means putting it on top of all the other open windows. You can enlarge or shrink a window, or move it about on the screen. In short, Windows lets you control the surface of the screen the way you control the items on your desk.

While the desktop model forms the foundation of the Windows 95 user interface, the program is not limited by it. In fact, several Windows 95 innovations are interface elements that emulate other types of familiar devices, such as slider controls, spin controls, tree lists, and toolbars. As you will see, Windows 95 gives you, the programmer, a large array of features from which you may choose those most appropriate to your specific application.

The Mouse

Like preceding versions of Windows, Windows 95 allows the use of the mouse for almost all control, selection, and drawing operations. Of course, to say that it *allows* the use of the mouse is an understatement. The fact is that the Windows 95 interface was *designed for the mouse*—it *allows* the use of the keyboard! Although it is certainly possible for an application program to ignore the mouse, it does so only in violation of a basic Windows design principle.

Icons and Bitmaps

Windows 95 encourages the use of icons and bitmaps (graphics images). The theory behind the use of icons and bitmaps is found in the old adage "a picture is worth a thousand words."

An icon is a small symbol that is used to represent some operation or program. Generally, the operation or program can be activated by selecting the icon. A bitmap is often used to convey information quickly and simply to the user. However, bitmaps can also be used as menu elements.

Menus, Toolbars, Status Bars, and Dialog Boxes

Aside from standard windows, Windows 95 also provides several special-purpose windows. The most common of these are the menu, the toolbar, the status bar, and the dialog box. A *menu* is, as you would expect, a special window that contains only a menu from which the user makes a selection. However, instead of having to provide the menu selection functions in your program, you simply create a standard menu using built-in menu-selection functions.

A *toolbar* is essentially a special type of menu that displays its options using small graphics images (icons). The user selects an object by clicking on the desired image. A *status bar* is a bar located on the bottom of a window that displays status information related to an application. Both toolbars and status bars are innovations added by Windows 95. They did not exist as standard elements in prior versions of Windows.

A *dialog box* is a special window that allows more complex interaction with the application than that allowed by a menu or toolbar. For example, your application might use a dialog box to request a filename. With few exceptions, non-menu input is accomplished via a dialog box.

How Windows 95 and Your Program Interact

When you write a program for many operating systems, it is your program that initiates interaction with the operating system. For example, in a DOS program, it is the program that requests such things as input and output. Put differently, programs written in the "traditional way" call the operating system. The operating system does not call your program. However, Windows 95 generally works in the opposite way. It is Windows 95 that calls your program. The process works like this: Your Windows 95 program waits until it is sent a *message* by Windows. The message is passed to your program through a special function that is called by Windows. Once a message is received, your program is expected to take an appropriate action. While your program may call one or more Windows 95 API functions when responding to a message, it is still Windows 95 that initiates the activity. More than anything else, it is the message-based interaction with Windows 95 that dictates the general form of all Windows 95 programs.

There are many different types of messages that Windows 95 may send your program. For example, each time the mouse is clicked on a window belonging to your program, a mouse-clicked message will be sent to your program. Another type of message is sent each time a window belonging to your program must be redrawn. Still another message is sent each time the user presses a key when your program is the focus of input. Keep one fact firmly in mind: as far as your program is concerned, messages arrive randomly. This is why Windows 95 programs resemble interrupt-driven programs. You can't know what message will be next.

2

The Win32 API: The Windows 95 API

In general, the Windows environment is accessed through a call-based interface called the Application Program Interface (API). The API consists of several hundred functions that your program calls as needed. The API functions provide all the system services performed by Windows 95. There is a subset to the API called the Graphics Device Interface (GDI), which is the part of Windows that provides device-independent graphics support. It is the GDI functions that make it possible for a Windows application to run on a variety of hardware.

Windows 95 programs use the Win32 API. For the most part, Win32 is a superset of the older Windows 3.1 API (Win16). Indeed, for the most part the functions are called by the same name and are used in the same way. However, even though similar in spirit and purpose, the two APIs differ because, as mentioned in Chapter 1, Win32 supports 32-bit addressing while Win16 supports only the 16-bit, segmented-memory model. Because of this difference, several of the older API functions have been widened to accept 32-bit arguments and return 32-bit values. Also, a few API functions have had to be altered to accommodate the 32-bit architecture. API functions have also been added to support the new approach to multitasking, its new interface elements, and the other enhanced Windows 95 features. If you are new to Windows programming in general, these changes will not affect you significantly. However, if you will be porting code from Windows 3.1 to Windows 95, then you will need to carefully examine the arguments you pass to each API function.

Because Windows 95 supports full 32-bit addressing, it makes sense that integers are also 32 bits long. This means that types **int** and **unsigned** are 32 bits long, not 16 bits, as is the case for Windows 3.1. If you want to use a 16-bit integer, it must be declared as **short**. (Windows 95 provides portable **typedef** names for these types, as you will see shortly.) Therefore, if you will be porting code from the 16-bit environment, you will need to check your use of integers because they will automatically be expanded from 16 to 32 bits and side effects may result.

Another result of 32-bit addressing is that pointers no longer need to be declared as **near** or **far**. Any pointer can access any part of memory. In Windows 95, both **far** and **near** are defined as nothing. This means you can leave **far** and **near** in your programs when porting to Windows 95, but they will have no effect.

The Components of a Window

Before we move on to specific aspects of Windows 95 programming, a few important terms need to be defined. Figure 2-1 shows a standard window with each of its elements pointed out.

All windows have a border that defines the limits of the window; the borders are also used when resizing the window. At the top of the window are several items. On the far left is the system menu icon (also called the title bar icon). Clicking on this box displays the system menu. To the right of the system menu icon is the window's title. At the far right are the minimize, maximize, and close icon boxes. (Previous versions of Windows did not include a close box. This is a Windows 95 innovation.) The client area is the part of the window in which your program activity takes place. Most windows also have horizontal and vertical scroll bars that are used to move information through the window.

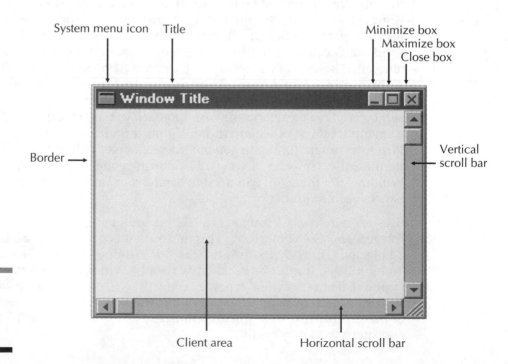

The elements of a standard window

Figure 2-1.

Some Windows 95 Application Basics

Some basic concepts common to all Windows 95 programs need to be discussed before we develop the Windows 95 application skeleton.

WinMain( )

All Windows 95 programs begin execution with a call to **WinMain( )**. (Windows programs do not have a **main( )** function.) **WinMain( )** has some special properties that differentiate it from other functions in your application. First, it must be compiled using the **WINAPI** calling convention. (You will see **APIENTRY** used as well. They both mean the same thing.) By default, functions in your C or C++ programs use the C calling convention. However, it is possible to compile a function so that it uses a different calling convention; Pascal is a common alternative. For various technical reasons, the calling convention Windows 95 uses to call **WinMain( )** is **WINAPI**. The return type of **WinMain( )** should be **int**.

 In older Windows 3.1 programs, the calling convention used for WinMain( ) was FAR PASCAL. However, this should be changed to WINAPI when porting existing applications to Windows 95.

The Window Function

All Windows 95 programs must contain a special function that is *not* called by your program, but is called by Windows 95. This function is generally called the *window function* or the *window procedure*. The window function is called by Windows 95 when it needs to pass a message to your program. It is through this function that Windows 95 communicates with your program. The window function receives the message in its parameters. All window functions must be declared as returning type **LRESULT CALLBACK**. The type **LRESULT** is a **typedef** that, at the time of this writing, is another name for a long integer. The **CALLBACK** calling convention is used with those functions that will be called by Windows 95. In Windows terminology, any function that is called by Windows is referred to as a *callback* function.

 Windows 3.1 code specifies the window function as LONG FAR PASCAL. However, while Windows 95 still allows this definition, for the sake of portability, you should use LRESULT CALLBACK for all of your new Windows 95 code. This will allow future Windows changes to be transparent to your code.

In addition to receiving the messages sent by Windows 95, the window function must initiate any actions indicated by a message. Typically, a window function's body consists of a **switch** statement that links a specific response to each message that the program will respond to. Your program need not respond to every message that Windows 95 sends. For messages that your program doesn't care about, you can let Windows 95 provide default processing. Since there are hundreds of different messages that Windows 95 can generate, it is common for most messages simply to be processed by Windows 95 and not by your program.

All messages are 32-bit integer values. Furthermore, all messages are linked with any additional information that the messages require.

Window Classes

When your Windows 95 program first begins execution, it will need to define and register a *window class*. (Here, the word *class* is not being used in its C++ sense. Rather, it means *style* or *type*.) When you register a window class, you are telling Windows 95 about the form and function of the window. However, registering the window class does not cause a window to come into existence. To actually create a window requires additional steps.

The Message Loop

As explained earlier, Windows 95 communicates with your program by sending it messages. All Windows 95 applications must establish a *message loop* inside the **WinMain( )** function. This loop reads any pending message from the application's message queue and dispatches that message back to Windows 95, which then calls your program's window function with that message as a parameter. This may seem to be an overly complex way of passing messages, but it is, nevertheless, the way that all Windows programs must function. (Part of the reason for this scheme is to return control to Windows 95 so that the scheduler can allocate CPU time as it sees fit rather than waiting for your application's time slice to end.)

Windows Data Types

As you will soon see, Windows 95 programs do not make extensive use of standard C/C++ data types, such as **int** or **char ***. Instead, all data types used by Windows 95 have been **typedef**ed within the **windows.h** file and/or its related files. The **windows.h** file is supplied by Microsoft (and any other company that makes a Windows 95 C/C++ compiler) and must be included in all Windows 95 programs. Some of the most common types are **HANDLE, HWND, BYTE, WORD, DWORD, UINT, LONG, BOOL, LPSTR**, and **LPCSTR. HANDLE** is a 32-bit integer that is used as a handle. As you will see, there are a number of handle types, but they are all the same size as **HANDLE**. A *handle* is simply a value that identifies some resource.

Also, all handle types begin with an H. For example, **HWND** is a 32-bit integer used as a window handle. **BYTE** is an 8-bit unsigned character. **WORD** is a 16-bit unsigned short integer. **DWORD** is an unsigned long integer. **UINT** is a 32-bit unsigned integer. **LONG** is another name for **long**. **BOOL** is an integer. This type is used to indicate values that are either true or false. **LPSTR** is a pointer to a string, and **LPCSTR** is a **const** pointer to a string.

In addition to the basic types described above, Windows 95 defines several structures. The two that are needed by the skeleton program are **MSG** and **WNDCLASS**. The **MSG** structure holds a Windows 95 message, and **WNDCLASS** is a structure that defines a window class. These structures will be discussed later in this chapter.

 UINT is a 32-bit unsigned integer when compiling Windows 95 programs. It is a 16-bit unsigned integer if you compile your code for Windows 3.1. Remember this when porting applications to Windows 95.

A Windows 95 Skeleton

Now that the necessary background information has been covered, it's time to develop a minimal Windows 95 application. As stated, all Windows 95 programs have certain things in common. This section develops a Windows 95 skeleton that provides these necessary features. In the world of Windows programming, application skeletons are commonly used because there is a substantial "price of admission" when creating a Windows program. Unlike DOS programs that you may have written, in which a minimal program is about five lines long, a minimal Windows program is approximately 50 lines long.

A minimal Windows 95 program contains two functions: **WinMain( )** and the window function. The **WinMain( )** function must perform the following general steps:

1. Define a window class.
2. Register that class with Windows 95.
3. Create a window of that class.
4. Display the window.
5. Begin running the message loop.

The window function must respond to all relevant messages. Since the skeleton program does nothing but display its window, the only message that it must respond to is the one telling the application that the user has terminated the program.

Before considering the specifics, examine the following program, which is a minimal Windows 95 skeleton. It creates a standard window that includes a title. The window also contains the system menu and is, therefore, capable of being minimized, maximized, moved, resized, and closed. It also contains the standard minimize, maximize, and close boxes.

```c
/* A minimal Windows 95 skeleton. */

#include <windows.h>

LRESULT CALLBACK WindowFunc(HWND, UINT, WPARAM, LPARAM);

char szWinName[] = "MyWin"; /* name of window class */

int WINAPI WinMain(HINSTANCE hThisInst, HINSTANCE hPrevInst,
                   LPSTR lpszArgs, int nWinMode)
{
  HWND hwnd;
  MSG msg;
  WNDCLASS wcl;

  /* Define a window class. */
  wcl.hInstance = hThisInst; /* handle to this instance */
  wcl.lpszClassName = szWinName; /* window class name */
  wcl.lpfnWndProc = WindowFunc; /* window function */
  wcl.style = 0; /* default style */

  wcl.hIcon = LoadIcon(NULL, IDI_APPLICATION); /* icon style */
  wcl.hCursor = LoadCursor(NULL, IDC_ARROW); /* cursor style */
  wcl.lpszMenuName = NULL; /* no menu */

  wcl.cbClsExtra = 0; /* no extra */
  wcl.cbWndExtra = 0; /* information needed */

  /* Make the window background white. */
  wcl.hbrBackground = (HBRUSH) GetStockObject(WHITE_BRUSH);

  /* Register the window class. */
  if(!RegisterClass (&wcl)) return 0;

  /* Now that a window class has been registered, a window
     can be created. */
  hwnd = CreateWindow(
    szWinName, /* name of window class */
    "Windows 95 Skeleton", /* title */
    WS_OVERLAPPEDWINDOW, /* window style - normal */
    CW_USEDEFAULT, /* X coordinate - let Windows decide */
```

2

```
      CW_USEDEFAULT, /* Y coordinate - let Windows decide */
      CW_USEDEFAULT, /* width - let Windows decide */
      CW_USEDEFAULT, /* height - let Windows decide */
      HWND_DESKTOP, /* no parent window */
      NULL, /* no menu */
      hThisInst, /* handle of this instance of the program */
      NULL /* no additional arguments */
    );

    /* Display the window. */
    ShowWindow(hwnd, nWinMode);
    UpdateWindow(hwnd);

    /* Create the message loop. */
    while(GetMessage(&msg, NULL, 0, 0))
    {
      TranslateMessage(&msg); /* allow use of keyboard */
      DispatchMessage(&msg); /* return control to Windows */
    }
    return msg.wParam;
}

/* This function is called by Windows 95 and is passed
   messages from the message queue.
*/
LRESULT CALLBACK WindowFunc(HWND hwnd, UINT message,
                            WPARAM wParam, LPARAM lParam)
{
  switch(message) {
    case WM_DESTROY: /* terminate the program */
      PostQuitMessage(0);
      break;
    default:
      /* Let Windows 95 process any messages not specified in
         the preceding switch statement. */
      return DefWindowProc(hwnd, message, wParam, lParam);
  }
  return 0;
}
```

Now let's go through this program step by step.

First, all Windows 95 programs must include the header file **windows.h**. As stated, this file (along with its support files) contains the API function prototypes and various types, macros, and definitions used by Windows 95. For example, the data types **HWND** and **WNDCLASS** are defined in **windows.h**.

The window function used by the program is called **WindowFunc( )**. It is declared as a callback function, because this is the function that Windows 95 calls to communicate with the program.

Program execution begins with **WinMain( ),** which is passed four parameters. **hThisInst** and **hPrevInst** are handles. **hThisInst** refers to the current instance of the program. Remember, Windows 95 is a multitasking system, so more than one instance of your program may be running at the same time. **hPrevInst** will always be NULL. (In Windows 3.1 programs, **hPrevInst** would be non-zero if there were other instances of the program currently executing, but this doesn't apply in Windows 95.) The **lpszArgs** parameter is a pointer to a string that holds any command line arguments specified when the application was begun. The **nWinMode** parameter contains a value that determines how the window will be displayed when your program begins execution.

Inside the function, three variables are created. The **hwnd** variable will hold the handle to the program's window. The **msg** structure variable will hold window messages, and the **wcl** structure variable will be used to define the window class.

As mentioned above, the hPrevInst parameter will always be NULL in a Windows 95 program. This is because of a fundamental change made between Windows 3.1 and Windows 95. In Windows 3.1, multiple instances of a program share window classes and various other bits of data. Therefore, it is important for an application to know if another version of itself is running in the system. However, in Windows 95 each process is isolated from the next; there is no automatic sharing of window classes and the like. The only reason that hPrevInst exists in Windows 95 is for the sake of compatibility.

Defining the Window Class

The first two actions that **WinMain( )** takes are to define a window class and then register it. A window class is defined by filling in the fields defined by the **WNDCLASS** structure. Its fields are shown here:

```
UINT style; /* type of window */
WNDPROC lpfnWndProc; /* address to window func */
int cbClsExtra; /* extra class info */
int cbWndExtra; /* extra window info */
HINSTANCE hInstance; /* handle of this instance */
HICON hIcon; /* handle of minimized icon */
HCURSOR hCursor; /* handle of mouse cursor */
HBRUSH hbrBackground; /* background color */
LPCSTR lpszMenuName; /* name of main menu */
LPCSTR lpszClassName; /* name of window class */
```

As you can see by looking at the program, the **hInstance** field is assigned the current instance handle as specified by **hThisInst**. The name of the window class is pointed to by **lpszClassName**, which points to the string "MyWin" in this case. The address of the window function is assigned to **lpfnWndProc**. No default style is specified, and no extra information is needed.

In Windows 3.1, each window class must be registered only once. Therefore, if another instance of the program is running, then the current instance must not define and register the window class. To avoid this possibility, the value of hPrevInst is tested. If it is non-zero, then the window class has already been registered by a previous instance. If not, then the window class is defined and registered. However, this test is no longer needed by Windows 95 and is not included in any of the examples in this book. You may wish to include it for downward compatibility with Windows 3.1, though, since doing so causes no harm.

All Windows applications need to define a default shape for the mouse cursor and for the application's icon. An application can define its own custom version of these resources, or it may use one of the built-in styles, as the skeleton does. The style of the icon is loaded by the API function **LoadIcon( )**, whose prototype is shown here:

HICON LoadIcon(HINSTANCE *hInst*, LPCSTR *lpszName*);

This function returns a handle to an icon. Here, *hInst* specifies the handle of the module that contains the icon, and the icon name is specified in *lpszName*. However, to use one of the built-in icons, you must use **NULL** for the first parameter and specify one of the following macros for the second.

Icon Macro	Shape
IDI_APPLICATION	Default icon
IDI_ASTERISK	Information icon
IDI_EXCLAMATION	Exclamation point icon
IDI_HAND	Stop sign
IDI_QUESTION	Question mark icon

To load the mouse cursor, use the API **LoadCursor( )** function. This function has the following prototype:

HCURSOR LoadCursor(HINSTANCE *hInst*, LPCSTR *lpszName*);

This function returns a handle to a cursor resource. Here, *hInst* specifies the handle of the module that contains the mouse cursor, and the name of the mouse cursor is specified in *lpszName*. However, to use one of the built-in cursors, you must use **NULL** for the first parameter and specify one of the built-in cursors, using its macro, for the second parameter. Some of the most common built-in cursors are shown here.

Cursor Macro	Shape
IDC_ARROW	Default arrow pointer
IDC_CROSS	Cross hairs
IDC_IBEAM	Vertical I-beam
IDC_WAIT	Hourglass

The background color of the window created by the skeleton is specified as white, and a handle to this *brush* is obtained using the API function **GetStockObject( )**. A brush is a resource that paints the screen using a predetermined size, color, and pattern. The function **GetStockObject( )** is used to obtain a handle to a number of standard display objects, including brushes, pens (which draw lines), and character fonts. It has this prototype:

HGDIOBJ GetStockObject(int *object*);

The function returns a handle to the object specified by *object*. (The type **HGDIOBJ** is a GDI handle.) Here are some of the built-in brushes available to your program:

Brush Macro	Background Type
BLACK_BRUSH	Black
DKGRAY_BRUSH	Dark gray
HOLLOW_BRUSH	See-through window
LTGRAY_BRUSH	Light gray
WHITE_BRUSH	White

You can use these macros as parameters to **GetStockObject( )** to obtain a brush.

Once the window class has been fully specified, it is registered with Windows 95 using the API function **RegisterClass( )**, whose prototype is shown here:

ATOM RegisterClass(CONST WNDCLASS *lpWClass*);

The function returns a value that identifies the window class. **ATOM** is a **typedef** that means **WORD**. Each window class is given a unique value. *lpWClass* must be the address of the **WNDCLASS** structure.

In Windows 3.1, Register Class( ) returns a Boolean value indicating success (true) or failure (false). This has been changed in Windows 95 to a return value that identifies the class.

Creating a Window

Once a window class has been defined and registered, your application can actually create a window of that class using the API function **CreateWindow( )**, whose prototype is shown here.

```
HWND CreateWindow(
  LPCSTR lpClassName, /* name of window class */
  LPCSTR lpWinName, /* title of window */
  DWORD dwStyle, /* type of window */
  int X, int Y, /* upper-left coordinates */
  int Width, int Height, /* dimensions of window */
  HWND hParent, /* handle of parent window */
  HMENU hMenu, /* handle of main menu */
  HINSTANCE hThisInst, /* handle of creator */
  LPVOID lpszAdditional /* pointer to additional info */
);
```

As you can see by looking at the skeleton program, many of the parameters to **CreateWindow( )** may be defaulted or specified as NULL. In fact, most often the *X, Y, Width*, and *Height* parameters will simply use the macro **CW_USEDEFAULT**, which tells Windows 95 to select an appropriate size and location for the window. If the window has no parent, which is the case in the skeleton, then *hParent* must be specified as **HWND_DESKTOP**. (You may also use NULL for this parameter.) If the window does not contain a main menu, then *hMenu* must be NULL. Also, if no additional information is required, as is most often the case, then *lpszAdditional* is NULL. (The type **LPVOID** is **typedef**ed as **void ***. Historically, **LPVOID** stands for "long pointer to **void**.")

The remaining four parameters must be set explicitly by your program. First, *lpszClassName* must point to the name of the window class. (This is the name you gave it when it was registered.) The title of the window is a string pointed to by *lpszWinName*. This can be a null string, but usually a window will be given a title. The style (or type) of window actually created is determined by the value of *dwStyle*. The macro **WS_OVERLAPPEDWINDOW** specifies a standard window that has a system menu, a border, and minimize, maximize, and close boxes. While this style of window is the most common, you can construct one to your own specifications. To accomplish this, you simply OR together the various style macros that you want. Some other common styles are shown next:

Style Macros	Window Feature
WS_OVERLAPPED	Overlapped window with border
WS_MAXIMIZEBOX	Maximize box
WS_MINIMIZEBOX	Minimize box
WS_SYSMENU	System menu
WS_HSCROLL	Horizontal scroll bar
WS_VSCROLL	Vertical scroll bar

The *hThisInst* parameter must contain the current instance handle of the application.

The **CreateWindow( )** function returns the handle of the window it creates or NULL if the window cannot be created.

Once the window has been created, it still is not displayed on the screen. To cause the window to be displayed, call the **ShowWindow( )** API function. This function has the following prototype:

BOOL ShowWindow(HWND *hwnd*, int *nHow*);

The handle of the window to display is specified in *hwnd*. The display mode is specified in *nHow*. The first time the window is displayed, you will want to pass **WinMain( )**'s **nWinMode** as the *nHow* parameter. Remember, the value of **nWinMode** determines how the window will be displayed when the program begins execution. Subsequent calls can display (or remove) the window as necessary. Some common values for *nHow* are shown here:

Display Macros	Effect
SW_HIDE	Removes the window
SW_MINIMIZE	Minimizes the window into an icon
SW_MAXIMIZE	Maximizes the window
SW_RESTORE	Returns a window to normal size

The **ShowWindow( )** function returns the previous display status of the window. If the window was displayed, then non-zero is returned. If the window has not been displayed, zero is returned.

Although not technically necessary for the skeleton, a call to **UpdateWindow( )** is included because it is needed by virtually every Windows 95 application that you will create. It essentially tells Windows 95 to send a message to your application that the main window needs to be updated. (This message will be discussed in the next chapter.)

The Message Loop

The final part of the skeletal **WinMain( )** is the *message loop*. The message loop is a part of all Windows applications. Its purpose is to receive and process messages sent by Windows 95. When an application is running, it is continually being sent messages. These messages are stored in the application's message queue until they can be read and processed. Each time your application is ready to read another message, it must call the API function **GetMessage( )**, which has this prototype:

BOOL GetMessage(LPMSG *msg*, HWND *hwnd*, UINT *min*, UINT *max*);

The message will be received by the structure pointed to by *msg*. All Windows messages are of structure type **MSG**, shown here.

```
/* Message structure */
typedef struct tagMSG
{
  HWND hwnd; /* window that message is for */
  UINT message; /* message */
  WPARAM wParam; /* message-dependent info */
  LPARAM lParam; /* more message-dependent info */
  DWORD time; /* time message posted */
  POINT pt; /* X,Y location of mouse */
} MSG;
```

In **MSG**, the handle of the window for which the message is intended is contained in **hwnd**. All Win32 messages are 32-bit integers, and the message is contained in **message**. Additional information relating to each message is passed in **wParam** and **lParam.** The type **WPARAM** is a **typedef** for **UINT**, and **LPARAM** is a **typedef** for **LONG**.

 The message field of MSG is 16 bits long in Windows 3.1, but it is widened to 32 bits for Win32. Also, the wParam field, which is 16 bits in Windows 3.1, has been widened to 32 bits in Win32. Be aware of these changes when porting code.

The time the message was sent (posted) is specified in milliseconds in the **time** field.

The **pt** member will contain the coordinates of the mouse when the message was sent. The coordinates are held in a **POINT** structure, which is defined like this:

```
typedef struct tagPOINT {
  LONG x, y;
} POINT;
```

 In Windows 3.1, the x and y in the POINT structure are declared as integers. However, in Windows 95 (Win32), they are widened to LONG.

If there are no messages in the application's message queue, then a call to **GetMessage( )** will pass control back to Windows 95. (We will explore messages in greater detail in the next chapter.)

The *hwnd* parameter to **GetMessage( )** specifies the window for which messages will be obtained. It is possible, and even likely, that an application will contain several windows, but you only want to receive messages for a specific window. If you want to receive all messages directed at your application, this parameter must be NULL.

The remaining two parameters to **GetMessage( )** specify a range of messages that will be received. Generally, you want your application to receive all messages. To accomplish this, specify both *min* and *max* as 0, as the skeleton does.

GetMessage( ) returns zero when the user terminates the program, causing the message loop to terminate. Otherwise it returns non-zero.

Inside the message loop, two functions are called. The first is the API function **TranslateMessage( )**. This function translates virtual key codes generated by Windows 95 into character messages. (Virtual keys are discussed in Chapter 4.) Although it is not necessary for all applications, most applications call **TranslateMessage( )** because it is needed to allow full integration of the keyboard into your application program.

Once the message has been read and translated, it is dispatched back to Windows 95 using the **DispatchMessage( )** API function. Windows 95 then holds this message until it can be passed to the program's window function.

Once the message loop terminates, the **WinMain( )** function ends by returning the value of **msg.wParam** to Windows 95. This value contains the return code generated when your program terminates.

The Window Function

The second function in the application skeleton is its window function. In this case the function is called **WindowFunc( )**, but it could have any name you like. The window function is passed the first four members of the **MSG** structure as parameters. For the skeleton, the only parameter used is the message itself. However, in the next chapter you will learn more about other parameters to this function.

The skeleton's window function responds to only one message explicitly: **WM_DESTROY**. This message is sent when the user terminates the program. When this message is received, your program must execute a call to the API function **PostQuitMessage( )**. The argument to this function is an exit code that is returned in **msg.wParam** inside **WinMain( )**. Calling **PostQuitMessage( )** causes a **WM_QUIT** message to be sent to your application, which causes **GetMessage( )** to return false, thus stopping your program.

Any other messages received by **WindowFunc( )** are passed to Windows 95, via a call to **DefWindowProc( )**, for default processing. This step is necessary, because all messages must be dealt with in one fashion or another.

2

Using a Definition File

If you are familiar with Windows 3.1 programming, then you have used *definition files*. In Windows 3.1, all programs need to have a definition file associated with them. A definition file is simply a text file that specifies certain information and settings needed by your Windows 3.1 program. However, because of the 32-bit architecture of Windows 95 (and other improvements), definition files are no longer needed. There is no harm in supplying a definition file, and if you want to include one for the sake of downward compatibility with Windows 3.1, then you are free to do so.

If you are new to Windows programming in general and you don't know what a definition file is, the following discussion gives a brief overview.

All definition files use the extension .DEF. For example, the definition file for the skeleton program could be called SKEL.DEF. Here is a definition file that you can use to provide downward compatibility with Windows 3.1:

```
DESCRIPTION 'Skeleton Program'
EXETYPE WINDOWS
CODE PRELOAD MOVEABLE DISCARDABLE
DATA PRELOAD MOVEABLE MULTIPLE
HEAPSIZE 8192
STACKSIZE 8192
EXPORTS WindowFunc
```

This file specifies the name of the program and its description, both of which are optional. It also states that the executable file will be compatible with Windows (rather than DOS, for example). The **CODE** statement tells Windows 95 to load all of the program at startup (**PRELOAD**), that the code may be moved in memory (**MOVEABLE**), and that the code may be removed from memory and reloaded if (and when) necessary (**DISCARDABLE**). The file states that your program's data must be loaded upon execution and may be moved about in memory. It also specifies that each instance of the program has its own data (**MULTIPLE**). Next, the size of the heap and stack allocated to the program are specified. Finally, the name of the window function is exported. Exporting allows Windows 3.1 to call the function.

Remember: Definition files are not needed when programming for Windows 95. However, they cause no harm and may be included for downward compatibility with Windows 3.1. (The heap size and stack size may need to be increased for real applications.)

Naming Conventions

If you are new to Windows 95 programming, several of the variable and parameter names in the skeleton program and its description probably seemed rather unusual. This is because they follow a set of naming conventions that was invented for Windows programming by Microsoft. For functions, the name consists of a verb followed by a noun. The first character of the verb and noun are capitalized. For the most part, we will use this convention for function names in this book.

For variable names, Microsoft chose to use a rather complex system of embedding the data type into the name. To accomplish this, a lowercase type prefix is added to the start of the variable's name. The name itself begins with a capital letter. The type prefixes are shown in Table 2-1. Frankly, the use of type prefixes is controversial and is not universally supported. Many Windows programmers use this method, but many do not. This method will be used by the Windows 95 programs in this book when it seems reasonable to do so. However, you are free to use any naming convention you like.

2

Prefix	Data Type
b	Boolean (one byte)
c	Character (one byte)
dw	Long unsigned integer
f	16-bit bitfield (flags)
fn	Function
h	Handle
l	Long integer
lp	Long pointer
n	Short integer
p	Pointer
pt	Long integer holding screen coordinates
w	Short unsigned integer
sz	Pointer to null-terminated string
lpsz	Long pointer to null-terminated string
rgb	Long integer holding RGB color values

Variable Type
Prefix
Characters
Table 2-1.

Chapter 3

Processing Messages

As explained in Chapter 2, Windows 95 communicates with your application by sending it messages. For this reason, the processing of these messages is at the core of all Windows 95 applications. In the previous chapter you learned how to create a skeletal Windows 95 application. In this chapter, that skeleton will be expanded to receive and process several common messages.

What Are Messages?

There are many different Windows 95 messages. Each message is represented by a unique 32-bit integer value. In the header file **windows.h** there are standard names for these messages. Generally, you will use the macro name, not the actual integer value, when referring to a message. Here are some common Windows 95 message macros:

    WM_CHAR
    WM_PAINT
    WM_MOVE
    WM_CLOSE
    WM_LBUTTONUP
    WM_LBUTTONDOWN
    WM_COMMAND

Two other values accompany each message and contain information related to the specific message. One of these values is of type **WPARAM**; the other is of type **LPARAM**. For Windows 95, both of these types translate into 32-bit integers. These values are commonly called **wParam** and **lParam**, respectively. They typically hold things like cursor or mouse coordinates, the value of a keypress, or a system-related value, such as character size. As each message is discussed, the meaning of the values contained in **wParam** and **lParam** will be described.

 In Windows 3.1, wParam is a 16-bit value. However, in Windows 95, it is a 32-bit value. This change causes a few messages to be different between the two versions of Windows. These differences will be noted.

As mentioned in Chapter 2, the function that actually processes messages is your program's window function. As you should recall, this function is passed four parameters: the handle of the window that the message is for, the message itself, and, finally, **wParam** and **lParam**.

Sometimes two pieces of information are encoded into the two words that comprise the **wParam** and **lParam** parameters. To provide easy access to each half of **wParam** and **lParam**, Windows defines two macros called **LOWORD** and **HIWORD**. They return the low-order and high-order words of a long integer, respectively. They are used like this:

```
x = LOWORD(lParam);

x = HIWORD(lParam);
```

You will soon see these macros in use.

Responding to a Keypress

One of the most common Windows 95 messages is generated when a key is pressed. This message is called **WM_CHAR**. It is important to understand that your application never receives, per se, keystrokes directly from the keyboard. Instead, each time a key is pressed, a **WM_CHAR** message is sent to the active window. To show how this process works, this section extends the skeletal application developed in Chapter 2 so that it processes keystroke messages.

Each time a **WM_CHAR** is sent, **wParam** contains the ASCII value of the key pressed. **LOWORD(lParam)** contains the number of times the key has been repeated as a result of the key being held down. The bits of **HIWORD(lParam)** are encoded as shown here:

15: Set if the key is being released; cleared if the
     key is being pressed.

14: Set if the key was pressed before the message sent;
     cleared if it was not pressed.

13: Set if the ALT key is also being pressed; cleared
     if ALT is not pressed.

12: Used by Windows 95

11: Used by Windows 95

10: Used by Windows 95

9: Used by Windows 95

8: Set if the key pressed is a function key or an extended
     key; cleared otherwise.

7 - 0: Manufacturer-dependent key code (i.e., the scan code)

For our purposes, the only value that is important at this time is **wParam**, since it holds the key that was pressed. However, notice how detailed the information is that Windows 95 supplies about the state of the system. Of course, you are free to use as much or as little of this information as you like.

To process a **WM_CHAR** message, you must add it to the **switch** statement inside your program's window function. For example, here is a window function that processes a keystroke by displaying it on the screen:

```
char str[80] = ""; /* holds output string */

LRESULT CALLBACK WindowFunc(HWND hwnd, UINT message,
                            WPARAM wParam, LPARAM lParam)
```

3

```
{
  HDC hdc;

  switch(message) {
    case WM_CHAR: /* process keystroke */
      hdc = GetDC(hwnd); /* get device context */
      TextOut(hdc, 1, 1, "  ", 2); /* erase old character */
      sprintf(str, "%c", (char) wParam); /* stringize character */
      TextOut(hdc, 1, 1, str, strlen(str)); /* output char */
      ReleaseDC(hwnd, hdc); /* release device context */
      break;
    case WM_DESTROY: /* terminate the program */
      PostQuitMessage(0);
      break;
    default:
      /* Let Windows 95 process any messages not specified in
         the preceding switch statement. */
      return DefWindowProc(hwnd, message, wParam, lParam);
  }
  return 0;
}
```

The purpose of the code inside the **WM_CHAR** case is very simple: it echoes the key to the screen! You are probably surprised that it takes so many lines of code to accomplish this seemingly trivial feat. The reason is that Windows must establish a link between your program and the screen. This is called a *device context* (DC for short), and it is acquired by calling **GetDC( )**. For now, don't worry about precisely what a device context is. It will be discussed in the next section. However, after you obtain a device context, you may write to the screen. At the end of the process, the device context is released using **ReleaseDC( )**. Your program *must* release the device context when done with it. There are a finite number of device contexts. If your program doesn't release the DC, the available DCs will eventually be exhausted, and a subsequent call to **GetDC( )** will fail. Both **GetDC( )** and **ReleaseDC( )** are API functions. Their prototypes are shown here:

HDC GetDC(HWND *hwnd*);

int ReleaseDC(HWND *hwnd*, HDC *hdc*);

GetDC( ) returns a device context associated with the window whose handle is specified by *hwnd*. The type **HDC** specifies a handle to a device context.

ReleaseDC( ) returns true if the device context was released, false otherwise. The *hwnd* parameter is the handle of the window for which the device context is released. The *hdc* parameter is the handle of device context obtained through the call to **GetDC( )**.

The function that actually outputs the character is the API function **TextOut( )**. Its prototype is shown here.

> BOOL TextOut(HDC *DC*, int *x*, int *y*, LPCSTR *lpstr*, int *nlength*);

The **TextOut( )** function outputs the string pointed to by *lpstr* at the window coordinates specified by *x, y*. (By default, these coordinates are given in terms of pixels.) The length of the string is specified by *nlength*. The **TextOut( )** function returns non-zero if successful, zero otherwise.

In the function, each time a **WM_CHAR** message is received, the character typed by the user is converted, using **sprintf( )**, into a string that is one character long, and then displayed using **TextOut( )** at location 1, 1. (The string **str** is global because it will need to keep its value between function calls in later examples.) In a window, the upper-left corner of the client area is location 0, 0. Window coordinates are always relative to the window, not the screen. Therefore, as characters are entered, they are displayed in the upper-left corner no matter where the window is physically located on the screen.

The reason for the first call to **TextOut( )** is to erase whatever previous character was just displayed. Because Windows is a graphics-based system, characters are of different sizes, and the overwriting of one character by another does not necessarily cause all of the previous character to be erased. For example, if you overwrote a *w* with an *i*, part of the *w* would still be displayed unless it was manually erased. (Try commenting out the first call to **TextOut( )** and observe what happens.)

It is important to understand that no Windows 95 API function will allow output beyond the borders of a window. Output will automatically be clipped to prevent the boundaries from being crossed.

At first you might think that using **TextOut( )** to output a single character is not an efficient application of the function. The fact is that Windows 95 (and Windows, in general) does not contain a function that simply outputs a character. As you will see, Windows 95 performs much of its user interaction through dialog boxes, menus, toolbars, and so on. For this reason it only contains a few functions that output text to the client area.

Here is the entire skeleton that processes keystrokes. Figure 3-1 shows the window produced by this program.

```
/* Processing WM_CHAR messages. */

#include <windows.h>
```

3

```c
#include <string.h>
#include <stdio.h>

LRESULT CALLBACK WindowFunc(HWND, UINT, WPARAM, LPARAM);

char szWinName[] = "MyWin"; /* name of window class */

char str[80] = ""; /* holds output string */

int WINAPI WinMain(HINSTANCE hThisInst, HINSTANCE hPrevInst,
                   LPSTR lpszArgs, int nWinMode)
{
  HWND hwnd;
  MSG msg;
  WNDCLASS wcl;

  /* Define a window class. */
  wcl.hInstance = hThisInst; /* handle to this instance */
  wcl.lpszClassName = szWinName; /* window class name */
  wcl.lpfnWndProc = WindowFunc; /* window function */
  wcl.style = 0; /* default style */

  wcl.hIcon = LoadIcon(NULL, IDI_APPLICATION); /* icon style */
  wcl.hCursor = LoadCursor(NULL, IDC_ARROW); /* cursor style */
  wcl.lpszMenuName = NULL; /* no menu */

  wcl.cbClsExtra = 0; /* no extra */
  wcl.cbWndExtra = 0; /* information needed */

  /* Make the window white. */
  wcl.hbrBackground = GetStockObject(WHITE_BRUSH);

  /* Register the window class. */
  if(!RegisterClass (&wcl)) return 0;

  /* Now that a window class has been registered, a window
     can be created. */
  hwnd = CreateWindow(
    szWinName, /* name of window class */
    "Processing WM_CHAR Messages", /* title */
    WS_OVERLAPPEDWINDOW, /* window style - normal */
    CW_USEDEFAULT, /* X coordinate - let Windows decide */
    CW_USEDEFAULT, /* Y coordinate - let Windows decide */
    CW_USEDEFAULT, /* width - let Windows decide */
    CW_USEDEFAULT, /* height - let Windows decide */
    HWND_DESKTOP, /* no parent window */
    NULL, /* no menu */
    hThisInst, /* handle of this instance of the program */
```

```
          NULL /* no additional arguments */
  );

  /* Display the window. */
  ShowWindow(hwnd, nWinMode);
  UpdateWindow(hwnd);

  /* Create the message loop. */
  while(GetMessage(&msg, NULL, 0, 0))
  {
    TranslateMessage(&msg); /* allow use of keyboard */
    DispatchMessage(&msg); /* return control to Windows */
  }
  return msg.wParam;
}


/* This function is called by Windows 95 and is passed
   messages from the message queue.
*/
LRESULT CALLBACK WindowFunc(HWND hwnd, UINT message,
                            WPARAM wParam, LPARAM lParam)
{
  HDC hdc;

  switch(message) {
    case WM_CHAR: /* process keystroke */
      hdc = GetDC(hwnd); /* get device context */
      TextOut(hdc, 1, 1, "  ", 2); /* erase old character */
      sprintf(str, "%c", (char) wParam); /* stringize character */
      TextOut(hdc, 1, 1, str, strlen(str)); /* output char */
      ReleaseDC(hwnd, hdc); /* release device context */
      break;
    case WM_DESTROY: /* terminate the program */
      PostQuitMessage(0);
      break;
    default:
      /* Let Windows 95 process any messages not specified in
         the preceding switch statement. */
      return DefWindowProc(hwnd, message, wParam, lParam);
  }
  return 0;
}
```

Device Contexts

The program in the previous section had to obtain a device context prior to
outputting to the window. Also, that device context had to be released after

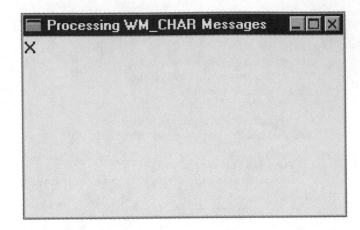

Sample
window
produced
by the
WM_CHAR
program
Figure 3-1.

output had been accomplished. It is now time for you to understand what a *device context* is. It is an output path that goes from your Windows 95 application, through the appropriate device driver, to the client area of your window. The device context also fully defines the state of the device driver.

Before your application can output information to the client area of the window, a device context must be obtained. Until this is done, there is no linkage between your program and the window relative to output. Thus, it is necessary to obtain a device context prior to performing any output to a window. Since **TextOut( )** and other output functions require a handle to a device context, this is a self-enforcing rule.

Processing the WM_PAINT Message

Before you continue reading, run the program from the previous section again and enter a few characters. Next, minimize and then restore the window. As you will see, the last character typed is not displayed after the window is restored. Also, if the window is overwritten by another window and then uncovered, the character is not redisplayed. The reason for this is simple: In general, Windows does not keep a record of what a window contains. Instead, it is your program's job to maintain the contents of a window. To help your program accomplish this, each time the contents of a window must be redisplayed, your program will be sent a **WM_PAINT** message. (This message will also be sent when your window is first displayed.) Each time your program receives this message, it must redisplay the contents of the window. In this section, you will add a **case** statement that processes the **WM_PAINT** message.

Note: For various technical reasons, when the window is moved or resized, its contents are automatically redisplayed. However, this will not occur when the window is minimized or overwritten and then redisplayed.

Before explaining how to respond to a **WM_PAINT** message, it might be useful to explain why Windows does not automatically rewrite your window. The answer is short and to the point. In many situations, it is easier for your program, which has intimate knowledge of the contents of the window, to rewrite it than it would be for Windows to do so. While the merits of this approach have been much debated by programmers, you should simply accept it, because it is unlikely to change.

The first step to processing a **WM_PAINT** message is to add its **case** to the **switch** statement inside the window function, as shown here.

3

```
case WM_PAINT: /* process a repaint request */
  hdc = BeginPaint(hwnd, &paintstruct); /* get DC */
  TextOut(hdc, 1, 1, str, strlen(str)); /* output string */
  EndPaint(hwnd, &paintstruct); /* release DC */
  break;
```

Let's look at this closely. First, notice that a device context is obtained using a call to **BeginPaint( )** instead of **GetDC( )**. For various reasons, when you process a **WM_PAINT** message, you must obtain a device context using **BeginPaint( )**, which has this prototype:

HDC BeginPaint(HWND *hwnd*, LPPAINTSTRUCT *lpPS*);

The second parameter is a pointer to a structure of type **PAINTSTRUCT**, which is defined like this:

```
typedef struct tagPAINTSTRUCT {
  HDC hdc; /* handle to device context */
  BOOL fErase; /* true if background must be erased */
  RECT rcPaint; /* coordinates of region to redraw */
  BOOL fRestore;  /* reserved */
  BOOL fIncUpdate; /* reserved */
  BYTE rgbReserved[32]; /* reserved */
} PAINTSTRUCT;
```

The type **RECT** is a structure that specifies the upper-left and lower-right coordinates of a rectangular region. This structure is shown here:

```
typedef tagRECT {
  LONG left, top; /* upper left */
```

```
LONG right, bottom; /* lower right */
} RECT;
```

In **PAINTSTRUCT**, the **rcPaint** element contains the coordinates of the region of the window that needs to be repainted. For now, you will not need to use the contents of this structure; you can assume that the entire window must be redisplayed.

Here is the full program that now processes **WM_PAINT** messages.

```
/* Process WM_PAINT messages. */

#include <windows.h>
#include <string.h>
#include <stdio.h>

LRESULT CALLBACK WindowFunc(HWND, UINT, WPARAM, LPARAM);

char szWinName[] = "MyWin"; /* name of window class */

char str[80] = "Sample Output"; /* holds output string */

int WINAPI WinMain(HINSTANCE hThisInst, HINSTANCE hPrevInst,
                   LPSTR lpszArgs, int nWinMode)
{
  HWND hwnd;
  MSG msg;
  WNDCLASS wcl;

  /* Define a window class. */
  wcl.hInstance = hThisInst; /* handle to this instance */
  wcl.lpszClassName = szWinName; /* window class name */
  wcl.lpfnWndProc = WindowFunc; /* window function */
  wcl.style = 0; /* default style */

  wcl.hIcon = LoadIcon(NULL, IDI_APPLICATION); /* icon style */
  wcl.hCursor = LoadCursor(NULL, IDC_ARROW); /* cursor style */
  wcl.lpszMenuName = NULL; /* no menu */

  wcl.cbClsExtra = 0; /* no extra */
  wcl.cbWndExtra = 0; /* information needed */

  /* Make the window white. */
  wcl.hbrBackground = GetStockObject(WHITE_BRUSH);

  /* Register the window class. */
  if(!RegisterClass (&wcl)) return 0;
```

```
      /* Now that a window class has been registered, a window
         can be created. */
      hwnd = CreateWindow(
        szWinName, /* name of window class */
        "Processing WM_PAINT Messages", /* title */
        WS_OVERLAPPEDWINDOW, /* window style - normal */
        CW_USEDEFAULT, /* X coordinate - let Windows decide */
        CW_USEDEFAULT, /* Y coordinate - let Windows decide */
        CW_USEDEFAULT, /* width - let Windows decide */
        CW_USEDEFAULT, /* height - let Windows decide */
        HWND_DESKTOP, /* no parent window */
        NULL, /* no menu */
        hThisInst, /* handle of this instance of the program */
        NULL /* no additional arguments */
      );

      /* Display the window. */
      ShowWindow(hwnd, nWinMode);
      UpdateWindow(hwnd);

      /* Create the message loop. */
      while(GetMessage(&msg, NULL, 0, 0))
      {
        TranslateMessage(&msg); /* allow use of keyboard */
        DispatchMessage(&msg); /* return control to Windows */
      }
      return msg.wParam;
}


/* This function is called by Windows 95 and is passed
   messages from the message queue.
*/
LRESULT CALLBACK WindowFunc(HWND hwnd, UINT message,
                            WPARAM wParam, LPARAM lParam)
{
  HDC hdc;
  PAINTSTRUCT paintstruct;

  switch(message) {
    case WM_CHAR: /* process keystroke */
      hdc = GetDC(hwnd); /* get device context */
      TextOut(hdc, 1, 1, " ", 2); /* erase old character */
      sprintf(str, "%c", (char) wParam); /* stringize character */
      TextOut(hdc, 1, 1, str, strlen(str)); /* output char */
      ReleaseDC(hwnd, hdc); /* release device context */
      break;
    case WM_PAINT: /* process a repaint request */
```

```
       hdc = BeginPaint(hwnd, &paintstruct); /* get DC */
       TextOut(hdc, 1, 1, str, strlen(str)); /* output string */
       EndPaint(hwnd, &paintstruct); /* release DC */
       break;
     case WM_DESTROY: /* terminate the program */
       PostQuitMessage(0);
       break;
     default:
        /* Let Windows 95 process any messages not specified in
           the preceding switch statement. */
        return DefWindowProc(hwnd, message, wParam, lParam);
   }
   return 0;
}
```

Before you continue, first enter, compile, and run this program. Try typing a few characters and then minimizing and restoring the window. As you will see, each time the window is redisplayed, the last character you typed is automatically redrawn. Notice that the global array **str** is initialized to **Sample Output** and that this string is displayed when the program begins execution. The reason is that when a window is created, a **WM_PAINT** message is automatically generated.

While the handling of the **WM_PAINT** message in the skeleton is quite simple, it must be emphasized that most real-world versions of this will be more complex because most windows contain considerably more output.

Since it is your program's responsibility to restore the contents of the window if it is resized or overwritten, you must always provide some mechanism to accomplish this. In real-world programs, this is usually accomplished in one of three ways: First, your program can simply regenerate the output by computational means. This is most feasible when no user input is required. Second, in some instances, you can keep a record of events and replay the events when the window needs to be redrawn. Finally, your program can maintain a virtual screen that you simply copy to the window each time it must be redrawn. This is the most general method. (The implementation of this approach is described later in this book.) Which approach is best depends completely upon the application. Most of the examples in this book won't bother to redraw the window, because doing so typically involves substantial additional code that would just muddy the point of an example. However, your programs will need to restore their windows in order to be conforming Windows 95 applications.

Responding to Mouse Messages

Since Windows is largely a mouse-based operating system, all Windows programs should respond to mouse input. Windows 95 is no exception. Because the mouse is so important, there are several different types of mouse messages. This section examines the two most common. These are **WM_LBUTTONDOWN** and **WM_RBUTTONDOWN**, which are generated when the left button and right button are pressed, respectively.

To begin, you must add to the **switch** statement in the window function the code that responds to the two mouse messages, as shown here.

```
case WM_RBUTTONDOWN: /* process right button */
  hdc = GetDC(hwnd); /* get DC */
  strcpy(str, "Right button is down.");
  TextOut(hdc, LOWORD(lParam), HIWORD(lParam),
          str, strlen(str));
  ReleaseDC(hwnd, hdc); /* Release DC */
  break;
case WM_LBUTTONDOWN: /* process left button */
  hdc = GetDC(hwnd); /* get DC */
  strcpy(str, "Left button is down.");
  TextOut(hdc, LOWORD(lParam), HIWORD(lParam),
          str, strlen(str));
  ReleaseDC(hwnd, hdc); /* Release DC */
  break;
```

When either button is pressed, the mouse's current *x, y* location is specified in **LOWORD(lParam)** and **HIWORD(lParam)**, respectively. The code that responds to the mouse messages uses these coordinates as the location to display its output. That is, each time you press a mouse button, a message will be displayed at the current location of the mouse pointer.

Here is the complete program that responds to the mouse messages:

```
/* Process Mouse Messages. */

#include <windows.h>
#include <string.h>
#include <stdio.h>

LRESULT CALLBACK WindowFunc(HWND, UINT, WPARAM, LPARAM);

char szWinName[] = "MyWin"; /* name of window class */
```

3

```
char str[80] = "Sample Output"; /* holds output string */

int WINAPI WinMain(HINSTANCE hThisInst, HINSTANCE hPrevInst,
                   LPSTR lpszArgs, int nWinMode)
{
  HWND hwnd;
  MSG msg;
  WNDCLASS wcl;

  /* Define a window class. */
  wcl.hInstance = hThisInst; /* handle to this instance */
  wcl.lpszClassName = szWinName; /* window class name */
  wcl.lpfnWndProc = WindowFunc; /* window function */
  wcl.style = 0; /* default style */

  wcl.hIcon = LoadIcon(NULL, IDI_APPLICATION); /* icon style */
  wcl.hCursor = LoadCursor(NULL, IDC_ARROW); /* cursor style */
  wcl.lpszMenuName = NULL; /* no menu */

  wcl.cbClsExtra = 0; /* no extra */
  wcl.cbWndExtra = 0; /* information needed */

  /* Make the window white. */
  wcl.hbrBackground = GetStockObject(WHITE_BRUSH);

  /* Register the window class. */
  if(!RegisterClass (&wcl)) return 0;

  /* Now that a window class has been registered, a window
     can be created. */
  hwnd = CreateWindow(
    szWinName, /* name of window class */
    "Processing Mouse Messages", /* title */
    WS_OVERLAPPEDWINDOW, /* window style - normal */
    CW_USEDEFAULT, /* X coordinate - let Windows decide */
    CW_USEDEFAULT, /* Y coordinate - let Windows decide */
    CW_USEDEFAULT, /* width - let Windows decide */
    CW_USEDEFAULT, /* height - let Windows decide */
    HWND_DESKTOP, /* no parent window */
    NULL, /* no menu */
    hThisInst, /* handle of this instance of the program */
    NULL /* no additional arguments */
  );

  /* Display the window. */
  ShowWindow(hwnd, nWinMode);
  UpdateWindow(hwnd);
```

```
    /* Create the message loop. */
    while(GetMessage(&msg, NULL, 0, 0))
    {
      TranslateMessage(&msg); /* allow use of keyboard */
      DispatchMessage(&msg); /* return control to Windows */
    }
    return msg.wParam;
}


/* This function is called by Windows 95 and is passed
   messages from the message queue.
*/
LRESULT CALLBACK WindowFunc(HWND hwnd, UINT message,
                            WPARAM wParam, LPARAM lParam)
{
  HDC hdc;
  PAINTSTRUCT paintstruct;

  switch(message) {
    case WM_CHAR: /* process keystroke */
      hdc = GetDC(hwnd); /* get device context */
      TextOut(hdc, 1, 1, "  ", 2); /* erase old character */
      sprintf(str, "%c", (char) wParam); /* stringize character */
      TextOut(hdc, 1, 1, str, strlen(str)); /* output char */
      ReleaseDC(hwnd, hdc); /* release device context */
      break;
    case WM_PAINT: /* process a repaint request */
      hdc = BeginPaint(hwnd, &paintstruct); /* get DC */
      TextOut(hdc, 1, 1, str, strlen(str)); /* output string */
      EndPaint(hwnd, &paintstruct); /* release DC */
      break;
    case WM_RBUTTONDOWN: /* process right button */
      hdc = GetDC(hwnd); /* get DC */
      strcpy(str, "Right button is down.");
      TextOut(hdc, LOWORD(lParam), HIWORD(lParam),
              str, strlen(str));
      ReleaseDC(hwnd, hdc); /* Release DC */
      break;
    case WM_LBUTTONDOWN: /* process left button */
      hdc = GetDC(hwnd); /* get DC */
      strcpy(str, "Left button is down.");
      TextOut(hdc, LOWORD(lParam), HIWORD(lParam),
              str, strlen(str));
      ReleaseDC(hwnd, hdc); /* Release DC */
      break;
    case WM_DESTROY: /* terminate the program */
      PostQuitMessage(0);
```

3

```
          break;
     default:
        /* Let Windows 95 process any messages not specified in
           the preceding switch statement. */
        return DefWindowProc(hwnd, message, wParam, lParam);
  }
  return 0;
}
```

Figure 3-2 shows sample output from this program.

A Closer Look at the Mouse Messages

Each time a **WM_LBUTTONDOWN** or a **WM_RBUTTONDOWN** message is generated, several pieces of information are also supplied in the **wParam** parameter. It may contain any combination of the following values:

MK_CONTROL
MK_SHIFT
MK_RBUTTON
MK_LBUTTON
MK_MBUTTON

If the CTRL key is pressed when a mouse button is pressed, then **wParam** will contain **MK_CONTROL**. If the SHIFT key is pressed when a mouse button is pressed, then **wParam** will contain **MK_SHIFT**. If the right

Sample output from the Mouse Messages program
Figure 3-2.

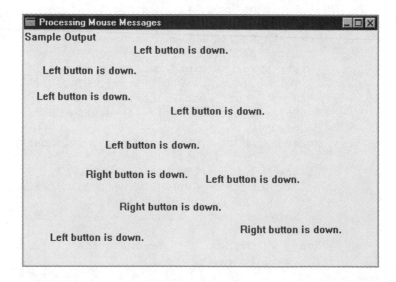

mouse button is down when the left button is pressed, then **wParam** will contain **MK_RBUTTON**. If the left mouse button is down when the right button is pressed, then **wParam** will contain **MK_LBUTTON**. If the middle mouse button (if it exists) is down when one of the other buttons is pressed, then **wParam** will contain **MK_MBUTTON**. Before moving on, you might want to try experimenting with these messages. More than one of these values may be present.

Generating a WM_PAINT Message

It is possible for your program to cause a **WM_PAINT** message to be generated. At first, you might wonder why your program would need to generate a **WM_PAINT** message, since it seems as though it can repaint its window whenever it wants. However, this is a false assumption. Remember, updating a window is a costly process in terms of time. Because Windows is a multitasking system that might be running other programs that also demand CPU time, your program should simply tell Windows that it wants to output information, but let Windows decide when it is best to actually perform that output. This allows Windows to better manage the system and efficiently allocate CPU time to all the tasks in the system. Using this approach, your program simply holds all output until a **WM_PAINT** message is received.

In the previous examples, the **WM_PAINT** message was only received when the window was resized or uncovered. However, if all output is held until a **WM_PAINT** message is received, then to achieve interactive I/O, there must be some way to tell Windows that it needs to send a **WM_PAINT** to your window whenever output is pending. As expected, Windows 95 includes such a feature. Thus, when your program has information to output, it simply requests that a **WM_PAINT** message be sent when Windows is ready to do so.

To cause Windows to send a **WM_PAINT** message, your program will call the **InvalidateRect( )** API function. Its prototype is shown here.

BOOL InvalidateRect(HWND *hwnd*, CONST RECT **lpRect*, BOOL *bErase*);

Here, *hwnd* is the handle of the window to which you want to send the **WM_PAINT** message. The **RECT** structure pointed to by *lpRect* specifies the coordinates within the window that must be redrawn. If this value is NULL, then the entire window will be specified. If *bErase* is true, then the background will be erased. If it is zero, then the background is left unchanged. The function returns non-zero if successful; zero otherwise. (In general, this function will succeed.)

3

When **InvalidateRect( )** is called, it tells Windows that the window is invalid and must be redrawn. This, in turn, causes Windows to send a **WM_PAINT** message to the program's window function.

Here is a reworked version of the previous application skeleton that performs all output by generating a **WM_PAINT** message. The other message response code simply prepares the information to be displayed and then calls **InvalidateRect( )**.

```c
/* A Windows skeleton that routes all output
   through the WM_PAINT message. */

#include <windows.h>
#include <string.h>
#include <stdio.h>

LRESULT CALLBACK WindowFunc(HWND, UINT, WPARAM, LPARAM);

char szWinName[] = "MyWin"; /* name of window class */

char str[80] = "Sample Output"; /* holds output string */

int X = 1, Y = 1; /* screen location */

int WINAPI WinMain(HINSTANCE hThisInst, HINSTANCE hPrevInst,
                   LPSTR lpszArgs, int nWinMode)
{
  HWND hwnd;
  MSG msg;
  WNDCLASS wcl;

  /* Define a window class. */
  wcl.hInstance = hThisInst; /* handle to this instance */
  wcl.lpszClassName = szWinName; /* window class name */
  wcl.lpfnWndProc = WindowFunc; /* window function */
  wcl.style = 0; /* default style */

  wcl.hIcon = LoadIcon(NULL, IDI_APPLICATION); /* icon style */
  wcl.hCursor = LoadCursor(NULL, IDC_ARROW); /* cursor style */
  wcl.lpszMenuName = NULL; /* no menu */

  wcl.cbClsExtra = 0; /* no extra */
  wcl.cbWndExtra = 0; /* information needed */

  /* Make the window white. */
  wcl.hbrBackground = GetStockObject(WHITE_BRUSH);

  /* Register the window class. */
```

```
      if(!RegisterClass (&wcl)) return 0;

      /* Now that a window class has been registered, a window
         can be created. */
      hwnd = CreateWindow(
        szWinName, /* name of window class */
        "Routing Output Through WM_PAINT", /* title */
        WS_OVERLAPPEDWINDOW, /* window style - normal */
        CW_USEDEFAULT, /* X coordinate - let Windows decide */
        CW_USEDEFAULT, /* Y coordinate - let Windows decide */
        CW_USEDEFAULT, /* width - let Windows decide */
        CW_USEDEFAULT, /* height - let Windows decide */
        HWND_DESKTOP, /* no parent window */
        NULL, /* no menu */
        hThisInst, /* handle of this instance of the program */
        NULL /* no additional arguments */
      );

      /* Display the window. */
      ShowWindow(hwnd, nWinMode);
      UpdateWindow(hwnd);

      /* Create the message loop. */
      while(GetMessage(&msg, NULL, 0, 0))
      {
        TranslateMessage(&msg); /* allow use of keyboard */
        DispatchMessage(&msg); /* return control to Windows */
      }
      return msg.wParam;
  }

  /* This function is called by Windows 95 and is passed
     messages from the message queue.
  */
  LRESULT CALLBACK WindowFunc(HWND hwnd, UINT message,
                              WPARAM wParam,LPARAM lParam)
  {
    HDC hdc;
    PAINTSTRUCT paintstruct;

    switch(message) {
      case WM_CHAR: /* process keystroke */
        X = Y = 1; /* display chars in upper left corner */
        sprintf(str, "%c", (char) wParam); /* stringize character */
        InvalidateRect(hwnd, NULL, 1); /* paint the screen */
        break;
      case WM_PAINT: /* process a repaint request */
        hdc = BeginPaint(hwnd, &paintstruct); /* get DC */
```

```
      TextOut(hdc, X, Y, str, strlen(str)); /* output string */
      EndPaint(hwnd, &paintstruct); /* release DC */
      break;
    case WM_RBUTTONDOWN: /* process right button */
      strcpy(str, "Right button is down.");
      X = LOWORD(lParam); /* set X,Y to current */
      Y = HIWORD(lParam); /* mouse location */
      InvalidateRect(hwnd, NULL, 1); /* paint the screen */
      break;
    case WM_LBUTTONDOWN: /* process left button */
      strcpy(str, "Left button is down.");
      X = LOWORD(lParam); /* set X,Y to current */
      Y = HIWORD(lParam); /* mouse location */
      InvalidateRect(hwnd, NULL, 1); /* paint the screen */
      break;
    case WM_DESTROY: /* terminate the program */
      PostQuitMessage(0);
      break;
    default:
      /* Let Windows 95 process any messages not specified in
         the preceding switch statement. */
      return DefWindowProc(hwnd, message, wParam, lParam);
  }
  return 0;
}
```

Notice that the program adds two new global variables called **X** and **Y** that hold the location at which the text will be displayed when a **WM_PAINT** message is received.

As you can see, by channeling all output through **WM_PAINT**, the program has actually become smaller and, in some ways, easier to understand. Also, as stated at the start of this section, the program allows Windows 95 to decide when it is most appropriate to update the window.

Note: Many Windows applications route all (or most) output through **WM_PAINT**, for the reasons given above. However, the previous programs are not technically wrong by outputting text when they respond to a message. It's just that this approach may not be the best one for all purposes.

Generating Timer Messages

The last message that will be discussed here is **WM_TIMER**. Using Windows, it is possible to establish a timer that will interrupt your program at periodic intervals. Each time the timer goes off, it sends a **WM_TIMER** message to your window function. Using a timer is a good way to "wake up" your program every so often. This is particularly useful when a program is running as a background task.

To start a timer, use the **SetTimer( )** API function, whose prototype is shown here:

    UINT SetTimer(HWND *hwnd*, UINT *nID*, UINT *wLength*,
            TIMERPROC *lpTFunc*);

Here, *hwnd* is the handle of the window that uses the timer. *nID* specifies a value that will be associated with this timer. (More than one timer can be active.) The value of *wLength* specifies the length of the period, in milliseconds. That is, *wLength* specifies how much time there is between interrupts. The function pointed to by *lpTFunc* is the timer function that will be called when the timer goes off. This must be a callback function that returns **VOID CALLBACK** and takes the same type of parameters as the window function. However, if the value of *lpTFunc* is NULL, as it commonly is, then your program's window function will be used for this purpose. In this case, whenever the timer goes off, a **WM_TIMER** message is put into the message queue for your program, and your program's window function processes it like any other message. This is the approach used by the example that follows. The function returns *nID* if successful. If the timer cannot be allocated, zero is returned.

Once a timer has been started, it continues to interrupt your program until either you terminate the application or your program executes a call to the **KillTimer( )** API function, whose prototype is shown here.

    BOOL KillTimer(HWND *hwnd*, UINT *nID*);

Here, *hwnd* is the window that contains the timer and *nID* is the value that identifies that particular timer.

Each time a **WM_TIMER** message is generated, the value of **wParam** contains the ID of the timer and **lParam** contains the address of the timer callback function (if one was specified). For the example that follows, **lParam** will be NULL.

To demonstrate the use of a timer, the following program uses a timer to create a clock. It uses the standard C/C++ time and date functions to obtain and display the current system time and date. Whenever the timer goes off, which is approximately once each second, the time is updated. Thus, the time displayed is accurate to within 1 second.

3

```
/* A clock program. */

#include <windows.h>
#include <string.h>
#include <stdio.h>
#include <time.h>

LRESULT CALLBACK WindowFunc(HWND, UINT, WPARAM, LPARAM);

char szWinName[] = "WinClock"; /* name of window class */

char str[80] = ""; /* holds output string */

int X = 1, Y = 1; /* screen location */

int WINAPI WinMain(HINSTANCE hThisInst, HINSTANCE hPrevInst,
                   LPSTR lpszArgs, int nWinMode)
{
  HWND hwnd;
  MSG msg;
  WNDCLASS wcl;

  /* Define a window class. */
  wcl.hInstance = hThisInst; /* handle to this instance */
  wcl.lpszClassName = szWinName; /* window class name */
  wcl.lpfnWndProc = WindowFunc; /* window function */
  wcl.style = 0; /* default style */

  wcl.hIcon = LoadIcon(NULL, IDI_APPLICATION); /* icon style */
  wcl.hCursor = LoadCursor(NULL, IDC_ARROW); /* cursor style */
  wcl.lpszMenuName = NULL; /* no menu */

  wcl.cbClsExtra = 0; /* no extra */
  wcl.cbWndExtra = 0; /* information needed */

  /* Make the window white. */
  wcl.hbrBackground = GetStockObject(WHITE_BRUSH);

  /* Register the window class. */
  if(!RegisterClass (&wcl)) return 0;

  /* Now that a window class has been registered, a window
     can be created. */
  hwnd = CreateWindow(
    szWinName, /* name of window class */
    "Clock", /* title */
    WS_OVERLAPPEDWINDOW, /* window style - normal */
    CW_USEDEFAULT, /* X coordinate - let Windows decide */
```

```
      CW_USEDEFAULT, /* Y coordinate - let Windows decide */
      CW_USEDEFAULT, /* width - let Windows decide */
      CW_USEDEFAULT, /* height - let Windows decide */
      HWND_DESKTOP, /* no parent window */
      NULL, /* no menu */
      hThisInst, /* handle of this instance of the program */
      NULL /* no additional arguments */
    );

    /* Display the window. */
    ShowWindow(hwnd, nWinMode);

    /* start a timer — interrupt once per second */
    SetTimer(hwnd, 1, 1000, NULL);

    UpdateWindow(hwnd);

    /* Create the message loop. */
    while(GetMessage(&msg, NULL, 0, 0))
    {
      TranslateMessage(&msg); /* allow use of keyboard */
      DispatchMessage(&msg); /* return control to Windows */
    }

    KillTimer(hwnd, 1); /* stop the timer */

    return msg.wParam;
}

/* This function is called by Windows 95 and is passed
   messages from the message queue.
*/
LRESULT CALLBACK WindowFunc(HWND hwnd, UINT message,
                            WPARAM wParam, LPARAM lParam)
{
  HDC hdc;
  PAINTSTRUCT paintstruct;
  struct tm *newtime;
  time_t t;

  switch(message) {
    case WM_PAINT: /* process a repaint request */
      hdc = BeginPaint(hwnd, &paintstruct); /* get DC */
      TextOut(hdc, X, Y, str, strlen(str)); /* output string */
      EndPaint(hwnd, &paintstruct); /* release DC */
      break;
    case WM_TIMER: /* timer went off */
      /* get the new time */
```

3

```
      t = time(NULL);
      newtime = localtime(&t);

      /* display the new time */
      strcpy(str, asctime(newtime));
      str[strlen(str)-1] = '\0'; /* remove /r/n */
      InvalidateRect(hwnd, NULL, 0); /* update screen */
      break;
    case WM_DESTROY: /* terminate the program */
      PostQuitMessage(0);
      break;
    default:
      /* Let Windows 95 process any messages not specified in
         the preceding switch statement. */
      return DefWindowProc(hwnd, message, wParam, lParam);
  }
  return 0;
}
```

Sample output from this program is shown here:

Now that you have learned how a Windows 95 program processes messages, you can move on to create message boxes and menus, which are discussed in Chapter 4.

Chapter

4

Message Boxes
and Menus

Now that you know how to construct a basic Windows 95 skeleton to receive and process messages, it is time to begin exploration of Windows' user interface components. If you are learning to program Windows for the first time, it is important to understand that your application will most often communicate with the user through one or more predefined interface components. There are several different types of interface elements supported by Windows 95. This chapter discusses two: message boxes and menus. These are the most basic and fundamental of Windows' interface components. Virtually any program you write will use both of them. As you will see, the basic style of the message box and the menu is predefined. You need only supply the specific information that relates to your application.

This chapter also introduces the resource, a crucial part of nearly all Windows applications.

Message Boxes

By far the simplest interface window is the message box. A message box simply displays a message to the user and waits for an acknowledgment. It is possible to construct message boxes that allow the user to select between a few basic alternatives, but in general, the purpose of a message box is simply to inform the user that some event has taken place.

To create a message box, use the **MessageBox( )** API function. Its prototype is shown here.

> int MessageBox(HWND *hwnd*, LPCSTR *lpText*, LPCSTR *lpCaption*,
> UINT *wMBType*);

Here, *hwnd* is the handle to the parent window. The *lpText* parameter is a pointer to a string that will appear inside the message box. The string pointed to by *lpCaption* is used as the caption for the box. The value of *wMBType* determines the exact nature of the message box, including what type of buttons will be present. Some of its most common values are shown in Table 4-1. These macros are defined by including **windows.h**; you can OR together two or more of these macros as long as they are not mutually exclusive. **MessageBox( )** returns the user's response to the box. The possible return values are shown here:

Button Pressed	Return Value
Abort	IDABORT
Retry	IDRETRY
Ignore	IDIGNORE
Cancel	IDCANCEL
No	IDNO
Yes	IDYES
OK	IDOK

Remember, depending upon the value of *wMBType*, only certain buttons will be present.

To display a message box, simply call the **MessageBox( )** function. Windows 95 will display the message box at its first opportunity. You do not need to obtain a device context or generate a **WM_PAINT** message. **MessageBox( )** handles all of these details for you. (Because message boxes are so easy to use, they make excellent debugging tools when you need a simple way to output something to the screen.)

Value	Effect
MB_ABORTRETRYIGNORE	Displays Abort, Retry, and Ignore push buttons
MB_ICONEXCLAMATION	Displays an exclamation point icon
MB_ICONHAND	Displays a stop sign icon
MB_ICONINFORMATION	Displays an information icon
MB_ICONQUESTION	Displays a question mark icon
MB_ICONSTOP	Same as MB_ICONHAND
MB_OK	Displays OK push button
MB_OKCANCEL	Displays OK and Cancel push buttons
MB_RETRYCANCEL	Displays Retry and Cancel push buttons
MB_YESNO	Displays Yes and No push buttons
MB_YESNOCANCEL	Displays Yes, No, and Cancel push buttons

Some
Common
Values for
wMBType
Table 4-1.

Here is a simple example that displays a message box when you press a
mouse button:

4

```
/* Demonstrate a Message Box. */

#include <windows.h>
#include <string.h>
#include <stdio.h>

LRESULT CALLBACK WindowFunc(HWND, UINT, WPARAM, LPARAM);

char szWinName[] = "MyWin"; /* name of window class */

int WINAPI WinMain(HINSTANCE hThisInst, HINSTANCE hPrevInst,
                   LPSTR lpszArgs, int nWinMode)
{
  HWND hwnd;
  MSG msg;
  WNDCLASS wcl;

  /* Define a window class. */
  wcl.hInstance = hThisInst; /* handle to this instance */
  wcl.lpszClassName = szWinName; /* window class name */
  wcl.lpfnWndProc = WindowFunc; /* window function */
  wcl.style = 0; /* default style */

  wcl.hIcon = LoadIcon(NULL, IDI_APPLICATION); /* icon style */
  wcl.hCursor = LoadCursor(NULL, IDC_ARROW); /* cursor style */
  wcl.lpszMenuName = NULL; /* no menu */
```

```
    wcl.cbClsExtra = 0; /* no extra */
    wcl.cbWndExtra = 0; /* information needed */

    /* Make the window white. */
    wcl.hbrBackground = GetStockObject(WHITE_BRUSH);

    /* Register the window class. */
    if(!RegisterClass (&wcl)) return 0;

    /* Now that a window class has been registered, a window
       can be created. */
    hwnd = CreateWindow(
      szWinName, /* name of window class */
      "Using Message Boxes", /* title */
      WS_OVERLAPPEDWINDOW, /* window style - normal */
      CW_USEDEFAULT, /* X coordinate - let Windows decide */
      CW_USEDEFAULT, /* Y coordinate - let Windows decide */
      CW_USEDEFAULT, /* width - let Windows decide */
      CW_USEDEFAULT, /* height - let Windows decide */
      HWND_DESKTOP, /* no parent window */
      NULL, /* no menu */
      hThisInst, /* handle of this instance of the program */
      NULL /* no additional arguments */
    );

    /* Display the window. */
    ShowWindow(hwnd, nWinMode);
    UpdateWindow(hwnd);

    /* Create the message loop. */
    while(GetMessage(&msg, NULL, 0, 0))
    {
      TranslateMessage(&msg); /* allow use of keyboard */
      DispatchMessage(&msg); /* return control to Windows */
    }
    return msg.wParam;
}

/* This function is called by Windows 95 and is passed
   messages from the message queue.
*/
LRESULT CALLBACK WindowFunc(HWND hwnd, UINT message,
                            WPARAM wParam, LPARAM lParam)
{
  int response;

  switch(message) {
    case WM_RBUTTONDOWN: /* process right button */
```

```
      response = MessageBox(hwnd, "Press One:", "Right Button",
                            MB_ABORTRETRYIGNORE);
      switch(response) {
        case IDABORT:
          MessageBox(hwnd, "", "Abort", MB_OK);
          break;
        case IDRETRY:
          MessageBox(hwnd, "", "Retry", MB_OK);
          break;
        case IDIGNORE:
          MessageBox(hwnd, "", "Ignore", MB_OK);
          break;
      }
      break;
    case WM_LBUTTONDOWN: /* process left button */
      response = MessageBox(hwnd, "Continue?", "Left Button",
                 MB_ICONHAND | MB_YESNO);
      switch(response) {
        case IDYES:
          MessageBox(hwnd, "Press Button", "Yes", MB_OK);
          break;
        case IDNO:
          MessageBox(hwnd, "Press Button", "No", MB_OK);
          break;
      }
      break;
    case WM_DESTROY: /* terminate the program */
      PostQuitMessage(0);
      break;
    default:
      /* Let Windows 95 process any messages not specified in
         the preceding switch statement. */
      return DefWindowProc(hwnd, message, wParam, lParam);
  }
  return 0;
}
```

Each time a button is pressed, a message box is displayed. For example, pressing the right button displays the message box shown here:

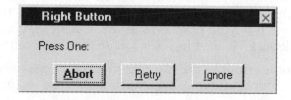

As you can see, the message box displays the buttons Abort, Retry, and Ignore. Depending upon your response, a second message box will be displayed that indicates which button you pressed. Pressing the left mouse button causes a message box that contains a stop sign to be displayed. This box allows a Yes or a No response.

Before you continue, experiment with message boxes, trying different types.

Introducing Menus

In Windows the most common element of control is the menu. Virtually all main windows have some type of menu associated with them. Because menus are so common and important in Windows applications, Windows provides substantial built-in support for them. As you will see, adding a menu to a window involves these few steps:

1. Define the form of the menu in a resource file.
2. Load the menu when your program creates its main window.
3. Process menu selections.

In Windows, the top level of a menu is displayed across the top of the window. Submenus are displayed as popup menus. (You should be accustomed to this approach, because it is used by virtually all Windows programs.)

Before moving on, it is important to understand what resources and resource files are.

Using Resources

Windows defines several common types of objects as *resources*. Resources are essentially objects that are used by your program but defined outside your program. They include things such as menus, icons, dialog boxes, and bitmapped graphics. Since a menu is a resource, you need to understand resources before you can add a menu to your program.

A resource is created separately from your program, but is added to the .EXE file when your program is linked. Resources are contained in *resource files*, which have the extension .RC. In general, the filename should be the same as that of your program's .EXE file. For example, if your program is called PROG.EXE, then its resource file should be called PROG.RC.

Some resources are text files that you create using a standard text editor. Text resources are typically defined within the resource file. Others, such as icons, are most easily generated using a resource editor, but they still must be referred to in the .RC file that is associated with your application. The example resource files in this chapter are simply text files because menus are text-based resources.

Resource files are not C or C++ files. Instead, they contain a special resource language, or *script*, that must be compiled using a *resource compiler*. The resource compiler converts an .RC file into a .RES file, which may be linked with your program.

Compiling .RC Files

Resource files are not used directly by your program. Instead, they must be converted into a linkable format. Once you have created an .RC file, you compile it into a .RES file using the resource compiler. (The resource compiler is often called RC.EXE, but this varies.) Exactly how you compile a resource file will depend upon what compiler you are using. Also, some integrated development environments automatically handle this phase for you. In any event, the output of the resource compiler will be a .RES file, and it is this file that you will link with your program to build the final Windows 95 application.

4

Note: You must consult your compiler's user manual for instructions on including resource files with your programs.

Creating a Simple Menu

Before a menu can be included, you must define its content in a resource file. All menu definitions have this general form:

MenuName MENU [*options*]
{
  menu items
}

Here, *MenuName* is the name of the menu. (It may also be an integer value identifying the menu, but all examples in this book will use the name when referring to the menu.) The keyword **MENU** tells the resource compiler that a menu is being created. There are several options that can be specified when creating the menu. They are shown in Table 4-2. (Again, these macros are defined by including **windows.h**.) The examples in this book simply use the default settings and do not specify options.

Option	Meaning
DISCARDABLE	Menu may be removed from memory when no longer needed.
FIXED	Menu is fixed in memory.
LOADONCALL	Menu is loaded when used.
MOVEABLE	Menu may be moved in memory.
PRELOAD	Menu is loaded when your program begins execution.

There are two types of items that can be used to define the menu: **MENUITEM**s and **POPUP**s. A **MENUITEM** specifies a final selection. A **POPUP** specifies a popup submenu, which may, in itself, contain other **MENUITEM**s or **POPUP**s. The general form of these two statements is shown here:

MENUITEM "*ItemName*", *MenuID* [*,options*]

POPUP "*PopupName*" [*,options*]

Here, *ItemName* is the name of the menu selection, such as Help or File. *MenuID* is a unique integer associated with a menu item that will be sent to your application when a selection is made. Typically, these values are defined as macros inside a header file that is included both in your application code and in the .RC resource file. *PopupName* is the name of the popup menu. For both cases, the values for *options* (defined by including **windows.h**) are shown in Table 4-3.

Option	Meaning
CHECKED	A checkmark is displayed next to the name (not applicable to top-level menus).
GRAYED	The name is shown in gray and may not be selected.
HELP	May be associated with a help selection. This applies to **MENUITEM**s only.
INACTIVE	The option may not be selected.
MENUBARBREAK	For menu bar, causes the item to be put on a new line. For popup menus, causes the item to be put in a different column. In this case, the item is separated using a bar.
MENUBREAK	Same as MENUBARBREAK except that no separator bar is used.

Here is an example of a simple menu that you should enter at this time. Call
the file MENU.RC.

```
; Sample menu resource file.
#include "menu.h"

MYMENU MENU
{
  POPUP "&One"
  {
    MENUITEM "&Alpha", IDM_ALPHA
    MENUITEM "&Beta", IDM_BETA
  }
  POPUP "&Two"
  {
    MENUITEM "&Gamma", IDM_GAMMA
    POPUP "&Delta"
    {
      MENUITEM "&Epsilon", IDM_EPSILON
      MENUITEM "&Zeta", IDM_ZETA
    }
    MENUITEM "&Eta", IDM_ETA
    MENUITEM "&Theta", IDM_THETA
  }
  MENUITEM "&Help", IDM_HELP
}
```

4

This menu, called **MYMENU**, contains three top-level menu bar options:
One, Two, and Help. The One and Two options contain popup submenus.
The Delta option activates a popup submenu of its own. Notice that options
that activate submenus do not have menu ID values associated with them.
Only actual menu items have ID numbers. In this menu, all menu ID values
are specified as macros beginning with IDM. (These macros are defined in
the header file **menu.h**.) How you name these values is arbitrary.

An & in an item's name causes the key that it precedes to become the
shortcut key associated with that option. That is, once that menu is active,
pressing the shortcut key causes that menu item to be selected. The shortcut
key doesn't have to be the first key in the name, but it should be unless a
conflict with another name exists.

Note: You can embed comments into resource files on a line-by-line
basis by beginning them with a semicolon, as the first line of the preceding
resource file example shows. You may also use C- and C++-style comments.

The **menu.h** header file, which is included in MENU.RC, contains the macro definitions of the menu ID values. It is shown here. Enter it at this time.

```
#define IDM_ALPHA    100
#define IDM_BETA     101
#define IDM_GAMMA    102
#define IDM_DELTA    103
#define IDM_EPSILON  104
#define IDM_ZETA     105
#define IDM_ETA      106
#define IDM_THETA    107
#define IDM_HELP     108
```

This file defines the menu ID values that will be returned when the various menu items are selected. This file will also be included in the program that uses the menu. Remember, the actual names and values you give the menu items are arbitrary, but each value must be unique. Also, the valid range for ID values is 0 through 65,565.

Including a Menu in Your Program

Once you have created a menu, you include that menu in a program by specifying its name when you create the window's class. Specifically, you assign the **lpszMenuName** field a pointer to a string that contains the name of the menu. For example, to load the menu **MYMENU**, you would use this line when defining the window's class:

```
wcl.lpszMenuName = "MYMENU"; // main menu
```

Responding to Menu Selections

Each time the user makes a menu selection, your program's window function is sent a **WM_COMMAND** message. When that message is received, the value of **LOWORD(wParam)** corresponds to the menu item's ID constant. (That is, **LOWORD(wParam)** contains the value you associated with the item when you defined the menu in its .RC file.) Since **WM_COMMAND** is sent whenever a menu item is selected and the value associated with that item is contained in **LOWORD(wParam)**, you will need to use a nested **switch** statement to determine which item was selected. For example, this fragment responds to a selection made from **MYMENU**:

```
switch(message) {
  case WM_COMMAND:
    switch(LOWORD(wParam)) {
```

```
      case IDM_ALPHA: MessageBox(hwnd, "Alpha", "", MB_OK);
        break;
      case IDM_BETA: MessageBox(hwnd, "Beta", "", MB_OK);
        break;
      case IDM_GAMMA: MessageBox(hwnd, "Gamma", "", MB_OK);
        break;
      case IDM_EPSILON: MessageBox(hwnd, "Epsilon", "", MB_OK);
        break;
      case IDM_ZETA: MessageBox(hwnd, "Zeta", "", MB_OK);
        break;
      case IDM_ETA: MessageBox(hwnd, "Eta", "", MB_OK);
        break;
      case IDM_THETA: MessageBox(hwnd, "Theta", "", MB_OK);
        break;
      case IDM_HELP: MessageBox(hwnd, "No Help", "Help", MB_OK);
        break;
    }
    break;
```

For the sake of illustration, the response to each selection simply displays an acknowledgment of that selection on the screen. However, in real-world applications, the response to menu selections will generally be more complex.

4

A Sample Menu Program

Here is a program that adds a menu to the previous program. Enter it at this time, calling it MENU.C. Sample output from the program is shown in Figure 4-1.

```
/* Demonstrate menus. */

#include <windows.h>
#include <string.h>
#include <stdio.h>
#include "menu.h"

LRESULT CALLBACK WindowFunc(HWND, UINT, WPARAM, LPARAM);

char szWinName[] = "MyWin"; /* name of window class */

int WINAPI WinMain(HINSTANCE hThisInst, HINSTANCE hPrevInst,
                   LPSTR lpszArgs, int nWinMode)
{
  HWND hwnd;
  MSG msg;
  WNDCLASS wcl;
```

```
/* Define a window class. */
wcl.hInstance = hThisInst; /* handle to this instance */
wcl.lpszClassName = szWinName; /* window class name */
wcl.lpfnWndProc = WindowFunc; /* window function */
wcl.style = 0; /* default style */

wcl.hIcon = LoadIcon(NULL, IDI_APPLICATION); /* icon style */
wcl.hCursor = LoadCursor(NULL, IDC_ARROW); /* cursor style */

/* specify name of menu resource */
wcl.lpszMenuName = "MYMENU"; /* main menu */

wcl.cbClsExtra = 0; /* no extra */
wcl.cbWndExtra = 0; /* information needed */

/* Make the window white. */
wcl.hbrBackground = GetStockObject(WHITE_BRUSH);

/* Register the window class. */
if(!RegisterClass (&wcl)) return 0;

/* Now that a window class has been registered, a window
   can be created. */
hwnd = CreateWindow(
  szWinName, /* name of window class */
  "Using Menus", /* title */
  WS_OVERLAPPEDWINDOW, /* window style - normal */
  CW_USEDEFAULT, /* X coordinate - let Windows decide */
  CW_USEDEFAULT, /* Y coordinate - let Windows decide */
  CW_USEDEFAULT, /* width - let Windows decide */
  CW_USEDEFAULT, /* height - let Windows decide */
  HWND_DESKTOP, /* no parent window */
  NULL, /* no menu */
  hThisInst, /* handle of this instance of the program */
  NULL /* no additional arguments */
);

/* Display the window. */
ShowWindow(hwnd, nWinMode);
UpdateWindow(hwnd);

/* Create the message loop. */
while(GetMessage(&msg, NULL, 0, 0))
{
  TranslateMessage(&msg); /* allow use of keyboard */
  DispatchMessage(&msg); /* return control to Windows */
}
return msg.wParam;
```

```
    }

    /* This function is called by Windows 95 and is passed
       messages from the message queue.
    */
    LRESULT CALLBACK WindowFunc(HWND hwnd, UINT message,
                                        WPARAM wParam, LPARAM lParam)
    {
      int response;

      switch(message) {
        case WM_COMMAND:
          switch(LOWORD(wParam)) {
            case IDM_ALPHA: MessageBox(hwnd, "Alpha", "", MB_OK);
              break;
            case IDM_BETA: MessageBox(hwnd, "Beta", "", MB_OK);
              break;
            case IDM_GAMMA: MessageBox(hwnd, "Gamma", "", MB_OK);
              break;
            case IDM_EPSILON: MessageBox(hwnd, "Epsilon", "", MB_OK);
              break;
            case IDM_ZETA: MessageBox(hwnd, "Zeta", "", MB_OK);
              break;
            case IDM_ETA: MessageBox(hwnd, "Eta", "", MB_OK);
              break;
            case IDM_THETA: MessageBox(hwnd, "Theta", "", MB_OK);
              break;
            case IDM_HELP: MessageBox(hwnd, "No Help", "Help", MB_OK);
              break;
          }
          break;
        case WM_RBUTTONDOWN: /* process right button */
          response = MessageBox(hwnd, "Press One:", "Right Button",
                                MB_ABORTRETRYIGNORE);
          switch(response) {
            case IDABORT:
              MessageBox(hwnd, "", "Abort", MB_OK);
              break;
            case IDRETRY:
              MessageBox(hwnd, "", "Retry", MB_OK);
              break;
            case IDIGNORE:
              MessageBox(hwnd, "", "Ignore", MB_OK);
              break;
          }
          break;
        case WM_LBUTTONDOWN: /* process left button */
          response = MessageBox(hwnd, "Continue?", "Left Button",
```

4

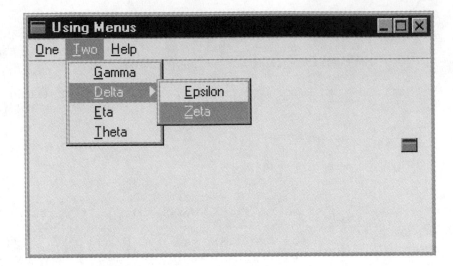

```
                 MB_ICONHAND | MB_YESNO);
    switch(response) {
      case IDYES:
        MessageBox(hwnd, "Press Button", "Yes", MB_OK);
        break;
      case IDNO:
        MessageBox(hwnd, "Press Button", "No", MB_OK);
        break;
    }
    break;
  case WM_DESTROY: /* terminate the program */
    PostQuitMessage(0);
    break;
  default:
    /* Let Windows 95 process any messages not specified in
       the preceding switch statement. */
    return DefWindowProc(hwnd, message, wParam, lParam);
  }
  return 0;
}
```

Adding Menu Accelerator Keys

Before leaving the topic of menus, one more feature relating to them will be
discussed. This feature is the accelerator key. *Accelerator keys* are special
keystrokes defined by you that, when pressed, automatically select a menu
option even though the menu in which that option resides is not displayed.
Put differently, you can select an item directly by pressing an accelerator key,
bypassing the menu entirely. The term *accelerator keys* is an accurate

description, because it is generally faster to select a menu item by pressing an accelerator key than by first activating the menu and then selecting the item.

To define accelerator keys relative to a menu, you must add an accelerator key table to your resource file. All accelerator table definitions have this general form:

```
TableName ACCELERATORS
{
 Key1, MenuID1 [,type] [option]
 Key2, MenuID2 [,type] [option]
 Key3, MenuID3 [,type] [option]
  .
  .
  .
 Keyn, MenuIDn [,type] [option]
}
```

Here, *TableName* is the name of the accelerator table. *Key* is the keystroke that selects the item, and *MenuID* is the ID value associated with the desired item. The *type* specifies whether the key is a standard key (the default) or a virtual key (discussed shortly). The options may be one of the following macros: **NOINVERT**, **ALT**, **SHIFT**, and **CONTROL**. **NOINVERT** prevents the selected menu item from being highlighted when its accelerator key is pressed. **ALT** specifies the ALT key. **SHIFT** specifies the SHIFT key. **CONTROL** specifies the CTRL key.

The value of *Key* will be a quoted character, an ASCII integer value corresponding to a key, or a virtual key code. If a quoted character is used, then it is assumed to be an ASCII character. If it is an integer value, then you must tell the resource compiler explicitly that this is an ASCII character by specifying *type* as **ASCII**. If it is a virtual key, then *type* must be **VIRTKEY**.

If the key is an uppercase quoted character, then its corresponding menu item will be selected if it is pressed while the user holds down SHIFT. If it is a lowercase character, then its menu item will be selected if the key is pressed by itself. If the key is specified as a lowercase character and **ALT** is specified as an option, then pressing ALT and the character will select the item. (If the key is uppercase and **ALT** is specified, then you must press SHIFT and ALT to select the item.) Finally, if you want the user to press CTRL and the character to select an item, precede the key with ^.

A *virtual key* is a system-independent code for a variety of keys. Virtual keys include the function keys F1 through F12, the arrow keys, and various non-ASCII keys. They are defined by macros in the header file **windows.h** (or one of its derivatives). All virtual-key macros begin with **VK_**. For

4

example, the macros for the function keys are **VK_F1** through **VK_F12**. You should refer to **windows.h** for the other virtual key code macros. To use a virtual key as an accelerator, simply specify its macro for the *key* and specify **VIRTKEY** for its *type*. You may also specify **ALT**, **SHIFT**, or **CONTROL** to achieve the desired key combination.

Here are some examples:

```
"A", IDM_x ; select by pressing Shift-A
"a", IDM_x ; select by pressing a
"^A", IDM_x ; select by pressing Ctrl-A
"a", IDM_x, ALT ; select by pressing Alt-A
VK_F2, IDM_x ; select by pressing F2
VK_F2, IDM_x, SHIFT ; select by pressing Shift-F2
```

Here is the MENU.RC resource file, with accelerator key definitions for the menu specified in the previous section added:

```
; Sample menu resource file
#include <windows.h>
#include "menu.h"

MYMENU MENU
{
  POPUP "&One"
  {
    MENUITEM "&Alpha\tF2", IDM_ALPHA
    MENUITEM "&Beta\tF3", IDM_BETA
  }
  POPUP "&Two"
  {
    MENUITEM "&Gamma\tShift-G", IDM_GAMMA
    POPUP "&Delta"
    {
      MENUITEM "&Epsilon\tCntl-E", IDM_EPSILON
      MENUITEM "&Zeta\tCntl-Z", IDM_ZETA
    }
    MENUITEM "&Eta\tCntl-F4", IDM_ETA
    MENUITEM "&Theta\tF5", IDM_THETA
  }
  MENUITEM "&Help", IDM_HELP
}

; Define menu accelerators
MYMENU ACCELERATORS
{
  VK_F2, IDM_ALPHA, VIRTKEY
  VK_F3, IDM_BETA, VIRTKEY
```

```
    "G", IDM_GAMMA
    "^E", IDM_EPSILON
    "^Z", IDM_ZETA
    VK_F4, IDM_ETA, VIRTKEY, CONTROL
    VK_F5, IDM_THETA, VIRTKEY
    VK_F1, IDM_HELP, VIRTKEY
}
```

Notice that the menu definition has been enhanced to display which accelerator key selects which option. Each item is separated from its accelerator key using a tab. The header file **windows.h** is included because it defines the virtual key macros.

Loading the Accelerator Table

Even though the accelerators are contained in the same resource file as the menu, they must be loaded separately using another API function called **LoadAccelerators( )**, whose prototype is shown here:

HACCEL LoadAccelerators(HINSTANCE *ThisInst*, LPCSTR *Name*);

4

ThisInst is the handle of the application and *Name* is the name of the accelerator table. The function returns a handle to the accelerator table or NULL if the table cannot be loaded.

You must call **LoadAccelerators( )** soon after the window is created. For example, this shows how to load the **MYMENU** accelerator table:

```
HACCEL hAccel;

hAccel = LoadAccelerators(hThisInst, "MYMENU");
```

The value of **hAccel** will be used later to help process accelerator keys.

Although the **LoadAccelerators( )** function loads the accelerator table, your program still cannot process the accelerators until you add another API function to the message loop. This function is called **TranslateAccelerator( )**, and its prototype is shown here:

int TranslateAccelerator(HWND *hwnd*, HACCEL *hAccel*, LPMSG *lpMess*);

Here, *hwnd* is the handle of the window for which accelerator keys will be translated. *hAccel* is the handle to the accelerator table that will be used. This is the handle returned by **LoadAccelerators( )**. Finally, *lpMess* is a pointer to the message. The **TranslateAccelerator( )** function returns true if an accelerator key was pressed and false otherwise. This function translates accelerator keystrokes into the proper **WM_COMMAND** message.

When using **TranslateAccelerator( )**, your message loop should look like this:

```
while(GetMessage(&msg, NULL, 0, 0))
{
  if(!TranslateAccelerator(hwnd, hAccel, &msg)) {
    TranslateMessage(&msg); /* allow use of keyboard */
    DispatchMessage(&msg); /* return control to Windows */
  }
}
```

To try using accelerators, substitute the following version of **WinMain( )** into the preceding application and add the accelerator table to your resource file.

```
/* Process accelerator keys. */
int WINAPI WinMain(HINSTANCE hThisInst, HINSTANCE hPrevInst,
                   LPSTR lpszArgs, int nWinMode)
{
  HWND hwnd;
  MSG msg;
  WNDCLASS wcl;
  HACCEL hAccel;

  /* Define a window class. */
  wcl.hInstance = hThisInst; /* handle to this instance */
  wcl.lpszClassName = szWinName; /* window class name */
  wcl.lpfnWndProc = WindowFunc; /* window function */
  wcl.style = 0; /* default style */

  wcl.hIcon = LoadIcon(NULL, IDI_APPLICATION); /* icon style */
  wcl.hCursor = LoadCursor(NULL, IDC_ARROW); /* cursor style */

  /* specify name of menu resource */
  wcl.lpszMenuName = "MYMENU"; /* main menu */

  wcl.cbClsExtra = 0; /* no extra */
  wcl.cbWndExtra = 0; /* information needed */

  /* Make the window white. */
  wcl.hbrBackground = GetStockObject(WHITE_BRUSH);

  /* Register the window class. */
  if(!RegisterClass (&wcl)) return 0;

  /* Now that a window class has been registered, a window
     can be created. */
  hwnd = CreateWindow(
```

```
      szWinName, /* name of window class */
      "Using Menus", /* title */
      WS_OVERLAPPEDWINDOW, /* window style - normal */
      CW_USEDEFAULT, /* X coordinate - let Windows decide */
      CW_USEDEFAULT, /* Y coordinate - let Windows decide */
      CW_USEDEFAULT, /* width - let Windows decide */
      CW_USEDEFAULT, /* height - let Windows decide */
      HWND_DESKTOP, /* no parent window */
      NULL, /* no menu */
      hThisInst, /* handle of this instance of the program */
      NULL /* no additional arguments */
    );

    /* load the keyboard accelerators */
    hAccel = LoadAccelerators(hThisInst, "MYMENU");

    /* Display the window. */
    ShowWindow(hwnd, nWinMode);
    UpdateWindow(hwnd);

    /* Create the message loop. */
    while(GetMessage(&msg, NULL, 0, 0))
    {
      if(!TranslateAccelerator(hwnd, hAccel, &msg)) {
        TranslateMessage(&msg); /* allow use of keyboard */
        DispatchMessage(&msg); /* return control to Windows */
      }
    }
    return msg.wParam;
}
```

4

Before moving on to the next chapter, you should experiment on your own using message boxes, menus, and accelerators. Try the various options and see what they do. Menus and message boxes will be used by most of the other programs in this book, so a thorough understanding is important.

Chapter

5

Introducing Dialog Boxes

This chapter introduces the *dialog box*. After menus, there is no more important interface element than the dialog box. A dialog box is a type of window that provides a more flexible means by which the user can interact with your application. In general, dialog boxes allow the user to select or enter information that would be difficult or impossible to enter using a menu.

Dialog boxes (and the controls that occur within them) are a large topic. In this chapter you will learn the basics of dialog box management, including how to create a dialog box and process dialog box messages. In subsequent chapters, we will use a dialog box to explore several elements of the Windows 95 interface.

How Dialog Boxes Interact with the User

A dialog box interacts with the user through one or more *controls*. A control is a specific type of input or output window. A control is owned by its parent window, which, in the examples presented in this chapter, is the dialog box. Windows 95 supports several controls, including push buttons, check boxes, radio buttons, list boxes, edit boxes, combination boxes, scroll bars, and static controls. Each is briefly described here:

♦ A *push button* is a control that the user "pushes on" (by clicking it with the mouse or by pressing TAB until the button is highlighted, and then pressing ENTER) to activate some response. You have already been using push buttons in message boxes. For example, the OK button that we have been using in most message boxes is a push button.

♦ A *check box* contains one or more items that are either checked or not checked. If the item is checked, that means it is selected. If there are two or more check boxes in the dialog box, more than one item may be selected.

♦ A *radio button* is essentially a check box. However, when there is more than one radio button, one and only one item may be selected. Thus, radio buttons are mutually exclusive check boxes.

♦ A *list box* displays a list of items from which the user may select one (or more). List boxes are commonly used to display things such as filenames.

♦ An *edit box* allows the user to enter a string. Edit boxes provide all necessary text editing features required by the user. Therefore, to request a string, the program simply displays an edit box and waits until the user has finished typing in the string.

♦ A *combination box* is a combination of a list box and an edit box.

♦ A *scroll bar* is used to scroll text in a window.

♦ A *static control* is used to output text (or graphics) that provides information to the user, but accepts no input.

The examples in this chapter illustrate three of these controls: push buttons, the list box, and the edit box. Later in this book, the other controls will be examined.

It is important to understand that controls both generate messages (when accessed by the user) and receive messages (from your application). A message generated by a control indicates what type of interaction the user has had with the control. A message sent to the control is essentially an instruction to which the control must respond. You will see examples of this type of message passing later in this chapter.

Modal and Modeless Dialog Boxes

There are two types of dialog boxes: *modal* and *modeless*. The most common dialog boxes are modal. A modal dialog box demands a response before the parent program will continue. That is, a modal dialog box will not allow you to refocus input to another part of the parent application without first responding to the dialog box.

A modeless dialog box does not prevent the parent program from running. That is, it does not demand a response before input can be refocused to another part of the program.

We will examine modal dialog boxes first, since they are the most common. A modeless dialog box example concludes this chapter.

Receiving Dialog Box Messages

A dialog box is a window (albeit, a special kind of window). Events that occur within it are sent to your program using the same message-passing mechanism the main window uses. However, dialog box messages are not sent to your program's main window function. Instead, each dialog box that you define will need its own window function, which is generally called a *dialog function*. This function must have this prototype (of course, the name of the function may be anything you like):

BOOL CALLBACK DFunc(HWND *hdwnd*, UINT *message*,
                 WPARAM *wParam*, LPARAM *lParam*);

5

As you can see, a dialog function receives the same parameters as your program's main window function. However, it differs from the main window function in that it returns a true or false result. Like your program's main window function, the dialog box window function will receive many messages. If it processes a message, then it must return true. If it does not respond to a message, it must return false.

In general, each control within a dialog box will be given its own resource ID. Each time that control is accessed by the user, a message will be sent to the dialog function, indicating the ID of the control and the type of action the user has taken. That function will then decode the message and take appropriate actions. This process parallels the way messages are decoded by your program's main window function.

In Windows 3.1, the dialog function must be exported in the .DEF file associated with your program. However, this is not required by Windows 95. (In fact, as mentioned earlier, .DEF files are no longer used by Windows 95.)

Activating a Dialog Box

To activate a modal dialog box (to cause it to be displayed), you must call the **DialogBox( )** API function, whose prototype is shown here:

int DialogBox(HINSTANCE *hThisInst*, LPCSTR *lpName*,
HWND *hwnd*, DLGPROC *lpDFunc*);

Here, *hThisInst* is a handle to the current application that is passed to your program in the instance parameter to **WinMain( )**.

The name of the dialog box as defined in the resource file is pointed to by *lpName*. The handle to the parent window that activates the dialog box is passed in *hwnd*. The *lpDFunc* parameter contains a pointer to the dialog function.

 In Windows 3.1, the *lpDFunc* parameter to DialogBox( ) is a pointer to a procedure-instance, which is a short piece of code that links the dialog function with the data segment that the program is currently using. A procedure-instance is obtained using the MakeProcInstance( ) API function. However, this no longer applies to Windows 95. The *lpDFunc* parameter is a pointer to the dialog function itself, and MakeProcInstance( ) is no longer needed. You should remove calls to MakeProcInstance( ) if you are converting older 3.1 code.

Creating a Simple Dialog Box

The first dialog box we create will be a simple example containing three push buttons—Red, Green, and Cancel. When either the Red or Green button is pressed, the button will activate a message box indicating the choice selected. The box will be removed from the screen when the Cancel button is pressed.

The program will have a top-level menu containing three options: Dialog 1, Dialog 2, and Help. Only Dialog 1 will have a dialog box associated with it. The Dialog 2 entry is a placeholder added so that you can define your own dialog box as you work through the examples.

While this and other examples in this chapter don't do much with the information provided by the dialog box, they illustrate the central features that you will use in your applications.

The Dialog Box Resource File

A dialog box is another resource that is contained in your program's resource file. Before developing a program that uses a dialog box, you will need a resource file that specifies one. Although it is possible to specify the contents of a dialog box using a text editor and to enter its specifications as you do when creating a menu, this is seldom done. Instead, most programmers use a dialog editor. This is mainly because dialog box definitions involve the positioning of the various controls inside the dialog box, which is best done interactively. However, since the complete .RC files for the examples in this chapter are supplied in their text form, you should simply enter them as text. Just remember that when creating your own dialog boxes, you will want to use a dialog editor.

Note: Since, in practice, most dialog boxes are created using a dialog editor, only a brief explanation of the dialog box definition in the resource file is given for the examples in this chapter.

Dialog boxes are defined within your program's resource file using the **DIALOG** statement. Its general form is shown here:

Dialog-name DIALOG [DISCARDABLE] *X, Y, Width, Height*
Features
{
  Dialog-items
}

Dialog-name is the name of the dialog box. The box's upper-left corner will be at *X,Y*, and the box will have the dimensions specified by *Width* x *Height*. If the box may be removed from memory when not in use, then specify it as **DISCARDABLE**. One or more features of the dialog box may be specified. As you will see, two of these are the caption and the style of the box. The *Dialog-items* are the controls that comprise the dialog box.

The following resource file defines the dialog box that will be used by the first example program. It includes a menu that is used to activate the dialog box, the menu accelerator keys, and then the dialog box itself. You should enter it into your computer at this time, calling it MYDIALOG.RC.

```
; Sample dialog box and menu resource file.
#include "mydialog.h"
#include <windows.h>

MYMENU MENU
{
  MENUITEM "Dialog &1", IDM_DIALOG1
  MENUITEM "Dialog &2", IDM_DIALOG2
  MENUITEM "&Help", IDM_HELP
}
```

5

```
MYMENU ACCELERATORS
{
  VK_F2, IDM_DIALOG1, VIRTKEY
  VK_F3, IDM_DIALOG2, VIRTKEY
  VK_F1, IDM_HELP, VIRTKEY
}


MYDB DIALOG 18, 18, 142, 92
CAPTION "Sample Dialog Box"
STYLE DS_MODALFRAME | WS_POPUP | WS_CAPTION | WS_SYSMENU
{
  DEFPUSHBUTTON "Red", IDD_RED, 32, 40, 30, 14,
            WS_CHILD | WS_VISIBLE | WS_TABSTOP
  PUSHBUTTON "Green", IDD_GREEN, 74, 40, 30, 14,
            WS_CHILD | WS_VISIBLE | WS_TABSTOP
  PUSHBUTTON "Cancel", IDCANCEL, 52, 65, 37, 14,
            WS_CHILD | WS_VISIBLE | WS_TABSTOP
}
```

This defines a dialog box called **MYDB** that has its upper-left corner at
location 18, 18. Its width is 142 and its height is 92. The string after
CAPTION becomes the title of the dialog box. The **STYLE** statement
determines what type of dialog box is created. Some common style values,
including those used in this chapter, are shown in Table 5-1. You can OR
together the values that are appropriate for the style of dialog box that you
desire. These style values may also be used by other controls.

Within the **MYDB** definition are defined three push buttons. The first is
the default push button. This button is automatically highlighted when the
dialog box is first displayed. The general form of a push-button declaration is

Value	Meaning
DS_MODALFRAME	Create modal dialog box
WS_BORDER	Include border
WS_CAPTION	Include title bar
WS_CHILD	Create as child window
WS_POPUP	Create as popup window
WS_MAXIMIZEBOX	Include maximize box
WS_MINIMIZEBOX	Include minimize box
WS_SYSMENU	Include system menu
WS_TABSTOP	Control may be selected by pressing TAB
WS_VISIBLE	Box is visible when activated

Some
Common
Dialog Box
Style Options
Table 5-1.

shown here:

PUSHBUTTON "*string*", *PBID*, *X*, *Y*, *Width*, *Height* [, *Style*]

Here, *string* is the text that will be shown inside the push button. *PBID* is the value associated with the push button. It is this value that is returned to your program when the button is pushed. The button's upper-left corner will be at *X,Y*, and the button will have the dimensions specified by *Width* x *Height*. *Style* determines the exact nature of the push button. To define a default push button, use the **DEFPUSHBUTTON** statement. It has the same parameters as the regular push buttons.

The header file **mydialog.h**, which is also used by the example program, is shown here. Enter this file now.

```
#define IDM_DIALOG1   100
#define IDM_DIALOG2   101
#define IDM_HELP      102

#define IDD_RED       103
#define IDD_GREEN     104
```

The Dialog Box Window Function

As stated earlier, events that occur with a dialog box are passed to the window function associated with that dialog box and not to your program's main window function. The following dialog box window function responds to the events that occur within the **MYDB** dialog box.

5

```
/* A simple dialog function. */
BOOL CALLBACK DialogFunc(HWND hdwnd, UINT message,
                         WPARAM wParam, LPARAM lParam)
{
  switch(message) {
    case WM_COMMAND:
      switch(LOWORD(wParam)) {
        case IDCANCEL:
          EndDialog(hdwnd, 0);
          return 1;
        case IDD_RED:
          MessageBox(hdwnd, "You Picked Red", "RED", MB_OK);
          return 1;
        case IDD_GREEN:
          MessageBox(hdwnd, "You Picked Green", "GREEN", MB_OK);
          return 1;
      }
  }
```

```
    return 0;
}
```

Each time a control within the dialog box is accessed, a **WM_COMMAND** message is sent to **DialogFunc( )**. **LOWORD(wParam)** contains the ID of the affected control.

DialogFunc( ) processes the three messages that can be generated by the box. If the user presses Cancel, then **IDCANCEL** is sent, causing the dialog box to be closed via a call to the API function **EndDialog( )**. (**IDCANCEL** is a standard ID defined by including **windows.h**.) **EndDialog( )** has this prototype:

BOOL EndDialog(HWND *hdwnd*, int *nStatus*);

Here, *hdwnd* is the handle to the dialog box and *nStatus* is a status code returned by the **DialogBox( )** function. (The value of *nStatus* may be ignored if it is not relevant to your program.) This function returns non-zero if successful and zero otherwise. (In normal situations, the function is successful.)

Pressing either of the other two buttons causes a message box to be displayed that confirms the selection.

A First Dialog Box Sample Program

Following is the entire dialog box example. When the program begins execution, only the top-level menu is displayed on the menu bar. By selecting Dialog 1, the user causes the dialog box to be displayed. Once the dialog box is displayed, selecting a push button causes the appropriate response. A sample screen is shown in Figure 5-1.

```
/* Demonstrate a modal dialog box. */

#include <windows.h>
#include <string.h>
#include <stdio.h>
#include "mydialog.h"

LRESULT CALLBACK WindowFunc(HWND, UINT, WPARAM, LPARAM);
BOOL CALLBACK DialogFunc(HWND, UINT, WPARAM, LPARAM);

char szWinName[] = "MyWin"; /* name of window class */

HINSTANCE hInst;

int WINAPI WinMain(HINSTANCE hThisInst, HINSTANCE hPrevInst,
                   LPSTR lpszArgs, int nWinMode)
```

```
{
  HWND hwnd;
  MSG msg;
  WNDCLASS wcl;
  HANDLE hAccel;

  /* Define a window class. */
  wcl.hInstance = hThisInst; /* handle to this instance */
  wcl.lpszClassName = szWinName; /* window class name */
  wcl.lpfnWndProc = WindowFunc; /* window function */
  wcl.style = 0; /* default style */

  wcl.hIcon = LoadIcon(NULL, IDI_APPLICATION); /* icon style */
  wcl.hCursor = LoadCursor(NULL, IDC_ARROW); /* cursor style */

  /* specify name of menu resource */
  wcl.lpszMenuName = "MYMENU"; /* main menu */

  wcl.cbClsExtra = 0; /* no extra */
  wcl.cbWndExtra = 0; /* information needed */

  /* Make the window white. */
  wcl.hbrBackground = GetStockObject(WHITE_BRUSH);

  /* Register the window class. */
  if(!RegisterClass (&wcl)) return 0;

  /* Now that a window class has been registered, a window
     can be created. */
  hwnd = CreateWindow(
    szWinName, /* name of window class */
    "Dialog Boxes", /* title */
    WS_OVERLAPPEDWINDOW, /* window style - normal */
    CW_USEDEFAULT, /* X coordinate - let Windows decide */
    CW_USEDEFAULT, /* Y coordinate - let Windows decide */
    CW_USEDEFAULT, /* width - let Windows decide */
    CW_USEDEFAULT, /* height - let Windows decide */
    NULL, /* no parent window */
    NULL, /* Use menu registers with this class */
    hThisInst, /* handle of this instance of the program */
    NULL /* no additional arguments */
  );

  hInst = hThisInst; /* save the current instance handle */

  /* load accelerators */
  hAccel = LoadAccelerators(hThisInst, "MYMENU");
```

5

```
    /* Display the window. */
    ShowWindow(hwnd, nWinMode);
    UpdateWindow(hwnd);

    /* Create the message loop. */
    while(GetMessage(&msg, NULL, 0, 0))
    {
      if(!TranslateAccelerator(hwnd, hAccel, &msg)) {
        TranslateMessage(&msg); /* allow use of keyboard */
        DispatchMessage(&msg); /* return control to Windows */
      }
    }
    return msg.wParam;
}

/* This function is called by Windows 95 and is passed
   messages from the message queue.
*/
LRESULT CALLBACK WindowFunc(HWND hwnd, UINT message,
                               WPARAM wParam, LPARAM lParam)
{
  switch(message) {
    case WM_COMMAND:
      switch(LOWORD(wParam)) {
        case IDM_DIALOG1:
          DialogBox(hInst, "MYDB", hwnd, DialogFunc);
          break;
        case IDM_DIALOG2:
          MessageBox(hwnd, "Dialog Not Implemented", "", MB_OK);
          break;
        case IDM_HELP:
          MessageBox(hwnd, "Help", "Help", MB_OK);
          break;
      }
      break;
    case WM_DESTROY: /* terminate the program */
      PostQuitMessage(0);
      break;
    default:
      /* Let Windows 95 process any messages not specified in
         the preceding switch statement. */
      return DefWindowProc(hwnd, message, wParam, lParam);
  }
  return 0;
}
```

```
/* A simple dialog function. */
BOOL CALLBACK DialogFunc(HWND hdwnd, UINT message,
                          WPARAM wParam, LPARAM lParam)
{
  switch(message) {
    case WM_COMMAND:
      switch(LOWORD(wParam)) {
        case IDCANCEL:
          EndDialog(hdwnd, 0);
          return 1;
        case IDD_RED:
          MessageBox(hdwnd, "You Picked Red", "RED", MB_OK);
          return 1;
        case IDD_GREEN:
          MessageBox(hdwnd, "You Picked Green", "GREEN", MB_OK);
          return 1;
      }
  }
  return 0;
}
```

Notice the global variable **hInst**. This variable is assigned a copy of the current instance handle passed to **WinMain( )**. The reason for the existence of this variable is that the dialog box needs access to the current instance handle. However, the dialog box is not created in **WinMain( )**. Instead, it is created in **WindowFunc( )**. Therefore, a copy of the instance parameter must be made so that it can be accessible outside of **WinMain( )**.

5

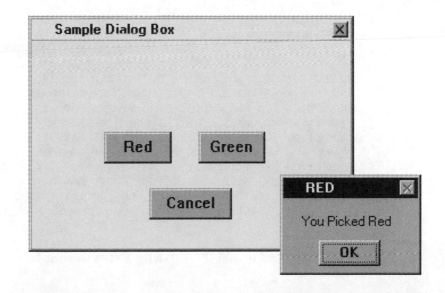

Sample output from the first dialog box program
Figure 5-1.

Adding a List Box

To continue exploring dialog boxes, let's add another control to the dialog box defined in the previous program. One of the most common controls after the push button is the list box. The **LISTBOX** statement has this general form:

LISTBOX *LBID*, *X*, *Y*, *Width*, *Height* [,*Style*]

Here, *LBID* is the value that identifies the list box. The box's upper-left corner will be at *X,Y,* and the box will have the dimensions specified by *Width* x *Height*. *Style* determines the exact nature of the list box. (The *Style* values used here are described in Table 5-1.)

To add a list box, you must change the dialog box definition in MYDIALOG.RC. First, add this list box description to the dialog box definition:

```
LISTBOX ID_LB1, 2, 10, 47, 28, LBS_NOTIFY ¦ WS_CHILD ¦
        WS_VISIBLE ¦ WS_BORDER ¦ WS_VSCROLL ¦ WS_TABSTOP
```

Next, add this push button to the dialog box definition:

```
PUSHBUTTON "Select Fruit", IDD_SELFRUIT, 5, 45, 42, 14,
        WS_CHILD ¦ WS_VISIBLE ¦ WS_TABSTOP
```

Finally, the positions of the Red and Green push buttons must be changed slightly, with the Red button located at 57, 45 and the Green button located at 95, 45. After you make these changes, your dialog box definition should look like this:

```
MYDB DIALOG 18, 18, 142, 92
CAPTION "Test Dialog Box"
STYLE DS_MODALFRAME ¦ WS_POPUP ¦ WS_CAPTION ¦ WS_SYSMENU
{
  DEFPUSHBUTTON "Red", IDD_RED, 57, 45, 30, 14,
             WS_CHILD ¦ WS_VISIBLE ¦ WS_TABSTOP
  PUSHBUTTON "Green", IDD_GREEN, 95, 45, 30, 14,
             WS_CHILD ¦ WS_VISIBLE ¦ WS_TABSTOP
  PUSHBUTTON "Cancel", IDCANCEL, 52, 65, 37, 14,
             WS_CHILD ¦ WS_VISIBLE ¦ WS_TABSTOP
  PUSHBUTTON "Select Fruit", IDD_SELFRUIT, 5, 45, 42, 14,
             WS_CHILD ¦ WS_VISIBLE ¦ WS_TABSTOP
  LISTBOX ID_LB1, 2, 10, 47, 28, LBS_NOTIFY ¦ WS_CHILD ¦
          WS_VISIBLE ¦ WS_BORDER ¦ WS_VSCROLL ¦ WS_TABSTOP
}
```

You will also need to add these macros to **mydialog.h**:

```
#define IDD_SELFRUIT 105
#define ID_LB1       106
```

ID_LB1 identifies the list box specified in the dialog box definition in the resource file. **IDD_SELFRUIT** is the ID value of the Select Fruit push button.

List Box Basics

When using a list box, you must perform two basic operations. First, you must initialize the list box when the dialog box is first displayed. This means sending the list box the list that it will display. (By default, the list box will be empty.) Second, once the list box has been initialized, your program will need to respond to the user's selection of an item from the list.

List boxes generate various types of messages. The only one we will use is **LBN_DBLCLK**. This message is sent when the user has double-clicked on an entry in the list. This message is contained in **HIWORD(wParam)** each time a **WM_COMMAND** is generated for the list box. (The list box must have the **LBS_NOTIFY** style flag included in its definition in order to generate **LBN_DBLCLK** messages.) Once a selection has been made, you will need to query the list box to find out which item has been selected.

Unlike a push button, a list box is a control that receives messages as well as generates them. You can send a list box several different messages. However, our example only sends these two:

Macro	Purpose
LB_ADDSTRING	Adds a string (selection) to the list box
LB_GETCURSEL	Requests the index of the selected item

LB_ADDSTRING is a message that tells the list box to add a specified string to the list. That is, the specified string becomes another selection within the box. You will see how to use this message shortly. The **LB_GETCURSEL** message causes the list box to return the index of the item within the list that the user selects. All list box indexes begin with 0.

To send a message to the list box (or any other control), use the **SendDlgItemMessage( )** API function. Its prototype is shown here:

```
LONG SendDlgItemMessage(HWND hdwnd, int ID,
                        UINT IDMsg, WPARAM wParam,
                        LPARAM lParam);
```

SendDlgItemMessage( ) sends to the control (within the dialog box) whose ID is specified by *ID* the message specified by *IDMsg*. The handle of the dialog box is specified in *hdwnd*. Any additional information required by the message is specified in *wParam* and *lParam*. The additional information, if any, varies from message to message. If there is no additional information to pass to a control, the *wParam* and *lParam* arguments should be 0. The value returned by **SendDlgItemMessage( )** contains the information requested by *IDMsg*.

Initializing the List Box

Since a list box is empty by default, you will need to initialize it each time the dialog box that contains it is displayed. This is quite simple, because each time a dialog box is activated, its window function is sent a **WM_INITDIALOG** message. Therefore, you will need to add this case to the outer **switch** statement in **DialogFunc( )**.

```
case WM_INITDIALOG: // initialize list box
  SendDlgItemMessage(hdwnd, ID_LB1,
                     LB_ADDSTRING, 0, (LPARAM)"Apple");
  SendDlgItemMessage(hdwnd, ID_LB1,
                     LB_ADDSTRING, 0, (LPARAM)"Orange");
  SendDlgItemMessage(hdwnd, ID_LB1,
                     LB_ADDSTRING, 0, (LPARAM)"Pear");
  SendDlgItemMessage(hdwnd, ID_LB1,
                     LB_ADDSTRING, 0, (LPARAM)"Grape");
  return 1;
```

This code loads the list box with the strings "Apple," "Orange," "Pear," and "Grape." Each string is added to the list box by calling **SendDlgItemMessage( )** with the **LB_ADDSTRING** message. The string to add is pointed to by the *lParam* parameter. (The type cast to **LPARAM** is necessary.) In this case, each string is added to the list box in the order it is sent. (However, depending upon how you construct the list box, it is possible to have the items displayed in alphabetical order.) If the number of items you send to a list box exceeds what it can display in its window, vertical scroll bars will be added automatically.

Processing a Selection

After the list box has been initialized, it is ready for use. There are essentially two ways a user can make a selection from a list box. First, the user can double-click on an item in the list box. This causes a **WM_COMMAND** message to be passed to the dialog box's window function. In this case, **LOWORD(wParam)** contains the ID associated with the list box, and **HIWORD(wParam)** contains the **LBN_DBLCLK** message. Double-clicking causes your program to be aware of the user's selection immediately. The other way to use a list box is to simply highlight a selection. This does *not* cause a message to be sent to your program, but the list box remembers the selection and waits until your program requests the selection. Both methods are demonstrated in the example program.

Once an item has been selected in a list box, you determine which item was chosen by sending the **LB_GETCURSEL** message to the list box. The list box then returns the index of the selected item. If this message is sent before an item has been selected, the list box returns **LB_ERR** (–1).

To demonstrate how to process a list box selection, add these cases to the inner switch inside **DialogFunc( )**. Each time a selection is made by double-clicking, a message box will display the index of the item selected. If the user presses the "Select Fruit" push button, the currently selected item is also reported.

```
case ID_LB1: /* process a list box LBN_DBLCLK */
  // see if user made a selection
  if(HIWORD(wParam)==LBN_DBLCLK) {
    i = SendDlgItemMessage(hdwnd, ID_LB1,
           LB_GETCURSEL, 0, 0L);  // get index
    sprintf(str, "Index in list is: %d", i);
    MessageBox(hdwnd, str, "Selection Made", MB_OK);
  }
  return 1;
case IDD_SELFRUIT: /* Select Fruit has been pressed */
  i = SendDlgItemMessage(hdwnd, ID_LB1,
         LB_GETCURSEL, 0, 0L);  // get index
  if(i > -1) sprintf(str, "Index in list is: %d", i);
  else sprintf(str, "No Fruit Selected");
  MessageBox(hdwnd, str, "Selection Made", MB_OK);
  return 1;
```

The Entire List Box Example

For your convenience, the entire expanded dialog box program is shown here. (Be sure to update **mydialog.h** and MYDIALOG.RC before compiling this program.)

```
/* Demonstrate List Boxes */

#include <windows.h>
#include <string.h>
#include <stdio.h>
#include "mydialog.h"

LRESULT CALLBACK WindowFunc(HWND, UINT, WPARAM, LPARAM);
BOOL CALLBACK DialogFunc(HWND, UINT, WPARAM, LPARAM);
```

5

```
char szWinName[] = "MyWin"; /* name of window class */

HINSTANCE hInst;

int WINAPI WinMain(HINSTANCE hThisInst, HINSTANCE hPrevInst,
                   LPSTR lpszArgs, int nWinMode)
{
  HWND hwnd;
  MSG msg;
  WNDCLASS wcl;
  HANDLE hAccel;

  /* Define a window class. */
  wcl.hInstance = hThisInst; /* handle to this instance */
  wcl.lpszClassName = szWinName; /* window class name */
  wcl.lpfnWndProc = WindowFunc; /* window function */
  wcl.style = 0; /* default style */

  wcl.hIcon = LoadIcon(NULL, IDI_APPLICATION); /* icon style */
  wcl.hCursor = LoadCursor(NULL, IDC_ARROW); /* cursor style */

  /* specify name of menu resource */
  wcl.lpszMenuName = "MYMENU"; /* main menu */

  wcl.cbClsExtra = 0; /* no extra */
  wcl.cbWndExtra = 0; /* information needed */

  /* Make the window white. */
  wcl.hbrBackground = GetStockObject(WHITE_BRUSH);

  /* Register the window class. */
  if(!RegisterClass (&wcl)) return 0;

  /* Now that a window class has been registered, a window
     can be created. */
  hwnd = CreateWindow(
    szWinName, /* name of window class */
    "Using a List Box", /* title */
    WS_OVERLAPPEDWINDOW, /* window style - normal */
    CW_USEDEFAULT, /* X coordinate - let Windows decide */
    CW_USEDEFAULT, /* Y coordinate - let Windows decide */
    CW_USEDEFAULT, /* width - let Windows decide */
    CW_USEDEFAULT, /* height - let Windows decide */
    NULL, /* no parent window */
    NULL, /* use menu registered with this class */
    hThisInst, /* handle of this instance of the program */
```

```
      NULL /* no additional arguments */
  );

  hInst = hThisInst; /* save the current instance handle */

  /* load accelerators */
  hAccel = LoadAccelerators(hThisInst, "MYMENU");

  /* Display the window. */
  ShowWindow(hwnd, nWinMode);
  UpdateWindow(hwnd);

  /* Create the message loop. */
  while(GetMessage(&msg, NULL, 0, 0))
  {
    if(!TranslateAccelerator(hwnd, hAccel, &msg)) {
      TranslateMessage(&msg); /* allow use of keyboard */
      DispatchMessage(&msg); /* return control to Windows */
    }
  }
  return msg.wParam;
}

/* This function is called by Windows 95 and is passed
   messages from the message queue.
*/
LRESULT CALLBACK WindowFunc(HWND hwnd, UINT message,
                            WPARAM wParam, LPARAM lParam)
{
  switch(message) {
    case WM_COMMAND:
      switch(LOWORD(wParam)) {
        case IDM_DIALOG1:
          DialogBox(hInst, "MYDB", hwnd, DialogFunc);
          break;
        case IDM_DIALOG2:
          MessageBox(hwnd, "Dialog Not Implemented", "", MB_OK);
          break;
        case IDM_HELP:
          MessageBox(hwnd, "Help", "Help", MB_OK);
          break;
      }
      break;
    case WM_DESTROY: /* terminate the program */
      PostQuitMessage(0);
      break;
    default:
      /* Let Windows 95 process any messages not specified in
```

```
              the preceding switch statement. */
        return DefWindowProc(hwnd, message, wParam, lParam);
  }
  return 0;
}

/* A simple dialog function. */
BOOL CALLBACK DialogFunc(HWND hdwnd, UINT message,
                         WPARAM wParam, LPARAM lParam)
{
  long i;
  char str[80];

  switch(message) {
    case WM_COMMAND:
      switch(LOWORD(wParam)) {
        case IDCANCEL:
          EndDialog(hdwnd, 0);
          return 1;
        case IDD_RED:
          MessageBox(hdwnd, "You Picked Red", "RED", MB_OK);
          return 1;
        case IDD_GREEN:
          MessageBox(hdwnd, "You Picked Green", "GREEN", MB_OK);
          return 1;
        case ID_LB1: /* process a list box LBN_DBLCLK */
          // see if user made a selection
          if(HIWORD(wParam)==LBN_DBLCLK) {
            i = SendDlgItemMessage(hdwnd, ID_LB1,
                    LB_GETCURSEL, 0, 0L);  // get index
            sprintf(str, "Index in list is: %d", i);
            MessageBox(hdwnd, str, "Selection Made", MB_OK);
          }
          return 1;
        case IDD_SELFRUIT: /* Select Fruit has been pressed */
          i = SendDlgItemMessage(hdwnd, ID_LB1,
                  LB_GETCURSEL, 0, 0L);  // get index
          if(i > -1) sprintf(str, "Index in list is: %d", i);
          else sprintf(str, "No Fruit Selected");
          MessageBox(hdwnd, str, "Selection Made", MB_OK);
          return 1;
      }
      break;
    case WM_INITDIALOG: // initialize list box
      SendDlgItemMessage(hdwnd, ID_LB1,
                         LB_ADDSTRING, 0, (LPARAM)"Apple");
      SendDlgItemMessage(hdwnd, ID_LB1,
                         LB_ADDSTRING, 0, (LPARAM)"Orange");
```

```
        SendDlgItemMessage(hdwnd, ID_LB1,
                        LB_ADDSTRING, 0, (LPARAM)"Pear");
        SendDlgItemMessage(hdwnd, ID_LB1,
                        LB_ADDSTRING, 0, (LPARAM)"Grape");
        return 1;
    }
    return 0;
}
```

Sample output from this program is shown in Figure 5-2.

Adding an Edit Box

The last control we will add to the sample dialog box in this chapter is the edit box. Edit boxes are particularly useful because they allow users to enter a string of their own choosing. Before you can use an edit box, you must define one in your resource file. For this example, change MYDIALOG.RC so that it looks like this:

```
MYDB DIALOG 18, 18, 142, 92
CAPTION "Test Dialog Box"
STYLE DS_MODALFRAME | WS_POPUP | WS_CAPTION | WS_SYSMENU
{
  DEFPUSHBUTTON "Red", IDD_RED, 57, 45, 30, 14,
            WS_CHILD | WS_VISIBLE | WS_TABSTOP
  PUSHBUTTON "Green", IDD_GREEN, 95, 45, 30, 14,
            WS_CHILD | WS_VISIBLE | WS_TABSTOP
  PUSHBUTTON "Cancel", IDCANCEL, 52, 65, 37, 14,
            WS_CHILD | WS_VISIBLE | WS_TABSTOP
```

5

Sample output
that includes a
list box
Figure 5-2.

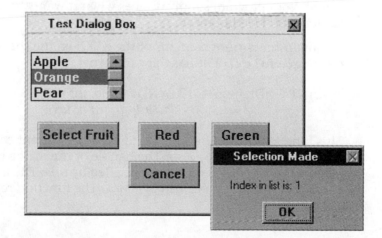

```
PUSHBUTTON "Select Fruit", IDD_SELFRUIT, 5, 45, 42, 14,
        WS_CHILD | WS_VISIBLE | WS_TABSTOP
PUSHBUTTON "Edit OK", IDOK, 68, 22, 30, 14,
        WS_CHILD | WS_VISIBLE | WS_TABSTOP
LISTBOX ID_LB1, 2, 10, 47, 28, LBS_NOTIFY | WS_CHILD |
        WS_VISIBLE | WS_BORDER | WS_VSCROLL | WS_TABSTOP
EDITTEXT ID_EB1, 68, 8, 72, 12, ES_LEFT | ES_AUTOHSCROLL |
        WS_CHILD | WS_VISIBLE | WS_BORDER | WS_TABSTOP
}
```

This version adds a push button called **Edit OK**, which will be used to tell the program that you are done editing text in the edit box. It also adds the list box itself. The ID for the list box is **ID_EB1**. This definition causes a standard edit box to be created.

The **EDITTEXT** statement has this general form:

EDITTEXT *EDID*, *X*, *Y*, *Width*, *Height* [,*Style*]

Here, *EDID* is the value that identifies the edit box. The box's upper-left corner will be at *X,Y,* and its dimensions are specified by *Width* x *Height*. *Style* determines the exact nature of the list box. (The *Style* values used here are described in Table 5-1.)

Next, add this macro definition to **mydialog.h**:

```
#define ID_EB1      107
```

Edit boxes recognize many messages and generate several of their own. However, for the purposes of this example, there is no need for the program to respond to any messages. As you will see, edit boxes perform the editing function on their own. There is no need for program interaction when text is edited. Your program simply decides when it wants to obtain the current contents of the edit box.

To obtain the current contents of the edit box, use the API function **GetDlgItemText( )**. It has this prototype:

UINT GetDlgItemText(HWND *hdwnd*, int *nID*,
                    LPSTR *lpstr*, int *nMax*);

This function causes the edit box to copy the current contents of the box to the string pointed to by *lpstr*. The handle of the dialog box is specified by *hdwnd*. The ID of the edit box is specified by *nID*. The maximum number of characters to copy is specified by *nMax*. The function returns the length of the string.

To add an edit box to the sample program, add the following **case** statement to the inner **switch** of the **DialogFunc( )** function. Each time the **Edit OK** button is pressed, a message window will be displayed that contains the current text inside the edit box.

```
case IDOK: /* edit box OK button selected */
  /* display contents of the edit box */
  GetDlgItemText(hdwnd, ID_EB1, str, 80);
  MessageBox(hdwnd, str, "Edit Box Contains", MB_OK);
  return 1;
```

The macro **IDOK** is a built-in value defined by including **windows.h**.

Figure 5-3 shows sample output created by the edit box.

Using a Modeless Dialog Box

To conclude this chapter, the modal dialog box used by the preceding program will be converted into a modeless dialog box. As you will see, using a modeless dialog box requires a little more work than using a modal one, mainly because a modeless dialog box is a more independent window than is a modal dialog box. Specifically, the rest of your program is still active when a modeless dialog box is displayed. Also, both it and your application's window function continue to receive messages. Thus, as you will see, some additional overhead is required in your application's message loop to accommodate the modeless dialog box.

5

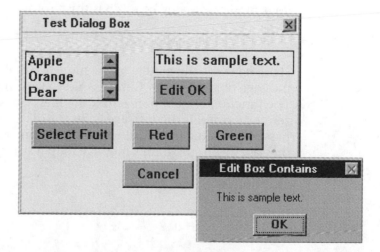

Sample output using the edit box

Figure 5-3.

To create a modeless dialog box, you do not use **DialogBox( )**. Instead, you must use the **CreateDialog( )** API function. Its prototype is shown here:

HWND CreateDialog(HINSTANCE *hThisInst*, LPCSTR *lpName*,
        HWND *hwnd*, DLGPROC *lpDFunc*);

Here, *hThisInst* is a handle to the current application that is passed to your program in the instance parameter to **WinMain( )**. The name of the dialog box as defined in the resource file is pointed to by *lpName*. The handle to the parent window that activates the dialog box is passed in *hwnd*. The *lpDFunc* parameter contains a pointer to the dialog function. The dialog function is the same type as used for a modal dialog box.

Unlike a modal dialog box, a modeless dialog box is not automatically visible, so you may need to call **ShowWindow( )** to cause it to be displayed after it has been created. However, if you add **WS_VISIBLE** to the dialog box's definition in its resource file, then it will be automatically displayed.

To close a modeless dialog box, your program must call **DestroyWindow( )** rather than **EndDialog( )**. The prototype for **DestroyWindow( )** is shown here.

BOOL DestroyWindow(HWND *hwnd*);

Here, *hwnd* is the handle to the window (in this case, dialog box) being closed.

Since your application's window function will continue receiving messages while a modeless dialog box is active, you must make a change to your program's message loop. Specifically, you must add a call to **IsDialogMessage( )**. This function routes dialog box messages to your modeless dialog box. It has this prototype:

BOOL IsDialogMessage(HWND *hdwnd*, LPMSG *msg*);

Here, *hdwnd* is the handle of the modeless dialog box, and *msg* is the message obtained from **GetMessage( )** within your program's message loop. The function returns non-zero if the message is for the dialog box. It returns zero otherwise. If the message is for the dialog box, then it is automatically passed to the dialog box function. Therefore, to process modeless dialog box messages, your program's message loop must look something like this:

```
while(GetMessage(&msg, NULL, 0, 0))
{
  if(!IsDialogMessage(hDlg, &msg)) {
    /* not for dialog box */
```

```
      if(!TranslateAccelerator(hwnd, hAccel, &msg)) {
        TranslateMessage(&msg); /* allow use of keyboard */
        DispatchMessage(&msg); /* return control to Windows */
      }
    }
  }
```

As you can see, the message is only processed by the rest of the message loop
if it is not a dialog box message.

Creating a Modeless Dialog Box

Surprisingly few changes are needed to convert the modal dialog box shown
in the preceding example into a modeless one. The first change that you need
to make is to the dialog box definition in the MYDIALOG.RC resource file.
Since a modeless dialog box is not automatically visible, add **WS_VISIBLE**
to the dialog box definition. Because we have made many changes to
MYDIALOG.RC since the beginning of this chapter, the entire file is
shown here for your convenience.

```
; Sample dialog box and menu resource file.
#include "mydialog.h"
#include <windows.h>

MYMENU MENU
{
  MENUITEM "Dialog &1", IDM_DIALOG1
  MENUITEM "Dialog &2", IDM_DIALOG2
  MENUITEM "&Help", IDM_HELP
}


MYMENU ACCELERATORS
{
  VK_F2, IDM_DIALOG1, VIRTKEY
  VK_F3, IDM_DIALOG2, VIRTKEY
  VK_F1, IDM_HELP, VIRTKEY
}


MYDB DIALOG 18, 18, 142, 92
CAPTION "Test Dialog Box"
STYLE DS_MODALFRAME | WS_POPUP | WS_CAPTION
      | WS_SYSMENU | WS_VISIBLE
{
  DEFPUSHBUTTON "Red", IDD_RED, 57, 45, 30, 14,
            WS_CHILD | WS_VISIBLE | WS_TABSTOP
  PUSHBUTTON "Green", IDD_GREEN, 95, 45, 30, 14,
            WS_CHILD | WS_VISIBLE | WS_TABSTOP
```

5

```
    PUSHBUTTON "Cancel", IDCANCEL, 52, 65, 37, 14,
            WS_CHILD | WS_VISIBLE | WS_TABSTOP
    PUSHBUTTON "Select Fruit", IDD_SELFRUIT, 5, 45, 42, 14,
            WS_CHILD | WS_VISIBLE | WS_TABSTOP
    PUSHBUTTON "Edit OK", IDOK, 68, 22, 30, 14,
            WS_CHILD | WS_VISIBLE | WS_TABSTOP
    LISTBOX ID_LB1, 2, 10, 47, 28, LBS_NOTIFY | WS_CHILD |
            WS_VISIBLE | WS_BORDER | WS_VSCROLL | WS_TABSTOP
    EDITTEXT ID_EB1, 68, 8, 72, 12, ES_LEFT | ES_AUTOHSCROLL |
            WS_CHILD | WS_VISIBLE | WS_BORDER | WS_TABSTOP
}
```

Next, you must make the following changes to the program:

1. Add **IsDialogMessage( )** to the message loop.
2. Create the dialog box using **CreateDialog( )** rather than **DialogBox( )**.
3. Close the dialog box using **DestroyWindow( )** instead of **EndDialog( )**.

The entire listing for the modeless dialog box example (incorporating these changes) is shown here.

Sample output from this program is shown in Figure 5-4. (You should try this program on your own to fully understand the difference between modal and modeless dialog boxes.)

```c
/* Demonstrate a modeless dialog box. */

#include <windows.h>
#include <string.h>
#include <stdio.h>
#include "mydialog.h"

LRESULT CALLBACK WindowFunc(HWND, UINT, WPARAM, LPARAM);
BOOL CALLBACK DialogFunc(HWND, UINT, WPARAM, LPARAM);

char szWinName[] = "MyWin"; /* name of window class */

HINSTANCE hInst;

HWND hDlg; /* dialog box handle */

int WINAPI WinMain(HINSTANCE hThisInst, HINSTANCE hPrevInst,
                   LPSTR lpszArgs, int nWinMode)
{
  HWND hwnd;
  MSG msg;
```

```
WNDCLASS wcl;
HANDLE hAccel;

/* Define a window class. */
wcl.hInstance = hThisInst; /* handle to this instance */
wcl.lpszClassName = szWinName; /* window class name */
wcl.lpfnWndProc = WindowFunc; /* window function */
wcl.style = 0; /* default style */

wcl.hIcon = LoadIcon(NULL, IDI_APPLICATION); /* icon style */
wcl.hCursor = LoadCursor(NULL, IDC_ARROW); /* cursor style */

/* specify name of menu resource */
wcl.lpszMenuName = "MYMENU"; /* main menu */

wcl.cbClsExtra = 0; /* no extra */
wcl.cbWndExtra = 0; /* information needed */

/* Make the window white. */
wcl.hbrBackground = GetStockObject(WHITE_BRUSH);

/* Register the window class. */
if(!RegisterClass (&wcl)) return 0;

/* Now that a window class has been registered, a window
   can be created. */
hwnd = CreateWindow(
  szWinName, /* name of window class */
  "A Modeless Dialog Box", /* title */
  WS_OVERLAPPEDWINDOW, /* window style - normal */
  CW_USEDEFAULT, /* X coordinate - let Windows decide */
  CW_USEDEFAULT, /* Y coordinate - let Windows decide */
  CW_USEDEFAULT, /* width - let Windows decide */
  CW_USEDEFAULT, /* height - let Windows decide */
  NULL, /* no parent window */
  NULL, /* Use menu registered with this class */
  hThisInst, /* handle of this instance of the program */
  NULL /* no additional arguments */
);

hInst = hThisInst; /* save the current instance handle */

/* load accelerators */
hAccel = LoadAccelerators(hThisInst, "MYMENU");

/* Display the window. */
ShowWindow(hwnd, nWinMode);
UpdateWindow(hwnd);
```

5

```
        /* Create the message loop. */
        while(GetMessage(&msg, NULL, 0, 0))
        {
          if(!IsDialogMessage(hDlg, &msg)) {
            /* not for dialog box */
            if(!TranslateAccelerator(hwnd, hAccel, &msg)) {
              TranslateMessage(&msg); /* allow use of keyboard */
              DispatchMessage(&msg); /* return control to Windows */
            }
          }
        }
        return msg.wParam;
}


/* This function is called by Windows 95 and is passed
   messages from the message queue.
*/
LRESULT CALLBACK WindowFunc(HWND hwnd, UINT message,
                            WPARAM wParam, LPARAM lParam)
{
  switch(message) {
    case WM_COMMAND:
      switch(LOWORD(wParam)) {
        case IDM_DIALOG1: /* this creates modeless dialog box */
          hDlg = CreateDialog(hInst, "MYDB", hwnd, DialogFunc);
          break;
        case IDM_DIALOG2:
          MessageBox(hwnd, "Dialog Not Implemented", "", MB_OK);
          break;
        case IDM_HELP:
          MessageBox(hwnd, "Help", "Help", MB_OK);
          break;
      }
      break;
    case WM_DESTROY: /* terminate the program */
      PostQuitMessage(0);
      break;
    default:
      /* Let Windows 95 process any messages not specified in
         the preceding switch statement. */
      return DefWindowProc(hwnd, message, wParam, lParam);
  }
  return 0;
}

/* A simple dialog function. */
BOOL CALLBACK DialogFunc(HWND hdwnd, UINT message,
                         WPARAM wParam, LPARAM lParam)
```

```
   {
     long i;
     char str[80];

     switch(message) {
       case WM_COMMAND:
         switch(LOWORD(wParam)) {
           case IDOK: /* edit box OK button selected */
             /* display contents of the edit box */
             GetDlgItemText(hdwnd, ID_EB1, str, 80);
             MessageBox(hdwnd, str, "Edit Box Contains", MB_OK);
             return 1;
           case IDCANCEL:
             DestroyWindow(hdwnd);
             return 1;
           case IDD_RED:
             MessageBox(hdwnd, "You Picked Red", "RED", MB_OK);
             return 1;
           case IDD_GREEN:
             MessageBox(hdwnd, "You Picked Green", "GREEN", MB_OK);
             return 1;
           case ID_LB1: /* process a list box LBN_DBLCLK */
             // see if user made a selection
             if(HIWORD(wParam)==LBN_DBLCLK) {
               i = SendDlgItemMessage(hdwnd, ID_LB1,
                        LB_GETCURSEL, 0, 0L);  // get index
               sprintf(str, "Index in list is: %d", i);
               MessageBox(hdwnd, str, "Selection Made", MB_OK);
             }
             return 1;
           case IDD_SELFRUIT: /* Select Fruit has been pressed */
             i = SendDlgItemMessage(hdwnd, ID_LB1,
                        LB_GETCURSEL, 0, 0L);  // get index
             if(i > -1) sprintf(str, "Index in list is: %d", i);
             else sprintf(str, "No Fruit Selected");
             MessageBox(hdwnd, str, "Selection Made", MB_OK);
             return 1;
         }
         break;
       case WM_INITDIALOG: // initialize list box
         SendDlgItemMessage(hdwnd, ID_LB1,
                        LB_ADDSTRING, 0, (LPARAM)"Apple");
         SendDlgItemMessage(hdwnd, ID_LB1,
                        LB_ADDSTRING, 0, (LPARAM)"Orange");
         SendDlgItemMessage(hdwnd, ID_LB1,
                        LB_ADDSTRING, 0, (LPARAM)"Pear");
         SendDlgItemMessage(hdwnd, ID_LB1,
                        LB_ADDSTRING, 0, (LPARAM)"Grape");
```

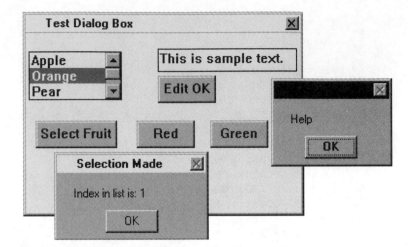

Sample output
using the
modeless
dialog box
Figure 5-4.

```
        return 1;
    }
    return 0;
}
```

This chapter only scratches the surface of what you can do using dialog
boxes and their various controls. Additional controls are covered later in this
book. Also, you will want to experiment on your own, exploring how the
various controls function and interact with your program.

Chapter

6

Creating Custom Icons, Cursors, and Bitmaps

This chapter explains how to control the appearance of two important items linked with all Windows applications: the design of the icon that is associated with an application and the shape of the mouse cursor. This chapter also shows how to display a bitmapped graphics image.

Icons, cursors, and bitmaps are resources that consist of graphical information. These resources are created using an *image editor*. (An image editor is generally supplied with a compiler that is capable of compiling Windows 95 programs.) Once you have defined the nature of the icon, cursor, or bitmap, the image must be incorporated into the resource file associated with your program. Finally, before the image is used, it must be loaded by your program. This chapter discusses the necessary details required to accomplish this.

Defining an Icon and a Cursor

As stated, when you create your own icons or cursors, you will need to use an image editor. An image editor displays an enlarged view of your icon or cursor. This allows you to easily construct or alter the image. For example, the custom icon shown in the examples is displayed inside the Microsoft Image Editor shown in Figure 6-1.

For the examples that follow, you will need both an icon and a cursor image. You must create these using the image editor supplied with your compiler. Each image must then be saved in its own file.

Once you have defined the icon and cursor images, you will need to add an **ICON** and a **CURSOR** statement to your program's resource file. The statements have these general forms:

> *IconName* ICON *filename*
> *CursorName* CURSOR *filename*

Here, *IconName* is the name that identifies the icon, and *CursorName* is the name that identifies the cursor. These names are used by your program to refer to the icon and cursor. *filename* specifies the file that holds the custom icon or cursor.

In the examples that follow, you should call your icon **MYICON** and your cursor **MYCURSOR**. Store your icon in a file called ICON.ICO and

A custom icon
within an
image editor

Figure 6-1.

your cursor in a file named CURSOR.CUR. Next, add these lines to your resource file:

```
MYCURSOR CURSOR CURSOR.CUR
MYICON ICON ICON.ICO
```

Changing the Icon and Cursor

As you know, all Windows 95 applications first create a window class that defines the attributes of the window, including the shape of the application's icon and mouse cursor. The handles to the icon and mouse cursor are stored in the **hIcon** and **hCursor** fields of the **WNDCLASS** structure. So far, we have been using one of the built-in icons and cursors supplied by Windows 95. To use a custom icon and mouse cursor, you must load the new icon and cursor before the window class is registered. To accomplish this, you must use the API functions **LoadIcon( )** and **LoadCursor( )**, which you learned about in Chapter 2. For example, the following loads the icon identified as **MYICON** and the cursor called **MYCURSOR** and stores their handles in the appropriate fields of the **wcl** **WNDCLASS** structure variable:

```
wcl.hIcon = LoadIcon(hThisInst, "MYICON"); /* load icon */
wcl.hCursor = LoadCursor(hThisInst, "MYCURSOR"); /* load cursor */
```

Here, **hThisInst** is the handle of the current instance of the program. In the previous programs in this book, these functions have been used to load default icons and cursors. Here, they will be used to load your custom icon and cursor.

A Sample Program That Demonstrates a Custom Icon and Cursor

6

The following program uses a custom icon and cursor. The icon is displayed in the main window's system menu box and in the program's entry in the task bar. The cursor will be used when the mouse pointer is over the window. That is, the shape of the mouse cursor will automatically change to the one defined by your program when the mouse moves over the program's window. It will automatically revert to its default shape when it moves off the program's window.

Remember, before you try to compile this program, you must define a custom icon and cursor using an image editor and then add these resources to the resource file associated with the program.

```c
/* Demonstrate a custom icon and mouse cursor. */

#include <windows.h>
#include <string.h>
#include <stdio.h>

LRESULT CALLBACK WindowFunc(HWND, UINT, WPARAM, LPARAM);

char szWinName[] = "MyWin"; /* name of window class */

int WINAPI WinMain(HINSTANCE hThisInst, HINSTANCE hPrevInst,
                   LPSTR lpszArgs, int nWinMode)
{
  HWND hwnd;
  MSG msg;
  WNDCLASS wcl;

  /* Define a window class. */
  wcl.hInstance = hThisInst; /* handle to this instance */
  wcl.lpszClassName = szWinName; /* window class name */
  wcl.lpfnWndProc = WindowFunc; /* window function */
  wcl.style = 0; /* default style */

  wcl.hIcon = LoadIcon(hThisInst, "MYICON"); /* load icon */
  wcl.hCursor = LoadCursor(hThisInst, "MYCURSOR"); /* load cursor */

  wcl.lpszMenuName = NULL; /* no main menu */

  wcl.cbClsExtra = 0; /* no extra */
  wcl.cbWndExtra = 0; /* information needed */

  /* Make the window white. */
  wcl.hbrBackground = GetStockObject(WHITE_BRUSH);

  /* Register the window class. */
  if(!RegisterClass (&wcl)) return 0;

  /* Now that a window class has been registered, a window
     can be created. */
  hwnd = CreateWindow(
    szWinName, /* name of window class */
    "Custom Icon and Cursor", /* title */
    WS_OVERLAPPEDWINDOW, /* window style - normal */
    CW_USEDEFAULT, /* X coordinate - let Windows decide */
    CW_USEDEFAULT, /* Y coordinate - let Windows decide */
    CW_USEDEFAULT, /* width - let Windows decide */
    CW_USEDEFAULT, /* height - let Windows decide */
    HWND_DESKTOP, /* no parent window */
```

```
      NULL, /* no menu */
      hThisInst, /* handle of this instance of the program */
      NULL /* no additional arguments */
    );

    /* Display the window. */
    ShowWindow(hwnd, nWinMode);
    UpdateWindow(hwnd);

    /* Create the message loop. */
    while(GetMessage(&msg, NULL, 0, 0))
    {
      TranslateMessage(&msg); /* allow use of keyboard */
      DispatchMessage(&msg); /* return control to Windows */
    }
    return msg.wParam;
}


/* This function is called by Windows 95 and is passed
   messages from the message queue.
*/
LRESULT CALLBACK WindowFunc(HWND hwnd, UINT message,
                            WPARAM wParam, LPARAM lParam)
{
  switch(message) {
    case WM_DESTROY: /* terminate the program */
      PostQuitMessage(0);
      break;
    default:
      /* Let Windows 95 process any messages not specified in
         the preceding switch statement. */
      return DefWindowProc(hwnd, message, wParam, lParam);
  }
  return 0;
}
```

6

The custom icon is shown in Figure 6-2. (Of course, your custom icon may look different.) The custom mouse cursor will appear when you move the mouse over the window. (Try this before continuing.)

Defining the Small Icon

As you may know from using Windows 95, the icon associated with an application appears in two different sizes. For example, when you move or copy an object to the desktop, a large icon is displayed. When you minimize an application, a small icon is shown. (The small icon is also shown as the

Custom icon

　Custom Icon and Cursor 　□□▣

The
customized
icon and
mouse cursor
Figure 6-2.

system menu icon.) Typically, large icons are 32 by 32 bitmaps and small icons are 16 by 16 bitmaps.

Up to now, you have only defined one icon (the large one) that is associated with an application. By default, Windows 95 uses the large icon for both the large and the small icon. (The large icon is simply "shrunk" to create the small one.) In this section, you will learn how to specify the small icon.

To specify the small icon, you must register your window class using **RegisterClassEx( )**. Its prototype is shown here:

ATOM RegisterClassEx(CONST LPWNDCLASSEX *lpWndClsEx*);

lpWndClsEx is a pointer to a structure of type **WNDCLASSEX**.
WNDCLASSEX is the same as **WNDCLASS** except that it includes two additional members. The first new member is an unsigned integer called **cbSize**. This member must be assigned the size of the **WNDCLASSESX** structure. The second new member is **hIconSm**, which holds the handle to the small icon. To load the small icon, use the standard **LoadIcon( )** function.

To illustrate the effect of defining both the large and the small icon, the preceding program is reworked to use **WNDCLASSEX** and **RegisterClassEx( )**. The standard **IDI_APPLICATION** icon is specified for the small icon. Sample output is shown in Figure 6-3.

```
/* Demonstrate both a large and small icon. */

#include <windows.h>
#include <string.h>
```

```c
#include <stdio.h>

LRESULT CALLBACK WindowFunc(HWND, UINT, WPARAM, LPARAM);

char szWinName[] = "MyWin"; /* name of window class */

int WINAPI WinMain(HINSTANCE hThisInst, HINSTANCE hPrevInst,
                   LPSTR lpszArgs, int nWinMode)
{
  HWND hwnd;
  MSG msg;
  WNDCLASSEX wcl; /* must use WNDCLASSEX to set small icon */

  /* Define a window class. */
  wcl.hInstance = hThisInst; /* handle to this instance */
  wcl.lpszClassName = szWinName; /* window class name */
  wcl.lpfnWndProc = WindowFunc; /* window function */
  wcl.style = 0; /* default style */

  wcl.cbSize = sizeof(WNDCLASSEX); /* set size of WNDCLASSEX */

  /* load both big and small icons */
  wcl.hIcon = LoadIcon(hThisInst, "MYICON"); /* load icon */
  wcl.hIconSm = LoadIcon(NULL, IDI_APPLICATION); /* small icon */

  wcl.hCursor = LoadCursor(hThisInst, "MYCURSOR"); /* load cursor */

  wcl.lpszMenuName = NULL; /* no main menu */

  wcl.cbClsExtra = 0; /* no extra */
  wcl.cbWndExtra = 0; /* information needed */

  /* Make the window white. */
  wcl.hbrBackground = GetStockObject(WHITE_BRUSH);

  /* Register the window class. */
  if(!RegisterClassEx(&wcl)) return 0;

  /* Now that a window class has been registered, a window
     can be created. */
  hwnd = CreateWindow(
    szWinName, /* name of window class */
    "Custom Icon and Cursor", /* title */
    WS_OVERLAPPEDWINDOW, /* window style - normal */
    CW_USEDEFAULT, /* X coordinate - let Windows decide */
    CW_USEDEFAULT, /* Y coordinate - let Windows decide */
    CW_USEDEFAULT, /* width - let Windows decide */
    CW_USEDEFAULT, /* height - let Windows decide */
```

6

```
    HWND_DESKTOP, /* no parent window */
    NULL, /* no menu */
    hThisInst, /* handle of this instance of the program */
    NULL /* no additional arguments */
  );

  /* Display the window. */
  ShowWindow(hwnd, nWinMode);
  UpdateWindow(hwnd);

  /* Create the message loop. */
  while(GetMessage(&msg, NULL, 0, 0))
  {
    TranslateMessage(&msg); /* allow use of keyboard */
    DispatchMessage(&msg); /* return control to Windows */
  }
  return msg.wParam;
}

/* This function is called by Windows 95 and is passed
   messages from the message queue.
*/
LRESULT CALLBACK WindowFunc(HWND hwnd, UINT message,
                            WPARAM wParam, LPARAM lParam)
{
  switch(message) {
    case WM_DESTROY: /* terminate the program */
      PostQuitMessage(0);
      break;
    default:
      /* Let Windows 95 process any messages not specified in
         the preceding switch statement. */
      return DefWindowProc(hwnd, message, wParam, lParam);
  }
  return 0;
}
```

Since there is no need for any of the programs in this book to specify
separate large and small icons, most of the subsequent examples do not do
so. Remember, Windows 95 automatically uses the icon associated with
hIcon for both small and large icons if no separate small icon is specified.
However, you may want to specify both the large and small icons in your
own applications. (Actually, for the best looking Windows 95 applications,
you will almost certainly want to define both icons.)

Small icon

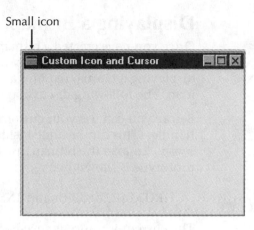

Sample output
from the large
and small
icons program
Figure 6-3.

Large icon

Windows 3.1 allowed only one icon (the large icon) to be defined for an application. You may want to define a small icon when porting applications to Windows 95. Also, Windows 3.1 does not support the RegisterClassEx( ) function or the WNDCLASSEX structure.

Using a Bitmap

A bitmap is a graphics image. Since Windows is a graphics-based operating system, it makes sense that you can include graphics images in your applications. It is important to understand that you can draw graphics images such as lines, circles, and boxes inside the client area of a window using the rich set of graphics functions contained in the Windows API. (These functions are discussed later in the book.) However, a bitmap, and the mechanism used to display one, is separate from those types of graphics. A bitmap is a self-contained graphical resource that your program utilizes as a single entity. A bitmap contains a bit-by-bit representation of the image that will ultimately be displayed on the screen. Put differently, a bitmap contains a complete image that your program generally displays in its totality.

6

Creating a Bitmap

If you wish to try the sample program that displays a bitmap, you must create a bitmap resource before continuing. As with other graphical resources, you must use an image editor to create your bitmap. Unlike icons and cursors, which have a fixed size, the size of a custom bitmap is under your control. To use the example that follows, your bitmap must be 64 x 64 pixels square. Call your bitmap file BP.BMP and then add this line to your program's resource file:

```
MYBP1 BITMAP BP.BMP
```

Displaying a Bitmap

Once you have created a bitmap and included it in your application's resource file, you may display it as many times as you want. However, displaying a bitmap requires a little more work than using a custom cursor or icon. The following discussion explains the proper procedure.

Before you can use your custom bitmap, you must load it and store its handle. (This can be done inside **WinMain( )** or any other place that makes sense.) To load the bitmap, use the **LoadBitmap( )** API function, whose prototype is shown here.

HBITMAP LoadBitmap(HINSTANCE *hThisInst*, LPCSTR *lpszName*);

The current instance is specified in *hThisInst,* and a pointer to the name of the bitmap, as specified in the resource file, is passed in *lpszName*. The function returns the handle to the bitmap, or NULL if an error occurs. For example:

```
HBITMAP hBit1; /* handle of bitmap */
/* ... */
hBit1 = LoadBitmap(hThisInst, "MYBP1"); /* load bitmap */
```

This fragment loads a bitmap called **MYBP1** and stores a handle to it in **hBit1**.

When it comes time to display the bitmap, your program must go through the following four steps:

1. Obtain the device context so that your program can output to the window.
2. Obtain an equivalent memory device context that will hold the bitmap until it is displayed. (A bitmap is held in memory until it is copied to your window.)
3. Select the bitmap into the memory device context.
4. Copy the bitmap from the memory device context to the window device context. This causes the bitmap to actually be displayed.

To see how these steps can be implemented, consider the following fragment. It causes a bitmap to be displayed each time the left mouse button is pressed. (It assumes that the bitmap has already been loaded.)

```
HDC DC, memDC;

/* ... */
```

```
case WM_LBUTTONDOWN:
  DC = GetDC(hwnd); /* get device context */
  memDC = CreateCompatibleDC(DC); /* create compatible DC */
  SelectObject(memDC, hBit1);
  BitBlt(DC, LOWORD(lParam), HIWORD(lParam), 64, 64,
         memDC, 0, 0, SRCCOPY); /* build image */
  ReleaseDC(hwnd, DC); /* free the device context */
  DeleteDC(memDC); /* free the memory context */
  break;
```

Let's examine this code, step by step. First, two device context handles are declared. **DC** will hold the current window device context as obtained by **GetDC( )**. The other, called **memDC**, will hold the device context of the memory that stores the bitmap until it is drawn in the window.

Inside the **case** statement, the window device context is obtained. This step is necessary because the bitmap will be displayed in the client area of the window and no output can occur until your program is granted a device context. Next, a memory context is created that will hold the bitmap. This memory device context will be compatible with the window device context. The compatible memory device context is created using the **CreateCompatibleDC( )** API function. Its prototype is shown here:

HDC CreateCompatibleDC(HDC *hdc*);

This function returns a handle to a region of memory that is compatible with the device context of the window, specified by *hdc*. This memory will be used to construct an image before it is actually displayed. The function returns NULL if an error occurs.

Before a bitmap can be displayed, it must be selected into the device context using the **SelectObject( )** API function. Since there can be several bitmaps associated with an application, you must select the one you want to display before it can actually be output to the window. The **SelectObject( )** prototype is shown here.

HGDIOBJ SelectObject(HDC *hMdc*, HGDIOBJ *hObject*);

Here, *hMdc* is the memory device context that holds the object, and *hObject* is the handle of that object. The function returns the handle of the previously selected object, allowing it to be reselected later, if desired.

To actually display the object once it has been selected, use the **BitBlt( )** API function. This function copies a bitmap from one device context to another. Its prototype is shown next.

6

BOOL BitBlt(HDC *hDest*, int *X*, int *Y*, int *Width*, int *Height*,
          HDC *hSource*, int *Sourcex*, int *Sourcey*,
          DWORD *dwRaster*);

Here, *hDest* is the handle of the target device context, and *X* and *Y* are the upper-left coordinates that indicate the location where the bitmap will be drawn. The width and height of the bitmap are specified in *Width* and *Height*. The *hSource* parameter contains the handle of the source device context, which in this case will be the memory context obtained using **CreateCompatibleDC( )**. *Sourcex* and *Sourcey* specify the upper-left coordinates in the bitmap. These values are usually 0. The value of *dwRaster* determines how the bit-by-bit contents of the bitmap will actually be drawn on the screen. Some of its most common values are shown here:

dwRaster Macro	Effect
SRCCOPY	Copies bitmap as is, overwriting existing information
SRCAND	ANDs bitmap with current destination
SRCPAINT	ORs bitmap with current destination
SRCINVERT	XORs bitmap with current destination

These macros are defined by including **windows.h**. The function returns non-zero if successful and zero otherwise.

In this example, the call to **BitBlt( )** displays the entire bitmap at the location where the left mouse button was pressed, copying the bitmap to the window.

After the bitmap is displayed, both device contexts are released. Only a device context obtained through a call to **GetDC( )** can be released using a call to **ReleaseDC( )**. To release the memory device context obtained using **CreateCompatibleDC( )**, you must use **DeleteDC( )**, which takes as its parameter the handle of the device context to release.

A bitmap is a resource that must be removed before your application ends. To do this, your program must call **DeleteObject( )** when the bitmap is no longer needed or when a **WM_DESTROY** message is received. **DeleteObject( )** has this prototype:

BOOL DeleteObject(HGDIOBJ *hObj*);

Here, *hObj* is the handle to the object being deleted. The function returns non-zero if successful and zero if it fails.

The Complete Bitmap Example Program

Here is a complete program that displays a bitmap. It displays your custom bitmap each time you press the left mouse button. The bitmap is displayed at the location pointed to by the mouse. Sample output is shown in Figure 6-4.

```c
/*  Demonstrate a bitmap. */

#include <windows.h>
#include <string.h>
#include <stdio.h>

LRESULT CALLBACK WindowFunc(HWND, UINT, WPARAM, LPARAM);

char szWinName[] = "MyWin"; /* name of window class */

HBITMAP hBit1; /* handle of bitmap */

int WINAPI WinMain(HINSTANCE hThisInst, HINSTANCE hPrevInst,
                   LPSTR lpszArgs, int nWinMode)
{
  HWND hwnd;
  MSG msg;
  WNDCLASS wcl;

  /* Define a window class. */
  wcl.hInstance = hThisInst; /* handle to this instance */
  wcl.lpszClassName = szWinName; /* window class name */
  wcl.lpfnWndProc = WindowFunc; /* window function */
  wcl.style = 0; /* default style */

  wcl.hIcon = LoadIcon(hThisInst, "MYICON"); /* icon style */
  wcl.hCursor = LoadCursor(hThisInst, "MYCURSOR"); /* cursor style */

  wcl.lpszMenuName = NULL; /* no main menu */

  wcl.cbClsExtra = 0; /* no extra */
  wcl.cbWndExtra = 0; /* information needed */

  /* Make the window white. */
  wcl.hbrBackground = GetStockObject(WHITE_BRUSH);

  /* Register the window class. */
  if(!RegisterClass (&wcl)) return 0;
```

6

```
/* Now that a window class has been registered, a window
   can be created. */
hwnd = CreateWindow(
  szWinName, /* name of window class */
  "Custom Bitmap", /* title */
  WS_OVERLAPPEDWINDOW, /* window style - normal */
  CW_USEDEFAULT, /* X coordinate - let Windows decide */
  CW_USEDEFAULT, /* Y coordinate - let Windows decide */
  CW_USEDEFAULT, /* width - let Windows decide */
  CW_USEDEFAULT, /* height - let Windows decide */
  HWND_DESKTOP, /* no parent window */
  NULL, /* no menu */
  hThisInst, /* handle of this instance of the program */
  NULL /* no additional arguments */
);

/* Display the window. */
ShowWindow(hwnd, nWinMode);
UpdateWindow(hwnd);

/* load the bitmap */
hBit1 = LoadBitmap(hThisInst, "MYBP1"); /* load bitmap */

/* Create the message loop. */
while(GetMessage(&msg, NULL, 0, 0))
{
  TranslateMessage(&msg); /* allow use of keyboard */
  DispatchMessage(&msg); /* return control to Windows */
}
return msg.wParam;
}

/* This function is called by Windows 95 and is passed
   messages from the message queue.
*/
LRESULT CALLBACK WindowFunc(HWND hwnd, UINT message,
                            WPARAM wParam, LPARAM lParam)
{
  HDC DC, memDC;

  switch(message) {
    case WM_LBUTTONDOWN:
      DC = GetDC(hwnd); /* get device context */
      memDC = CreateCompatibleDC(DC); /* create compatible DC */
      SelectObject(memDC, hBit1);
      BitBlt(DC, LOWORD(lParam), HIWORD(lParam), 64, 64,
             memDC, 0, 0, SRCCOPY); /* build image */
      ReleaseDC(hwnd, DC); /* free the device context */
```

```
        DeleteDC(memDC); /* free the memory context */
        break;
    case WM_DESTROY: /* terminate the program */
        DeleteObject(hBit1); /* remove the bitmap */
        PostQuitMessage(0);
        break;
    default:
        /* Let Windows 95 process any messages not specified in
           the preceding switch statement. */
        return DefWindowProc(hwnd, message, wParam, lParam);
    }
    return 0;
}
```

Using Multiple Bitmaps

Before concluding the topic of bitmaps, one last point must be emphasized:
It is possible (indeed, easy) to use more than one bitmap within your
program. Your application can include as many bitmaps as necessary.
Whenever you need to display one, simply load the desired bitmap and
display it using the method described in the previous section.

To illustrate how easy it is to use multiple bitmaps, let's add another one to
the preceding program. First, add this line to your resource file:

```
MYBP2 BITMAP BP2.BMP
```

6

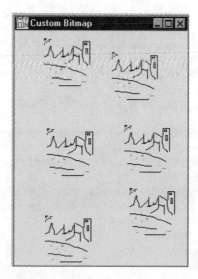

Sample output
using the
custom bitmap
Figure 6-4.

Then, using an image editor, create a second 64 x 64 bitmap. When you are done, save the second bitmap in a file called **BP2.BMP**.

Next, add a second bitmap handle to your program called **hBit2**. Also, add this line to **WinMain( )** to load the second bitmap:

```
hBit2 = LoadBitmap(hThisInst, "MYBP2"); /* load bitmap */
```

Inside **WindowFunc( )**, add this **case** to the preceding program. It will cause the second bitmap to be displayed each time the right mouse button is pressed.

```
case WM_RBUTTONDOWN: /* display second bitmap */
  DC = GetDC(hwnd); /* get device context */
  memDC = CreateCompatibleDC(DC); /* create compatible DC */
  SelectObject(memDC, hBit2);
  BitBlt(DC, LOWORD(lParam), HIWORD(lParam), 64, 64,
         memDC, 0, 0, SRCCOPY); /* build image */
  ReleaseDC(hwnd, DC); /* free the device context */
  DeleteDC(memDC); /* free the memory context */
  break;
```

Finally, add this line to the **WM_DESTROY** case:

```
DeleteObject(hBit2);
```

After you make these changes, your program should look like the one shown here. To display the first bitmap, press the left mouse button. To display the second bitmap, press the right mouse button.

```
/*  Demonstrate two bitmaps. */

#include <windows.h>
#include <string.h>
#include <stdio.h>

LRESULT CALLBACK WindowFunc(HWND, UINT, WPARAM, LPARAM);

char szWinName[] = "MyWin"; /* name of window class */

HBITMAP hBit1, hBit2; /* handle of bitmaps */

int WINAPI WinMain(HINSTANCE hThisInst, HINSTANCE hPrevInst,
                   LPSTR lpszArgs, int nWinMode)
{
  HWND hwnd;
  MSG msg;
  WNDCLASS wcl;
```

```
/* Define a window class. */
wcl.hInstance = hThisInst; /* handle to this instance */
wcl.lpszClassName = szWinName; /* window class name */
wcl.lpfnWndProc = WindowFunc; /* window function */
wcl.style = 0; /* default style */

wcl.hIcon = LoadIcon(hThisInst, "MYICON"); /* icon style */
wcl.hCursor = LoadCursor(hThisInst, "MYCURSOR"); /* cursor style */

wcl.lpszMenuName = NULL; /* no main menu */

wcl.cbClsExtra = 0; /* no extra */
wcl.cbWndExtra = 0; /* information needed */

/* Make the window white. */
wcl.hbrBackground = GetStockObject(WHITE_BRUSH);

/* Register the window class. */
if(!RegisterClass (&wcl)) return 0;

/* Now that a window class has been registered, a window
   can be created. */
hwnd = CreateWindow(
  szWinName, /* name of window class */
  "Two Custom Bitmaps", /* title */
  WS_OVERLAPPEDWINDOW, /* window style - normal */
  CW_USEDEFAULT, /* X coordinate - let Windows decide */
  CW_USEDEFAULT, /* Y coordinate - let Windows decide */
  CW_USEDEFAULT, /* width - let Windows decide */
  CW_USEDEFAULT, /* height - let Windows decide */
  HWND_DESKTOP, /* no parent window */
  NULL, /* no menu */
  hThisInst, /* handle of this instance of the program */
  NULL /* no additional arguments */
);

/* Display the window. */
ShowWindow(hwnd, nWinMode);
UpdateWindow(hwnd);

/* load the bitmaps */
hBit1 = LoadBitmap(hThisInst, "MYBP1"); /* load bitmap */
hBit2 = LoadBitmap(hThisInst, "MYBP2"); /* load bitmap */

/* Create the message loop. */
while(GetMessage(&msg, NULL, 0, 0))
  {
```

6

```
      TranslateMessage(&msg); /* allow use of keyboard */
      DispatchMessage(&msg); /* return control to Windows */
   }
   return msg.wParam;
}


/* This function is called by Windows 95 and is passed
   messages from the message queue.
*/
LRESULT CALLBACK WindowFunc(HWND hwnd, UINT message,
                            WPARAM wParam, LPARAM lParam)
{
   HDC DC, memDC;

   switch(message) {
     case WM_LBUTTONDOWN: /* display first bitmap */
       DC = GetDC(hwnd); /* get device context */
       memDC = CreateCompatibleDC(DC); /* create compatible DC */
       SelectObject(memDC, hBit1);
       BitBlt(DC, LOWORD(lParam), HIWORD(lParam), 64, 64,
              memDC, 0, 0, SRCCOPY); /* build image */
       ReleaseDC(hwnd, DC); /* free the device context */
       DeleteDC(memDC); /* free the memory context */
       break;
     case WM_RBUTTONDOWN: /* display second bitmap */
       DC = GetDC(hwnd); /* get device context */
       memDC = CreateCompatibleDC(DC); /* create compatible DC */
       SelectObject(memDC, hBit2);
       BitBlt(DC, LOWORD(lParam), HIWORD(lParam), 64, 64,
              memDC, 0, 0, SRCCOPY); /* build image */
       ReleaseDC(hwnd, DC); /* free the device context */
       DeleteDC(memDC); /* free the memory context */
       break;
     case WM_DESTROY: /* terminate the program */
       DeleteObject(hBit1); /* remove the bitmaps */
       DeleteObject(hBit2);
       PostQuitMessage(0);
       break;
     default:
       /* Let Windows 95 process any messages not specified in
          the preceding switch statement. */
       return DefWindowProc(hwnd, message, wParam, lParam);
   }
   return 0;
}
```

Sample output from the dual-bitmap program is shown in Figure 6-5.

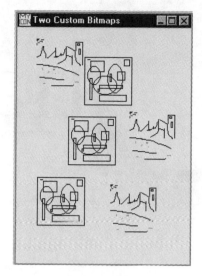

Sample output
from the
dual-bitmap
program
Figure 6-5.

In the next chapter, we will again take up the topic of controls by exploring
more of those supported by Windows 95.

Chapter 7

A Closer Look at Controls

Controls were introduced in Chapter 5, when dialog boxes were first discussed. This chapter examines several more controls, including check boxes, radio buttons, group boxes, static text controls, and scroll bars. As you will see, many of the techniques that you learned when using the controls in Chapter 5 will apply to the controls discussed here.

Note: If you have not yet read Chapter 5, which covers dialog boxes, you should do so at this time, because a dialog box is used to demonstrate the controls discussed in this chapter.

Using Check Boxes

A *check box* is a control that is used to turn an option on or off. It consists of a small box that can either contain a checkmark or not. There is a label associated with each check box to describe what option the box represents. If the box contains a checkmark, the box is said to be *checked* and the option selected. If the box is empty, then the box is unchecked, or *cleared,* and the option will be deselected. A check box is typically part of a dialog box and is generally defined within the dialog box's definition in your program's resource file. To add a check box to a dialog box definition, use the **CHECKBOX** command, which takes this general form:

CHECKBOX *"string"*, *CBID, X, Y, Width, Height* [, *Style*]

Here, *string* is the text that will be shown alongside the check box. *CBID* is the value associated with the check box. The box's upper-left corner will be at *X,Y,* and the box plus its associated text will have the dimensions specified by *Width* x *Height. Style* determines the exact nature of the check box. If no explicit style is specified, then the check box defaults to displaying *string* on the right, and the user can tab to the box. As you know from using Windows 95, check boxes are toggles. Each time you select a check box, its state changes from checked to unchecked, and vice versa. However, this is not necessarily accomplished automatically.

When you use the **CHECKBOX** resource command, you are creating a *manual check box,* which your program must manage by checking and unchecking the box each time it is selected. (You will see how, shortly.) However, you can have Windows 95 perform this housekeeping function for you if you create an *automatic check box*. An automatic check box is created using the **AUTOCHECKBOX** resource command. It has exactly the same form as the **CHECKBOX** command. When you use an automatic check box, Windows 95 automatically toggles its state (between checked and unchecked) each time the box is selected.

Windows 3.1 does not support the AUTOCHECKBOX resource command. When converting from Windows 3.1, you will want to watch for manual check boxes that can be converted to automatic check boxes.

Before continuing, you need to create the following resource file, which defines a dialog box that contains both a manual and an automatic check box. The file also defines a top-level menu. Enter this file into your computer now:

```
#include "mydialog.h"
#include <windows.h>

MYMENU MENU
{
  MENUITEM "&Dialog", ID_DIALOG1
  MENUITEM "&Status", ID_STATUS
  MENUITEM "&Help", ID_HELP
}

MYMENU ACCELERATORS
{
  VK_F2, ID_DIALOG1, VIRTKEY
  VK_F3, ID_STATUS, VIRTKEY
  VK_F1, ID_HELP, VIRTKEY
}

MYDB DIALOG 18, 18, 142, 92
CAPTION "Test Dialog Box"
STYLE DS_MODALFRAME | WS_POPUP | WS_CAPTION | WS_SYSMENU
{
  PUSHBUTTON "OK", IDOK, 77, 40, 30, 13,
             WS_CHILD | WS_VISIBLE | WS_TABSTOP
  PUSHBUTTON "Cancel", IDCANCEL, 74, 65, 37, 14,
             WS_CHILD | WS_VISIBLE | WS_TABSTOP
  CHECKBOX "Checkbox 1" , ID_CB1, 3, 10, 48, 12
  AUTOCHECKBOX "Checkbox 2" , ID_CB2, 3, 22, 48, 12
}
```

You will also need to create the header file **mydialog.h**, which is shown next. This file also defines values that will be needed by other examples later in this chapter.

7

```
#define ID_DIALOG1    100
#define ID_STATUS     101
#define ID_HELP       102

#define ID_CB1        103
#define ID_CB2        104

#define ID_CT1        105
```

```
#define ID_RB1          106
#define ID_RB2          107

#define ID_GB1          200
#define ID_GB2          201
```

Each time the user clicks on a check box or selects the check box and then presses the spacebar, a **WM_COMMAND** message is sent to the dialog function and the low-order word of **wParam** contains the identifier associated with that check box. If you are using a manual check box, then you will want to respond to this command by changing the state of the box. To do this, send the check box a **BM_SETCHECK** message using the **SendDlgItemMessage( )** API function. This function was discussed in Chapter 5. Its prototype is shown again here for your convenience:

LONG SendDlgItemMessage(HWND *hdwnd*, int *ID*,
                        UINT *IDMsg*, WPARAM *wParam*,
                        LPARAM *lParam*);

When the **BM_SETCHECK** message is sent, the value of *wParam* determines whether the box will be checked or cleared. If *wParam* is 1, then the box will be checked. If it is 0, the box will be cleared. By default, when a dialog box is first displayed, all check boxes will be unchecked. When sending **BM_SETCHECK**, *lParam* is unused.

Remember, if you use an automatic check box, then the state of the box will be changed automatically each time it is selected. You do not need to send an automatic check box a **BM_SETCHECK** message.

You can determine the status of a check box by sending it the message **BM_GETCHECK**. The check box returns 1 if the box is checked and 0 otherwise. In this case, both *wParam* and *lParam* are 0.

Here is a program that demonstrates both an automatic and a manual check box. To illustrate the difference between the two, in this example, once the manual check box is selected, it is always checked. It is not possible to clear the box. You will see how to manage a manual check box in the next example.

```
/* Demonstrate check boxes. */

#include <windows.h>
#include <string.h>
#include <stdio.h>
#include "mydialog.h"

LRESULT CALLBACK WindowFunc(HWND, UINT, WPARAM, LPARAM);
```

```
LRESULT CALLBACK DialogFunc(HWND, UINT, WPARAM, LPARAM);

char szWinName[] = "MyWin"; /* name of window class */

HINSTANCE hInst;

int status1=0, status2=0; /* holds status of check boxes */

int WINAPI WinMain(HINSTANCE hThisInst, HINSTANCE hPrevInst,
                   LPSTR lpszArgs, int nWinMode)
{
  HWND hwnd;
  MSG msg;
  WNDCLASS wcl;
  HANDLE hAccel;

  /* Define a window class. */
  wcl.hInstance = hThisInst; /* handle to this instance */
  wcl.lpszClassName = szWinName; /* window class name */
  wcl.lpfnWndProc = WindowFunc; /* window function */
  wcl.style = 0; /* default style */

  wcl.hIcon = LoadIcon(NULL, IDI_APPLICATION); /* icon style */
  wcl.hCursor = LoadCursor(NULL, IDC_ARROW); /* cursor style */

  /* specify name of menu resource */
  wcl.lpszMenuName = "MYMENU"; /* main menu */

  wcl.cbClsExtra = 0; /* no extra */
  wcl.cbWndExtra = 0; /* information needed */

  /* Make the window white. */
  wcl.hbrBackground = GetStockObject(WHITE_BRUSH);

  /* Register the window class. */
  if(!RegisterClass (&wcl)) return 0;

  /* Now that a window class has been registered, a window
     can be created. */
  hwnd = CreateWindow(
    szWinName, /* name of window class */
    "Using Check Boxes", /* title */
    WS_OVERLAPPEDWINDOW, /* window style - normal */
    CW_USEDEFAULT, /* X coordinate - let Windows decide */
    CW_USEDEFAULT, /* Y coordinate - let Windows decide */
    CW_USEDEFAULT, /* width - let Windows decide */
    CW_USEDEFAULT, /* height - let Windows decide */
    HWND_DESKTOP, /* no parent window */
```

7

```
        NULL, /* no menu */
        hThisInst, /* handle of this instance of the program */
        NULL /* no additional arguments */
      );

      hInst = hThisInst; /* save the current instance handle */

      /* load accelerators */
      hAccel = LoadAccelerators(hThisInst, "MYMENU");

      /* Display the window. */
      ShowWindow(hwnd, nWinMode);
      UpdateWindow(hwnd);

      /* Create the message loop. */
      while(GetMessage(&msg, NULL, 0, 0))
      {
        if(!TranslateAccelerator(hwnd, hAccel, &msg)) {
          TranslateMessage(&msg); /* allow use of keyboard */
          DispatchMessage(&msg); /* return control to Windows */
        }
      }
      return msg.wParam;
    }

    /* This function is called by Windows 95 and is passed
       messages from the message queue.
    */
    LRESULT CALLBACK WindowFunc(HWND hwnd, UINT message,
                                WPARAM wParam, LPARAM lParam)
    {
      char str[80];

      switch(message) {
        case WM_COMMAND:
          switch(LOWORD(wParam)) {
            case ID_DIALOG1:
              DialogBox(hInst, "MYDB", hwnd, DialogFunc);
              break;
            case ID_STATUS: /* show check box status */
              if(status1) strcpy(str, "Checkbox 1 is checked\n");
              else strcpy(str, "Checkbox 1 is not checked\n");
              if(status2) strcat(str, "Checkbox 2 is checked");
              else strcat(str, "Checkbox 2 is not checked");
              MessageBox(hwnd, str, "", MB_OK);
              break;
            case ID_HELP:
              MessageBox(hwnd, "Help", "", MB_OK);
```

```
                break;
          }
        break;
      case WM_DESTROY: /* terminate the program */
        PostQuitMessage(0);
        break;
      default:
        /* Let Windows 95 process any messages not specified in
           the preceding switch statement. */
        return DefWindowProc(hwnd, message, wParam, lParam);
  }
  return 0;
}


/* A simple dialog function. */
LRESULT CALLBACK DialogFunc(HWND hdwnd, UINT message,
                            WPARAM wParam, LPARAM lParam)
{
  switch(message) {
    case WM_COMMAND:
      switch(LOWORD(wParam)) {
        case IDCANCEL:
          EndDialog(hdwnd, 0);
          return 1;
        case IDOK:
          /* update global checkbox status variables */
          status1 = SendDlgItemMessage(hdwnd, ID_CB1,
            BM_GETCHECK, 0, 0);  // is box checked?
          status2 = SendDlgItemMessage(hdwnd, ID_CB2,
            BM_GETCHECK, 0, 0);  // is box checked?
          EndDialog(hdwnd, 0);
          return 1;
        case ID_CB1:
          /* user selected 1st check box, so check it */
          SendDlgItemMessage(hdwnd, ID_CB1, BM_SETCHECK, 1, 0);
          return 1;
      }
  }
  return 0;
}
```

7

This program contains two global variables, **status1** and **status2**, which hold the state of the two check boxes. These variables are set when the OK button is selected inside the dialog box. To set the state of the check boxes, select the **Dialog** main menu option. To see the status of the check boxes, select the **Status** main menu option. (The **Help** option is included only as a placeholder.)

When you run this program and select the **Dialog** main menu option, you will see the dialog box shown in Figure 7-1.

Managing Check Boxes

The check box program, as it stands, has two serious flaws. First, the state of each check box is reset each time the dialog box is displayed. That is, the previous setting of each box is lost. Secondly, while the manual check box can be set, it cannot be cleared. That is, the manual check box is not fully implemented as a toggle, the way check boxes are expected to function. In this section, you will learn how to manage check boxes more effectively.

Toggling a Check Box

First, while it is far easier to simply use automatic check boxes, it is possible to implement a toggled check box by managing a manual check box. This means that your program will have to perform all the necessary overhead itself, instead of letting Windows 95 handle it. To accomplish this, the program first finds out the current state of the check box and then sets it to the opposite state. The following change to the dialog function accomplishes this.

```
case ID_CB1: /* This is a manually managed check box. */
  /* user selected 1st check box, so change its state */
  if(!SendDlgItemMessage(hdwnd, ID_CB1, BM_GETCHECK, 0, 0))
    SendDlgItemMessage(hdwnd, ID_CB1, BM_SETCHECK, 1, 0);
  else /* turn it off */
    SendDlgItemMessage(hdwnd, ID_CB1, BM_SETCHECK, 0, 0);
  return 1;
```

Initializing a Check Box

As mentioned, both the manual and the automatic check boxes are cleared (that is, unchecked) each time the dialog box that contains them is activated. While this might be desirable in some situations, it is not what users

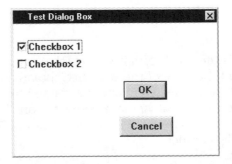

The test
dialog box
Figure 7-1.

normally expect. Generally, check boxes are set to their previous state each time the dialog box is displayed. If you want the check boxes to reflect their previous state, then you must initialize them each time the dialog box is activated. The easiest way to do this is to send them the appropriate **BM_SETCHECK** messages when the dialog box is created. Remember, each time a dialog box is activated, it is sent a **WM_INITDIALOG** message. When this message is received, you can set the state of the check boxes (and anything else) inside the dialog box.

The code to initialize the check boxes is shown here:

```
case WM_INITDIALOG:
  /* The dialog box has just been displayed.  Set
     the check boxes appropriately. */
  SendDlgItemMessage(hdwnd, ID_CB1, BM_SETCHECK, status1, 0);
  SendDlgItemMessage(hdwnd, ID_CB2, BM_SETCHECK, status2, 0);
  return 1;
```

The entire program listing, which incorporates the check box initialization and manages the manual check box, is shown here. Compare its operation to the preceding example's. As you might expect, it now behaves in a way common to most other Windows applications.

```
/* Demonstrates check boxes with enhancements. */

#include <windows.h>
#include <string.h>
#include <stdio.h>
#include "mydialog.h"

LRESULT CALLBACK WindowFunc(HWND, UINT, WPARAM, LPARAM);
LRESULT CALLBACK DialogFunc(HWND, UINT, WPARAM, LPARAM);

char szWinName[] = "MyWin"; /* name of window class */

HINSTANCE hInst;

int status1=0, status2=0; /* holds status of check boxes */

int WINAPI WinMain(HINSTANCE hThisInst, HINSTANCE hPrevInst,
                   LPSTR lpszArgs, int nWinMode)
{
  HWND hwnd;
  MSG msg;
  WNDCLASS wcl;
  HANDLE hAccel;
```

7

```
/* Define a window class. */
wcl.hInstance = hThisInst; /* handle to this instance */
wcl.lpszClassName = szWinName; /* window class name */
wcl.lpfnWndProc = WindowFunc; /* window function */
wcl.style = 0; /* default style */

wcl.hIcon = LoadIcon(NULL, IDI_APPLICATION); /* icon style */
wcl.hCursor = LoadCursor(NULL, IDC_ARROW); /* cursor style */

/* specify name of menu resource */
wcl.lpszMenuName = "MYMENU"; /* main menu */

wcl.cbClsExtra = 0; /* no extra */
wcl.cbWndExtra = 0; /* information needed */

/* Make the window white. */
wcl.hbrBackground = GetStockObject(WHITE_BRUSH);

/* Register the window class. */
if(!RegisterClass (&wcl)) return 0;

/* Now that a window class has been registered, a window
   can be created. */
hwnd = CreateWindow(
  szWinName, /* name of window class */
  "Using Check Boxes", /* title */
  WS_OVERLAPPEDWINDOW, /* window style - normal */
  CW_USEDEFAULT, /* X coordinate - let Windows decide */
  CW_USEDEFAULT, /* Y coordinate - let Windows decide */
  CW_USEDEFAULT, /* width - let Windows decide */
  CW_USEDEFAULT, /* height - let Windows decide */
  HWND_DESKTOP, /* no parent window */
  NULL, /* no menu */
  hThisInst, /* handle of this instance of the program */
  NULL /* no additional arguments */
);

hInst = hThisInst; /* save the current instance handle */

/* load accelerators */
hAccel = LoadAccelerators(hThisInst, "MYMENU");

/* Display the window. */
ShowWindow(hwnd, nWinMode);
UpdateWindow(hwnd);

/* Create the message loop. */
while(GetMessage(&msg, NULL, 0, 0))
```

```
    {
      if(!TranslateAccelerator(hwnd, hAccel, &msg)) {
        TranslateMessage(&msg); /* allow use of keyboard */
        DispatchMessage(&msg); /* return control to Windows */
      }
    }
    return msg.wParam;
}


/* This function is called by Windows 95 and is passed
   messages from the message queue.
*/
LRESULT CALLBACK WindowFunc(HWND hwnd, UINT message,
                            WPARAM wParam, LPARAM lParam)
{
  char str[80];

  switch(message) {
    case WM_COMMAND:
      switch(LOWORD(wParam)) {
        case ID_DIALOG1:
          DialogBox(hInst, "MYDB", hwnd, DialogFunc);
          break;
        case ID_STATUS:
          if(status1) strcpy(str, "Checkbox 1 is checked\n");
          else strcpy(str, "Checkbox 1 is not checked\n");
          if(status2) strcat(str, "Checkbox 2 is checked");
          else strcat(str, "Checkbox 2 is not checked");
          MessageBox(hwnd, str, "", MB_OK);
          break;
        case ID_HELP:
          MessageBox(hwnd, "Help", "", MB_OK);
          break;
      }
      break;
    case WM_DESTROY: /* terminate the program */
      PostQuitMessage(0);
      break;
    default:
      /* Let Windows 95 process any messages not specified in
         the preceding switch statement. */
      return DefWindowProc(hwnd, message, wParam, lParam);
  }
  return 0;
}

/* A simple dialog function. */
LRESULT CALLBACK DialogFunc(HWND hdwnd, UINT message,
```

7

```
                              WPARAM wParam, LPARAM lParam)
{
  switch(message) {
    case WM_INITDIALOG:
      /* The dialog box has just been displayed.  Set
         the check boxes appropriately. */
      SendDlgItemMessage(hdwnd, ID_CB1, BM_SETCHECK, status1, 0);
      SendDlgItemMessage(hdwnd, ID_CB2, BM_SETCHECK, status2, 0);
      return 1;
    case WM_COMMAND:
      switch(LOWORD(wParam)) {
        case IDCANCEL:
          EndDialog(hdwnd, 0);
          return 1;
        case IDOK:
          /* update global check box status variables */
          status1 = SendDlgItemMessage(hdwnd, ID_CB1,
            BM_GETCHECK, 0, 0);  // is box checked?
          status2 = SendDlgItemMessage(hdwnd, ID_CB2,
            BM_GETCHECK, 0, 0);  // is box checked?
          EndDialog(hdwnd, 0);
          return 1;
        case ID_CB1: /* This is a manually managed check box. */
          /* user selected 1st check box, so change its state */
          if (!SendDlgItemMessage(hdwnd, ID_CB1, BM_GETCHECK, 0, 0))
            SendDlgItemMessage(hdwnd, ID_CB1, BM_SETCHECK, 1, 0);
          else /* turn it off */
            SendDlgItemMessage(hdwnd, ID_CB1, BM_SETCHECK, 0, 0);
          return 1;
      }
  }
  return 0;
}
```

Adding Static Controls

A *static control* is one that neither receives nor generates any messages. In short, the term *static control* is a formal way of describing something that is simply displayed in a dialog box, such as a text message or a box used to group other controls. The two static controls that we will look at here are the *centered text box* and the *group box*. Both of these controls are included in the dialog definition in your program's resource file, using the commands **CTEXT** and **GROUPBOX**, respectively.

The **CTEXT** control outputs a string that is centered within a predefined area. The general form for **CTEXT** is shown next:

CTEXT *"text"*, *CTID, X, Y, Width, Height* [, *Style*]

Here, *text* is the text that will be displayed. *CTID* is the value associated with the text. The text will be shown in a box that has its upper-left corner at *X,Y* and its dimensions specified by *Width* x *Height*. *Style* determines the exact nature of the text box. If no explicit style is specified, then the check box defaults to displaying *text* centered within the box. Understand that the box itself is *not* displayed. The box simply defines the space that *text* is allowed to occupy.

The **GROUPBOX** control draws a box. This box is generally used to visually group other controls, and it may contain a title for the group. The general form for **GROUPBOX** is shown here:

GROUPBOX *"title"*, *GBID, X, Y, Width, Height* [, *Style*]

Here, *title* is the title to the box. *CTID* is the value associated with the text. The upper-left corner will be at *X,Y*, and its dimensions are specified by *Width* x *Height*. *Style* determines the exact nature of the group box. Generally, the default setting is sufficient.

To see the effects of using these two static controls, add the following definitions to the dialog box inside the resource file you created for the preceding examples.

```
GROUPBOX "Checkboxes", ID_GB1, 1, 1, 51, 34
CTEXT "This is text", ID_CT1, 1, 44, 50, 24
```

After you have added these lines, recompile the preceding example, execute the program, and select the **Dialog** main menu option. The dialog box will now look like the one shown in Figure 7-2. Remember that although the static controls make the dialog box look different, its function has not changed.

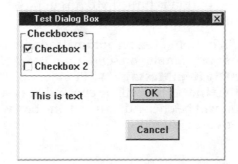

Adding static controls to the dialog box
Figure 7-2.

7

Adding Radio Buttons

The next control examined is the *radio button*. Radio buttons are used to present mutually exclusive options. A radio button consists of a label and a small button. If the button is empty, then the option is not selected. If the button is filled, then the option is selected. Windows 95 supports two types of radio buttons: manual and automatic. The manual radio button (like the manual check box) requires that you perform all management functions. The automatic radio button performs the management functions for you. Because managing radio buttons is more complex than managing check boxes, and because automatic radio buttons are the type generally used by applications, they are the only ones examined here.

Like other controls, automatic radio buttons are defined in your program's resource file, within a dialog definition. To create an automatic radio button, use **AUTORADIOBUTTON**, which has this general form:

AUTORADIOBUTTON *"string"*, *RBID*, *X*, *Y*, *Width*, *Height* [, *Style*]

Here, *string* is the text that will be shown alongside the button. *RBID* is the value associated with the radio button. The button's upper-left corner will be at *X,Y*, and the button plus its associated text will have the dimensions specified by *Width* x *Height*. *Style* determines the exact nature of the radio button. If no explicit style is specified, then the button defaults to displaying *string* on the right, and the user can tab to the button.

 Windows 3.1 does not support the AUTORADIOBUTTON resource command. Watch for opportunities to use AUTORADIOBUTTON when converting from Windows 3.1.

As stated, radio buttons are generally used to create groups of mutually exclusive options. When you use automatic radio buttons to create such a group, then Windows 95 automatically manages the buttons in a mutually exclusive manner. That is, each time you select one button, the previously selected button is turned off. It is impossible to select more than one button at a time.

A radio button (even an automatic one) may be set to a known state by your program if you send it the **BM_SETCHECK** message using the **SendDlgItemMessage( )** API function. The value of *wParam* determines whether the button will be checked or cleared. If *wParam* is 1, then the button will be checked. If it is 0, the box will be cleared. By default, all buttons are cleared.

Note: Even if you use automatic radio buttons, it is possible to manually set more than one option or to clear all options using **SendDlgItemMessage( )**. However, normal Windows style dictates that radio buttons be used in a mutually exclusive fashion, with one, and only one, option selected. It is strongly suggested that you not violate this rule.

You can obtain the status of a radio button by sending it the **BM_GETCHECK** message. The button returns 1 if the button is selected and 0 if it is not.

To add radio buttons to the example program, first add these lines to the dialog box definition inside your resource file. Notice that another group box is added to surround the radio buttons. This is not necessary, of course, but such groupings are common in dialog boxes.

```
AUTORADIOBUTTON "Radio 1", ID_RB1, 60, 10, 48, 12
AUTORADIOBUTTON "Radio 2", ID_RB2, 60, 22, 48, 12
GROUPBOX "Radio Group", ID_GB2, 58, 1, 51, 34
```

Following is the preceding sample program, expanded to accommodate the two radio buttons. Since the radio buttons are automatic, there are only a few additions to the program. Notice that the state of the radio buttons is stored in two global variables called **rbstatus1** and **rbstatus2**. The values of these variables are used to set the initial button states and to display the status of the buttons when the **Status** main menu option is selected.

```
/* Demonstrate radio buttons. */

#include <windows.h>
#include <string.h>
#include <stdio.h>
#include "mydialog.h"

LRESULT CALLBACK WindowFunc(HWND, UINT, WPARAM, LPARAM);
LRESULT CALLBACK DialogFunc(HWND, UINT, WPARAM, LPARAM);

char szWinName[] = "MyWin"; /* name of window class */

HINSTANCE hInst;

int cbstatus1=0, cbstatus2=0; /* holds status of check boxes */
int rbstatus1=1, rbstatus2=0; /* holds status of radio buttons */

int WINAPI WinMain(HINSTANCE hThisInst, HINSTANCE hPrevInst,
                   LPSTR lpszArgs, int nWinMode)
```

7

```c
{
  HWND hwnd;
  MSG msg;
  WNDCLASS wcl;
  HANDLE hAccel;

  /* Define a window class. */
  wcl.hInstance = hThisInst; /* handle to this instance */
  wcl.lpszClassName = szWinName; /* window class name */
  wcl.lpfnWndProc = WindowFunc; /* window function */
  wcl.style = 0; /* default style */

  wcl.hIcon = LoadIcon(NULL, IDI_APPLICATION); /* icon style */
  wcl.hCursor = LoadCursor(NULL, IDC_ARROW); /* cursor style */

  /* specify name of menu resource */
  wcl.lpszMenuName = "MYMENU"; /* main menu */

  wcl.cbClsExtra = 0; /* no extra */
  wcl.cbWndExtra = 0; /* information needed */

  /* Make the window white. */
  wcl.hbrBackground = GetStockObject(WHITE_BRUSH);

  /* Register the window class. */
  if(!RegisterClass (&wcl)) return 0;

  /* Now that a window class has been registered, a window
     can be created. */
  hwnd = CreateWindow(
    szWinName, /* name of window class */
    "Try Radio Buttons", /* title */
    WS_OVERLAPPEDWINDOW, /* window style - normal */
    CW_USEDEFAULT, /* X coordinate - let Windows decide */
    CW_USEDEFAULT, /* Y coordinate - let Windows decide */
    CW_USEDEFAULT, /* width - let Windows decide */
    CW_USEDEFAULT, /* height - let Windows decide */
    HWND_DESKTOP, /* no parent window */
    NULL, /* no menu */
    hThisInst, /* handle of this instance of the program */
    NULL /* no additional arguments */
  );

  hInst = hThisInst; /* save the current instance handle */

  /* load accelerators */
  hAccel = LoadAccelerators(hThisInst, "MYMENU");
```

```
    /* Display the window. */
    ShowWindow(hwnd, nWinMode);
    UpdateWindow(hwnd);

    /* Create the message loop. */
    while(GetMessage(&msg, NULL, 0, 0))
    {
      if(!TranslateAccelerator(hwnd, hAccel, &msg)) {
        TranslateMessage(&msg); /* allow use of keyboard */
        DispatchMessage(&msg); /* return control to Windows */
      }
    }
    return msg.wParam;
}


/* This function is called by Windows 95 and is passed
   messages from the message queue.
*/
LRESULT CALLBACK WindowFunc(HWND hwnd, UINT message,
                            WPARAM wParam, LPARAM lParam)
{
  char str[255];

  switch(message) {
    case WM_COMMAND:
      switch(LOWORD(wParam)) {
        case ID_DIALOG1:
          DialogBox(hInst, "MYDB", hwnd, DialogFunc);
          break;
        case ID_STATUS:
          if(cbstatus1) strcpy(str, "Checkbox 1 is checked\n");
          else strcpy(str, "Checkbox 1 is not checked\n");
          if(cbstatus2) strcat(str, "Checkbox 2 is checked\n");
          else strcat(str, "Checkbox 2 is not checked\n");
          if(rbstatus1) strcat(str, "Radio 1 is checked\n");
          else strcat(str, "Radio 1 is not checked\n");
          if(rbstatus2) strcat(str, "Radio 2 is checked");
          else strcat(str, "Radio 2 is not checked");
          MessageBox(hwnd, str, "", MB_OK);
          break;
        case ID_HELP:
          MessageBox(hwnd, "Help", "", MB_OK);
          break;
      }
      break;
    case WM_DESTROY: /* terminate the program */
      PostQuitMessage(0);
      break;
```

7

```
      default:
        /* Let Windows 95 process any messages not specified in
         the preceding switch statement. */
        return DefWindowProc(hwnd, message, wParam, lParam);
  }
  return 0;
}

/* A simple dialog function. */
LRESULT CALLBACK DialogFunc(HWND hdwnd, UINT message,
                            WPARAM wParam, LPARAM lParam)
{
  switch(message) {
    case WM_INITDIALOG:
      /* The dialog box has just been displayed.  Set
         the check boxes and radio buttons appropriately. */
      SendDlgItemMessage(hdwnd, ID_CB1, BM_SETCHECK, cbstatus1, 0);
      SendDlgItemMessage(hdwnd, ID_CB2, BM_SETCHECK, cbstatus2, 0);
      SendDlgItemMessage(hdwnd, ID_RB1, BM_SETCHECK, rbstatus1, 0);
      SendDlgItemMessage(hdwnd, ID_RB2, BM_SETCHECK, rbstatus2, 0);
      return 1;
    case WM_COMMAND:
      switch(LOWORD(wParam)) {
        case IDCANCEL:
          EndDialog(hdwnd, 0);
          return 1;
        case IDOK:
          /* update global check box status variables */
          cbstatus1 = SendDlgItemMessage(hdwnd, ID_CB1,
            BM_GETCHECK, 0, 0);  // is box checked?
          cbstatus2 = SendDlgItemMessage(hdwnd, ID_CB2,
            BM_GETCHECK, 0, 0);  // is box checked?

          /* now, update global check box status variables */
          rbstatus1 = SendDlgItemMessage(hdwnd, ID_RB1,
            BM_GETCHECK, 0, 0);  // is button checked?
          rbstatus2 = SendDlgItemMessage(hdwnd, ID_RB2,
            BM_GETCHECK, 0, 0);  // is button checked?

          EndDialog(hdwnd, 0);
          return 1;
        case ID_CB1: /* This is a manually managed check box. */
          /* user selected 1st check box, so change its state */
          if(!SendDlgItemMessage(hdwnd, ID_CB1, BM_GETCHECK, 0, 0))
```

```
                SendDlgItemMessage(hdwnd, ID_CB1, BM_SETCHECK, 1, 0);
            else /* turn it off */
                SendDlgItemMessage(hdwnd, ID_CB1, BM_SETCHECK, 0, 0);
            return 1;

        }
    }
    return 0;
}
```

When you run this program, the dialog box will now look like the one shown in Figure 7-3.

Using a Scroll Bar Control

The last control to be examined in this chapter is the scroll bar. Scroll bars exist in two forms in Windows. The first type of scroll bar is part of a normal window or dialog box. The other type of scroll bar exists separately, as a control. While both types of scroll bars are managed in essentially the same way, the control scroll bar requires some special techniques. For this reason, the scroll bar control is discussed here.

To add a scroll bar control to a dialog box, use the **SCROLLBAR** statement, which has this general form:

SCROLLBAR *SBID, X, Y, Width, Height* [, *Style*]

Here, *SBID* is the value associated with the scroll bar. The scroll bar's upper-left corner will be at *X,Y,* and the scroll bar will have the dimensions specified by *Width* x *Height*. *Style* determines the exact nature of the scroll bar. Its default style is **SBS_HORZ**, which creates a horizontal scroll bar. For a vertical scroll bar, specify the **SBS_VERT** style. If you want the scroll bar to be capable of receiving keyboard focus, include the **WS_TABSTOP** style

7

The dialog box with radio buttons

Figure 7-3.

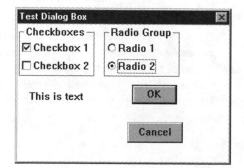

For example, the following creates a vertical scroll bar.

```
SCROLLBAR ID_SB1, 130, 10, 10, 70, SBS_VERT | WS_TABSTOP
```

Receiving Scroll Bar Messages

Unlike other controls, a scroll bar control does not generate a **WM_ COMMAND** message. Instead, scroll bars—whether control scroll bars or window scroll bars—send either a **WM_VSCROLL** or a **WM_HSCROLL** message when either a vertical or horizontal scroll bar is activated, respectively. The value of the low-order word of **wParam** contains a code that describes the activity. **lParam** contains the handle of the scroll bar control. (For a window scroll bar, **lParam** is 0.)

As mentioned, the value in **LOWORD(wParam)** specifies what activity has taken place. Here are some common scroll bar values:

    SB_LINEUP
    SB_LINEDOWN
    SB_PAGEUP
    SB_PAGEDOWN
    SB_THUMBPOSITION
    SB_THUMBTRACK

Each time the user moves the scroll bar up one position, **SB_LINEUP** is sent. Each time the scroll bar is moved down one position, **SB_LINEDOWN** is sent. **SB_PAGEUP** and **SB_PAGEDOWN** are sent when the scroll bar is moved up or down one page. The **SB_THUMBPOSITION** value is sent each time the slider box (thumb) of the scroll bar is dragged to a new position. The **SB_THUMBTRACK** message is sent each time the thumb passes over a new position. This allows you to "track" the movement of the thumb before it is released. When **SB_THUMBPOSITION** or **SB_THUMBTRACK** is received, the high-order word of **wParam** contains the current slider box position.

In Windows 3.1, the organization relative to scroll bar messages of lParam and wParam differ from their equivalents in Windows 95. Specifically, the handle of the scroll bar is in the high-order word of lParam. The position of the slider box is in the low-order word of lParam. The nature of the scroll bar action is in wParam. Because of these differences, you must rewrite all scroll bar code when porting from Windows 3.1 to Windows 95.

Setting the Scroll Bar Range

Before you can use a scroll bar control, you must define its range. The range of the scroll bar determines how many positions there are between one end and the other. By default, window scroll bars have a range of 0 to 100. However, control scroll bars have a default range of 0 to 0, which means that the range needs to be set before the scroll bar control can be used. To set the range of a scroll bar, use the **SetScrollRange( )** API function, shown here:

        BOOL SetScrollRange(HWND *hwnd*, int *which*, int *min*,
                        int *max*, BOOL *repaint*);

Here, *hwnd* is the handle that identifies the scroll bar. For window scroll bars, this is the handle of the window. For scroll bar controls, this is the handle of the scroll bar. (Remember, scroll bar controls pass their handle in **lParam**.) The value of *which* determines which scroll bar is having its range set. If you are setting the range of the vertical window scroll bar, then this parameter must be **SB_VERT**. If you are setting the range of the horizontal window scroll bar, this value must be **SB_HORZ**. However, to set a scroll bar control, this value must be **SB_CTL**. The values of *min* and *max* determine the range. These values must lie between 0 and 32,767. If *repaint* is true, then the scroll bar is redrawn after the range is set. If it is false, the bar is not redisplayed. The function returns non-zero if successful and zero on failure.

Setting the Scroll Bar Slider Box Position

Scroll bars are manually managed controls. Thus your program must move the slider box (thumb) as needed. To do this, use the **SetScrollPos( )** function, whose prototype is shown here:

        int SetScrollPos(HWND *hwnd*, int *which*, int *pos*,
                    BOOL *repaint*);

Here, *hwnd* is the handle that identifies the scroll bar. For window scroll bars, this is the handle of the window. For scroll bar controls, this is the handle of the scroll bar. The value of *which* determines which scroll bar is having its slider box set. If you are setting the position of the box of a vertical window scroll bar, then this parameter must be **SB_VERT**. If you are setting the position of the box in a horizontal window scroll bar, this value must be **SB_HORZ**. However, to set the slider box in a scroll bar control, this value must be **SB_CTL**. The value of *pos* determines where the slider box will be positioned. It must contain a value within the range of the scroll bar. If *repaint* is true, then the scroll bar is redrawn after the box is set. If it is false, the bar is not redisplayed.

7

A Sample Scroll Bar Program

This section shows a simple program that demonstrates how to create a vertical scroll bar, including managing scroll bar messages. The program requires the following resource file:

```
; Demonstrate a scroll bar.
#include "scroll.h"
#include <windows.h>

MYMENU MENU
{
  MENUITEM "&Scroll Bar", IDM_DIALOG1
  MENUITEM "&Help", IDM_HELP
}

MYMENU ACCELERATORS
{
  VK_F2, IDM_DIALOG1, VIRTKEY
  VK_F1, IDM_HELP, VIRTKEY
}

MYDB DIALOG 18, 18, 142, 92
CAPTION "Using a Scroll Bar"
STYLE DS_MODALFRAME | WS_POPUP | WS_CAPTION | WS_SYSMENU
{
  GROUPBOX "Thumb Position", ID_GB1, 1, 1, 60, 30
  SCROLLBAR ID_SB1, 130, 10, 10, 70, SBS_VERT | WS_TABSTOP
}
```

You will also need to create this header file, called **scroll.h**:

```
#define IDM_DIALOG1    100
#define IDM_HELP       101

#define ID_SB1         102
#define ID_GB1         103
```

The entire scroll bar demonstration program is shown next. It responds to the **SB_LINEUP**, **SB_LINEDOWN**, **SB_PAGEUP**, **SB_PAGEDOWN**, **SB_THUMBPOSITION**, and **SB_THUMBTRACK** messages when the slider box is moved appropriately. It also displays the current position of the thumb in the "Thumb Position" group box. The position will change as you move the slider. Figure 7-4 shows sample output from the program. One other point: notice that the thumb position is displayed by outputting text into the client area of the dialog box using **TextOut( )**. Although a dialog

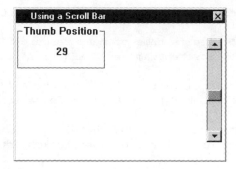

Sample
output from
the scroll bar
demonstration
Figure 7-4.

box performs a special purpose, it is still a window with the same basic
characteristics as the main window.

```c
/* Demonstrate A Scroll Bar */

#include <windows.h>
#include <string.h>
#include <stdio.h>
#include "scroll.h"

#define RANGEMAX 50

LRESULT CALLBACK WindowFunc(HWND, UINT, WPARAM, LPARAM);
BOOL CALLBACK DialogFunc(HWND, UINT, WPARAM, LPARAM);

char szWinName[] = "MyWin"; /* name of window class */

HINSTANCE hInst;

int WINAPI WinMain(HINSTANCE hThisInst, HINSTANCE hPrevInst,
                   LPSTR lpszArgs, int nWinMode)
{
  HWND hwnd;
  MSG msg;
  WNDCLASS wcl;
  HANDLE hAccel;

  /* Define a window class. */
  wcl.hInstance = hThisInst; /* handle to this instance */
  wcl.lpszClassName = szWinName; /* window class name */
  wcl.lpfnWndProc = WindowFunc; /* window function */
  wcl.style = 0; /* default style */

  wcl.hIcon = LoadIcon(NULL, IDI_APPLICATION); /* icon style */
```

7

```
wcl.hCursor = LoadCursor(NULL, IDC_ARROW); /* cursor style */

/* specify name of menu resource */
wcl.lpszMenuName = "MYMENU"; /* main menu */

wcl.cbClsExtra = 0; /* no extra */
wcl.cbWndExtra = 0; /* information needed */

/* Make the window white. */
wcl.hbrBackground = GetStockObject(WHITE_BRUSH);

/* Register the window class. */
if(!RegisterClass (&wcl)) return 0;

/* Now that a window class has been registered, a window
   can be created. */
hwnd = CreateWindow(
  szWinName, /* name of window class */
  "Using a Scroll Bar", /* title */
  WS_OVERLAPPEDWINDOW, /* window style - normal */
  CW_USEDEFAULT, /* X coordinate - let Windows decide */
  CW_USEDEFAULT, /* Y coordinate - let Windows decide */
  CW_USEDEFAULT, /* width - let Windows decide */
  CW_USEDEFAULT, /* height - let Windows decide */
  HWND_DESKTOP, /* no parent window */
  NULL, /* no menu */
  hThisInst, /* handle of this instance of the program */
  NULL /* no additional arguments */
);

hInst = hThisInst; /* save the current instance handle */

/* load accelerators */
hAccel = LoadAccelerators(hThisInst, "MYMENU");

/* Display the window. */
ShowWindow(hwnd, nWinMode);
UpdateWindow(hwnd);

/* Create the message loop. */
while(GetMessage(&msg, NULL, 0, 0))
{
  if(!TranslateAccelerator(hwnd, hAccel, &msg)) {
    TranslateMessage(&msg); /* allow use of keyboard */
    DispatchMessage(&msg); /* return control to Windows */
  }
}
return msg.wParam;
```

```
      }

   /* This function is called by Windows 95 and is passed
      messages from the message queue.
   */
   LRESULT CALLBACK WindowFunc(HWND hwnd, UINT message,
                                    WPARAM wParam, LPARAM lParam)
   {
     switch(message) {
       case WM_COMMAND:
         switch(LOWORD(wParam)) {
           case IDM_DIALOG1:
             DialogBox(hInst, "MYDB", hwnd, DialogFunc);
             break;
           case IDM_HELP:
             MessageBox(hwnd, "Help", "Use the Scroll Bar", MB_OK);
             break;
         }
         break;
       case WM_DESTROY: /* terminate the program */
         PostQuitMessage(0);
         break;
       default:
         /* Let Windows 95 process any messages not specified in
            the preceding switch statement. */
         return DefWindowProc(hwnd, message, wParam, lParam);
     }
     return 0;
   }

   /* A simple dialog function. */
   BOOL CALLBACK DialogFunc(HWND hdwnd, UINT message,
                              WPARAM wParam, LPARAM lParam)
   {
     char str[80];
     static int pos = 0; /* slider box position */

HDC hdc;

     switch(message) {
       case WM_COMMAND:
         switch(LOWORD(wParam)) {
           case IDCANCEL:
             EndDialog(hdwnd, 0);
             return 1;
         }
         break;
       case WM_VSCROLL:
```

7

```
SetScrollRange((HWND) lParam, SB_CTL, 0, RANGEMAX, 1);
switch(LOWORD(wParam)) {
  case SB_LINEDOWN:
    pos++;
    if(pos>RANGEMAX) pos = RANGEMAX;
    SetScrollPos((HWND) lParam, SB_CTL, pos, 1);
    hdc = GetDC(hdwnd);
    sprintf(str, "%d", pos);
    TextOut(hdc, 55, 30, "    ", 4);
    TextOut(hdc, 55, 30, str, strlen(str));
    ReleaseDC(hdwnd, hdc);
    return 1;
  case SB_LINEUP:
    pos--;
    if(pos<0) pos = 0;
    SetScrollPos((HWND) lParam, SB_CTL, pos, 1);
    hdc = GetDC(hdwnd);
    sprintf(str, "%d", pos);
    TextOut(hdc, 55, 30, "    ", 4);
    TextOut(hdc, 55, 30, str, strlen(str));
    ReleaseDC(hdwnd, hdc);
    return 1;
  case SB_THUMBPOSITION:
    pos = HIWORD(wParam); /* get current position */
    SetScrollPos((HWND) lParam, SB_CTL, pos, 1);
    hdc = GetDC(hdwnd);
    sprintf(str, "%d", pos);
    TextOut(hdc, 55, 30, "    ", 4);
    TextOut(hdc, 55, 30, str, strlen(str));
    ReleaseDC(hdwnd, hdc);
    return 1;
  case SB_THUMBTRACK:
    pos = HIWORD(wParam); /* get current position */
    SetScrollPos((HWND) lParam, SB_CTL, pos, 1);
    hdc = GetDC(hdwnd);
    sprintf(str, "%d", pos);
    TextOut(hdc, 55, 30, "    ", 4);
    TextOut(hdc, 55, 30, str, strlen(str));
    ReleaseDC(hdwnd, hdc);
    return 1;
  case SB_PAGEDOWN:
    pos += 5;
    if(pos>RANGEMAX) pos = RANGEMAX;
    SetScrollPos((HWND) lParam, SB_CTL, pos, 1);
    hdc = GetDC(hdwnd);
    sprintf(str, "%d", pos);
    TextOut(hdc, 55, 30, "    ", 4);
    TextOut(hdc, 55, 30, str, strlen(str));
```

```
               ReleaseDC(hdwnd, hdc);
               return 1;
           case SB_PAGEUP:
               pos -= 5;
               if(pos<0) pos = 0;
               SetScrollPos((HWND) lParam, SB_CTL, pos, 1);
               hdc = GetDC(hdwnd);
               sprintf(str, "%d", pos);
               TextOut(hdc, 55, 30, "      ", 4);
               TextOut(hdc, 55, 30, str, strlen(str));
               ReleaseDC(hdwnd, hdc);
               return 1;
       }
   }
   return 0;
}
```

Many beginning Windows programmers have the impression that using scroll bars is difficult. Actually, scroll bars are one of the easiest Windows controls.

In the next chapter, you will learn more about outputting text to a window.

7

Chapter 8

Working with Text

In the past several chapters, output has been handled using message and dialog boxes—the client area of the window has been ignored. However, this chapter returns to the client area and explores various aspects of how Windows 95 manages text. Also, some important techniques are developed that make it easier for you to repaint the window when it has been overwritten. The chapter concludes with a discussion of the way additional text fonts can be used by your application.

As with most other aspects of the Windows 95 environment, you, the programmer, have virtually unlimited control over the way that text is displayed and managed within the client area of a window. As such, it is far beyond the scope of this chapter to cover all aspects of text manipulation using Windows. However, you will be able to easily explore other aspects of text manipulation after understanding the basics introduced in this chapter.

This chapter begins with a discussion of the window coordinate system and how text is mapped to it. Then several text and screen API functions are described. These functions help you control and manage text output to the client area of a window.

Window Coordinates

As you know, **TextOut( )** is Windows' text output function. It displays a string at the specified coordinates, which are always relative to the window. Therefore, a window's position on the screen has no effect upon the coordinates passed to **TextOut( )**. By default, the upper-left corner of the client area of the window is location 0, 0. The *X* value increases as you go to the right and the *Y* value increases as you move downward.

So far, we have been using window coordinates for **TextOut( )** and for positioning various elements within a dialog box without any specific mention of what those coordinates actually refer to. Now is the time to clarify a few details. First, the coordinates that are specified in **TextOut( )** are *logical coordinates*. That is, the units used by **TextOut( )** (and other window display functions, including the graphics functions described in the next chapter) are *logical units*. Windows maps these logical units onto pixels when output is actually displayed. We haven't had to worry about this distinction until now because, by default, logical units are the same as pixels. It is important to understand, however, that different mapping modes can be selected in which this convenient default will not be the case.

Setting the Text and Background Colors

By default, when you output text to the window using **TextOut( )**, it is shown as black text against the current background. However, you can determine both the color of the text and the background color using the API functions **SetTextColor( )** and **SetBkColor( )**, whose prototypes are shown here:

COLORREF SetTextColor(HDC *hdc*, COLORREF *color*);

COLORREF SetBkColor(HDC *hdc*, COLORREF *color*);

The **SetTextColor( )** function sets the current text color of the device associated with *hdc* to that specified by *color* (or to the closest color the display device is capable of displaying). The **SetBkColor( )** function sets the current text background color to that specified by *color* (or the nearest possible shade). For both functions, the previous color setting is returned. If an error occurs, then the value **CLR_INVALID** is returned.

The color is specified as a value of type **COLORREF**, which is a 32-bit integer. Windows allows colors to be specified in three different ways. The first, and by far most common way, is as an *RGB* (red, green, blue) value. In an RGB value, the relative intensities of the three colors are combined to produce the actual color. The second way a color can be specified is as an index into a logical palette. The third is as an RGB value relative to a palette. In this chapter, only the first way will be discussed.

A long integer value that holds an RGB color is passed to either **SetTextColor( )** or **SetBkColor( )** using the following encoding:

Byte	Color
Byte 0 (low-order byte)	Red
Byte 1	Green
Byte 2	Blue
Byte 3 (high-order byte)	Must be zero

Each color in an RGB value is in the range 0 through 255, with 0 being the lowest intensity and 255 being the highest intensity. For example, the following long integer produces a bright magenta color:

00	255	00	255

Although you are free to manually construct a COLORREF value, Windows defines the macro **RGB( )** that does this for you. It has this general form:

    COLORREF RGB(int *red*, int *green*, int *blue*);

Here, *red*, *green*, and *blue* must be values in the range 0 through 255. Therefore, to create bright magenta, use **RGB(255, 0, 255)**. To create white, use **RGB(255, 255, 255)**. To create black, use **RGB(0, 0, 0)**. To create other colors, you combine the three basic colors in varying intensities. For example, **RGB(0, 100, 100)** creates a light aqua. You can experiment to determine which colors are best for your application.

Setting the Background Display Mode

You can control the way the background is affected when text is displayed on the screen by using the **SetBkMode( )** API function, whose prototype is shown here:

    int SetBkMode(HDC *hdc*, int *mode*);

8

This function determines what happens to the current background color when text (and some other types of output) is displayed. The handle of the device context affected is specified by *hdc*. The background mode is specified in *mode* and must be one of these two macros: **OPAQUE** or **TRANSPARENT**. The function returns the previous setting or 0 if an error occurs.

If *mode* is **OPAQUE**, then each time text is output, the background is changed to that of the current background color. If *mode* is **TRANSPARENT**, then the background is not altered. In this case, any effects of a call to **SetBkColor( )** are essentially ignored. By default, the background mode is **OPAQUE**.

Obtaining the Text Metrics

As you know from Chapter 3, characters are not all of the same dimension. That is, in Windows, most text fonts are proportional. Therefore, the character *i* is not as wide as the character *w*. Also, the height of each character and the length of descenders (the hanging parts of letters like *p* and *g*) vary among fonts. In addition, the amount of space between horizontal lines is also changeable. That these (and other) attributes are variable would not be of too much consequence except for the fact that Windows demands that you, the programmer, manually manage virtually all text output.

Windows provides only minimal support for text output to the client area of a window. The main output function is **TextOut( )**. This function will only display a string of text beginning at a specified location. It will not format output or even automatically perform a carriage return/linefeed sequence, for example. Managing output to the client window is completely up to you.

Given that the size of each font may be different (and that fonts may be changed while your program is executing), there must be some way to determine the dimensions and various other attributes of the currently selected font. For example, the capability to write one line of text after another implies that you have some way of knowing how tall the font is and how many pixels are between lines. The API function that obtains information about the current font is called **GetTextMetrics( )**, and it has this prototype:

BOOL GetTextMetrics(HDC *hdc*, LPTEXTMETRIC *lpTAttrib*);

Here, *hdc* is the handle of the output device, which is generally obtained using **GetDC( )** or **BeginPaint( )**, and *lpTAttrib* is a pointer to a structure of type **TEXTMETRIC**, which will, upon return, contain the text metrics for the currently selected font. The **TEXTMETRIC** structure is defined as shown here:

```
typedef struct tagTEXTMETRIC
{
  LONG tmHeight; /* total height of font */
  LONG tmAscent; /* height above base line */
  LONG tmDescent; /* length of descenders */
  LONG tmInternalLeading; /* space above characters */
  LONG tmExternalLeading; /* space between rows */
  LONG tmAveCharWidth; /* average width */
  LONG tmMaxCharWidth; /* maximum width */
  LONG tmWeight; /* weight */
  LONG tmOverhang; /* extra width added to special fonts */
  LONG tmDigitizedAspectX; /* horizontal aspect */
  LONG tmDigitizedAspectY; /* vertical aspect */
  BYTE tmFirstChar; /* first character in font */
  BYTE tmLastChar; /* last character in font */
  BYTE tmDefaultChar; /* default character */
  BYTE tmBreakChar; /* character used to break words */
  BYTE tmItalic; /* non-zero if italic */
  BYTE tmUnderlined; /* non-zero if underlined */
  BYTE tmStruckOut; /* non-zero if struckout */
  BYTE tmPitchAndFamily; /* pitch and family of font */
  BYTE tmCharSet; /* character set identifier */
} TEXTMERIC;
```

While most of the values obtained by this function will not be used in this chapter, two are very important because they are used to compute the vertical distance between lines of text. This value is needed if you want to output more than one line of text to a window. Unlike a console-based application in which there is only one font and its size is fixed, there may be several Windows fonts and they may vary in size. Specifically, each font defines the height of its characters and the amount of space required between lines. This means that it is not possible to know in advance the vertical (*Y*) coordinate of the next line of text. To determine where the next line of text will begin, you must call **GetTextMetrics( )** to acquire two values: the character height and the amount of space between lines. These values are given in the **tmHeight** and **tmExternalLeading** fields, respectively. By adding together these two values, you obtain the number of vertical units between lines.

Remember: The value **tmExternalLeading** contains, in essence, the number of vertical units that should be left blank between lines of text. This value is separate from the height of the font. Thus, both values are needed in order to compute where the next line of text will begin. You will see this applied, shortly.

8

There is an enhanced version of **TEXTMETRIC**, called
NEWTEXTMETRIC. **NEWTEXTMETRIC** is exactly the same as
TEXTMETRIC except that it adds four additional fields at the end. These
fields provide support for TrueType fonts. (TrueType fonts provide superior
scalability features.) The new fields in **NEWTEXTMETRIC** are shown here:

```
DWORD ntmFlags; /* indicates type of font */
UINT ntmSizeEM; /* size of an em */
UINT ntmCellHeight; /* font height */
UINT ntmAvgWidth; /* average character width */
```

For the purposes of this chapter, none of these fields are needed. However,
they may be of value to applications you create. You should consult your API
reference manual for details.

Computing the Length of a String

Because characters in the current font are not the same size, it's impossible
to know the length of a string in logical units by simply knowing how many
characters are in it. That is, the result returned by **strlen( )** is not
meaningful to managing output to a window because characters are of
differing widths. To solve this problem, Windows 95 includes the API
function **GetTextExtentPoint32( )**, whose prototype is shown here:

BOOL GetTextExtentPoint32(HDC *hdc*, LPCSTR *lpszString*,
        int *len*, LPSIZE *lpSize*);

Here, *hdc* is the handle of the output device. The string that you want the
length of is pointed to by *lpszString*. The number of characters in the string is
specified in *len*. The width and height of the string is returned, in logical
units, in the **SIZE** structure pointed to by *lpSize*. The **SIZE** structure is
defined as shown here:

```
typedef struct tagSIZE {
  LONG cx; /* width */
  LONG cy; /* height */
} SIZE;
```

Upon return from a call to **GetTextExtentPoint32( )**, the **cx** field will
contain the length of the string. Therefore, this value can be used to
determine the starting point for the next string to be displayed if you want
to continue where the previous output left off.

GetTextExtentPoint32( ) replaces the older GetTextExtentPoint( ) function. Be aware of this when converting programs from Windows 3.1.

Obtaining the System Metrics

Although Windows maintains and automatically translates logical coordinates into pixels, sometimes you will want to know the actual display size of the computer being used to run your application. To obtain this and other information, use the **GetSystemMetrics( )** API function, whose prototype is shown here:

```
int GetSystemMetrics(int what);
```

Here, *what* will specify the value you want to obtain. **GetSystemMetrics( )** can obtain 39 different values. The values for screen coordinates are returned in pixel units. Here are the macros for some common values:

Value	Metric Obtained
SM_CXFULLSCREEN	Width of maximized client area
SM_CYFULLSCREEN	Height of maximized client area
SM_CXICON	Width of large icon
SM_CYICON	Height of large icon
SM_CXSMICON	Width of small icon
SM_CYSMICON	Height of small icon
SM_CXSCREEN	Width of entire screen
SM_CYSCREEN	Height of entire screen

A Short Text Demonstration

Now that you have learned about some of Windows 95's text functions, a short demonstration of these features will be useful. Here is a short program that does just that:

```
/* Demonstrate Text Output */

#include <windows.h>
#include <string.h>
#include <stdio.h>
```

8

```
#include "text.h"

LRESULT CALLBACK WindowFunc(HWND, UINT, WPARAM, LPARAM);

char szWinName[] = "MyWin"; /* name of window class */

char str[255]; /* holds output strings */

int X=0, Y=0; /* current output location */
int maxX, maxY; /* screen dimensions */

int WINAPI WinMain(HINSTANCE hThisInst, HINSTANCE hPrevInst,
                   LPSTR lpszArgs, int nWinMode)
{
  HWND hwnd;
  MSG msg;
  WNDCLASS wcl;
  HANDLE hAccel;

  /* Define a window class. */
  wcl.hInstance = hThisInst; /* handle to this instance */
  wcl.lpszClassName = szWinName; /* window class name */
  wcl.lpfnWndProc = WindowFunc; /* window function */
  wcl.style = 0; /* default style */

  wcl.hIcon = LoadIcon(NULL, IDI_APPLICATION); /* icon style */
  wcl.hCursor = LoadCursor(NULL, IDC_ARROW); /* cursor style */

  /* specify name of menu resource */
  wcl.lpszMenuName = "MYMENU"; /* main menu */

  wcl.cbClsExtra = 0; /* no extra */
  wcl.cbWndExtra = 0; /* information needed */

  /* Make the window white. */
  wcl.hbrBackground = GetStockObject(WHITE_BRUSH);

  /* Register the window class. */
  if(!RegisterClass (&wcl)) return 0;

  /* Now that a window class has been registered, a window
     can be created. */
  hwnd = CreateWindow(
    szWinName, /* name of window class */
    "Fun with Text", /* title */
    WS_OVERLAPPEDWINDOW, /* window style - normal */
    CW_USEDEFAULT, /* X coordinate - let Windows decide */
    CW_USEDEFAULT, /* Y coordinate - let Windows decide */
```

```
            CW_USEDEFAULT, /* width - let Windows decide */
            CW_USEDEFAULT, /* height - let Windows decide */
            HWND_DESKTOP, /* no parent window */
            NULL, /* no menu */
            hThisInst, /* handle of this instance of the program */
            NULL /* no additional arguments */
          );

          /* load accelerators */
          hAccel = LoadAccelerators(hThisInst, "MYMENU");

          /* Display the window. */
          ShowWindow(hwnd, nWinMode);
          UpdateWindow(hwnd);

          /* Create the message loop. */
          while(GetMessage(&msg, NULL, 0, 0))
          {
            if(!TranslateAccelerator(hwnd, hAccel, &msg)) {
              TranslateMessage(&msg); /* allow use of keyboard */
              DispatchMessage(&msg); /* return control to Windows */
            }
          }
          return msg.wParam;
        }


        /* This function is called by Windows 95 and is passed
           messages from the message queue.
        */
        LRESULT CALLBACK WindowFunc(HWND hwnd, UINT message,
                                    WPARAM wParam, LPARAM lParam)
        {
          HDC hdc;
          TEXTMETRIC tm;
          SIZE size;

          switch(message) {
            case WM_CREATE:
              /* get screen coordinates */
              maxX = GetSystemMetrics(SM_CXSCREEN);
              maxY = GetSystemMetrics(SM_CYSCREEN);
              break;
            case WM_COMMAND:
              switch(LOWORD(wParam)) {
                case ID_SHOW:
                  hdc = GetDC(hwnd); /* get device context */

                  /* set text color to black */
```

8

```
              SetTextColor(hdc, RGB(0, 0, 0));
              /* set background color to turquoise */
              SetBkColor(hdc, RGB(0, 255, 255));

              /* get text metrics */
              GetTextMetrics(hdc, &tm);

              sprintf(str, "The font is %ld pixels high.", tm.tmHeight);
              TextOut(hdc, X, Y, str, strlen(str)); /* output string */
              Y = Y + tm.tmHeight + tm.tmExternalLeading; /* next line */

              strcpy(str, "This is on the next line. ");
              TextOut(hdc, X, Y, str, strlen(str)); /* output string */

              /* compute length of a string */
              GetTextExtentPoint32(hdc, str, strlen(str), &size);
              sprintf(str, "Previous string is %ld units long", size.cx);
              X = size.cx; /* advance to end of previous string */
              TextOut(hdc, X, Y, str, strlen(str));
              Y = Y + tm.tmHeight + tm.tmExternalLeading; /* next line */
              X = 0; /* reset X */

              sprintf(str, "Screen dimensions: %d %d", maxX, maxY);
              TextOut(hdc, X, Y, str, strlen(str));
              Y = Y + tm.tmHeight + tm.tmExternalLeading; /* next line */
              ReleaseDC(hwnd, hdc); /* Release DC */
              break;
            case ID_RESET:
              X = Y = 0;
              break;
            case ID_HELP:
              MessageBox(hwnd, "F2: Display\nF3: Reset", "Help", MB_OK);
              break;
        }
        break;
      case WM_DESTROY: /* terminate the program */
        PostQuitMessage(0);
        break;
      default:
        /* Let Windows 95 process any messages not specified in
        the preceding switch statement. */
        return DefWindowProc(hwnd, message, wParam, lParam);
  }
  return 0;
}
```

This program requires the following resource file:

```
#include <windows.h>
#include "text.h"

MYMENU MENU
{
  MENUITEM "&Show", ID_SHOW
  MENUITEM "&Reset", ID_RESET
  MENUITEM "&Help", ID_HELP
}


MYMENU ACCELERATORS
{
  VK_F2, ID_SHOW, VIRTKEY
  VK_F3, ID_RESET, VIRTKEY
  VK_F1, ID_HELP, VIRTKEY
}
```

It also requires the header file **text.h**, shown here:

```
#define ID_SHOW      100
#define ID_RESET     101
#define ID_HELP      102
```

Enter these files and then compile and run the program. Each time you select Show from the main menu, you will cause a few lines of text to be displayed. The text will be black and the background turquoise (if you have a color monitor, of course). Sample output is shown in Figure 8-1.

When the window is first created and **WM_CREATE** is received, the global integers **maxX** and **maxY** are initialized to the coordinates of the screen using the **GetSystemMetrics( )** function. While these values serve no purpose in this program, they will be used in later examples.

Notice that the program declares two global variables, called **X** and **Y**, and initializes both to 0. These variables will contain the current window location at which text will be displayed. They will be continually updated by the program after each output sequence.

The interesting part of this program is mostly contained within the **WM_COMMAND** message. Let's examine it closely, beginning with the **ID_SHOW** case. Each time an **ID_SHOW** message is received, a device context is obtained. Then the text color is set to black and the background

8

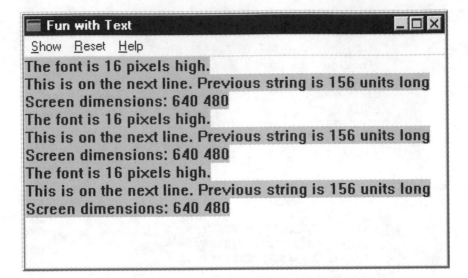

Sample output
from the text
demonstration
program
Figure 8-1.

color is set to turquoise. Since the device context is obtained each time an
ID_SHOW message is received, the colors must be set each time. That is,
they cannot be set only once (at the start of the program, for example).

After the colors have been set, the text metrics are obtained. Next, the first
line of text is output. Notice that it is constructed using **sprintf( )** and then
actually output using **TextOut( )**. As you know from previous chapters,
neither **TextOut( )** nor any other API function performs text formatting, so
it is up to you, the programmer, to construct your output first and then
display it using **TextOut( )**. After the string is displayed, the **Y** coordinate is
advanced to the next line by applying the formula developed earlier.

The program continues by next outputting the line "This is on the next line."
Then, before that string is overwritten by the next call to **sprintf( )**, its
length is computed using a call to **GetTextExtentPoint32( )**. This value is
then used to advance the **X** coordinate to the end of the previous line before
the next line is printed. Notice that here, the **Y** coordinate is unchanged.
This causes the next string to be displayed immediately after the previous
one. Before continuing, the program advances **Y** to the next line and resets
X to 0, which is the leftmost coordinate. This causes subsequent output once
again to start at the beginning of the next line.

Finally, the screen dimensions are displayed and the **Y** coordinate is
advanced to the next line. Each time you select Show, the text is displayed
lower in the window and does not overwrite the preceding text. Instead,
each set of lines is displayed beneath the previous one.

To start over, select Reset. This causes the coordinates to be reset to 0, 0.
However, it does not erase what is already in the window.

Solving the Repaint Problem

While the preceding program demonstrates several text and system functions, it reintroduces a fundamental problem that was first discussed in Chapter 3. The problem is this: When you run the program, display some text, and then overlay the window with another, the text is lost. Specifically, when the window is uncovered, the part of the text that was covered is missing. Of course, the reason for this is that each program must repaint its window when it receives a **WM_PAINT** message, and the preceding program does not do this. However, this raises the larger question: What mechanism should one use to restore the contents of a window that has been overwritten? As mentioned earlier, there are three basic methods. To review: First, you can regenerate the output if that output is created by some computational method. Second, you can store a record of display events and "replay" those events. Third, you can maintain a virtual window and simply copy the contents of the virtual window each time a **WM_CREATE** message is received. The most general of these is, of course, the third, and this is the method that will be developed here. As you will see, Windows provides substantial support for this method.

Virtual Window Theory

In general, here is how output will be accomplished using a virtual window. First, a virtual device context is created that is compatible with the actual device context. Then, all output is written to the virtual device context. Each time a **WM_PAINT** message is received, the contents of the virtual device context (i.e. the virtual window) are copied into the actual device context, causing output to be displayed in the window on the screen. Therefore, there is always a record of the current contents of the window. If the window is overwritten and then uncovered, a **WM_PAINT** message will be received and the window's contents will automatically be restored.

Some Additional API Functions

To implement a virtual window requires the use of several API functions. Four have been discussed already. These are **CreateCompatibleDC( )**, **SelectObject( )**, **GetStockObject( )**, and **BitBlt( )**. We will also be using **CreateCompatibleBitmap( )** and **PatBlt( )**, which are described next.

The **CreateCompatibleBitmap( )** function creates a bitmap that is compatible with a specified device context. This bitmap can also be used by any memory device context (created by **CreateCompatibleDC( )**) that is compatible with the specified device context. Its prototype is shown here:

HBITMAP CreateCompatibleBitmap(HDC *hdc*, int *width*, int *height*);

Here, *hdc* is the handle for the device context with which the bitmap will be compatible. The dimensions of the bitmap are specified in *width* and *height*. These values are given in pixels. The function returns a handle to the compatible bitmap or NULL on failure.

The **PatBlt( )** function fills a rectangle with the color and pattern of the currently selected *brush*. A brush is an object that specifies how a window (or region) will be filled. Filling an area using a brush is also commonly referred to as *painting* the region. The **PatBlt( )** function has this prototype:

BOOL PatBlt(HDC *hdc*, int *X*, int *Y*, int *width*, int *height*, DWORD *dwRaster*);

Here, *hdc* is the handle of the device to fill. The coordinates *X* and *Y* specify the upper-left corner of the region to be filled. The width and height of the region are specified in *width* and *height*. The value passed in *dwRaster* determines how the brush will be applied. It must be one of these macros:

dwRaster	Meaning
BLACKNESS	Region is black (brush is ignored)
WHITENESS	Region is white (brush is ignored)
PATCOPY	Brush is copied to region
PATINVERT	Brush is ORed to region
DSTINVERT	Region is inverted (brush is ignored)

Therefore, if you wish to apply the current brush unaltered, you would select **PATCOPY** for the value of *dwRaster*. The function returns non-zero if successful; zero otherwise.

Now that you know about the functions that will be used, it is time to see how to implement a virtual window.

Creating and Using a Virtual Window

Let's begin by restating the procedure that will be implemented. To create an easy and convenient means of restoring a window after a **WM_PAINT** message has been received, a virtual window will be maintained and all output will be written to that virtual window. Each time a repaint request is received, the contents of that window are copied into the window that is physically on the screen. Now, let's implement this approach.

Creating the Virtual Window

First, a virtual device context must be created that is compatible with the current device context. This will be done only once, as the program begins execution, when a **WM_CREATE** message is received. This compatible device context will stay in existence the entire time the program is executing. Here is the code that performs this function:

```
case WM_CREATE:
  /* get screen coordinates */
  maxX = GetSystemMetrics(SM_CXSCREEN);
  maxY = GetSystemMetrics(SM_CYSCREEN);

  /* make a compatible memory image */
  hdc = GetDC(hwnd);
  memdc = CreateCompatibleDC(hdc);
  hbit = CreateCompatibleBitmap(hdc, maxX, maxY);
  SelectObject(memdc, hbit);
  hbrush = GetStockObject(WHITE_BRUSH);
  SelectObject(memdc, hbrush);
  PatBlt(memdc, 0, 0, maxX, maxY, PATCOPY);
  ReleaseDC(hwnd, hdc);
  break;
```

Let's examine this code closely. First, the dimensions of the screen are obtained. They will be used to create a compatible bitmap. Then, the current device context is obtained. Next, a compatible device context is created in memory, using **CreateCompatibleDC( )**. The handle to this device context is stored in **memdc**, which is a global variable. Then, a compatible bitmap is created. This establishes a one-to-one mapping between the virtual window and the physical window. The dimensions of the bitmap are those of the maximum screen size. This ensures that the bitmap will always be large enough to fully restore the window, no matter how large the window is. (Actually, slightly smaller values could be used, since the borders aren't repainted, but this minor improvement is left to you, as an exercise.) The handle to the bitmap is stored in the global variable **hbit**. Next, a stock white brush is obtained and its handle is stored in the global variable **hbrush**. This brush is selected into the memory device context, and then **PatBlt( )** paints the entire virtual window using the brush. Thus the virtual window will have a white background, which matches the background of the physical window in the example program that follows. (Remember, these colors are under your control. The colors used here are arbitrary.) Finally, the physical device context is released. However, the memory device context stays in existence until the program ends.

8

Using the Virtual Window

Once the virtual window has been created, all output is directed to it. (The only time output is actually directed to the physical window is when a **WM_PAINT** message is received.) For example, here is a reworked version of the **ID_SHOW** message from the previous program, which uses the virtual window:

```
case ID_SHOW:
  /* set text color to black */
  SetTextColor(memdc, RGB(0, 0, 0));
  /* set background mode to transparent */
  SetBkMode(memdc, TRANSPARENT);

  /* get text metrics */
  GetTextMetrics(memdc, &tm);

  sprintf(str, "The font is %ld pixels high.", tm.tmHeight);
          TextOut(memdc, X, Y, str, strlen(str)); /* output string */
  Y = Y + tm.tmHeight + tm.tmExternalLeading; /* next line */

  strcpy(str, "This is on the next line. ");
  TextOut(memdc, X, Y, str, strlen(str)); /* output string */

  /* compute length of a string */
  GetTextExtentPoint32(memdc, str, strlen(str), &size);
  sprintf(str, "Previous string is %ld units long", size.cx);
  X = size.cx; /* advance to end of previous string */
  TextOut(memdc, X, Y, str, strlen(str));
  Y = Y + tm.tmHeight + tm.tmExternalLeading; /* next line */
  X = 0; /* reset X */

  sprintf(str, "Screen dimensions: %d %d", maxX, maxY);
  TextOut(memdc, X, Y, str, strlen(str));
  Y = Y + tm.tmHeight + tm.tmExternalLeading; /* next line */
  InvalidateRect(hwnd, NULL, 1);
  break;
```

This version directs all output to **memdc** and then calls **InvalidateRect( )** to cause the physical window to be updated.

Notice that this version also sets the background mode to **TRANSPARENT**. This causes the text to be displayed in the window without the background color being altered.

Each time a **WM_PAINT** message is received, the contents of the virtual device are copied into the physical device. This is accomplished with the following code.

```
case WM_PAINT: /* process a repaint request */
  hdc = BeginPaint(hwnd, &paintstruct); /* get DC */

  /* now, copy memory image onto screen */
  BitBlt(hdc, 0, 0, maxX, maxY, memdc, 0, 0, SRCCOPY);

  EndPaint(hwnd, &paintstruct); /* release DC */
  break;
```

As you can see, the **BitBlt( )** function is used to copy the image from **memdc** into **hdc**. Remember, the parameter **SRCCOPY** simply copies the image as is, without alteration, directly from the source to the target. Because all output has been stored in **memdc**, this statement causes that output to actually be displayed. Therefore, if the window is covered and then uncovered, **WM_PAINT** will be received and the contents of that window will be automatically restored.

As stated earlier, there are many ways to approach the restoring of a window, but the method just developed is applicable to a wide range of situations and is generally quite efficient. Also, since your program is passed the coordinates of the region that must be repainted, you can actually make the preceding routine more efficient by simply restoring that part of the window that had been destroyed. (You might want to try implementing this enhancement on your own.)

The Entire Virtual Window Demonstration Program

Here is the complete program that demonstrates a virtual window.

```
/* Repaint using a virtual window. */

#include <windows.h>
#include <string.h>
#include <stdio.h>
#include "text.h"

LRESULT CALLBACK WindowFunc(HWND, UINT, WPARAM, LPARAM);

char szWinName[] = "MyWin"; /* name of window class */

char str[255]; /* holds output strings */

int X=0, Y=0; /* current output location */
int maxX, maxY; /* screen dimensions */

HDC memdc; /* store the virtual device handle */
HBITMAP hbit; /* store the virtual bitmap */
```

8

```
HBRUSH hbrush; /* store the brush handle */

int WINAPI WinMain(HINSTANCE hThisInst, HINSTANCE hPrevInst,
                   LPSTR lpszArgs, int nWinMode)
{
  HWND hwnd;
  MSG msg;
  WNDCLASS wcl;
  HANDLE hAccel;

  /* Define a window class. */
  wcl.hInstance = hThisInst; /* handle to this instance */
  wcl.lpszClassName = szWinName; /* window class name */
  wcl.lpfnWndProc = WindowFunc; /* window function */
  wcl.style = 0; /* default style */

  wcl.hIcon = LoadIcon(NULL, IDI_APPLICATION); /* icon style */
  wcl.hCursor = LoadCursor(NULL, IDC_ARROW); /* cursor style */

  /* specify name of menu resource */
  wcl.lpszMenuName = "MYMENU"; /* main menu */

  wcl.cbClsExtra = 0; /* no extra */
  wcl.cbWndExtra = 0; /* information needed */

  /* Make the window white. */
  wcl.hbrBackground = GetStockObject(WHITE_BRUSH);

  /* Register the window class. */
  if(!RegisterClass (&wcl)) return 0;

  /* Now that a window class has been registered, a window
     can be created. */
  hwnd = CreateWindow(
    szWinName, /* name of window class */
    "Fun with Text", /* title */
    WS_OVERLAPPEDWINDOW, /* window style - normal */
    CW_USEDEFAULT, /* X coordinate - let Windows decide */
    CW_USEDEFAULT, /* Y coordinate - let Windows decide */
    CW_USEDEFAULT, /* width - let Windows decide */
    CW_USEDEFAULT, /* height - let Windows decide */
    HWND_DESKTOP, /* no parent window */
    NULL, /* no menu */
    hThisInst, /* handle of this instance of the program */
    NULL /* no additional arguments */
  );
```

```
      /* load accelerators */
      hAccel = LoadAccelerators(hThisInst, "MYMENU");

      /* Display the window. */
      ShowWindow(hwnd, nWinMode);
      UpdateWindow(hwnd);

      /* Create the message loop. */
      while(GetMessage(&msg, NULL, 0, 0))
      {
        if(!TranslateAccelerator(hwnd, hAccel, &msg)) {
          TranslateMessage(&msg); /* allow use of keyboard */
          DispatchMessage(&msg); /* return control to Windows */
        }
      }
      return msg.wParam;
    }

    /* This function is called by Windows 95 and is passed
       messages from the message queue.
    */
    LRESULT CALLBACK WindowFunc(HWND hwnd, UINT message,
                                WPARAM wParam, LPARAM lParam)
    {
      HDC hdc;
      PAINTSTRUCT paintstruct;
      TEXTMETRIC tm;
      SIZE size;

      switch(message) {
        case WM_CREATE:
          /* get screen coordinates */
          maxX = GetSystemMetrics(SM_CXSCREEN);
          maxY = GetSystemMetrics(SM_CYSCREEN);

          /* make a compatible memory image */
          hdc = GetDC(hwnd);
          memdc = CreateCompatibleDC(hdc);
          hbit = CreateCompatibleBitmap(hdc, maxX, maxY);
          SelectObject(memdc, hbit);
          hbrush = GetStockObject(WHITE_BRUSH);
          SelectObject(memdc, hbrush);
          PatBlt(memdc, 0, 0, maxX, maxY, PATCOPY);
          ReleaseDC(hwnd, hdc);
          break;
```

8

```
case WM_COMMAND:
  switch(LOWORD(wParam)) {
    case ID_SHOW:
      /* set text color to black */
      SetTextColor(memdc, RGB(0, 0, 0));
      /* set background mode to transparent */
      SetBkMode(memdc, TRANSPARENT);

      /* get text metrics */
      GetTextMetrics(memdc, &tm);

      sprintf(str, "The font is %ld pixels high.", tm.tmHeight);
      TextOut(memdc, X, Y, str, strlen(str)); /* output string */
      Y = Y + tm.tmHeight + tm.tmExternalLeading; /* next line */

      strcpy(str, "This is on the next line. ");
      TextOut(memdc, X, Y, str, strlen(str)); /* output string */

      /* compute length of a string */
      GetTextExtentPoint32(memdc, str, strlen(str), &size);
      sprintf(str, "Previous string is %ld units long", size.cx);
      X = size.cx; /* advance to end of previous string */
      TextOut(memdc, X, Y, str, strlen(str));
      Y = Y + tm.tmHeight + tm.tmExternalLeading; /* next line */
      X = 0; /* reset X */

      sprintf(str, "Screen dimensions: %d %d", maxX, maxY);
      TextOut(memdc, X, Y, str, strlen(str));
      Y = Y + tm.tmHeight + tm.tmExternalLeading; /* next line */
      InvalidateRect(hwnd, NULL, 1);
      break;
    case ID_RESET:
      X = Y = 0;
      /* erase by repainting background */
      PatBlt(memdc, 0, 0, maxX, maxY, PATCOPY);
      InvalidateRect(hwnd, NULL, 1);
      break;
    case ID_HELP:
      MessageBox(hwnd, "F2: Display\nF3: Reset", "Help", MB_OK);
      break;
  }
  break;
case WM_PAINT: /* process a repaint request */
```

```
      hdc = BeginPaint(hwnd, &paintstruct); /* get DC */

      /* now, copy memory image onto screen */
      BitBlt(hdc, 0, 0, maxX, maxY, memdc, 0, 0, SRCCOPY);
      EndPaint(hwnd, &paintstruct); /* release DC */
      break;
    case WM_DESTROY: /* terminate the program */
      DeleteDC(memdc); /* delete the memory device */
      PostQuitMessage(0);
      break;
    default:
     /* Let Windows 95 process any messages not specified in
     the preceding switch statement. */
      return DefWindowProc(hwnd, message, wParam, lParam);
  }
  return 0;
}
```

When you run this program you will see two immediate improvements. First, each time you cover and then uncover the window, the contents are restored. Second, when you select Reset, the window is cleared. This occurs because the call to **PatBlt( )** inside the **ID_RESET** message causes the white brush to paint the window, thus erasing any preexisting contents.

Changing Fonts

As you probably know, one of the main purposes of Windows in general, and Windows 95 specifically, is to provide complete control over the user interface. As such, it has a rich and varied set of text-based features that you can use. One of its strongest text-based features is its collection of various type fonts. Using Windows 95, you have several built-in type fonts to choose from. You can also create custom fonts. These topics are discussed in the following sections.

Using Built-in Fonts

The built-in fonts are stock objects that are selected using **GetStockObject( )**. At the time of this writing, Windows 95 supports seven built-in fonts. The macros associated with these fonts are shown here:

8

Macro	Font Description
ANSI_FIXED_FONT	Fixed-pitch font
ANSI_VAR_FONT	Variable-pitch font
DEVICE_DEFAULT_FONT	Default device font
DEFAULT_GUI_FONT	Default GUI font
OEM_FIXED_FONT	OEM-defined font
SYSTEM_FONT	Font used by Windows 95
SYSTEM_FIXED_FONT	Font used by older versions of Windows

The system fonts are those character fonts used by Windows for things like menus and dialog boxes. Older versions of Windows used a fixed-pitch system font, but in more recent versions, beginning with Windows 3.0, a variable font is used. Windows 95 also uses the variable font.

Selecting and using a built-in font is very easy. To do so, your program must first create a font handle, which is of type **HFONT**. Next, it must load the desired font, using **GetStockObject( )**, which returns a handle to the font. To switch to the font, select the font using **SelectObject( )** with the new font as a parameter. **SelectObject( )** will return a handle to the old font (which you may want to save so that you can switch back to it after you are done using the other font).

The following program demonstrates changing fonts. It adds another menu selection called Font. Each time it is selected, the font is toggled between the default system font and the ANSI variable font.

```
/* Demonstrate built-in fonts. */

#include <windows.h>
#include <string.h>
#include <stdio.h>
#include "text.h"

LRESULT CALLBACK WindowFunc(HWND, UINT, WPARAM, LPARAM);

char szWinName[] = "MyWin"; /* name of window class */

char str[255]; /* holds output strings */

int X=0, Y=0; /* current output location */
int maxX, maxY; /* screen dimensions */

HDC memdc; /* store the virtual device handle */
HBITMAP hbit; /* store the virtual bitmap */
HBRUSH hbrush; /* store the brush handle */
```

```
HFONT holdf, hnewf; /* store the font handles */

int WINAPI WinMain(HINSTANCE hThisInst, HINSTANCE hPrevInst,
                   LPSTR lpszArgs, int nWinMode)
{
  HWND hwnd;
  MSG msg;
  WNDCLASS wcl;
  HANDLE hAccel;

  /* Define a window class. */
  wcl.hInstance = hThisInst; /* handle to this instance */
  wcl.lpszClassName = szWinName; /* window class name */
  wcl.lpfnWndProc = WindowFunc; /* window function */
  wcl.style = 0; /* default style */

  wcl.hIcon = LoadIcon(NULL, IDI_APPLICATION); /* icon style */
  wcl.hCursor = LoadCursor(NULL, IDC_ARROW); /* cursor style */

  /* specify name of menu resource */
  wcl.lpszMenuName = "MYMENU"; /* main menu */

  wcl.cbClsExtra = 0; /* no extra */
  wcl.cbWndExtra = 0; /* information needed */

  /* Make the window white. */
  wcl.hbrBackground = GetStockObject(WHITE_BRUSH);

  /* Register the window class. */
  if(!RegisterClass (&wcl)) return 0;

  /* Now that a window class has been registered, a window
     can be created. */
  hwnd = CreateWindow(
    szWinName, /* name of window class */
    "Fun with Text", /* title */
    WS_OVERLAPPEDWINDOW, /* window style - normal */
    CW_USEDEFAULT, /* X coordinate - let Windows decide */
    CW_USEDEFAULT, /* Y coordinate - let Windows decide */
    CW_USEDEFAULT, /* width - let Windows decide */
    CW_USEDEFAULT, /* height - let Windows decide */
    HWND_DESKTOP, /* no parent window */
    NULL, /* no menu */
    hThisInst, /* handle of this instance of the program */
    NULL /* no additional arguments */
  );

  /* load accelerators */
```

8

```
    hAccel = LoadAccelerators(hThisInst, "MYMENU");

    /* Display the window. */
    ShowWindow(hwnd, nWinMode);
    UpdateWindow(hwnd);

    /* Create the message loop. */
    while(GetMessage(&msg, NULL, 0, 0))
    {
      if(!TranslateAccelerator(hwnd, hAccel, &msg)) {
        TranslateMessage(&msg); /* allow use of keyboard */
        DispatchMessage(&msg); /* return control to Windows */
      }
    }
    return msg.wParam;
}

/* This function is called by Windows 95 and is passed
   messages from the message queue.
*/
LRESULT CALLBACK WindowFunc(HWND hwnd, UINT message,
                            WPARAM wParam, LPARAM lParam)
{
  HDC hdc;
  PAINTSTRUCT paintstruct;
  static TEXTMETRIC tm;
  SIZE size;
  static fontswitch = 0;

  switch(message) {
    case WM_CREATE:
      /* get screen coordinates */
      maxX = GetSystemMetrics(SM_CXSCREEN);
      maxY = GetSystemMetrics(SM_CYSCREEN);

      /* make a compatible memory image device */
      hdc = GetDC(hwnd);
      memdc = CreateCompatibleDC(hdc);
      hbit = CreateCompatibleBitmap(hdc, maxX, maxY);
      SelectObject(memdc, hbit);
      hbrush = GetStockObject(WHITE_BRUSH);
      SelectObject(memdc, hbrush);
      PatBlt(memdc, 0, 0, maxX, maxY, PATCOPY);

      /* get new font */
      hnewf = GetStockObject(ANSI_VAR_FONT);

      ReleaseDC(hwnd, hdc);
```

```
        break;
case WM_COMMAND:
  switch(LOWORD(wParam)) {
    case ID_SHOW:
        /* set text color to black and mode to transparent */
        SetTextColor(memdc, RGB(0, 0, 0));
        SetBkMode(memdc, TRANSPARENT);

        /* get text metrics */
        GetTextMetrics(memdc, &tm);

        sprintf(str, "The font is %ld pixels high.", tm.tmHeight);
        TextOut(memdc, X, Y, str, strlen(str)); /* output string */
        Y = Y + tm.tmHeight + tm.tmExternalLeading; /* next line */

        strcpy(str, "This is on the next line. ");
        TextOut(memdc, X, Y, str, strlen(str)); /* output string */

        /* compute length of a string */
        GetTextExtentPoint32(memdc, str, strlen(str), &size);
        sprintf(str, "Previous string is %ld units long", size.cx);
        X = size.cx; /* advance to end of previous string */
        TextOut(memdc, X, Y, str, strlen(str));
        Y = Y + tm.tmHeight + tm.tmExternalLeading; /* next line */
        X = 0; /* reset X */

        sprintf(str, "Screen dimensions: %d %d", maxX, maxY);
        TextOut(memdc, X, Y, str, strlen(str));
        Y = Y + tm.tmHeight + tm.tmExternalLeading; /* next line */
        InvalidateRect(hwnd, NULL, 1);
        break;
    case ID_RESET:
      X = Y = 0;
      /* erase by repainting background */
      PatBlt(memdc, 0, 0, maxX, maxY, PATCOPY);
      InvalidateRect(hwnd, NULL, 1);
      break;
    case ID_FONT:
      if(!fontswitch) {  /* switch to new font */
        holdf = SelectObject(memdc, hnewf);
        fontswitch = 1;
      }
      else { /* switch to old font */
        SelectObject(memdc, holdf);
        fontswitch = 0;
      }
      break;
```

8

```
      case ID_HELP:
        MessageBox(hwnd, "F2: Display\nF3: Change font\nF4: Reset",
                   "Text Fun", MB_OK);
        break;
    }
    break;
  case WM_PAINT: /* process a repaint request */
    hdc = BeginPaint(hwnd, &paintstruct); /* get DC */

    /* now, copy memory image onto screen */
    BitBlt(hdc, 0, 0, maxX, maxY, memdc, 0, 0, SRCCOPY);
    EndPaint(hwnd, &paintstruct); /* release DC */
    break;
  case WM_DESTROY: /* terminate the program */
    DeleteDC(memdc);
    PostQuitMessage(0);
    break;
  default:
    /* Let Windows 95 process any messages not specified in
    the preceding switch statement. */
    return DefWindowProc(hwnd, message, wParam, lParam);
  }
  return 0;
}
```

Before you compile this program, change your resource file to the following:

```
#include <windows.h>
#include "text.h"

MYMENU MENU
{
  MENUITEM "&Show", ID_SHOW
  MENUITEM "Change &Font", ID_FONT
  MENUITEM "&Reset", ID_RESET
  MENUITEM "&Help", ID_HELP
}

MYMENU ACCELERATORS
{
  VK_F2, ID_SHOW, VIRTKEY
  VK_F3, ID_FONT, VIRTKEY
  VK_F4, ID_RESET, VIRTKEY
  VK_F1, ID_HELP, VIRTKEY
}
```

Finally, add this line to the **text.h** header file:

```
#define ID_FONT    103
```

Sample output produced by this program is shown in Figure 8-2.

Creating Custom Fonts

Although it may sound complex, it is actually very easy to create a custom type font. There are two major advantages to doing this. First, a custom font gives your application a unique look that will set it apart. Second, creating your own font lets you control precisely what occurs when text is output. Before beginning, it is important to understand that you will not be defining a new font. Instead, you will be tailoring an existing font so that it meets the specifications you desire. (That is, you don't need to define the shape of each character in the font you create.)

To create your own font, use the **CreateFont( )** API function, whose prototype is shown here:

```
HFONT CreateFont(int Height, int Width, int Escapement,
              int Orientation, int Weight,
              DWORD Ital, DWORD Underline,
              DWORD StrikeThru, DWORD Charset,
              DWORD Precision, DWORD ClipPrecision,
              DWORD Quality, DWORD Pitch,
              LPCSTR FontName);
```

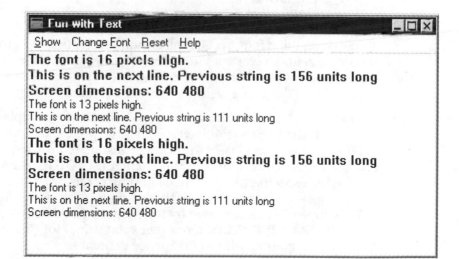

Sample output from the built-in font program
Figure 8-2.

8

The height of the font is passed in *Height,* and the width of the font is specified in *Width*. If *Width* is zero, then Windows chooses an appropriate value based on the current aspect ratio. Both *Height* and *Width* are specified in terms of logical units.

Text can be output at any angle within the window. The angle at which it is displayed is determined by the *Escapement* parameter. For normal, horizontal text, this value should be 0. Otherwise, it specifies the number of 1/10-degree increments the text should be rotated. For example, a value of 900 causes the text to be rotated 90 degrees so that output is vertical.

The angle of each individual character can also be specified using the *Orientation* parameter. It, too, uses 1/10-degree increments to specify the angle of each character relative to horizontal.

Weight specifies the preferred weight of the font in the range 0 to 1000. A value of 0 specifies the default weight. To specify a normal weight, use 400. For bold, use 700. You can also use any of these macros to specify the font weight:

    FW_DONTCARE
    FW_THIN
    FW_EXTRALIGHT
    FW_LIGHT
    FW_NORMAL
    FW_MEDIUM
    FW_SEMIBOLD
    FW_BOLD
    FW_EXTRABOLD
    FW_HEAVY

To create an italic font, specify *Ital* as non-zero. Otherwise, this parameter should be zero. To create an underlined font, specify *Underline* as non-zero. Otherwise, this parameter should be zero. To create a strike-through font, specify *StrikeThru* as non-zero. Otherwise, this parameter should be zero.

Charset indicates which character set is desired. The example that follows uses **ANSI_CHARSET**. *Precision* specifies the preferred output precision. This determines just how closely the output must match the requested font's characteristics. The example in this chapter uses **OUT_DEFAULT_PRECIS**. *ClipPrecision* specifies the preferred clipping precision. "Clipping precision" refers to just how each character that extends beyond the clipping region is to be "clipped." The value used by the example in this chapter is **CLIP_DEFAULT_PRECIS**. (For other valid values for *Charset, Precision,* and *ClipPrecision*, consult your API reference manual.)

Quality determines how closely the logical font will be matched with the actual physical fonts provided for the requested output device. It can be one of these values:

DEFAULT_QUALITY
DRAFT_QUALITY
PROOF_QUALITY

Pitch specifies the pitch and family of the font. There are three pitch choices:

DEFAULT_PITCH
FIXED_PITCH
VARIABLE_PITCH

There are six possible font families:

FF_DECORATIVE
FF_DONTCARE
FF_MODERN
FF_ROMAN
FF_SCRIPT
FF_SWISS

To create the value for *Pitch*, OR together one pitch value and one font family value.

A pointer to the name of the font is passed in *FontName*. This name can be no longer than 32 characters. The font you specify must be installed in your system.

If successful, **CreateFont( )** returns a handle to the font. On failure, NULL is returned.

Note: It is important to understand that the **CreateFont( )** function does not technically create a new font. It simply tailors as closely as possible, based on the information that you specify, the actual physical fonts available in the system.

Fonts created using **CreateFont( )** must be deleted before your program ends. To delete a font, call **DeleteObject( )**.

Here is a program that demonstrates two custom fonts. The first is based upon the Courier New font, the second upon Century Gothic. Each time you choose the Change Font menu item, a new font is selected and displayed.

8

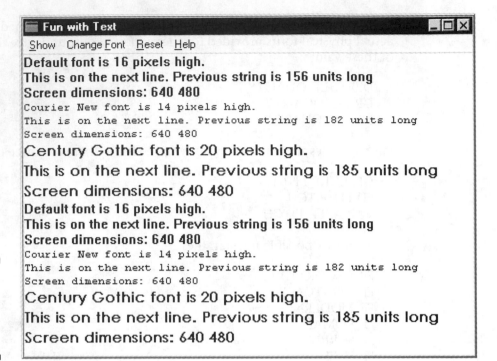

This program uses the same resource file as the program in the preceding
section. Sample output is shown in Figure 8-3.

```
/* Create a custom font. */

#include <windows.h>
#include <string.h>
#include <stdio.h>
#include "text.h"

LRESULT CALLBACK WindowFunc(HWND, UINT, WPARAM, LPARAM);

char szWinName[] = "MyWin"; /* name of window class */

char str[255]; /* holds output strings */
char fname[40] = "Default"; /* name of font */

int X=0, Y=0; /* current output location */
int maxX, maxY; /* screen dimensions */

HDC memdc; /* store the virtual device handle */
HBITMAP hbit; /* store the virtual bitmap */
HBRUSH hbrush; /* store the brush handle */
```

```
HFONT holdf, hnewf1, hnewf2; /* store the font handles */

int WINAPI WinMain(HINSTANCE hThisInst, HINSTANCE hPrevInst,
                   LPSTR lpszArgs, int nWinMode)
{
  HWND hwnd;
  MSG msg;
  WNDCLASS wcl;
  HANDLE hAccel;

  /* Define a window class. */
  wcl.hInstance = hThisInst; /* handle to this instance */
  wcl.lpszClassName = szWinName; /* window class name */
  wcl.lpfnWndProc = WindowFunc; /* window function */
  wcl.style = 0; /* default style */

  wcl.hIcon = LoadIcon(NULL, IDI_APPLICATION); /* icon style */
  wcl.hCursor = LoadCursor(NULL, IDC_ARROW); /* cursor style */

  /* specify name of menu resource */
  wcl.lpszMenuName = "MYMENU"; /* main menu */

  wcl.cbClsExtra = 0; /* no extra */
  wcl.cbWndExtra = 0; /* information needed */

  /* Make the window white. */
  wcl.hbrBackground = GetStockObject(WHITE_BRUSH);

  /* Register the window class. */
  if(!RegisterClass (&wcl)) return 0;

  /* Now that a window class has been registered, a window
     can be created. */
  hwnd = CreateWindow(
    szWinName, /* name of window class */
    "Fun with Text", /* title */
    WS_OVERLAPPEDWINDOW, /* window style - normal */
    CW_USEDEFAULT, /* X coordinate - let Windows decide */
    CW_USEDEFAULT, /* Y coordinate - let Windows decide */
    CW_USEDEFAULT, /* width - let Windows decide */
    CW_USEDEFAULT, /* height - let Windows decide */
    HWND_DESKTOP, /* no parent window */
    NULL, /* no menu */
    hThisInst, /* handle of this instance of the program */
    NULL /* no additional arguments */
  );

  /* load accelerators */
```

8

```
      hAccel = LoadAccelerators(hThisInst, "MYMENU");

      /* Display the window. */
      ShowWindow(hwnd, nWinMode);
      UpdateWindow(hwnd);

      /* Create the message loop. */
      while(GetMessage(&msg, NULL, 0, 0))
      {
        if(!TranslateAccelerator(hwnd, hAccel, &msg)) {
          TranslateMessage(&msg); /* allow use of keyboard */
          DispatchMessage(&msg); /* return control to Windows */
        }
      }
      return msg.wParam;
}

/* This function is called by Windows 95 and is passed
   messages from the message queue.
*/
LRESULT CALLBACK WindowFunc(HWND hwnd, UINT message,
                            WPARAM wParam, LPARAM lParam)
{
  HDC hdc;
  PAINTSTRUCT paintstruct;
  static TEXTMETRIC tm;
  SIZE size;
  static fontswitch = 0;

  switch(message) {
    case WM_CREATE:
      /* get screen coordinates */
      maxX = GetSystemMetrics(SM_CXSCREEN);
      maxY = GetSystemMetrics(SM_CYSCREEN);

      /* make a compatible memory image device */
      hdc = GetDC(hwnd);
      memdc = CreateCompatibleDC(hdc);
      hbit = CreateCompatibleBitmap(hdc, maxX, maxY);
      SelectObject(memdc, hbit);
      hbrush = GetStockObject(WHITE_BRUSH);
      SelectObject(memdc, hbrush);
      PatBlt(memdc, 0, 0, maxX, maxY, PATCOPY);

      /* create a new font */
      hnewf1 = CreateFont(14, 0, 0, 0, FW_NORMAL,
                          0, 0, 0, ANSI_CHARSET,
                          OUT_DEFAULT_PRECIS,
```

```
                       CLIP_DEFAULT_PRECIS,
                       DEFAULT_QUALITY,
                       DEFAULT_PITCH | FF_DONTCARE,
                       "Courier New");
        hnewf2 = CreateFont(20, 0, 0, 0, FW_SEMIBOLD,
                       0, 0, 0, ANSI_CHARSET,
                       OUT_DEFAULT_PRECIS,
                       CLIP_DEFAULT_PRECIS,
                       DEFAULT_QUALITY,
                       DEFAULT_PITCH | FF_DONTCARE,
                       "Century Gothic");
    ReleaseDC(hwnd, hdc);
    break;
  case WM_COMMAND:
    switch(LOWORD(wParam)) {
      case ID_SHOW:
        /* set text color to black and mode to transparent */
        SetTextColor(memdc, RGB(0, 0, 0));
        SetBkMode(memdc, TRANSPARENT);

        /* get text metrics */
        GetTextMetrics(memdc, &tm);

        sprintf(str, "%s font is %ld pixels high.",
                fname, tm.tmHeight);
        TextOut(memdc, X, Y, str, strlen(str)); /* output string */
        Y = Y + tm.tmHeight + tm.tmExternalLeading; /* next line */

        strcpy(str, "This is on the next line. ");
        TextOut(memdc, X, Y, str, strlen(str)); /* output string */

        /* compute length of a string */
        GetTextExtentPoint32(memdc, str, strlen(str), &size);
        sprintf(str, "Previous string is %ld units long", size.cx);
        X = size.cx; /* advance to end of previous string */
        TextOut(memdc, X, Y, str, strlen(str));
        Y = Y + tm.tmHeight + tm.tmExternalLeading; /* next line */
        X = 0; /* reset X */

        sprintf(str, "Screen dimensions: %d %d", maxX, maxY);
        TextOut(memdc, X, Y, str, strlen(str));
        Y = Y + tm.tmHeight + tm.tmExternalLeading; /* next line */
        InvalidateRect(hwnd, NULL, 1);
        break;
      case ID_RESET:
        X = Y = 0;
        /* erase by repainting background */
        PatBlt(memdc, 0, 0, maxX, maxY, PATCOPY);
```

8

```
                InvalidateRect(hwnd, NULL, 1);
                break;
              case ID_FONT:
                switch(fontswitch) {
                  case 0: /* switch to new font1 */
                    holdf = SelectObject(memdc, hnewf1);
                    fontswitch = 1;
                        strcpy(fname, "Courier New");
                    break;
                  case 1: /* switch to new font2 */
                    SelectObject(memdc, hnewf2);
                    fontswitch = 2;
                        strcpy(fname, "Century Gothic");
                    break;
                  default: /* switch to old font */
                    SelectObject(memdc, holdf);
                    fontswitch = 0;
                        strcpy(fname, "Default");
                }
                break;
              case ID_HELP:
                MessageBox(hwnd, "F2: Display\nF3: Change font\nF4: Reset",
                          "Text Fun", MB_OK);
                break;
          }
          break;
        case WM_PAINT: /* process a repaint request */
          hdc = BeginPaint(hwnd, &paintstruct); /* get DC */

          /* now, copy memory image onto screen */
          BitBlt(hdc, 0, 0, maxX, maxY, memdc, 0, 0, SRCCOPY);
          EndPaint(hwnd, &paintstruct); /* release DC */
          break;
        case WM_DESTROY: /* terminate the program */
          DeleteDC(memdc);
           DeleteObject(hnewf1);
           DeleteObject(hnewf2);
          PostQuitMessage(0);
          break;
        default:
          /* Let Windows 95 process any messages not specified in
          the preceding switch statement. */
          return DefWindowProc(hwnd, message, wParam, lParam);
      }
      return 0;
}
```

Remember, Windows' support for fonts and text is quite rich. You will want to explore this area on your own. In the next chapter, we will continue exploring window output by working with graphics.

8

Chapter

9

Working with Graphics

Windows 95 has a rich and flexible set of graphics functions available to the programmer. This is not too surprising, since it is a graphical operating system. However, what you might find surprising is how tightly the graphics are integrated into the Windows display system. In fact, much of what you learned in the preceding chapter about text is also applicable to graphics. For example, the same brush that is used to paint the window is used to fill an object. This chapter discusses and demonstrates several of Windows' graphics functions.

This chapter also examines several features that precisely control how output is mapped to a window. Specifically, it discusses how to set the current mapping mode, how to change the logical coordinates associated with a window, and how to define a viewport. These factors have a profound effect on how both graphics and text are displayed.

Keep in mind that the discussion of graphics and related topics in this chapter only scratches the surface. The Windows 95 graphics system is quite powerful, and you will want to explore it further on your own.

The Graphics Coordinate System

The graphics coordinate system is the same as that used by the text-based functions (discussed in Chapter 8). This means that, by default, the upper-left corner is located at 0,0 and that logical units are equivalent to pixels. Remember that the coordinate system and the mapping of logical units to pixels are under your control and may be changed. (You will see how later in this chapter.)

Windows 95 (and Windows in general) maintains a *current position* that is used and updated by certain graphics functions. When your program begins, the current location is set to 0,0. Keep in mind that the location of the current position is completely invisible. That is, no graphics "cursor" is displayed. Instead, the current position is simply the next place in the window at which certain graphics functions will begin.

Pens and Brushes

The Windows graphics system is based on two important objects: pens and brushes. You learned about brushes in Chapter 8. All of that information applies to the graphics functions described here, as well. By default, closed graphics shapes, such as rectangles and ellipses, are filled using the currently selected brush. *Pens* are resources that draw the lines and curves specified by the various graphics functions. The default pen is black and one pixel thick. However, you can alter these attributes.

Until now, we have only been working with stock objects. In this chapter you will learn how to create custom brushes and pens. There is one important thing to remember about custom objects: they must be deleted before your program ends. This is accomplished using **DeleteObject( )**.

Setting a Pixel

You can set the color of any specific pixel using the API function **SetPixel( )**, whose prototype is shown here:

COLORREF SetPixel(HDC *hdc*, int *X*, int *Y*, COLORREF *color*);

Here, *hdc* is the handle to the desired device context. The coordinates of the point to set are specified by *X,Y*, and the color is specified in *color*. (Refer to Chapter 8 for a discussion of the **COLORREF** data type.) The function returns the original color of the pixel, –1 if an error occurs or if the location specified is outside the window.

Drawing a Line

To draw a line, use the **LineTo( )** function. This function draws a line using the currently selected pen. Its prototype is shown here:

> BOOL LineTo(HDC *hdc*, int *X*, int *Y*);

The handle of the device context in which to draw the line is specified by *hdc*. The line is drawn from the current graphics position to the coordinates specified by *X,Y*. The current position is then changed to *X,Y*. The function returns non-zero if successful (i.e., the line is drawn) and zero on failure.

Some programmers are surprised by the fact that **LineTo( )** uses the current position as its starting location and then sets the current position to the end point of the line that is drawn (instead of leaving it unchanged). However, there is a good reason for this. Many times, when displaying lines, one line will begin at the end of the previous line. When this is the case, **LineTo( )** operates extremely efficiently by avoiding the additional overhead of passing an extra set of coordinates. When this is not the case, you can set the current location to any position you like using the **MoveToEx( )** function, described next, prior to calling **LineTo( )**.

Setting the Current Location

To set the current position, use the **MoveToEx()** function, whose prototype is shown here:

> BOOL MoveToEx(HDC *hdc*, int *X*, int *Y*, LPPOINT *lpCoord*);

The handle to the device context is specified in *hdc*. The coordinates of the new current position are specified by *X,Y*. The previous current position is returned in the **POINT** structure pointed to by *lpCoord*. **POINT** is defined like this:

```
typedef struct tagPOINT {
  LONG x;
  LONG y;
} POINT;
```

However, if you use NULL for the *lpCoord* parameter, then **MoveToEx( )** does not return the previous current position.

MoveToEx( ) returns non-zero if successful and zero on failure.

In Windows 3.1, the function that moves the current location is called MoveTo( ). It has only three parameters, which are the same as the first three parameters of MoveToEx( ). It returns the previous location as a double word. This function is not supported by Win32 (the Windows 95 API library). If you are porting code that uses this function, make appropriate changes. If your program doesn't need the previous location, simply make the *lpCoord* parameter NULL.

Drawing an Arc

You can draw an elliptical arc (a portion of an ellipse) in the current pen color using the **Arc( )** function. Its prototype is shown here:

BOOL Arc(HDC *hdc*, int *upX*, int *upY*, int *lowX*, int *lowY*,
int *startX*, int *startY*, int *endX*, int *endY*);

Here, *hdc* is the handle of the device context in which the arc will be drawn. The arc is defined by two objects. First, the arc is a portion of an ellipse that is bounded by the rectangle whose upper-left corner is at *upX,upY,* and whose lower-right corner is at *lowX,lowY*. The portion of the ellipse that is actually drawn (i.e., the arc) starts at the intersection of a line from the center of the rectangle through the point specified by *startX,startY,* and ends at the intersection of a line from the center of the rectangle through the point *endX,endY*. The arc is drawn counterclockwise starting from *startX,startY*. Figure 9-1 illustrates how **Arc( )** works.

Arc( ) returns non-zero if successful and zero on failure.

Displaying Rectangles

You can display a rectangle in the current pen using the **Rectangle( )** function, whose prototype is shown here:

BOOL Rectangle(HDC *hdc*, int *upX*, int *upY*, int *lowX*, int *lowY*);

As usual, *hdc* is the handle of the device context. The upper-left corner of the rectangle is specified by *upX,upY,* and the lower-right corner is specified by *lowX,lowY*. The function returns non-zero if successful and zero if an error occurs. The rectangle is automatically filled using the current brush.

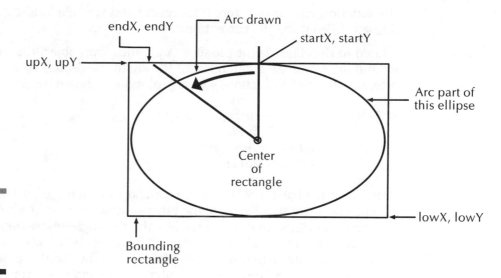

You can display a *rounded rectangle* (a rectangle with slightly rounded corners) using the **RoundRect( )** function. The prototype for **RoundRect( )** is shown here:

BOOL RoundRect(HDC *hdc*, int *upX*, int *upY*, int *lowX*, int *lowY*,
    int *curveX*, int *curveY*);

The first five parameters are the same as for **Rectangle( )**. How the corners are curved is determined by the values of *curveX* and *curveY*, which define the width and the height of the ellipse that describes the curve. The function returns non-zero if successful and zero if a failure occurs. The rounded rectangle is automatically filled using the current brush.

Drawing Ellipses and Pie Slices

To draw an ellipse or a circle with the current pen, use the **Ellipse( )** function, whose prototype is shown here:

BOOL Ellipse(HDC *hdc*, int *upX*, int *upY*, int *lowX*, int *lowY*);

Here, *hdc* is the handle of the device context in which the ellipse will be drawn. The ellipse is defined by specifying its bounding rectangle. The upper-left corner of the rectangle is specified by *upX,upY,* and the lower-right corner is specified by *lowX,lowY*. To draw a circle, specify a square rectangle.

The function returns non-zero if successful and zero if a failure occurs. The ellipse is filled using the current brush.

Related to the ellipse is the pie slice. A pie slice is an object that includes an arc and lines from each end point of the arc to the center. To draw a pie slice, use the **Pie( )** function, whose prototype is shown here:

```
BOOL Pie(HDC hdc, int upX, int upY,
         int lowX, int lowY,
         int startX, int startY,
         int endX, int endY);
```

Here, *hdc* is the handle of the device context in which the pie slice will be drawn. The arc of the slice is defined by two objects. First, the arc is a portion of an ellipse that is bounded by the rectangle whose upper-left corner is at *upX,upY,* and whose lower-right corner is at *lowX,lowY*. The portion of the ellipse that is actually drawn (i.e., the arc of the slice) starts at the intersection of a line from the center of the rectangle through the point specified by *startX,startY,* and ends at the intersection of a line from the center of the rectangle through the point *endX,endY*. The slice is drawn in the current pen and filled using the current brush.

The **Pie( )** function returns non-zero if successful and zero if an error occurs.

Working with Pens

Graphics objects are drawn using the current pen. There are three stock pens: black, white, and null. A handle to each of these can be obtained using **GetStockObject( )**, discussed earlier in this book. The macros for these stock pens are **BLACK_PEN**, **WHITE_PEN**, and **NULL_PEN**, respectively. Pen handles are of type **HPEN**.

Frankly, the stock pens are quite limited, and usually you will want to define your own pens for your application. This is accomplished using the function **CreatePen( )**, whose prototype is shown here:

```
HPEN CreatePen(int style, int width, COLORREF color);
```

The *style* parameter determines what type of pen is created. It must be one of these values:

Macro	Pen Style
PS_DASH	Dashed
PS_DASHDOT	Dash-dot
PS_DASHDOTDOT	Dash-dot-dot
PS_DOT	Dotted
PS_INSIDEFRAME	Solid pen that is within a bounded region
PS_NULL	None
PS_SOLID	Solid line

The dotted and/or dashed styles may only be applied to pens that are one unit thick. The **PS_INSIDEFRAME** pen is a solid pen that will be completely within the dimensions of any object that is drawn, even when that pen is more than one unit thick. For example, if a pen with **PS_INSIDEFRAME** style and a width greater than one is used to draw a rectangle, then the outside of the line will be within the coordinates of the rectangle. (When a wide pen of a different style is used, the line may be partially outside the dimensions of the object.)

The thickness of a pen is specified by *width*, which is in logical units. The color of the pen is specified by *color*, which is a **COLORREF** value (discussed in Chapter 8). For the examples in this chapter, all colors are specified as RGB values.

Once a pen has been created, it is selected into a device context using **SelectObject( )**. For example, the following fragment creates a red pen and then selects it for use:

```
HPEN hRedpen;

hRedpen = CreatePen(PS_SOLID, 1, RGB(255,0,0));
SelectObject(dc, hRedpen);
```

Remember, you must delete any custom pens you create by calling **DeleteObject( )** before your program terminates.

Creating Custom Brushes

Custom brushes are created in a way similar to custom pens. There are various styles of brushes. The most common custom brush is a *solid brush*. A solid brush is created using the **CreateSolidBrush( )** API function, whose prototype is shown here:

HBRUSH CreateSolidBrush(COLORREF *color*);

The color of the brush is specified in *color,* and a handle to the brush is returned.

Once a custom brush has been created, it is selected into the device context using **SelectObject( )**. For example, the following fragment creates a green brush and then selects it for use.

```
HBRUSH hGreenbrush

hGreenbrush = CreateSolidBrush(RGB(0, 255 ,0));
SelectObject(dc, hGreenbrush);
```

Like custom pens, custom brushes must be deleted before your program terminates.

Other types of brushes you might want to explore on your own are hatch and pattern brushes, which are created using **CreateHatchBrush( )** and **CreatePatternBrush( )**, respectively.

Deleting Custom Objects

You must delete custom objects before your program terminates. You do this using the **DeleteObject( )** API function. Remember, you do not need to delete stock objects. Also, the object being deleted must not be currently selected into any device context.

A Graphics Demonstration

The following program demonstrates the various graphics functions just discussed. The program uses the virtual window technique developed in Chapter 8. It directs output to a memory device context, which is then copied to the physical window when a **WM_PAINT** message is received. (Remember, this approach to output allows a window's contents to be automatically updated each time a **WM_PAINT** message is received.)

```
/* Demonstrate the basic graphics functions. */

#include <windows.h>
#include <string.h>
#include <stdio.h>
#include "graph.h"

LRESULT CALLBACK WindowFunc(HWND, UINT, WPARAM, LPARAM);
```

```
char szWinName[] = "MyWin"; /* name of window class */

char str[255]; /* holds output strings */

int maxX, maxY; /* screen dimensions */

HDC memdc; /* handle of memory DC */
HBITMAP hbit; /* handle of compatible bitmap */
HBRUSH hbrush, hOldbrush; /* handles of brushes */

/* create pens */
HPEN hOldpen; /* handle of old pen */
HPEN hRedpen, hGreenpen, hBluepen, hYellowpen;

int WINAPI WinMain(HINSTANCE hThisInst, HINSTANCE hPrevInst,
                   LPSTR lpszArgs, int nWinMode)
{
  HWND hwnd;
  MSG msg;
  WNDCLASS wcl;
  HANDLE hAccel;

  /* Define a window class. */
  wcl.hInstance = hThisInst; /* handle to this instance */
  wcl.lpszClassName = szWinName; /* window class name */
  wcl.lpfnWndProc = WindowFunc; /* window function */
  wcl.style = 0; /* default style */

  wcl.hIcon = LoadIcon(NULL, IDI_APPLICATION); /* icon style */
  wcl.hCursor = LoadCursor(NULL, IDC_ARROW); /* cursor style */

  /* specify name of menu resource */
  wcl.lpszMenuName = "MYMENU"; /* main menu */

  wcl.cbClsExtra = 0; /* no extra */
  wcl.cbWndExtra = 0; /* information needed */

  /* Make the window white. */
  wcl.hbrBackground = GetStockObject(WHITE_BRUSH);

  /* Register the window class. */
  if(!RegisterClass (&wcl)) return 0;

  /* Now that a window class has been registered, a window
     can be created. */
  hwnd = CreateWindow(
    szWinName, /* name of window class */
    "Fun with Graphics", /* title */
```

```
      WS_OVERLAPPEDWINDOW, /* window style - normal */
      CW_USEDEFAULT, /* X coordinate - let Windows decide */
      CW_USEDEFAULT, /* Y coordinate - let Windows decide */
      CW_USEDEFAULT, /* width - let Windows decide */
      CW_USEDEFAULT, /* height - let Windows decide */
      HWND_DESKTOP, /* no parent window */
      NULL, /* no menu */
      hThisInst, /* handle of this instance of the program */
      NULL /* no additional arguments */
    );

  /* load accelerators */
  hAccel = LoadAccelerators(hThisInst, "MYMENU");

  /* Display the window. */
  ShowWindow(hwnd, nWinMode);
  UpdateWindow(hwnd);

  /* Create the message loop. */
  while(GetMessage(&msg, NULL, 0, 0))
  {
    if(!TranslateAccelerator(hwnd, hAccel, &msg)) {
      TranslateMessage(&msg); /* allow use of keyboard */
      DispatchMessage(&msg); /* return control to Windows */
    }
  }
  return msg.wParam;
}

/* This function is called by Windows 95 and is passed
   messages from the message queue.
*/
LRESULT CALLBACK WindowFunc(HWND hwnd, UINT message,
                            WPARAM wParam, LPARAM lParam)
{
  HDC hdc;
  PAINTSTRUCT paintstruct;

  switch(message) {
    case WM_CREATE:
      /* get screen coordinates */
      maxX = GetSystemMetrics(SM_CXSCREEN);
      maxY = GetSystemMetrics(SM_CYSCREEN);

      /* make a compatible memory image device */
      hdc = GetDC(hwnd);
      memdc = CreateCompatibleDC(hdc);
      hbit = CreateCompatibleBitmap(hdc, maxX, maxY);
```

```
        SelectObject(memdc, hbit);
        hbrush = GetStockObject(WHITE_BRUSH);
        SelectObject(memdc, hbrush);
        PatBlt(memdc, 0, 0, maxX, maxY, PATCOPY);

        hRedpen = CreatePen(PS_SOLID, 1, RGB(255,0,0));
        hGreenpen = CreatePen(PS_SOLID, 2, RGB(0,255,0));
        hBluepen = CreatePen(PS_SOLID, 3, RGB(0,0,255));
        hYellowpen = CreatePen(PS_SOLID, 4, RGB(255, 255, 0));

        /* save default pen */
        hOldpen = SelectObject(memdc, hRedpen);
        SelectObject(memdc, hOldpen);

        ReleaseDC(hwnd, hdc);
        break;
    case WM_COMMAND:
      switch(LOWORD(wParam)) {
        case ID_LINES:
          /* set 2 pixels */
          SetPixel(memdc, 40, 14, RGB(0, 0, 0));
          SetPixel(memdc, 40, 15, RGB(0, 0, 0));

          LineTo(memdc, 100, 50);
          MoveToEx(memdc, 100, 50, NULL);

          /* change to green pen */
          hOldpen = SelectObject(memdc, hGreenpen);
          LineTo(memdc, 200, 100);

          /* change to yellow pen */
          SelectObject(memdc, hYellowpen);
          LineTo(memdc, 0, 200);

          /* change to blue pen */
          SelectObject(memdc, hBluepen);
          LineTo(memdc, 200, 200);

          /* change to red pen */
          SelectObject(memdc, hRedpen);
          LineTo(memdc, 0, 0);

          /* return to default pen */
          SelectObject(memdc, hOldpen);

          Arc(memdc, 0, 0, 300, 300, 0, 50, 200, 50);
          /* show intersecting lines that define arc */
          MoveToEx(memdc, 150, 150, NULL);
```

```
      LineTo(memdc, 0, 50);
      MoveToEx(memdc, 150, 150, NULL);
      LineTo(memdc, 200, 50);

      InvalidateRect(hwnd, NULL, 1);
      break;
    case ID_RECTANGLES:
      /* display, but don't fill */
      hOldbrush = SelectObject(memdc,
                              GetStockObject(HOLLOW_BRUSH));

      /* draw some rectangles */
      Rectangle(memdc, 50, 50, 300, 300);
      RoundRect(memdc, 125, 125, 220, 240, 15, 13);

      /* use a red pen */
      SelectObject(memdc, hRedpen);
      Rectangle(memdc, 100, 100, 200, 200);
      SelectObject(memdc, hOldpen); /* return to default pen */

      /* restore default brush */
      SelectObject(memdc, hOldbrush);

      InvalidateRect(hwnd, NULL, 1);
      break;
    case ID_ELLIPSES:
      /* make blue brush */
      hbrush = CreateSolidBrush(RGB(0, 0, 255));
      hOldbrush = SelectObject(memdc, hbrush);

      /* fill these ellipses with blue */
      Ellipse(memdc, 50, 200, 100, 280);
      Ellipse(memdc, 75, 25, 280, 100);

      /* use a red pen and fill with green */
      SelectObject(memdc, hRedpen);
      DeleteObject(hbrush); /* delete brush */
      /* create green brush */
      hbrush = CreateSolidBrush(RGB(0, 255, 0));
      SelectObject(memdc, hbrush); /* select green brush */
      Ellipse(memdc, 100, 100, 200, 200);

      /* draw a pie slice */
      Pie(memdc, 200, 200, 340, 340, 225, 200, 200, 250);

      SelectObject(memdc, hOldpen); /* return to default pen */
      SelectObject(memdc, hOldbrush); /* select default brush */
      DeleteObject(hbrush); /* delete green brush */
```

```
                InvalidateRect(hwnd, NULL, 1);
                break;
              case ID_RESET:
                /* reset current position to 0,0 */
                MoveToEx(memdc, 0, 0, NULL);
                /* erase by repainting background */
                PatBlt(memdc, 0, 0, maxX, maxY, PATCOPY);
                InvalidateRect(hwnd, NULL, 1);
                break;
              case ID_HELP:
                MessageBox(hwnd, "F2: Lines\nF3: Rectangles\n"
                          "F4: Ellipses\nF5: Reset",
                          "Graphics Fun", MB_OK);
                break;
          }
          break;
        case WM_PAINT: /* process a repaint request */
          hdc = BeginPaint(hwnd, &paintstruct); /* get DC */

          /* now, copy memory image onto screen */
          BitBlt(hdc, 0, 0, maxX, maxY, memdc, 0, 0, SRCCOPY);
          EndPaint(hwnd, &paintstruct); /* release DC */
          break;
        case WM_DESTROY: /* terminate the program */
          DeleteObject(hRedpen); /* delete pens */
          DeleteObject(hGreenpen);
          DeleteObject(hBluepen);
          DeleteObject(hYellowpen);

          DeleteDC(memdc);
          PostQuitMessage(0);
          break;
        default:
          /* Let Windows 95 process any messages not specified in
          the preceding switch statement. */
          return DefWindowProc(hwnd, message, wParam, lParam);
      }
      return 0;
}
```

This program requires the resource file shown here:

```
#include <windows.h>
#include "graph.h"

MYMENU MENU
{
  MENUITEM "&Lines", ID_LINES
```

```
    MENUITEM "&Rectangles", ID_RECTANGLES
    MENUITEM "&Ellipses", ID_ELLIPSES
    MENUITEM "&Reset", ID_RESET
    MENUITEM "&Help", ID_HELP
}

MYMENU ACCELERATORS
{
  VK_F2, ID_LINES, VIRTKEY
  VK_F3, ID_RECTANGLES, VIRTKEY
  VK_F4, ID_ELLIPSES, VIRTKEY
  VK_F5, ID_RESET, VIRTKEY
  VK_F1, ID_HELP, VIRTKEY
}
```

It also requires the header file **graph.h** shown here:

```
#define ID_LINES       100
#define ID_RECTANGLES 101
#define ID_ELLIPSES   102
#define ID_RESET      103
#define ID_HELP       104
```

The program displays a main menu that lets you display lines (plus two
pixels), rectangles, and ellipses. It also lets you reset the window, erasing its
contents and resetting the current position. Sample output is shown in
Figure 9-2.

Understanding Mapping Modes and Viewports

As you know, the Windows text and graphics functions operate on logical
units. These logical units are then translated by Windows into physical units
(i.e., pixels) when an object is displayed. How the translation from logical
units to physical units is made is determined by the current *mapping mode*.
By default, logical units are the same as pixels. However, you can change the
ratio of logical units to physical units by changing the mapping mode.

In addition to changing the way Windows maps output to a window,
you can also set two other attributes that affect the translation of logical
to physical units. First, you can define the length and width of a window
in terms of logical units that you select. Second, you can set the physical
extents of a viewport. A *viewport* is a region that exists within a window.
Once a viewport has been selected, all output is confined to its boundaries.

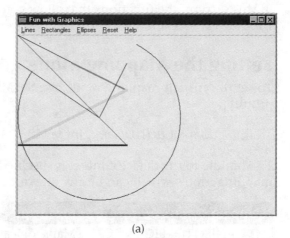

(a)

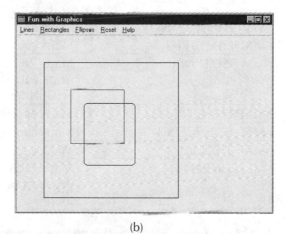

(b)

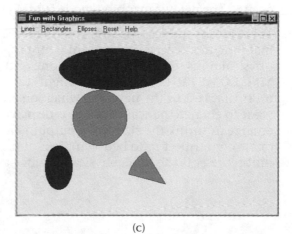

(c)

Sample output
from the
graphics
demonstration
program
Figure 9-2.

9

In this section, the functions that allow you to set the mapping mode, window extents, and viewport extents are examined.

Setting the Mapping Mode

To set the current mapping mode, use **SetMapMode( )**. It has this prototype:

    int SetMapMode(HDC *hdc*, int *mode*);

The handle to the device context is specified by *hdc*. *mode* specifies the new mapping mode, which can be any one of the following constants:

Mapping Mode	Meaning
MM_ANISOTROPIC	Maps logical units to programmer-defined units with arbitrarily scaled axes
MM_HIENGLISH	Maps each logical unit to 0.001 inch
MM_HIMETRIC	Maps each logical unit to 0.01 millimeter
MM_ISOTROPIC	Maps logical units to programmer-defined units with equally scaled axes (This establishes a one-to-one aspect ratio.)
MM_LOMETRIC	Maps each logical unit to 0.1 millimeter
MM_LOENGLISH	Maps each logical unit to 0.01 inch
MM_TEXT	Maps each logical unit to one device pixel
MM_TWIPS	Maps each logical unit to one-twentieth of a printer's point, or approximately 1/1440 inch

SetMapMode( ) returns the previous mapping mode, or zero if an error occurs. The default mapping mode is **MM_TEXT**.

There are several reasons why you might want to change the current mapping mode. First, if you want your program's output to be displayed in physical units, then you can select one of the real-world modes, such as **MM_LOMETRIC**. Second, you might want to define for your program the units that best fit the nature of what you are displaying. Third, you might want to change the scale of what is displayed. (That is, you might want to enlarge or shrink the size of the output.) Finally, you may want to establish a one-to-one aspect ratio between the X and Y axis. When this is done, each X unit represents the same physical distance as each Y unit.

Remember: Changing the mapping mode changes the way logical units are translated into physical units (pixels).

Defining the Window Extents

Selecting either the **MM_ISOTROPIC** or **MM_ ANISOTROPIC** mapping mode allows you to define the size of the window in terms of logical units. In fact, if you select either of these mapping modes, you must define the dimensions of the window. (Since **MM_ISOTROPIC** and **MM_ANISOTROPIC** operate on programmer-defined units, technically the limits are undefined until you define them.) To define the *X* and *Y* extents of a window, use the **SetWindowExtEx( )** function, shown here:

BOOL SetWindowExtEx(HDC *hdc*, int *Xextent*, int *Yextent*, LPSIZE *size*);

The handle of the device context is specified in *hdc*. *Xextent* and *Yextent* specify the new horizontal and vertical extents measured in logical units. The previous window extents are copied into the **SIZE** structure pointed to by *size*. However, if *size* is NULL, then the previous extents are ignored. The function returns non-zero if successful and zero on failure. **SetWindowExtEx( )** only has an effect when the mapping mode is **MM_ANISOTROPIC** or **MM_ISOTROPIC**.

The **SIZE** structure is defined like this:

```
typedef struct tagSIZE {
  LONG cx;
  LONG cy;
} SIZE;
```

Keep in mind that when you change the logical dimensions of a window, you are not changing the physical size of the window on the screen. You are simply defining the size of the window in terms of logical units that you choose. (Or, more precisely, you are defining the relationship between the logical units used by the window and the physical units (pixels) used by the device.) For example, the same window could be given logical dimensions of 100 x 100 or 50 x 75. The only difference is the ratio of logical units to pixels when an image is displayed.

SetWindowExtEx( ) replaces the older SetWindowExt( ) function. Be aware of this when porting older code.

Defining a Viewport

As mentioned, a viewport is a region within a window that receives output. A viewport is defined using the **SetViewportExtEx( )** function. Its prototype is shown here:

BOOL SetViewportExtEx(HDC *hdc*, int *Xextent,* int *Yextent,* LPSIZE *size*);

The handle of the device context is specified in *hdc*. *Xextent* and *Yextent* specify the new horizontal and vertical viewport extents, in pixels. The function returns non-zero if successful and zero on failure. The previous viewport extents are returned in the **SIZE** structure pointed to by *size*. However, if *size* is NULL, then the previous extents are ignored. **SetViewportExtEx( )** only has an effect when the mapping mode is **MM_ANISOTROPIC** or **MM_ISOTROPIC**.

A viewport may be any size you desire. That is, it may encompass the entire window or simply a part of it. For the default mapping mode of **MM_TEXT**, the viewport and the window are the same.

Output is automatically mapped from the window device context (logical units) to the viewport (pixels) and scaled accordingly. Therefore, by changing the X and Y extents of the viewport, you are in effect changing the size of anything displayed within it. Thus, if you make the viewport extents larger, the contents of the viewport will get larger. Conversely, if you make the extents smaller, the contents of the viewport will shrink. This is shown in the following demonstration program.

 SetViewportExtEx( ) replaces the older SetViewportExt( ) function. Be sure to make this change when porting code.

Setting the Viewport Origin

By default, the origin of the viewport is at 0,0 within the window. However, you can change this using **SetViewportOrgEx( )**, shown here:

BOOL SetViewportOrgEx(HDC *hdc*, int *X*, int *Y*, LPPOINT *OldOrg*);

The handle of the device context is passed in *hdc*. The new origin for the viewport, specified in pixels, is passed in *X,Y*. The previous origin is returned in the **POINT** structure pointed to by *OldOrg*. If this parameter is NULL, the previous origin is ignored.

Changing the origin of the viewport changes where images are drawn in the window. You will see the effects of this in the sample program that follows.

 SetViewportOrgEx( ) replaces the older SetViewportOrg( ) function. Be sure to make this change when porting code.

A Sample Mapping Mode Program

The following program is an expanded version of the preceding graphics program that sets the mapping mode, window extents, and viewport extents. Sample output from this program is shown in Figure 9-3. It sets the mapping mode to **MM_ANISOTROPIC**, sets the window extents to 200 x 200, and sets the initial viewport extents to 10 x 10. When you run this program, each time you select the Magnify main menu option, the viewport extents will be increased by 10 units in each dimension, causing the image to become larger within the window. Selecting the Origin menu option will cause the viewport origin to be moved 50 pixels in both the X and Y directions.

```
/* Set the mapping mode, the window and the viewport
   extents. */

#include <windows.h>
#include <string.h>
#include <stdio.h>
#include "graph.h"

LRESULT CALLBACK WindowFunc(HWND, UINT, WPARAM, LPARAM);

char szWinName[] = "MyWin"; /* name of window class */

char str[255]; /* holds output strings */

int maxX, maxY; /* screen dimensions */

int X = 10, Y = 10; /* viewport extents */
int orgX=0, orgY=0; /* viewport origin */

HDC memdc; /* handle of memory DC */
HBITMAP hbit; /* handle of compatible bitmap */
HBRUSH hbrush, hOldbrush; /* handles of brushes */

/* create pens */
HPEN hOldpen; /* handle of old pen */
```

```
HPEN hRedpen, hGreenpen, hBluepen, hYellowpen;

int WINAPI WinMain(HINSTANCE hThisInst, HINSTANCE hPrevInst,
                   LPSTR lpszArgs, int nWinMode)
{
  HWND hwnd;
  MSG msg;
  WNDCLASS wcl;
  HANDLE hAccel;

  /* Define a window class. */
  wcl.hInstance = hThisInst; /* handle to this instance */
  wcl.lpszClassName = szWinName; /* window class name */
  wcl.lpfnWndProc = WindowFunc; /* window function */
  wcl.style = 0; /* default style */

  wcl.hIcon = LoadIcon(NULL, IDI_APPLICATION); /* icon style */
  wcl.hCursor = LoadCursor(NULL, IDC_ARROW); /* cursor style */

  /* specify name of menu resource */
  wcl.lpszMenuName = "MYMENU"; /* main menu */

  wcl.cbClsExtra = 0; /* no extra */
  wcl.cbWndExtra = 0; /* information needed */

  /* Make the window white. */
  wcl.hbrBackground = GetStockObject(WHITE_BRUSH);

  /* Register the window class. */
  if(!RegisterClass (&wcl)) return 0;

  /* Now that a window class has been registered, a window
     can be created. */
  hwnd = CreateWindow(
    szWinName, /* name of window class */
    "Changing Mapping Modes", /* title */
    WS_OVERLAPPEDWINDOW, /* window style - normal */
    CW_USEDEFAULT, /* X coordinate - let Windows decide */
    CW_USEDEFAULT, /* Y coordinate - let Windows decide */
    CW_USEDEFAULT, /* width - let Windows decide */
    CW_USEDEFAULT, /* height - let Windows decide */
    HWND_DESKTOP, /* no parent window */
    NULL, /* no menu */
    hThisInst, /* handle of this instance of the program */
    NULL /* no additional arguments */
  );

  /* load accelerators */
```

```
      hAccel = LoadAccelerators(hThisInst, "MYMENU");

      /* Display the window. */
      ShowWindow(hwnd, nWinMode);
      UpdateWindow(hwnd);

      /* Create the message loop. */
      while(GetMessage(&msg, NULL, 0, 0))
      {
        if(!TranslateAccelerator(hwnd, hAccel, &msg)) {
          TranslateMessage(&msg); /* allow use of keyboard */
          DispatchMessage(&msg); /* return control to Windows */
        }
      }
      return msg.wParam;
}


/* This function is called by Windows 95 and is passed
   messages from the message queue.
*/
LRESULT CALLBACK WindowFunc(HWND hwnd, UINT message,
                            WPARAM wParam, LPARAM lParam)
{
  HDC hdc;
  PAINTSTRUCT paintstruct;

  switch(message) {
    case WM_CREATE:
      /* get screen coordinates */
      maxX = GetSystemMetrics(SM_CXSCREEN);
      maxY = GetSystemMetrics(SM_CYSCREEN);

      /* make a compatible memory image device */
      hdc = GetDC(hwnd);
      memdc = CreateCompatibleDC(hdc);
      hbit = CreateCompatibleBitmap(hdc, maxX, maxY);
      SelectObject(memdc, hbit);
      hbrush = GetStockObject(WHITE_BRUSH);
      SelectObject(memdc, hbrush);
      PatBlt(memdc, 0, 0, maxX, maxY, PATCOPY);

      hRedpen = CreatePen(PS_SOLID, 1, RGB(255,0,0));
      hGreenpen = CreatePen(PS_SOLID, 2, RGB(0,255,0));
      hBluepen = CreatePen(PS_SOLID, 3, RGB(0,0,255));
      hYellowpen = CreatePen(PS_SOLID, 4, RGB(255, 255, 0));

      /* save default pen */
      hOldpen = SelectObject(memdc, hRedpen);
```

```
      SelectObject(memdc, hOldpen);

      ReleaseDC(hwnd, hdc);
      break;
    case WM_COMMAND:
      switch(LOWORD(wParam)) {
        case ID_LINES:
          /* set 2 pixels */
          SetPixel(memdc, 40, 14, RGB(0, 0, 0));
          SetPixel(memdc, 40, 15, RGB(0, 0, 0));

          LineTo(memdc, 100, 50);
          MoveToEx(memdc, 100, 50, NULL);

          /* change to green pen */
          hOldpen = SelectObject(memdc, hGreenpen);
          LineTo(memdc, 200, 100);

          /* change to yellow pen */
          SelectObject(memdc, hYellowpen);
          LineTo(memdc, 0, 200);

          /* change to blue pen */
          SelectObject(memdc, hBluepen);
          LineTo(memdc, 200, 200);

          /* change to red pen */
          SelectObject(memdc, hRedpen);
          LineTo(memdc, 0, 0);

          /* return to default pen */
          SelectObject(memdc, hOldpen);

          Arc(memdc, 0, 0, 300, 300, 0, 50, 200, 50);
          /* show intersecting lines that define arc */
          MoveToEx(memdc, 150, 150, NULL);
          LineTo(memdc, 0, 50);
          MoveToEx(memdc, 150, 150, NULL);
          LineTo(memdc, 200, 50);
          InvalidateRect(hwnd, NULL, 1);
          break;
        case ID_RECTANGLES:
          /* display, but don't fill */
          hOldbrush = SelectObject(memdc,
                              GetStockObject(HOLLOW_BRUSH));

          /* draw some rectangles */
          Rectangle(memdc, 50, 50, 300, 300);
```

```
    RoundRect(memdc, 125, 125, 220, 240, 15, 13);

    /* use a red pen */
    SelectObject(memdc, hRedpen);
    Rectangle(memdc, 100, 100, 200, 200);
    SelectObject(memdc, hOldpen); /* return to default pen */


   /* restore default brush */
    SelectObject(memdc, hOldbrush);

    InvalidateRect(hwnd, NULL, 1);
    break;
  case ID_ELLIPSES:
    /* make blue brush */
    hbrush = CreateSolidBrush(RGB(0, 0, 255));
    hOldbrush = SelectObject(memdc, hbrush);

    /* fill these ellipses with blue */
    Ellipse(memdc, 50, 200, 100, 280);
    Ellipse(memdc, 75, 25, 280, 100);

    /* use a red pen and fill with green */
    SelectObject(memdc, hRedpen);
    DeleteObject(hbrush); /* delete brush */
    /* create green brush */
    hbrush = CreateSolidBrush(RGB(0, 255, 0));
    SelectObject(memdc, hbrush); /* select green brush */
    Ellipse(memdc, 100, 100, 200, 200);

    /* draw a pie slice */
    Pie(memdc, 200, 300, 340, 340, 235, 200, 200, 250);

    SelectObject(memdc, hOldpen); /* return to default pen */
    SelectObject(memdc, hOldbrush); /* select default brush */
    DeleteObject(hbrush); /* delete green brush */

    InvalidateRect(hwnd, NULL, 1);
    break;
  case ID_SIZE: /* increment size by 10 each time */
    X += 10;
    Y += 10;
    InvalidateRect(hwnd, NULL, 1);
    break;
  case ID_ORG: /* change viewport origin */
    orgX += 50;
    orgY += 50;
    InvalidateRect(hwnd, NULL, 1);
    break;
```

```
        case ID_RESET:
          /* reset current position to 0,0 */
          MoveToEx(memdc, 0, 0, NULL);
          /* erase by repainting background */
          PatBlt(memdc, 0, 0, maxX, maxY, PATCOPY);
          InvalidateRect(hwnd, NULL, 1);
           break;
        case ID_HELP:
          MessageBox(hwnd, "F2: Lines\nF3: Rectangles\n"
                     "F4: Ellipses\nF5: Magnify\n"
                     "F6: Origin\nF7: Reset",
                     "Graphics Fun", MB_OK);
          break;
      }
      break;
    case WM_PAINT: /* process a repaint request */
      hdc = BeginPaint(hwnd, &paintstruct); /* get DC */

     /* set mapping mode, window and viewport extents */
      SetMapMode(hdc, MM_ANISOTROPIC);
      SetWindowExtEx(hdc, 200, 200, NULL);
      SetViewportExtEx(hdc, X, Y, NULL);
      SetViewportOrgEx(hdc, orgX, orgY, NULL);

      /* now, copy memory image onto screen */
      BitBlt(hdc, 0, 0, maxX, maxY, memdc, 0, 0, SRCCOPY);
      EndPaint(hwnd, &paintstruct); /* release DC */
      break;
    case WM_DESTROY: /* terminate the program */
      DeleteObject(hRedpen); /* delete pens */
      DeleteObject(hGreenpen);
      DeleteObject(hBluepen);
      DeleteObject(hYellowpen);

      DeleteDC(memdc);
      PostQuitMessage(0);
      break;
    default:
     /* Let Windows 95 process any messages not specified in
     the preceding switch statement. */
     return DefWindowProc(hwnd, message, wParam, lParam);
  }
  return 0;
}
```

This program uses the following resource file:

```
#include <windows.h>
#include "graph.h"

MYMENU MENU
{
  MENUITEM "&Lines", ID_LINES
  MENUITEM "&Rectangles", ID_RECTANGLES
  MENUITEM "&Ellipses", ID_ELLIPSES
  MENUITEM "&Magnify", ID_SIZE
  MENUITEM "&Origin", ID_ORG
  MENUITEM "&Reset", ID_RESET
  MENUITEM "&Help", ID_HELP
}

MYMENU ACCELERATORS
{
  VK_F2, ID_LINES, VIRTKEY
  VK_F3, ID_RECTANGLES, VIRTKEY
  VK_F4, ID_ELLIPSES, VIRTKEY
  VK_F5, ID_SIZE, VIRTKEY
  VK_F6, ID_ORG, VIRTKEY
  VK_F7, ID_RESET, VIRTKEY
  VK_F1, ID_HELP, VIRTKEY
}
```

The header file **graph.h** must be modified to look like this:

```
#define ID_LINES      100
#define ID_RECTANGLES 101
#define ID_ELLIPSES   102
#define ID_SIZE       103
#define ID_ORG        104
#define ID_RESET      105
#define ID_HELP       106
```

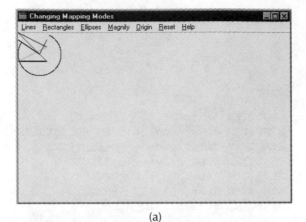

(a)

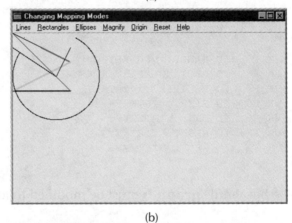

(b)

Sample output
from the
mapping
mode program
at various
magnifications
and positions
Figure 9-3.

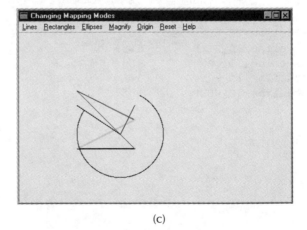

(c)

In the next chapter, we will return to the subject of controls, beginning our examination of the Windows 95 common controls.

Chapter 10

Introducing Common Controls

This chapter introduces one of the most exciting new features of Windows 95: common controls. In the preceding chapters you learned about the standard controls that are supported by Windows 95 (and by earlier versions of Windows). However, Windows 95 defines several new controls that add excitement to your application and greatly enhance the interface to any Windows application. The common controls are intended to supplement the standard controls and give you added power and flexibility. They can also help give your application a "custom" look.

The following table describes the common controls supported by Windows 95:

Control	Description
Drag list boxes	A list box that allows items to be dragged
Header controls	A column heading
Hot-key controls	Supports user-created hot keys
Image lists	A list of graphical images
List view controls	A list of icons and labels
Progress bars	A visual gauge used to indicate the degree to which a task is completed
Property sheets	A properties dialog box
Rich edit controls	A sophisticated edit box
Status windows	A bar that displays information related to an application
Tab controls	A tab-based menu (looks like the tabs on file folders)
Toolbars	A graphics-based menu
Tooltips	Small pop-up text boxes (typically used to describe toolbar buttons)
Trackbars	A slider-based control (similar in concept to a scroll bar, but looks like a fader control on a stereo)
Tree view controls	A tree-structured display
Up/down (spin) controls	Up and down arrows. Called a spin control when linked with an edit box

These controls are called *common controls* because they represent an extended set of controls that will be used by many applications. You have certainly encountered several (if not all) of these controls if you have been using Windows 95 for very long.

This chapter discusses the theory and general procedure for using a common control in your program. It then explores toolbars and tooltips. (Other common controls are examined in the following chapters.)

None of the common controls are supported by Windows 3.1. You will want to watch for opportunities to apply them when converting older programs to Windows 95. Without question, the use of the common controls will give your applications the modern look that users will come to expect from a Windows 95 program.

Including and Initializing the Common Controls

Before you can use the common controls, you must include the standard header file **commctrl.h** in your program. You must also make sure that the common controls library is linked into your program. (At the time of this writing, the common controls library is called COMCTL32.LIB, but you should check your compiler's user manual.)

Applications that use one or more common controls must call **InitCommonControls( )** prior to using the first common control. **InitCommonControls( )** ensures that the common controls dynamic link library (DLL) is loaded and that the common controls subsystem is initialized. The prototype for **InitCommonControls( )** is shown here:

```
void InitCommonControls(void);
```

A good place to call **InitCommonControls( )** is after your main window class has been registered.

Common Controls Are Windows

Before continuing, it is important to understand that all of the common controls are child windows. They will be created using one of three methods: by calling **CreateWindow( )**, by calling **CreateWindowEx( )**, or by calling a control-specific API function. (The **CreateWindowEx( )** function allows extended style attributes to be specified.) Because the common controls are windows, they can be managed in more or less the same way as you manage other windows used by your program.

Many common controls send your program either **WM_COMMAND** or **WM_NOTIFY** messages when they are accessed by the user. For many common controls, your program communicates by sending the control a message using the **SendMessage( )** API function, whose prototype is shown here:

```
LRESULT SendMessage(HWND hwnd, UINT Msg, WPARAM wParam,
                    LPARAM lParam);
```

Here, *hwnd* is the handle of the control, *Msg* is the message that you want to send to the control, and *wParam* and *lParam* contain any additional information associated with the message. The function returns the control's response, if any.

Using a Toolbar

Perhaps the most sought-after common control is the *toolbar*. A toolbar is essentially a graphical menu. In the toolbar, menu items are represented by icons, which form graphical buttons. Often, a toolbar is used in conjunction with a standard menu. As such, it provides an alternative means of making a menu selection.

To create a toolbar, use the **CreateToolbarEx( )** function, which is shown here:

```
HWND CreateToolbarEx(HWND hwnd, DWORD dwStyle, WORD ID,
                int NumButtons, HINSTANCE hInst,
                WORD BPID, LPCTBBUTTON Buttons,
                int NumButtons,
                int ButtonWidth, int ButtonHeight,
                int BMPWidth, int BMPHeight,
                UINT Size);
```

Here, *hwnd* is the handle of the parent window that owns the toolbar.

The style of the toolbar is passed in *dwStyle*. The toolbar style must include **WS_CHILD**. It can also include other standard styles, such as **WS_BORDER** or **WS_VISIBLE**. There are two toolbar-specific styles that you might want to specify. One is **TBSTYLE_TOOLTIPS**. This style allows tooltips to be used. (Tooltips are discussed later in this chapter.) The other is **TBSTYLE_WRAPABLE**. This allows a long toolbar to be wrapped to the next line.

The identifier associated with the toolbar is passed in *ID*. The number of buttons in the toolbar is passed in *NumButtons*. The instance handle of the application is passed in *hInst*. The identifier of the bitmap resource that forms the toolbar is passed in *BPID*.

Information about each button is passed in an array of **TBBUTTON** structures pointed to by *Buttons*. The number of buttons in the toolbar is specified in *NumButtons*. The width and height of the buttons are passed in *ButtonWidth* and *ButtonHeight*. The width and height of the icons within each button are passed in *BMPWidth* and *BMPHeight*. If *ButtonWidth* and *ButtonHeight* are zero, then appropriate button dimensions that fit the bitmap size are supplied automatically. The size of the **TBBUTTON** structure is passed in *Size*.

The function returns a handle to the toolbar window.

Each button has a **TBBUTTON** structure associated with it that defines its various characteristics. The **TBBUTTON** structure is shown here:

```
typedef struct _TBBUTTON {
  int iBitmap;
  int idCommand;
  BYTE fsState;
  BYTE fsStyle;
  DWORD dwData;
  int iString;
} TBBUTTON;
```

The index of the bitmap image associated with the button is contained in **iBitmap**. The buttons begin their indexing at zero and are displayed left to right.

The command associated with the button is stored in **idCommand**. Each time the button is pressed, a **WM_COMMAND** message will be generated and sent to the parent window. The value of **idCommand** will be contained in the low-order word **wParam**.

The initial state of the button is stored in **fsState**. It can be one (or more) of the values in the following table:

State	Meaning
TBSTATE_CHECKED	Button is pressed
TBSTATE_ENABLE	Button is active
TBSTATE_HIDDEN	Button is hidden and inactive
TBSTATE_INDETERMINATE	Button is gray and inactive
TBSTATE_PRESSED	Button is pressed
TBSTATE_WRAP	Following buttons are on new line

The style of the button is contained in **fsStyle**. It can be any valid combination of the following values:

Style	Meaning
TBSTYLE_BUTTON	Standard button
TBSTYLE_CHECK	Button toggles between checked and unchecked each time it is pressed
TBSTYLE_CHECKGROUP	A check button that is part of a mutually exclusive group
TBSTYLE_GROUP	A standard button that is part of a mutually exclusive group
TBSTYLE_SEP	Separates buttons (**idCommand** must be zero when this style is used)

Notice the **TBSTYLE_SEP** style. This style is used to provide a gap between buttons on the toolbar. This allows you to visually group buttons into clusters.

The **dwData** field contains user-defined data. The **iString** field is the index of an optional string associated with the button. These fields should be zero if they are unused.

In their default configuration, toolbars are fully automated controls and require virtually no management by your program in order to be used. However, you can manually manage a toolbar if you like by sending it explicit control messages. These messages are sent to the toolbar using **SendMessage( )**. Three common toolbar messages are shown here:

Message	Meaning
TB_CHECKBUTTON	Presses or clears a toolbar button. *wParam* must contain the ID of the button. *lParam* must be non-zero to press or zero to clear.
TB_ENABLEBUTTON	Enables or disables a toolbar button. *wParam* must contain the ID of the button. *lParam* must be non-zero to enable or zero to disable.
TB_HIDEBUTTON	Hides or shows a toolbar button. *wParam* must contain the ID of the button. *lParam* must be non-zero to hide or zero to show.

Toolbars can also generate notification messages that inform your program about various activities related to the toolbar. For simple toolbars, you won't need to worry about these messages. (The notification messages all begin with **TBN_,** and you can find information on them by examining the **commctrl.h** header file or your API library reference.)

Creating the Toolbar Bitmap

Before you can use a toolbar, you must create the icons that form the graphics images inside each button. To do this, you must use an image editor. The process is similar to creating a single icon (the way you did when working with custom icons in Chapter 6). However, there is one important point to remember: There is only one bitmap associated with the toolbar, and this bitmap must contain *all* of the button images. Thus, if your toolbar will have six buttons, then the bitmap associated with your toolbar must define six images. For example, if your toolbar images are each 16 x 16 bits and your toolbar has six buttons, then your toolbar bitmap will have to be 16 bits high by 96 (6 x 16) bits long.

For the toolbar examples presented in this chapter, you will need five images. Each image must be 16 x 16 bits. This means that you will need to create a bitmap that is 16 x 80. Figure 10-1 shows how the toolbar bitmap used by the sample programs in this chapter looks inside the image editor. (The fourth image is left blank intentionally.) The toolbar will be used as an alternative menu for the graphics program developed in Chapter 9. Store your bitmap in a file called TOOLBAR.BMP.

A Simple Toolbar Sample Program

The following program adds a toolbar to the graphics program developed in Chapter 9. The toolbar duplicates the menu options. It allows you to displays lines, rectangles, and ellipses. You can also reset the window and choose Help.

The toolbar program is shown here:

```
/* Demonstrate a toolbar. */

#include <windows.h>
#include <commctrl.h>
#include <string.h>
#include <stdio.h>
#include "tb.h"

#define NUMBUTTONS 6
```

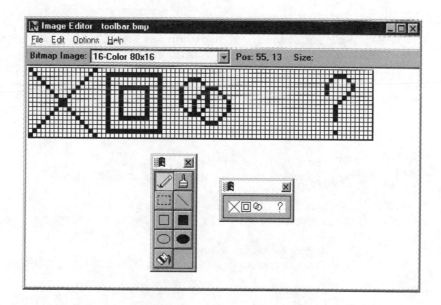

The toolbar bitmap being edited

Figure 10-1.

```
void InitToolbar(); /* initialize the tool bar */

LRESULT CALLBACK WindowFunc(HWND, UINT, WPARAM, LPARAM);

char szWinName[] = "MyWin"; /* name of window class */

int maxX, maxY; /* screen dimensions */

HDC memdc; /* handle of memory DC */
HBITMAP hbit; /* handle of compatible bitmap */
HBRUSH hbrush, hOldbrush; /* handles of brushes */

/* create pens */
HPEN hOldpen; /* handle of old pen */
HPEN hRedpen, hGreenpen, hBluepen, hYellowpen;

TBBUTTON tbButtons[NUMBUTTONS];

HWND tbwnd; /* toolbar handle */

int WINAPI WinMain(HINSTANCE hThisInst, HINSTANCE hPrevInst,
                   LPSTR lpszArgs, int nWinMode)
{
  HWND hwnd;
  MSG msg;
  WNDCLASS wcl;
  HANDLE hAccel;

  /* Define a window class. */
  wcl.hInstance = hThisInst; /* handle to this instance */
  wcl.lpszClassName = szWinName; /* window class name */
  wcl.lpfnWndProc = WindowFunc; /* window function */
  wcl.style = 0; /* default style */

  wcl.hIcon = LoadIcon(NULL, IDI_APPLICATION);
  wcl.hCursor = LoadCursor(NULL, IDC_ARROW);

  /* specify name of menu resource */
  wcl.lpszMenuName = "MYMENU"; /* main menu */

  wcl.cbClsExtra = 0; /* no extra */
  wcl.cbWndExtra = 0; /* information needed */

  /* Make the window white. */
  wcl.hbrBackground = GetStockObject(WHITE_BRUSH);

  /* Register the window class. */
  if(!RegisterClass(&wcl)) return 0;
```

```
    /* Now that a window class has been registered, a window
       can be created. */
    hwnd = CreateWindow(
      szWinName, /* name of window class */
      "Using a Toolbar", /* title */
      WS_OVERLAPPEDWINDOW, /* window style - normal */
      CW_USEDEFAULT, /* X coordinate - let Windows decide */
      CW_USEDEFAULT, /* Y coordinate - let Windows decide */
      CW_USEDEFAULT, /* width - let Windows decide */
      CW_USEDEFAULT, /* height - let Windows decide */
      HWND_DESKTOP, /* no parent window */
      NULL, /* no menu */
      hThisInst, /* handle of this instance of the program */
      NULL /* no additional arguments */
    );

    /* load accelerators */
    hAccel = LoadAccelerators(hThisInst, "MYMENU");

    InitToolbar(); /* initialize the toolbar */

    InitCommonControls(); /* activate the common controls */

    tbwnd = CreateToolbarEx(hwnd,
                    WS_VISIBLE | WS_CHILD | WS_BORDER,
                    ID_TOOLBAR,
                    NUMBUTTONS,
                    hThisInst,
                    IDTB_BMP,
                    tbButtons,
                    NUMBUTTONS,
                    0, 0, 16, 16,
                    sizeof(TBBUTTON));

    /* Display the window. */
    ShowWindow(hwnd, nWinMode);
    UpdateWindow(hwnd);

    /* Create the message loop. */
    while(GetMessage(&msg, NULL, 0, 0))
    {
      if(!TranslateAccelerator(hwnd, hAccel, &msg)) {
        TranslateMessage(&msg); /* allow use of keyboard */
        DispatchMessage(&msg); /* return control to Windows */
      }
    }
    return msg.wParam;
```

```
}

/* This function is called by Windows 95 and is passed
   messages from the message queue.
*/
LRESULT CALLBACK WindowFunc(HWND hwnd, UINT message,
                             WPARAM wParam, LPARAM lParam)
{
  HDC hdc;
  PAINTSTRUCT paintstruct;

  switch(message) {
    case WM_CREATE:
      /* get screen coordinates */
      maxX = GetSystemMetrics(SM_CXSCREEN);
      maxY = GetSystemMetrics(SM_CYSCREEN);

      /* make a compatible memory image device */
      hdc = GetDC(hwnd);
      memdc = CreateCompatibleDC(hdc);
      hbit = CreateCompatibleBitmap(hdc, maxX, maxY);
      SelectObject(memdc, hbit);
      hbrush = GetStockObject(WHITE_BRUSH);
      SelectObject(memdc, hbrush);
      PatBlt(memdc, 0, 0, maxX, maxY, PATCOPY);

      hRedpen = CreatePen(PS_SOLID, 1, RGB(255,0,0));
      hGreenpen = CreatePen(PS_SOLID, 2, RGB(0,255,0));
      hBluepen = CreatePen(PS_SOLID, 3, RGB(0,0,255));
      hYellowpen = CreatePen(PS_SOLID, 4, RGB(255, 255, 0));

      /* save default pen */
      hOldpen = SelectObject(memdc, hRedpen);
      SelectObject(memdc, hOldpen);

      ReleaseDC(hwnd, hdc);
      break;
    case WM_COMMAND:
      switch(LOWORD(wParam)) {
        case ID_LINES:
          /* set 2 pixels */
          SetPixel(memdc, 40, 14, RGB(0, 0, 0));
          SetPixel(memdc, 40, 15, RGB(0, 0, 0));

          LineTo(memdc, 100, 50);
          MoveToEx(memdc, 100, 50, NULL);

          /* change to green pen */
```

10

```
      hOldpen = SelectObject(memdc, hGreenpen);
      LineTo(memdc, 200, 100);

      /* change to yellow pen */
      SelectObject(memdc, hYellowpen);
      LineTo(memdc, 0, 200);

      /* change to blue pen */
      SelectObject(memdc, hBluepen);
      LineTo(memdc, 200, 200);

      /* change to red pen */
      SelectObject(memdc, hRedpen);
      LineTo(memdc, 0, 0);

      /* return to default pen */
      SelectObject(memdc, hOldpen);

      Arc(memdc, 0, 0, 300, 300, 0, 50, 200, 50);
      /* show intersecting lines that define arc */
      MoveToEx(memdc, 150, 150, NULL);
      LineTo(memdc, 0, 50);
      MoveToEx(memdc, 150, 150, NULL);
      LineTo(memdc, 200, 50);

      InvalidateRect(hwnd, NULL, 1);
      break;
    case ID_RECTANGLES:
      /* display, but don't fill */
      hOldbrush = SelectObject(memdc,
                             GetStockObject(HOLLOW_BRUSH));

      /* draw some rectangles */
      Rectangle(memdc, 50, 50, 300, 300);
      RoundRect(memdc, 125, 125, 220, 240, 15, 13);

      /* use a red pen */
      SelectObject(memdc, hRedpen);
      Rectangle(memdc, 100, 100, 200, 200);
      SelectObject(memdc, hOldpen); /* return to default pen */

      /* restore default brush */
      SelectObject(memdc, hOldbrush);

      InvalidateRect(hwnd, NULL, 1);
      break;
    case ID_ELLIPSES:
      /* make blue brush */
```

```
      hbrush = CreateSolidBrush(RGB(0, 0, 255));
      hOldbrush = SelectObject(memdc, hbrush);

      /* fill these ellipses with blue */
      Ellipse(memdc, 50, 200, 100, 280);
      Ellipse(memdc, 75, 25, 280, 100);

      /* use a red pen and fill with green */
      SelectObject(memdc, hRedpen);
      DeleteObject(hbrush); /* delete brush */
      /* create green brush */
      hbrush = CreateSolidBrush(RGB(0, 255, 0));
      SelectObject(memdc, hbrush); /* select green brush */
      Ellipse(memdc, 100, 100, 200, 200);

      /* draw a pie slice */
      Pie(memdc, 200, 200, 340, 340, 225, 200, 200, 250);

      SelectObject(memdc, hOldpen); /* return to default pen */
      SelectObject(memdc, hOldbrush); /* select default brush */
      DeleteObject(hbrush); /* delete green brush */

      InvalidateRect(hwnd, NULL, 1);
      break;
    case ID_RESET:
      /* reset current position to 0,0 */
      MoveToEx(memdc, 0, 0, NULL);
      /* erase by repainting background */
      PatBlt(memdc, 0, 0, maxX, maxY, PATCOPY);
      InvalidateRect(hwnd, NULL, 1);
      break;
    case ID_SHOW: /* show toolbar */
      ShowWindow(tbwnd, SW_RESTORE);
      break;
    case ID_HIDE: /* hide toolbar */
      ShowWindow(tbwnd, SW_HIDE);
      break;
    case ID_HELP:
      /* show help button as pressed */
      SendMessage(tbwnd, TB_CHECKBUTTON,
                  (LPARAM) ID_HELP, (WPARAM) 1);

      MessageBox(hwnd, "F2: Lines\nF3: Rectangles\n"
                 "F4: Ellipses\nF5: Reset\n"
                 "F6: Show Toolbar\n"
                 "F7: Hide Toolbar",
```

```
                         "Graphics Fun", MB_OK);

          /* reset the help button */
          SendMessage(tbwnd, TB_CHECKBUTTON,
                      (LPARAM) ID_HELP, (WPARAM) 0);
          break;
      }
      break;
   case WM_PAINT: /* process a repaint request */
     hdc = BeginPaint(hwnd, &paintstruct); /* get DC */

     /* now, copy memory image onto screen */
     BitBlt(hdc, 0, 0, maxX, maxY, memdc, 0, 0, SRCCOPY);
     EndPaint(hwnd, &paintstruct); /* release DC */
     break;
   case WM_DESTROY: /* terminate the program */
     DeleteObject(hRedpen); /* delete pens */
     DeleteObject(hGreenpen);
     DeleteObject(hBluepen);
     DeleteObject(hYellowpen);

     DeleteDC(memdc);
     PostQuitMessage(0);
     break;
   default:
     /* Let Windows 95 process any messages not specified in
     the preceding switch statement. */
     return DefWindowProc(hwnd, message, wParam, lParam);
  }
  return 0;
}

/* Initialize the toolbar structures. */
void initToolbar()
{
  tbButtons[0].iBitmap = 0;
  tbButtons[0].idCommand = ID_LINES;
  tbButtons[0].fsState = TBSTATE_ENABLED;
  tbButtons[0].fsStyle = TBSTYLE_BUTTON;
  tbButtons[0].dwData = 0L;
  tbButtons[0].iBitmap = 0;
  tbButtons[0].iString = 0;

  tbButtons[1].iBitmap = 1;
  tbButtons[1].idCommand = ID_RECTANGLES;
  tbButtons[1].fsState = TBSTATE_ENABLED;
  tbButtons[1].fsStyle = TBSTYLE_BUTTON;
  tbButtons[1].dwData = 0L;
```

```
  tbButtons[1].iString = 0;

  tbButtons[2].iBitmap = 2;
  tbButtons[2].idCommand = ID_ELLIPSES;
  tbButtons[2].fsState = TBSTATE_ENABLED;
  tbButtons[2].fsStyle = TBSTYLE_BUTTON;
  tbButtons[2].dwData = 0L;
  tbButtons[2].iString = 0;

  tbButtons[3].iBitmap = 3;
  tbButtons[3].idCommand = ID_RESET;
  tbButtons[3].fsState = TBSTATE_ENABLED;
  tbButtons[3].fsStyle = TBSTYLE_BUTTON;
  tbButtons[3].dwData = 0L;
  tbButtons[3].iString = 0;

  /* button separator */
  tbButtons[4].iBitmap = 0;
  tbButtons[4].idCommand = 0;
  tbButtons[4].fsState = TBSTATE_ENABLED;
  tbButtons[4].fsStyle = TBSTYLE_SEP;
  tbButtons[4].dwData = 0L;
  tbButtons[4].iString = 0;

  tbButtons[5].iBitmap = 4;
  tbButtons[5].idCommand = ID_HELP;
  tbButtons[5].fsState = TBSTATE_ENABLED;
  tbButtons[5].fsStyle = TBSTYLE_BUTTON;
  tbButtons[5].dwData = 0L;
  tbButtons[5].iString = 0;
}
```

This program requires the following resource file:

```
#include <windows.h>
#include "tb.h"

IDTB_BMP BITMAP "toolbar.bmp"

MYMENU MENU
{
  POPUP "&Draw"
  {
    MENUITEM "&Lines", ID_LINES
    MENUITEM "&Rectangles", ID_RECTANGLES
    MENUITEM "&Ellipses", ID_ELLIPSES
  }
  POPUP "&Options"
```

```
   {
     MENUITEM "&Reset", ID_RESET
     MENUITEM "&Show Toolbar", ID_SHOW
     MENUITEM "&Hide Toolbar", ID_HIDE
   }
    MENUITEM "&Help", WM_HELP
}

MYMENU ACCELERATORS
{
  VK_F2, ID_LINES, VIRTKEY
  VK_F3, ID_RECTANGLES, VIRTKEY
  VK_F4, ID_ELLIPSES, VIRTKEY
  VK_F5, ID_RESET, VIRTKEY
  VK_F6, ID_SHOW, VIRTKEY
  VK_F7, ID_HIDE, VIRTKEY
  VK_F1, ID_HELP, VIRTKEY
}
```

The **tb.h** header file is shown here:

```
#define ID_LINES       100
#define ID_RECTANGLES 101
#define ID_ELLIPSES    102
#define ID_SHOW        103
#define ID_HIDE        104
#define ID_RESET       105
#define ID_HELP        106

#define ID_TOOLBAR     200

#define IDTB_BMP       300
```

Most of the code in this program is straightforward. Here is a brief description. (Remember, the non-toolbar-related code was discussed in Chapter 9.) The toolbar information is held in the **tbButtons** array. This array is initialized in **InitToolBar( )**. Notice that the fifth structure is simply a button separator. In **WinMain( )**, the **InitCommonControls( )** function is called. Next, the toolbar is created and a handle to it is assigned to **tbwnd**.

Each button in the toolbar corresponds to a menu entry in the main menu. Specifically, each of the buttons (other than the separator) is associated with a menu ID. When a button is pressed, its associated ID will be sent to the program as part of a **WM_COMMAND** message in the same way as if a menu item had been selected. In fact, the same **case** statement handles both toolbar button presses and menu selections.

Since a toolbar is a window, it may be displayed or hidden like any other window using the **ShowWindow( )** function. To hide the window, select Hide Toolbar in the Options menu. To redisplay the toolbar, select Show Toolbar. Since the toolbar overlays part of the client area of the main window, you should always allow the user to remove the toolbar if it is not needed. As the program illustrates, this is very easy to do.

There is one other point of interest in the program. Notice the code inside the **ID_HELP** case. When Help is selected (either through the main menu or by pressing the Help button), the Help toolbar button is manually pressed by sending it a **TB_CHECKBUTTON** message. After the user closes the Help message box, the button is manually released. Thus, the Help button remains pressed while the Help message box is displayed. This is an example of how a toolbar can be manually managed by your program when necessary.

Sample output from the toolbar program is shown in Figure 10-2.

Adding Tooltips

As you have probably already noticed when using Windows 95, some toolbars automatically pop up small text windows after the mouse pointer has paused for about one second over a toolbar button. These small text windows are called *tooltips*. Although not technically required, tooltips should be included with most toolbars, because users will expect to see them. In this section, tooltips will be added to the toolbar.

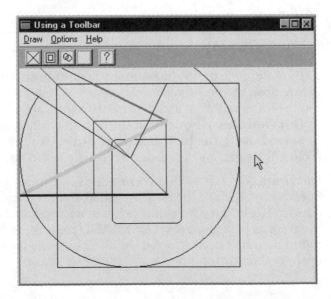

Sample output
from the
toolbar
program
Figure 10-2.

To add tooltips to a toolbar, you must first include the
TBSTYLE_TOOLTIPS style when you create the toolbar. This enables
WM_NOTIFY messages to be sent when the mouse pointer lingers over a
button for more than about one second. When a **WM_NOTIFY** message is
received, **lParam** will point to a **TOOLTIPTEXT** structure, which is
defined like this:

```
typedef struct {
  NMHDR hdr;
  LPSTR lpszText;
  char szText[80];
  HINSTANCE hinst;
  UINT uFlags;
} TOOLTIPTEXT;
```

The first member of **TOOLTIPTEXT** is an **NMHDR** structure, which is
defined like this:

```
typedef struct tagNMHDR
{
  HWND  hwndFrom; /* handle of control */
  UINT  idFrom; /* control ID */
  UINT  code; /* notification code */
} NMHDR;
```

If a tooltip is being requested, then **code** will contain **TTN_NEEDTEXT**
and **idFrom** will contain the ID of the button for which the tip is needed.
There are three ways to supply the required tooltip. You must either copy
the tooltip text into the **szText** array of **TOOLTIPTEXT**, point **lpszText**
to the text, or supply the resource ID of a string resource. When using a
string resource, the string ID is assigned to **lpszText**, and **hinst** must be
the handle of the string resource. By far the easiest way is to simply point
lpszText to a string supplied by your program. For example, the following
case responds to tooltip requests for the graphics program:

```
LPTOOLTIPTEXT TTtext;
// ...
case WM_NOTIFY: /* respond to tooltip request */
  TTtext = (LPTOOLTIPTEXT) lParam;
  if(TTtext->hdr.code == TTN_NEEDTEXT)
    switch(TTtext->hdr.idFrom) {
      case ID_LINES: TTtext->lpszText = "Lines";
        break;
      case ID_RECTANGLES: TTtext->lpszText = "Rectangles";
        break;
      case ID_ELLIPSES: TTtext->lpszText = "Ellipses";
        break;
```

```
      case ID_RESET: TTtext->lpszText = "Reset and Clear";
        break;
      case ID_HELP: TTtext->lpszText = "Help";
        break;
    }
  break;
```

Once the tooltip text has been set and control passes back to Windows, the tooltip will automatically be displayed. Your program need perform no further action. As you can see, tooltips are largely automated and easy to add to your application.

The Entire Toolbar Program, Including Tooltips

The entire toolbar program, with tooltips, is shown here. It uses the same resource file and header file as the preceding version. Sample output from this program is shown in Figure 10-3.

```
/* Add tooltips to the toolbar. */

#include <windows.h>
#include <commctrl.h>
#include <string.h>
#include <stdio.h>
#include "tb.h"

#define NUMBUTTONS 6

void InitToolbar(); /* initialize the toolbar */

LRESULT CALLBACK WindowFunc(HWND, UINT, WPARAM, LPARAM);

char szWinName[] = "MyWin"; /* name of window class */

int maxX, maxY; /* screen dimensions */

HDC memdc; /* handle of memory DC */
HBITMAP hbit; /* handle of compatible bitmap */
HBRUSH hbrush, hOldbrush; /* handles of brushes */

/* create pens */
HPEN hOldpen; /* handle of old pen */
HPEN hRedpen, hGreenpen, hBluepen, hYellowpen;

TBBUTTON tbButtons[NUMBUTTONS];

HWND tbwnd; /* toolbar handle */
```

```
int WINAPI WinMain(HINSTANCE hThisInst, HINSTANCE hPrevInst,
                   LPSTR lpszArgs, int nWinMode)
{
  HWND hwnd;
  MSG msg;
  WNDCLASS wcl;
  HANDLE hAccel;

  /* Define a window class. */
  wcl.hInstance = hThisInst; /* handle to this instance */
  wcl.lpszClassName = szWinName; /* window class name */
  wcl.lpfnWndProc = WindowFunc; /* window function */
  wcl.style = 0; /* default style */

  wcl.hIcon = LoadIcon(NULL, IDI_APPLICATION);
  wcl.hCursor = LoadCursor(NULL, IDC_ARROW);

  /* specify name of menu resource */
  wcl.lpszMenuName = "MYMENU"; /* main menu */

  wcl.cbClsExtra = 0; /* no extra */
  wcl.cbWndExtra = 0; /* information needed */

  /* Make the window white. */
  wcl.hbrBackground = GetStockObject(WHITE_BRUSH);

  /* Register the window class. */
  if(!RegisterClass(&wcl)) return 0;

  /* Now that a window class has been registered, a window
     can be created. */
  hwnd = CreateWindow(
    szWinName, /* name of window class */
    "Using a Toolbar", /* title */
    WS_OVERLAPPEDWINDOW, /* window style - normal */
    CW_USEDEFAULT, /* X coordinate - let Windows decide */
    CW_USEDEFAULT, /* Y coordinate - let Windows decide */
    CW_USEDEFAULT, /* width - let Windows decide */
    CW_USEDEFAULT, /* height - let Windows decide */
    HWND_DESKTOP, /* no parent window */
    NULL, /* no menu */
    hThisInst, /* handle of this instance of the program */
    NULL /* no additional arguments */
  );

  /* load accelerators */
```

```
      hAccel = LoadAccelerators(hThisInst, "MYMENU");

      InitToolbar(); /* initialize the toolbar structures */

      InitCommonControls(); /* activate the common controls */

      /* create the toolbar */
      tbwnd = CreateToolbarEx(hwnd,
                              WS_VISIBLE | WS_CHILD |
                              WS_BORDER | TBSTYLE_TOOLTIPS,
                              ID_TOOLBAR,
                              NUMBUTTONS,
                              hThisInst,
                              IDTB_BMP,
                              tbButtons,
                              NUMBUTTONS,
                              0, 0, 16, 16,
                              sizeof(TBBUTTON));

      /* Display the window. */
      ShowWindow(hwnd, nWinMode);
      UpdateWindow(hwnd);

      /* Create the message loop. */
      while(GetMessage(&msg, NULL, 0, 0))
      {
        if(!TranslateAccelerator(hwnd, hAccel, &msg)) {
          TranslateMessage(&msg); /* allow use of keyboard */
          DispatchMessage(&msg); /* return control to Windows */
        }
      }
      return msg.wParam;
    }

    /* This function is called by Windows 95 and is passed
       messages from the message queue.
    */
    LRESULT CALLBACK WindowFunc(HWND hwnd, UINT message,
                                WPARAM wParam, LPARAM lParam)
    {
      HDC hdc;
      PAINTSTRUCT paintstruct;
      LPTOOLTIPTEXT TTtext;

      switch(message) {
        case WM_CREATE:
          /* get screen coordinates */
          maxX = GetSystemMetrics(SM_CXSCREEN);
```

```
        maxY = GetSystemMetrics(SM_CYSCREEN);

        /* make a compatible memory image device */
        hdc = GetDC(hwnd);
        memdc = CreateCompatibleDC(hdc);
        hbit = CreateCompatibleBitmap(hdc, maxX, maxY);
        SelectObject(memdc, hbit);
        hbrush = GetStockObject(WHITE_BRUSH);
        SelectObject(memdc, hbrush);
        PatBlt(memdc, 0, 0, maxX, maxY, PATCOPY);

        hRedpen = CreatePen(PS_SOLID, 1, RGB(255,0,0));
        hGreenpen = CreatePen(PS_SOLID, 2, RGB(0,255,0));
        hBluepen = CreatePen(PS_SOLID, 3, RGB(0,0,255));
        hYellowpen = CreatePen(PS_SOLID, 4, RGB(255, 255, 0));

        /* save default pen */
        hOldpen = SelectObject(memdc, hRedpen);
        SelectObject(memdc, hOldpen);

        ReleaseDC(hwnd, hdc);
        break;
      case WM_NOTIFY: /* respond to tooltip request */
        TTtext = (LPTOOLTIPTEXT) lParam;
        if(TTtext->hdr.code == TTN_NEEDTEXT)
          switch(TTtext->hdr.idFrom) {
            case ID_LINES: TTtext->lpszText = "Lines";
              break;
            case ID_RECTANGLES: TTtext->lpszText = "Rectangles";
              break;
            case ID_ELLIPSES: TTtext->lpszText = "Ellipses";
              break;
            case ID_RESET: TTtext->lpszText = "Reset and Clear";
              break;
            case ID_HELP: TTtext->lpszText = "Help";
              break;
          }
        break;
      case WM_COMMAND:
        switch(LOWORD(wParam)) {
          case ID_LINES:
            /* set 2 pixels */
            SetPixel(memdc, 40, 14, RGB(0, 0, 0));
            SetPixel(memdc, 40, 15, RGB(0, 0, 0));

            LineTo(memdc, 100, 50);
            MoveToEx(memdc, 100, 50, NULL);
```

```
/* change to green pen */
hOldpen = SelectObject(memdc, hGreenpen);
LineTo(memdc, 200, 100);

/* change to yellow pen */
SelectObject(memdc, hYellowpen);
LineTo(memdc, 0, 200);

/* change to blue pen */
SelectObject(memdc, hBluepen);
LineTo(memdc, 200, 200);

/* change to red pen */
SelectObject(memdc, hRedpen);
LineTo(memdc, 0, 0);

/* return to default pen */
SelectObject(memdc, hOldpen)

Arc(memdc, 0, 0, 300, 300, 0, 50, 200, 50);
/* show intersecting lines that define arc */
MoveToEx(memdc, 150, 150, NULL);
LineTo(memdc, 0, 50);
MoveToEx(memdc, 150, 150, NULL);
LineTo(memdc, 200, 50);

InvalidateRect(hwnd, NULL, 1);
break;
case ID_RECTANGLES:
/* display, but don't fill */
hOldbrush = SelectObject(memdc,
                    GetStockObject(HOLLOW_BRUSH));

/* draw some rectangles */
Rectangle(memdc, 50, 50, 300, 300);
RoundRect(memdc, 125, 125, 220, 240, 15, 13);

/* use a red pen */
SelectObject(memdc, hRedpen);
Rectangle(memdc, 100, 100, 200, 200);
SelectObject(memdc, hOldpen); /* return to default pen */

/* restore default brush */
SelectObject(memdc, hOldbrush);

InvalidateRect(hwnd, NULL, 1);
break;
```

```
case ID_ELLIPSES:
  /* make blue brush */
  hbrush = CreateSolidBrush(RGB(0, 0, 255));
  hOldbrush = SelectObject(memdc, hbrush);

  /* fill these ellipses with blue */
  Ellipse(memdc, 50, 200, 100, 280);
  Ellipse(memdc, 75, 25, 280, 100);

  /* use a red pen and fill with green */
  SelectObject(memdc, hRedpen);
  DeleteObject(hbrush); /* delete brush */
  /* create green brush */
  hbrush = CreateSolidBrush(RGB(0, 255, 0));
  SelectObject(memdc, hbrush); /* select green brush */
  Ellipse(memdc, 100, 100, 200, 200);

  /* draw a pie slice */
  Pie(memdc, 200, 200, 340, 340, 225, 200, 200, 250);

  SelectObject(memdc, hOldpen); /* return to default pen */
  SelectObject(memdc, hOldbrush); /* select default brush */
  DeleteObject(hbrush); /* delete green brush */

  InvalidateRect(hwnd, NULL, 1);
  break;
case ID_SHOW: /* show toolbar */
  ShowWindow(tbwnd, SW_RESTORE);
  break;
case ID_HIDE: /* hide toolbar */
  ShowWindow(tbwnd, SW_HIDE);
  break;
case ID_RESET:
  /* reset current position to 0,0 */
  MoveToEx(memdc, 0, 0, NULL);
  /* erase by repainting background */
  PatBlt(memdc, 0, 0, maxX, maxY, PATCOPY);
  InvalidateRect(hwnd, NULL, 1);
  break;
case ID_HELP:
  /* show help button as pressed */
  SendMessage(tbwnd, TB_CHECKBUTTON,
```

```
                                   (LPARAM) ID_HELP, (WPARAM) 1);

                MessageBox(hwnd, "F2: Lines\nF3: Rectangles\n"
                                 "F4: Ellipses\nF5: Reset\n"
                                 "F6: Show Toolbar\n"
                                 "F7: Hide Toolbar",
                                 "Graphics Fun", MB_OK);


                /* reset the help button */
                SendMessage(tbwnd, TB_CHECKBUTTON,
                            (LPARAM) ID_HELP, (WPARAM) 0);
                break;
          }
          break;
        case WM_PAINT: /* process a repaint request */
          hdc = BeginPaint(hwnd, &paintstruct); /* get DC */

          /* now, copy memory image onto screen */
          BitBlt(hdc, 0, 0, maxX, maxY, memdc, 0, 0, SRCCOPY);
          EndPaint(hwnd, &paintstruct); /* release DC */
          break;
        case WM_DESTROY: /* terminate the program */
          DeleteObject(hRedpen); /* delete pens */
          DeleteObject(hGreenpen);
          DeleteObject(hBluepen);
          DeleteObject(hYellowpen);

          DeleteDC(memdc);
          PostQuitMessage(0);
          break;
        default:
          /* Let Windows 95 process any messages not specified in
          the preceding switch statement. */
          return DefWindowProc(hwnd, message, wParam, lParam);
      }
      return 0;
}

/* Initialize the toolbar structures. */
void InitToolbar()
{
  tbButtons[0].iBitmap = 0;
  tbButtons[0].idCommand = ID_LINES;
  tbButtons[0].fsState = TBSTATE_ENABLED;
  tbButtons[0].fsStyle = TBSTYLE_BUTTON;
  tbButtons[0].dwData = 0L;
  tbButtons[0].iBitmap = 0;
  tbButtons[0].iString = 0;
```

10

```
            tbButtons[1].iBitmap = 1;
            tbButtons[1].idCommand = ID_RECTANGLES;
            tbButtons[1].fsState = TBSTATE_ENABLED;
            tbButtons[1].fsStyle = TBSTYLE_BUTTON;
            tbButtons[1].dwData = 0L;
            tbButtons[1].iString = 0;

            tbButtons[2].iBitmap = 2;
            tbButtons[2].idCommand = ID_ELLIPSES;
            tbButtons[2].fsState = TBSTATE_ENABLED;
            tbButtons[2].fsStyle = TBSTYLE_BUTTON;
            tbButtons[2].dwData = 0L;
            tbButtons[2].iString = 0;

            tbButtons[3].iBitmap = 3;
            tbButtons[3].idCommand = ID_RESET;
            tbButtons[3].fsState = TBSTATE_ENABLED;
            tbButtons[3].fsStyle = TBSTYLE_BUTTON;
            tbButtons[3].dwData = 0L;
            tbButtons[3].iString = 0;

            /* button separator */
            tbButtons[4].iBitmap = 0;
            tbButtons[4].idCommand = 0;
            tbButtons[4].fsState = TBSTATE_ENABLED;
            tbButtons[4].fsStyle = TBSTYLE_SEP;
            tbButtons[4].dwData = 0L;
            tbButtons[4].iString = 0;

            tbButtons[5].iBitmap = 4;
            tbButtons[5].idCommand = ID_HELP;
            tbButtons[5].fsState = TBSTATE_ENABLED;
            tbButtons[5].fsStyle = TBSTYLE_BUTTON;
            tbButtons[5].dwData = 0L;
            tbButtons[5].iString = 0;
        }
```

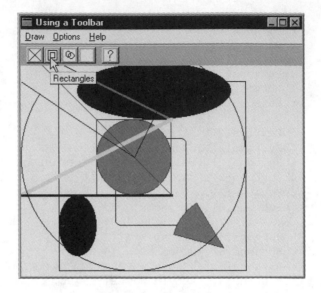

Sample output
from the
complete
toolbar
program,
including
tooltips

Figure 10-3.

In the next chapter you will continue to explore the common controls, examining up/down controls (also called spin controls), track bars, and progress bars.

Chapter 11

More Common Controls

This chapter continues our look at the Windows 95 common controls. It examines the up-down control, the trackbar, and the progress bar.

Remember, none of the common controls are supported by Windows 3.1. When converting older code to Windows 95, look for opportunities to use the new controls. Doing so will give your programs a modern look and feel.

Using Up-Down Controls

One new control that you will find useful in a number of situations is the *up-down* control. An up-down control is essentially a scroll bar without the bar! That is, it consists only of the arrows found on the ends of a scroll bar, but there is no bar between them. As you may have noticed while using various Windows applications, some scroll bars are so small that the bar is essentially pointless anyway. Also, some situations don't lend themselves to the concept of the bar but benefit from the use of the up and down arrows. To accommodate these situations, the designers of Windows 95 decided to define the up-down control. As you will see, using an up-down control is much like using a scroll bar.

An up-down control may be used in two different ways. First, it may be used more or less like a stand-alone scroll bar. Second, it can be used in conjunction with another control, called its *buddy window*. The most common buddy window is an edit box. When this is the case, a *spin control* (or *spinner*) is created. When you use a spin control, almost all of the overhead required to manage the control is provided automatically. This makes the spin control easy to add to your application. This chapter presents two up-down examples. The first creates a stand-alone up-down control. The second example uses a buddy window to create a spin control.

Creating an Up-Down Control

To create an up-down control, use the **CreateUpDownControl( )** function, shown here:

```
HWND CreateUpDownControl(DWORD Style, int X, int Y,
                int Width, int Height, HWND hParent,
                int ID, HINSTANCE hInst,
                HWND hBuddy, int Max, int Min, int StartPos);
```

Here, *Style* specifies the style of the up-down control. This parameter must include the standard styles **WS_CHILD**, **WS_VISIBLE**, and **WS_BORDER**. It may also include one or more of the up-down styles shown in Table 11-1.

The location of the upper-left corner of the up-down control is passed in *X* and *Y*. The width and height of the control are specified in *Width* and *Height*.

The handle of the parent window is passed in *hParent*. The ID associated with the up-down control is specified in *ID*. The instance handle of the application is passed in *hInst*. The handle of the buddy window is passed in *hBuddy*. If there is no buddy window, then this parameter must be *NULL*.

Style	Meaning
UDS_ALIGNLEFT	Aligns up-down control to the left of its buddy window.
UDS_ALIGNRIGHT	Aligns up-down control to the right of its buddy window.
UDS_ARROWKEYS	Enables arrows keys (that is, arrow keys may be used to move the control).
UDS_AUTOBUDDY	Buddy window is previous window in z-order.
UDS_HORZ	Up-down control is horizontal (up-down controls are vertical by default).
UDS_NOTHOUSANDS	Commas not used in large values (applies to spin controls only).
UDS_SETBUDDYINT	Automatically sets the text within the buddy window when the control position is changed. This allows the buddy window to show the current position of the up-down control.
UDS_WRAP	Position of up-down control will "wrap around" when moved past an end.

The Up-Down
Control Styles
Table 11-1.

11

The range of the control is passed in *Max* and *Min*. If *Max* is less than *Min*, then the control runs backward. The initial position of the control (which must be within the specified range) is passed in *StartPos*.

The function returns a handle to the control.

Up-Down Control Messages

When one of the arrows of an up-down control is pressed, it sends a **WM_VSCROLL** message to its parent window. The handle of the up-down control will be in *lParam*. Since there may be more than one control that generates **WM_VSCROLL** messages, you will need to check the handle in *lParam* to determine if it is that of the up-down control. To obtain the new position, send the control a **UDM_GETPOS** message. (You can send the control messages using **SendMessage( )**.) The current position of the control is returned.

In addition to the **UDM_GETPOS** message, up-down controls respond to several others. Commonly used up-down messages are shown in Table 11-2. For example, your program can set the position of an up-down control using the **UDM_SETPOS** message.

Message	Meaning
UDM_GETBUDDY	Obtains handle of buddy window. The handle is in the low-order word of the return value. *wParam* is 0. *lParam* is 0.
UDM_GETPOS	Obtains the current position. The current position is in the low-order word of the return value. *wParam* is 0. *lParam* is 0.
UDM_GETRANGE	Obtains the current range. The maximum value is in the low-order word of the return value; the minimum value is in the high-order word of the return value. *wParam* is 0. *lParam* is 0.
UDM_SETBUDDY	Specifies a new buddy window. The handle of the old buddy window is returned. *wParam* is the handle of the new buddy window. *lParam* is 0.
UDM_SETPOS	Sets the current position. *wParam* is 0. *lParam* is new current position.
UDM_SETRANGE	Sets the current range. *wParam* is 0. *lParam*: low-order word contains maximum; high-order word contains minimum.

Common
Up-Down
Messages
Table 11-2.

Using an Up-Down Control

The following program creates a stand-alone up-down control within a dialog box. In this example, the up-down control is not linked to a buddy window. The up-down control has a range of 0 to 100, with an initial position of 50. Each time the position of the control is changed (by pressing an arrow), the new position is displayed in the client area of the dialog box. Sample output from the program is shown in Figure 11-1.

```
/* Demonstrate up-down control basics. */

#include <windows.h>
#include <commctrl.h>
#include <stdio.h>
#include "updown.h"
```

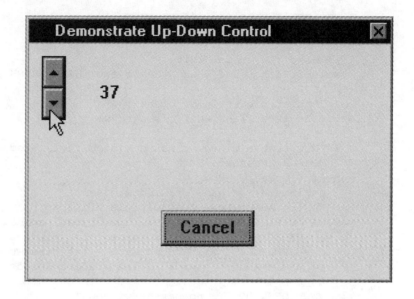

```
LRESULT CALLBACK WindowFunc(HWND, UINT, WPARAM, LPARAM);
BOOL CALLBACK DialogFunc(HWND, UINT, WPARAM, LPARAM);

char szWinName[] = "MyWin"; /* name of window class */

HINSTANCE hInst;

int WINAPI WinMain(HINSTANCE hThisInst, HINSTANCE hPrevInst,
                   LPSTR lpszArgs, int nWinMode)
{
  HWND hwnd;
  MSG msg;
  WNDCLASS wcl;
  HANDLE hAccel;

  /* Define a window class. */
  wcl.hInstance = hThisInst; /* handle to this instance */
  wcl.lpszClassName = szWinName; /* window class name */
  wcl.lpfnWndProc = WindowFunc; /* window function */
  wcl.style = 0; /* default style */

  wcl.hIcon = LoadIcon(NULL, IDI_APPLICATION);
  wcl.hCursor = LoadCursor(NULL, IDC_ARROW);

  /* specify name of menu resource */
  wcl.lpszMenuName = "MYMENU"; /* main menu */
```

```
wcl.cbClsExtra = 0; /* no extra */
wcl.cbWndExtra = 0; /* information needed */

/* Make the window white. */
wcl.hbrBackground = GetStockObject(WHITE_BRUSH);

/* Register the window class. */
if(!RegisterClass(&wcl)) return 0;

/* Now that a window class has been registered, a window
   can be created. */
hwnd = CreateWindow(
  szWinName, /* name of window class */
  "Using an Up-Down Control", /* title */
  WS_OVERLAPPEDWINDOW, /* window style - normal */
  CW_USEDEFAULT, /* X coordinate - let Windows decide */
  CW_USEDEFAULT, /* Y coordinate - let Windows decide */
  CW_USEDEFAULT, /* width - let Windows decide */
  CW_USEDEFAULT, /* height - let Windows decide */
  HWND_DESKTOP, /* no parent window */
  NULL, /* no menu */
  hThisInst, /* handle of this instance of the program */
  NULL /* no additional arguments */
);

hInst = hThisInst; /* save the current instance handle */

/* load accelerators */
hAccel = LoadAccelerators(hThisInst, "MYMENU");

InitCommonControls();

/* Display the window. */
ShowWindow(hwnd, nWinMode);
UpdateWindow(hwnd);

/* Create the message loop. */
while(GetMessage(&msg, NULL, 0, 0))
{
  if(!TranslateAccelerator(hwnd, hAccel, &msg)) {
    TranslateMessage(&msg); /* allow use of keyboard */
    DispatchMessage(&msg); /* return control to Windows */
  }
}
return msg.wParam;
}

/* This function is called by Windows 95 and is passed
```

```
        messages from the message queue.
*/
LRESULT CALLBACK WindowFunc(HWND hwnd, UINT message,
                            WPARAM wParam, LPARAM lParam)
{
  switch(message) {
    case WM_COMMAND:
      switch(LOWORD(wParam)) {
        case IDM_DIALOG:
          DialogBox(hInst, "MYDB", hwnd, DialogFunc);
          break;
        case IDM_HELP:
          MessageBox(hwnd, "Help", "Help", MB_OK);
          break;
      }
      break;
    case WM_DESTROY: /* terminate the program */
      PostQuitMessage(0);
      break;
    default:
      /* Let Windows 95 process any messages not specified in
         the preceding switch statement. */
      return DefWindowProc(hwnd, message, wParam, lParam);
  }
  return 0;
}

/* A simple dialog function. */
BOOL CALLBACK DialogFunc(HWND hdwnd, UINT message,
                         WPARAM wParam, LPARAM lParam)
{
  char str[80];
  long udpos = 0;
  HDC hdc;
  static HWND udWnd;

  switch(message) {
    case WM_INITDIALOG:
      udWnd = CreateUpDownControl(
                  WS_CHILD | WS_BORDER | WS_VISIBLE,
                  10, 10, 50, 50,
                  hdwnd,
                  ID_UPDOWN,
                  hInst,
                  NULL,
                  100, 0, 50);
      return 1;
    case WM_COMMAND:
```

```
      switch(LOWORD(wParam)) {
        case IDCANCEL:
          EndDialog(hdwnd, 0);
          return 1;
      }
    case WM_VSCROLL:  /* manually process an up-down control */
      if(udWnd==(HWND)lParam) {
        udpos = SendMessage(udWnd, UDM_GETPOS, 0, 0);
        sprintf(str, "%d", LOWORD(udpos));
        hdc = GetDC(hdwnd);
        TextOut(hdc, 55, 30, "      ", 6);
        TextOut(hdc, 55, 30, str, strlen(str));
        ReleaseDC(hdwnd, hdc);
        return 1;
      }
  }
  return 0;
}
```

The program also requires the following resource file:

```
#include <windows.h>
#include "updown.h"

MYMENU MENU
{
  MENUITEM "&Dialog", IDM_DIALOG
  MENUITEM "&Help", IDM_HELP
}

MYMENU ACCELERATORS
{
  VK_F2, IDM_DIALOG, VIRTKEY
  VK_F1, IDM_HELP, VIRTKEY
}

MYDB DIALOG 18, 18, 142, 92
CAPTION "Demonstrate Up-Down Control"
STYLE DS_MODALFRAME | WS_POPUP | WS_CAPTION | WS_SYSMENU
{
  PUSHBUTTON "Cancel", IDCANCEL, 52, 65, 37, 14,
             WS_CHILD | WS_VISIBLE | WS_TABSTOP
}
```

You will also need the header file **updown.h**, shown here. (The value **ID_EB1** will be used in the next example.)

```
#define IDM_DIALOG  100
#define IDM_HELP    101
#define ID_UPDOWN   102
#define ID_EB1      103
```

In the program, the up-down control is contained within the dialog box. The control is created when the dialog box is initialized, using the following code:

```
case WM_INITDIALOG:
  udWnd = CreateUpDownControl(
              WS_CHILD | WS_BORDER | WS_VISIBLE,
              10, 10, 50, 50,
              hdwnd,
              ID_UPDOWN,
              hInst,
              NULL,
              100, 0, 50);
    return 1;
```

This call to **CreateUpDownControl( )** creates an up-down control that is at location 10,10 within the dialog box. The control is 50 pixels wide and 50 pixels tall. Because the control is a child window of the dialog box, the dialog box's handle (**hdwnd**) is passed as the parent handle. The ID of the up-down control is **ID_UPDOWN**. Although this value is not required by this simple example, other programs will make use of it. **hInst** is the instance handle of the program. Because there is no buddy window, **NULL** is passed for the buddy parameter. The range of the up-down control is 0 to 100, and the initial position is 50.

Each time the up-down control is accessed, a **WM_VSCROLL** message is sent to the dialog box. The code that processes this message is shown next. The handle of the up-down control is contained in **lParam**. This handle is tested against that returned by **CreateUpDownControl( )** to confirm that it is the up-down control that generated the message. While there is only one control in this example, real world applications may have several controls capable of generating a **WM_VSCROLL** message, so you should always confirm which control has been accessed.

```
case WM_VSCROLL:  /* manually process an up-down control */
  if(udWnd==(HWND)lParam) {
    udpos = SendMessage(udWnd, UDM_GETPOS, 0, 0);
    sprintf(str, "%d", LOWORD(udpos));
    hdc = GetDC(hdwnd);
    TextOut(hdc, 55, 30, "       ", 6);
    TextOut(hdc, 55, 30, str, strlen(str));
    ReleaseDC(hdwnd, hdc);
```

```
    return 1;
}
```

To obtain the new up-down position, the **UDM_GETPOS** message is sent using **SendMessage( )**. The position is found in the low-order word of the return value. This value is then displayed in the client area of the dialog box.

 Remember, up-down controls were not supported by Windows 3.1. Therefore, you must be careful when adding one to an older program. It is not uncommon for older programs to assume that a WM_VSCROLL message is generated by a standard scroll bar. When adding an up-down control, you will frequently need to add a test to the portion of the program that processes scroll bar messages to confirm that it was actually the scroll bar and not an up-down control that generated the WM_VSCROLL message.

Creating a Spin Control

While there is nothing whatsoever wrong with creating and using a stand-alone up-down control, the up-down control is most commonly linked with an edit box. As mentioned, this combination is called a spin control. Because the spin control is such a common use of an up-down control, Windows 95 provides special support for it. In fact, a spin control is completely automated—your program itself contains virtually no management overhead for it.

To create a spin control, you must specify an edit control as a buddy window to an up-down control. After you have done this, each time the up-down control is changed, its new position is automatically displayed in the edit box. Furthermore, if you manually change the value in the edit box, the up-down control is automatically set to reflect that value.

A Spin Control Sample Program

Creating a spin control is an easy, two-step process. First, add an edit box to your program's resource file. Second, pass the handle of that box as the buddy window when the up-down control is created. The following program applies these steps:

```
/* Demonstrate a spin control. */

#include <windows.h>
#include <commctrl.h>
#include <stdio.h>
#include "updown.h"

LRESULT CALLBACK WindowFunc(HWND, UINT, WPARAM, LPARAM);
```

```
BOOL CALLBACK DialogFunc(HWND, UINT, WPARAM, LPARAM);

char szWinName[] = "MyWin"; /* name of window class */

HINSTANCE hInst;

int WINAPI WinMain(HINSTANCE hThisInst, HINSTANCE hPrevInst,
                   LPSTR lpszArgs, int nWinMode)
{
  HWND hwnd;
  MSG msg;
  WNDCLASS wcl;
  HANDLE hAccel;

  /* Define a window class. */
  wcl.hInstance = hThisInst; /* handle to this instance */
  wcl.lpszClassName = szWinName; /* window class name */
  wcl.lpfnWndProc = WindowFunc; /* window function */
  wcl.style = 0; /* default style */

  wcl.hIcon = LoadIcon(NULL, IDI_APPLICATION);
  wcl.hCursor = LoadCursor(NULL, IDC_ARROW);

  /* specify name of menu resource */
  wcl.lpszMenuName = "MYMENU"; /* main menu */

  wcl.cbClsExtra = 0; /* no extra */
  wcl.cbWndExtra = 0; /* information needed */

  /* Make the window white. */
  wcl.hbrBackground = GetStockObject(WHITE_BRUSH);

  /* Register the window class. */
  if(!RegisterClass(&wcl)) return 0;

  /* Now that a window class has been registered, a window
     can be created. */
  hwnd = CreateWindow(
    szWinName, /* name of window class */
    "Using a Spin Control", /* title */
    WS_OVERLAPPEDWINDOW, /* window style - normal */
    CW_USEDEFAULT, /* X coordinate - let Windows decide */
    CW_USEDEFAULT, /* Y coordinate - let Windows decide */
    CW_USEDEFAULT, /* width - let Windows decide */
    CW_USEDEFAULT, /* height - let Windows decide */
    HWND_DESKTOP, /* no parent window */
    NULL, /* no menu */
    hThisInst, /* handle of this instance of the program */
```

```
      NULL /* no additional arguments */
);

hInst = hThisInst; /* save the current instance handle */

/* load accelerators */
hAccel = LoadAccelerators(hThisInst, "MYMENU");

InitCommonControls();

/* Display the window. */
ShowWindow(hwnd, nWinMode);
UpdateWindow(hwnd);

/* Create the message loop. */
while(GetMessage(&msg, NULL, 0, 0))
{
  if(!TranslateAccelerator(hwnd, hAccel, &msg)) {
    TranslateMessage(&msg); /* allow use of keyboard */
    DispatchMessage(&msg); /* return control to Windows */
  }
}
return msg.wParam;
}

/* This function is called by Windows 95 and is passed
   messages from the message queue.
*/
LRESULT CALLBACK WindowFunc(HWND hwnd, UINT message,
                            WPARAM wParam, LPARAM lParam)
{
  switch(message) {
    case WM_COMMAND:
      switch(LOWORD(wParam)) {
        case IDM_DIALOG:
          DialogBox(hInst, "MYDB", hwnd, DialogFunc);
          break;
        case IDM_HELP:
          MessageBox(hwnd, "Help", "Help", MB_OK);
          break;
      }
      break;
    case WM_DESTROY: /* terminate the program */
      PostQuitMessage(0);
      break;
    default:
      /* Let Windows 95 process any messages not specified in
         the preceding switch statement. */
```

```
                    return DefWindowProc(hwnd, message, wParam, lParam);
       }
     return 0;
   }

   /* A simple dialog function. */
   BOOL CALLBACK DialogFunc(HWND hdwnd, UINT message,
                            WPARAM wParam, LPARAM lParam)
   {
     static HWND hEboxWnd;
     static HWND udWnd;

     switch(message) {
       case WM_INITDIALOG:
         hEboxWnd = GetDlgItem(hdwnd, ID_EB1);
         udWnd = CreateUpDownControl(
                     WS_CHILD | WS_BORDER | WS_VISIBLE |
                     UDS_SETBUDDYINT | UDS_ALIGNRIGHT,
                     10, 10, 50, 50,
                     hdwnd,
                     ID_UPDOWN,
                     hInst,
                     hEboxWnd,
                     100, 0, 50);
         return 1;
       case WM_COMMAND:
         switch(LOWORD(wParam)) {
           case IDCANCEL:
             EndDialog(hdwnd, 0);
             return 1;
         }
     }
     return 0;
   }
```

This program uses the following resource file. Notice that an edit box has been included in the dialog box's definition.

```
#include <windows.h>
#include "updown.h"

MYMENU MENU
{
  MENUITEM "&Dialog", IDM_DIALOG
  MENUITEM "&Help", IDM_HELP
}

MYMENU ACCELERATORS
```

```
{
  VK_F2, IDM_DIALOG, VIRTKEY
  VK_F1, IDM_HELP, VIRTKEY
}

MYDB DIALOG 18, 18, 142, 92
CAPTION "Demonstrate Spin Control"
STYLE DS_MODALFRAME | WS_POPUP | WS_CAPTION | WS_SYSMENU
{
  PUSHBUTTON "Cancel", IDCANCEL, 52, 65, 37, 14,
             WS_CHILD | WS_VISIBLE | WS_TABSTOP
  EDITTEXT ID_EB1, 10, 10, 30, 12, ES_LEFT | WS_CHILD |
           WS_VISIBLE | WS_BORDER
}
```

Sample output from the program is shown in Figure 11-2.

To understand how the spin control is created, look at the
WM_INITDIALOG case code, shown here:

```
case WM_INITDIALOG:
  hEboxWnd = GetDlgItem(hdwnd, ID_EB1);
  udWnd = CreateUpDownControl(
                WS_CHILD | WS_BORDER | WS_VISIBLE |
                UDS_SETBUDDYINT | UDS_ALIGNRIGHT,
                10, 10, 50, 50,
                hdwnd,
                ID_UPDOWN,
                hInst,
                hEboxWnd,
                100, 0, 50);
  return 1;
```

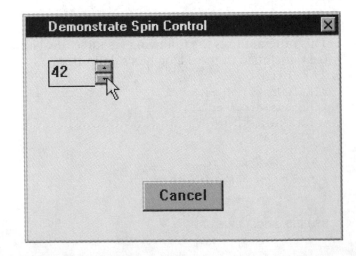

Sample output
from the spin
control
demonstration
program
Figure 11-2.

Since the dialog box is defined in the resource file, the program must call **GetDlgItem( )** to obtain its handle. **GetDlgItem( )** is defined like this:

HWND GetDlgItem(HWND *hDialog*, int *ID*);

GetDlgItem( ) returns a handle to the specified control. The handle of the dialog box that contains the control is specified in *hDialog*. The ID of the control is passed in *ID*. The function returns NULL if an error occurs.

Once the handle of the dialog box has been obtained, it is passed as the buddy window to the **CreateUpDownControl( )** function. Once the up-down control has been created with an edit box as its buddy window, the two controls are automatically linked together, forming the spin control.

11

Using a Trackbar

One of the most visually appealing common controls is the *trackbar* (sometimes called a *slider control*). A trackbar resembles a slide control found on various types of electronic equipment, such as stereos. It consists of a pointer that moves within a track. Although it looks quite different from a scroll bar, a trackbar is handled similarly by your program.

Trackbars are particularly useful when your program is emulating a real device. For example, if your program is controlling a graphics equalizer, then trackbars are an excellent choice for representing and setting the frequency curve.

To create a trackbar, use either **CreateWindow( )** or **CreateWindowEx( )**. **CreateWindowEx( )** allows some extended style specifications. For the trackbar example in this chapter we won't need to use any extended styles, but you may find them useful in your own applications. The window class of a trackbar is **TRACKBAR_CLASS**.

Trackbar Styles

When creating the trackbar, you can specify various style options. The most common ones are shown in Table 11-3. You will almost always want to include **TBS_AUTOTICKS**, because this style causes small tick marks to be automatically shown on the bar. The tick marks provide a scale for the bar.

Style	Effect
TBS_AUTOTICKS	Automatically adds tick marks to the trackbar
TBS_HORZ	Trackbar is horizontal (this is the default)
TBS_VERT	Trackbar is vertical
TBS_BOTTOM	Tick marks on bottom of bar (this is the default)
TBS_TOP	Tick marks on top of bar
TBS_LEFT	Tick marks on left of bar
TBS_RIGHT	Tick marks on right of bar (this is the default)
TBS_BOTH	Tick marks on both sides of bar

Common
Trackbar Style
Options
Table 11-3.

Sending Trackbar Messages

Like the other common controls we have examined, you send a trackbar a message using the **SendMessage( )** function. Common trackbar messages are shown in Table 11-4. Two messages that you will almost always need to send to a trackbar are **TBM_SETRANGE** and **TBM_SETPOS**. These set the range of the trackbar and establish its initial position, respectively. These items cannot be set when the trackbar is created using **CreateWindow( )**.

Processing a Trackbar Notification Message

When a trackbar is accessed, it generates a **WM_HSCROLL** scroll message. A value describing the nature of the activity is passed in the low-order word *wParam*. This value is referred to as a notification message. The handle of the trackbar that generated the message is in *lParam*. Table 11-5 lists some common trackbar notification messages.

A Trackbar Demonstration Program

The following program adds a trackbar to the previous spin control program. As you will see when you run the program, whenever you change the trackbar, the spin control is updated. If you change the spin control, the trackbar is changed. Thus, both the sending of messages to the trackbar and the receipt of messages from the trackbar are illustrated. Sample output is

Message	Meaning
TBM_GETPOS	Obtains the current position. *wParam* is 0. *lParam* is 0.
TBM_GETRANGEMAX	Gets the maximum trackbar range. *wParam* is 0. *lParam* is 0.
TBM_GETRANGEMIN	Gets the minimum trackbar range. *wParam* is 0. *lParam* is 0.
TBM_SETPOS	Sets the current position. *wParam* is non-zero to redraw the trackbar and zero otherwise. *lParam* contains the new position.
TBM_SETRANGE	Sets the trackbar range. *wParam* is non-zero to redraw trackbar and zero otherwise. *lParam* contains the range. The minimum value is in the low-order word. The maximum value is in the high-order word.
TBM_SETRANGEMAX	Sets the maximum range. *wParam* is non-zero to redraw trackbar and zero otherwise. *lParam* contains the maximum range value.
TBM_SETRANGEMIN	Sets the minimum range. *wParam* is non-zero to redraw trackbar and zero otherwise. *lParam* contains the minimum range value.

Common Trackbar Messages
Table 11-4.

Message	Meaning
TB_BOTTOM	END key pressed; slider moved to minimum value
TB_ENDTRACK	End of trackbar activity
TB_LINEDOWN	RIGHT ARROW or DOWN ARROW key pressed
TB_LINEUP	LEFT ARROW or UP ARROW key pressed
TB_PAGEDOWN	PGDN key pressed or mouse click before slider
TB_PAGEUP	PGUP key pressed or mouse click after slider
TB_THUMBPOSITION	Slider moved using the mouse
TB_THUMBTRACK	Slider dragged using the mouse
TB_TOP	HOME key pressed; slider moved to maximum value

Common Trackbar Notification Messages
Table 11-5.

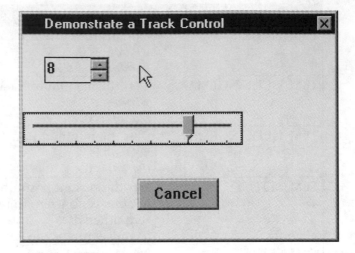

shown in Figure 11-3.

```
/* Demonstrate a trackbar. */

#include <windows.h>
#include <commctrl.h>
#include "track.h"

LRESULT CALLBACK WindowFunc(HWND, UINT, WPARAM, LPARAM);
BOOL CALLBACK DialogFunc(HWND, UINT, WPARAM, LPARAM);

char szWinName[] = "MyWin"; /* name of window class */

HINSTANCE hInst;

int WINAPI WinMain(HINSTANCE hThisInst, HINSTANCE hPrevInst,
                   LPSTR lpszArgs, int nWinMode)
{
  HWND hwnd;
  MSG msg;
  WNDCLASS wcl;
  HANDLE hAccel;

  /* Define a window class. */
  wcl.hInstance = hThisInst; /* handle to this instance */
  wcl.lpszClassName = szWinName; /* window class name */
  wcl.lpfnWndProc = WindowFunc; /* window function */
  wcl.style = 0; /* default style */

  wcl.hIcon = LoadIcon(NULL, IDI_APPLICATION);
```

```
wcl.hCursor = LoadCursor(NULL, IDC_ARROW);

/* specify name of menu resource */
wcl.lpszMenuName = "MYMENU"; /* main menu */

wcl.cbClsExtra = 0; /* no extra */
wcl.cbWndExtra = 0; /* information needed */

/* Make the window white. */
wcl.hbrBackground = GetStockObject(WHITE_BRUSH);

/* Register the window class. */
if(!RegisterClass(&wcl)) return 0;

/* Now that a window class has been registered, a window
   can be created. */
hwnd = CreateWindow(
  szWinName, /* name of window class */
  "Using a Trackbar", /* title */
  WS_OVERLAPPEDWINDOW, /* window style - normal */
  CW_USEDEFAULT, /* X coordinate - let Windows decide */
  CW_USEDEFAULT, /* Y coordinate - let Windows decide */
  CW_USEDEFAULT, /* width - let Windows decide */
  CW_USEDEFAULT, /* height - let Windows decide */
  HWND_DESKTOP, /* no parent window */
  NULL, /* no menu */
  hThisInst, /* handle of this instance of the program */
  NULL /* no additional arguments */
);

hInst = hThisInst; /* save the current instance handle */

/* load accelerators */
hAccel = LoadAccelerators(hThisInst, "MYMENU");

InitCommonControls();

/* Display the window. */
ShowWindow(hwnd, nWinMode);
UpdateWindow(hwnd);

/* Create the message loop. */
while(GetMessage(&msg, NULL, 0, 0))
{
  if(!TranslateAccelerator(hwnd, hAccel, &msg)) {
    TranslateMessage(&msg); /* allow use of keyboard */
    DispatchMessage(&msg); /* return control to Windows */
```

```
      }
    }
    return msg.wParam;
}

/* This function is called by Windows 95 and is passed
   messages from the message queue.
*/
LRESULT CALLBACK WindowFunc(HWND hwnd, UINT message,
                              WPARAM wParam, LPARAM lParam)
{
  switch(message) {
    case WM_COMMAND:
      switch(LOWORD(wParam)) {
        case IDM_DIALOG:
          DialogBox(hInst, "MYDB", hwnd, DialogFunc);
          break;
        case IDM_HELP:
          MessageBox(hwnd, "Help", "Help", MB_OK);
          break;
      }
      break;
    case WM_DESTROY: /* terminate the program */
      PostQuitMessage(0);
      break;
    default:
      /* Let Windows 95 process any messages not specified in
         the preceding switch statement. */
      return DefWindowProc(hwnd, message, wParam, lParam);
  }
  return 0;
}

/* A simple dialog function. */
BOOL CALLBACK DialogFunc(HWND hdwnd, UINT message,
                          WPARAM wParam, LPARAM lParam)
{
  static long udpos = 0;
  static long trackpos = 0;
  static HWND hEboxWnd;
  static HWND hTrackWnd;
  static HWND udWnd;
  int low=0, high=10;

  switch(message) {
    case WM_INITDIALOG:
      hEboxWnd = GetDlgItem(hdwnd, ID_EB1);
```

```
                udWnd = CreateUpDownControl(
                        WS_CHILD | WS_BORDER | WS_VISIBLE |
                        UDS_SETBUDDYINT | UDS_ALIGNRIGHT,
                        10, 10, 50, 50,
                        hdwnd,
                        ID_UPDOWN,
                        hInst,
                        hEboxWnd,
                        high, low, high/2);

            /* Create a trackbar */
            hTrackWnd = CreateWindow(TRACKBAR_CLASS,
                        "Trackbar", /* not used in this example */
                        WS_CHILD | WS_VISIBLE | WS_TABSTOP |
                        TBS_AUTOTICKS | WS_BORDER,
                        0, 70,
                        200, 30,
                        hdwnd,
                        NULL,
                        hInst,
                        NULL
            );
            SendMessage(hTrackWnd, TBM_SETRANGE,
                        (WPARAM) 1, (LPARAM) MAKELONG(low, high));

            SendMessage(hTrackWnd, TBM_SETPOS,
                        (WPARAM) 1, (LPARAM) high/2);
            return 1;
        case WM_VSCROLL: /* process up-down control */
            if(udWnd==(HWND)lParam) {
                trackpos = GetDlgItemInt(hdwnd, ID_EB1, NULL, 1);
                SendMessage(hTrackWnd, TBM_SETPOS,
                            (WPARAM) 1, (LPARAM) trackpos);
            }
            return 1;
        case WM_HSCROLL: /* trackbar was activated */
            if(hTrackWnd != (HWND)lParam) break; /* not trackbar */

            switch(LOWORD(wParam)) {
                case TB_TOP:
                case TB_BOTTOM:         /* For this example */
                case TB_LINEDOWN:       /* all messages will be */
                case TB_LINEUP:         /* processed in the same */
                case TB_THUMBPOSITION:  /* way. */
                case TB_THUMBTRACK:
                case TB_PAGEUP:
                case TB_PAGEDOWN:
                    trackpos = SendMessage(hTrackWnd, TBM_GETPOS,
```

```
                         0, 0);
            SetDlgItemInt(hdwnd, ID_EB1, trackpos, 1);
            return 1;
        }
        break;
      case WM_COMMAND:
        switch(LOWORD(wParam)) {
          case IDCANCEL:
            EndDialog(hdwnd, 0);
            return 1;
        }
    }
    return 0;
}
```

This program uses the following resource file:

```
#include <windows.h>
#include "track.h"

MYMENU MENU
{
  MENUITEM "&Dialog", IDM_DIALOG
  MENUITEM "&Help", IDM_HELP
}

MYMENU ACCELERATORS
{
  VK_F2, IDM_DIALOG, VIRTKEY
  VK_F1, IDM_HELP, VIRTKEY
}

MYDB DIALOG 18, 18, 142, 92
CAPTION "Demonstrate a Track Control"
STYLE DS_MODALFRAME | WS_POPUP | WS_CAPTION | WS_SYSMENU
{
  PUSHBUTTON "Cancel", IDCANCEL, 52, 65, 37, 14,
            WS_CHILD | WS_VISIBLE | WS_TABSTOP
  EDITTEXT ID_EB1, 10, 10, 30, 12, ES_LEFT | WS_CHILD |
          WS_VISIBLE | WS_BORDER
}
```

The header file **track.h** is shown here. (It is the same as **updown.h,** which was used by the previous program.)

```
#define IDM_DIALOG   100
#define IDM_HELP     101
```

```
#define ID_UPDOWN    102
#define ID_EB1       103
```

Inside the program, both a trackbar and a spin control are created when the dialog box is first displayed. After the trackbar is created, its range is set to 0 through 10. Its initial position is set at 5. (The same range and initial value are also given to the spin control.) Notice that the range is set using the macro **MAKELONG( )**. This macro assembles two integers into a long integer. It has this prototype:

DWORD MAKELONG(WORD *low*, WORD *high*);

The low-order part of the double word value is specified in *low*, and the high-order portion is specified in *high*. **MAKELONG( )** is quite useful when you need to encode two word values into a long integer.

Whenever the spin control is changed, a **WM_VSCROLL** message is received and the position of the trackbar is adjusted accordingly, as shown here:

```
case WM_VSCROLL: /* process up-down control */
  if(udWnd==(HWND)lParam) {
    trackpos = GetDlgItemInt(hdwnd, ID_EB1, NULL, 1);
    SendMessage(hTrackWnd, TBM_SETPOS,
                (WPARAM) 1, (LPARAM) trackpos);
  }
  return 1;
```

This **case** obtains the new value from the edit box by calling **GetDlgItemInt( )**. This function is similar to **GetDlgItemText( )**, which you learned about in Chapter 5. However, instead of obtaining the text from an edit box, it returns the integer equivalent of the contents of the box. For example, if the box contains the string 102, then **GetDlgItemInt( )** will return the value 102. For obvious reasons, this function only applies to edit boxes that contain numeric values. The prototype for **GetDlgItemInt( )** is shown here:

UINT GetDlgItemInt(HWND *hDialog*, int *ID*, BOOL **error*, BOOL *signed*);

The handle of the dialog box that contains the edit control is passed in *hDialog*. The ID of the dialog box is passed in *ID*. If the edit box does not contain a valid numeric string, zero is returned. However, zero is also a valid value. For this reason, the success or failure of the function is returned in the variable pointed to by *error*. After the call, the variable pointed to by *error* will be non-zero if the return value is valid. It will be zero if an error occurred. If you don't care about errors, you can use NULL for this parameter. If *signed* is a non-zero value, then a signed value will be returned by **GetDlgItemInt( )**. Otherwise, an unsigned value is returned.

After the setting in the edit box has been obtained, it is passed to the trackbar using the **SendMessage( )** function. In this way, if you change the value of the spin control, the trackbar will automatically be moved to reflect the new value.

Whenever the trackbar is moved, a **WM_HSCROLL** message is received and processed by the following code:

```
case WM_HSCROLL: /* trackbar was activated */
  if(hTrackWnd != (HWND)lParam) break; /* not trackbar */

  switch(LOWORD(wParam)) {
    case TB_TOP:
    case TB_BOTTOM:            /* For this example */
    case TB_LINEDOWN:          /* all messages will be */
    case TB_LINEUP:            /* processed in the same */
    case TB_THUMBPOSITION:     /* way. */
    case TB_THUMBTRACK:
    case TB_PAGEUP:
    case TB_PAGEDOWN:
      trackpos = SendMessage(hTrackWnd, TBM_GETPOS,
                     0, 0);
      SetDlgItemInt(hdwnd, ID_EB1, trackpos, 1);
      return 1;
  }
  break;
```

When the user moves the slider within the trackbar, the trackbar's position is automatically updated; your program does not have to do this itself. After the trackbar has been moved, the program obtains its new value and then uses this value to update the spin control. The value within the spin control's edit box is set using **SetDlgItemInt( )**. This function is essentially the reverse of **GetDlgItemInt( )**, just discussed. It has the following prototype:

BOOL SetDlgItemInt(HWND *hDialog*, int *ID*, UINT *value*, BOOL *signed*);

The handle of the dialog box that contains the edit control is passed in *hDialog*. The ID of the dialog box is passed in *ID*. The value to put into the edit box is passed in *value*. If *signed* is a non-zero value, then negative values are allowed. Otherwise, an unsigned value is assumed. The function returns non-zero if successful and zero on failure.

In this example, the trackbar may be moved using either the mouse or the keyboard. In fact, the reason that so many **TB_** messages are included is to support the keyboard interface. You might want to try taking some of these messages out and observing the results.

The linkage of the trackbar with the spin control within this program is purely arbitrary and for the sake of illustration. Trackbars can be used entirely on their own.

Using a Progress Bar

11

One of the simpler of the new common controls is the *progress bar*. You have probably seen progress bars in action. They are small windows in which the degree of completion of a long task is depicted. For example, progress bars are commonly displayed by installation programs, file transfer programs, and during sorts.

Progress bars are created using either **CreateWindow( )** or **CreateWindowEx( )** by specifying the **PROGRESS_CLASS** window class.

Sending Progress Bar Messages

Your program sends a progress bar a message using the standard **SendMessage( )** function. (Progress bars do not generate messages.) Generally, you will send messages to set a progress bar's range and to increment its progress. Table 11-6 lists some common progress bar messages.

By default, a progress bar has the range 0 through 100. However, you can set it to any value from 0 through 65,535. Typically, you will advance the bar by sending it a **PBM_STEPIT** message. This causes the bar's current position to advance by a predetermined increment called a *step*. By default, the step increment is 10, but it can be any value you like. As you increment the bar's position, more of the bar is filled. Since a progress bar is used to display the degree of completion of a long task, the fully filled bar should represent 100 percent completion.

A Simple Progress Bar Program

The following short program illustrates how to use a progress bar. It creates a dialog box that contains a progress bar and a push button named Progress. The progress bar has a range of 0 to 50 and a step increment of 5. Each time you press the Progress push button, the progress bar is incremented another step. When the bar is filled, the dialog box automatically removes itself.

Message	Meaning
PBM_SETPOS	Sets the progress bar's position. The old position is returned. *wParam* contains the new position. *lParam* is 0.
PBM_SETRANGE	Sets the progress bar's range. The old range is returned with the maximum in the high-order word and the minimum in the low-order word. *wParam* is 0. *lParam* contains the range. The maximum value is in the high-order word. The minimum value is in the low-order word.
PBM_SETSTEP	Sets the increment (or step) value. The old increment is returned. *wParam* contains the new increment. *lParam* is 0.
PBM_STEPIT	Advances the bar's progress by the step value. *wParam* is 0. *lParam* is 0.

Common
Progress Bar
Messages
Table 11-6.

Sample output is shown in Figure 11-4.

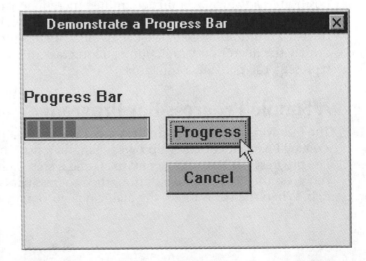

Sample output
from the
progress bar
program
Figure 11-4.

```
/* Demonstrate a progress bar. */

#include <windows.h>
#include <commctrl.h>
#include "prog.h"

#define MAX 50

LRESULT CALLBACK WindowFunc(HWND, UINT, WPARAM, LPARAM);
BOOL CALLBACK DialogFunc(HWND, UINT, WPARAM, LPARAM);

char szWinName[] = "MyWin"; /* name of window class */

HINSTANCE hInst;

int WINAPI WinMain(HINSTANCE hThisInst, HINSTANCE hPrevInst,
                   LPSTR lpszArgs, int nWinMode)
{
  HWND hwnd;
  MSG msg;
  WNDCLASS wcl;
  HANDLE hAccel;

  /* Define a window class. */
  wcl.hInstance = hThisInst; /* handle to this instance */
  wcl.lpszClassName = szWinName; /* window class name */
  wcl.lpfnWndProc = WindowFunc; /* window function */
  wcl.style = 0; /* default style */

  wcl.hIcon = LoadIcon(NULL, IDI_APPLICATION);
  wcl.hCursor = LoadCursor(NULL, IDC_ARROW);

  /* specify name of menu resource */
  wcl.lpszMenuName = "MYMENU"; /* main menu */

  wcl.cbClsExtra = 0; /* no extra */
  wcl.cbWndExtra = 0; /* information needed */

  /* Make the window white. */
  wcl.hbrBackground = GetStockObject(WHITE_BRUSH);

  /* Register the window class. */
  if(!RegisterClass(&wcl)) return 0;

  /* Now that a window class has been registered, a window
     can be created. */
  hwnd = CreateWindow(
    szWinName, /* name of window class */
```

```
       "Using a Progess Bar", /* title */
       WS_OVERLAPPEDWINDOW, /* window style - normal */
       CW_USEDEFAULT, /* X coordinate - let Windows decide */
       CW_USEDEFAULT, /* Y coordinate - let Windows decide */
       CW_USEDEFAULT, /* width - let Windows decide */
       CW_USEDEFAULT, /* height - let Windows decide */
       HWND_DESKTOP, /* no parent window */
       NULL, /* no menu */
       hThisInst, /* handle of this instance of the program */
       NULL /* no additional arguments */
  );

  hInst = hThisInst; /* save the current instance handle */

  /* load accelerators */
  hAccel = LoadAccelerators(hThisInst, "MYMENU");

  InitCommonControls();

  /* Display the window. */
  ShowWindow(hwnd, nWinMode);
  UpdateWindow(hwnd);

  /* Create the message loop. */
  while(GetMessage(&msg, NULL, 0, 0))
  {
    if(!TranslateAccelerator(hwnd, hAccel, &msg)) {
      TranslateMessage(&msg); /* allow use of keyboard */
      DispatchMessage(&msg); /* return control to Windows */
    }
  }
  return msg.wParam;
}

/* This function is called by Windows 95 and is passed
   messages from the message queue.
*/
LRESULT CALLBACK WindowFunc(HWND hwnd, UINT message,
                            WPARAM wParam, LPARAM lParam)
{
  switch(message) {
    case WM_COMMAND:
      switch(LOWORD(wParam)) {
        case IDM_DIALOG:
          DialogBox(hInst, "MYDB", hwnd, DialogFunc);
          break;
        case IDM_HELP:
          MessageBox(hwnd, "Help", "Help", MB_OK);
```

```
          break;
      }
      break;
    case WM_DESTROY: /* terminate the program */
      PostQuitMessage(0);
      break;
    default:
      /* Let Windows 95 process any messages not specified in
         the preceding switch statement. */
      return DefWindowProc(hwnd, message, wParam, lParam);
  }
  return 0;
}

/* A simple dialog function. */
BOOL CALLBACK DialogFunc(HWND hdwnd, UINT message,
                         WPARAM wParam, LPARAM lParam)
{
  static HWND hProgWnd;
  static int pos = 0;

  switch(message) {
    case WM_INITDIALOG:
      pos = 0;
      hProgWnd = CreateWindowEx(0, /* no extended style */
                    PROGRESS_CLASS,
                    "Progress Bar", /* not used in this example */
                    WS_CHILD | WS_VISIBLE | WS_BORDER,
                    0, 70,
                    110, 20,
                    hdwnd,
                    NULL,
                    hInst,
                    NULL);

      /* set range and increment */
      SendMessage(hProgWnd, PBM_SETRANGE, 0,
                  (LPARAM) MAKELONG(0, 50));
      SendMessage(hProgWnd, PBM_SETSTEP, (WPARAM) 5, 0);
      return 1;
    case WM_COMMAND:
      switch(LOWORD(wParam)) {
        case IDCANCEL:
          EndDialog(hdwnd, 0);
          return 1;
        case ID_PROG:
          SendMessage(hProgWnd, PBM_STEPIT, 0, 0);
          pos += 5; /* step unit is 5 */
```

```
            if(pos==50) EndDialog(hdwnd, 0);
            return 1;
        }
    }
    return 0;
}
```

The program requires the following resource file:

```
#include <windows.h>
#include "prog.h"

MYMENU MENU
{
  MENUITEM "&Dialog", IDM_DIALOG
  MENUITEM "&Help", IDM_HELP
}

MYMENU ACCELERATORS
{
  VK_F2, IDM_DIALOG, VIRTKEY
  VK_F1, IDM_HELP, VIRTKEY
}

MYDB DIALOG 18, 18, 142, 92
CAPTION "Demonstrate a Progress Bar"
STYLE DS_MODALFRAME | WS_POPUP | WS_CAPTION | WS_SYSMENU
{
  DEFPUSHBUTTON "Progress", ID_PROG, 62, 35, 37, 14,
            WS_CHILD | WS_VISIBLE | WS_TABSTOP
  PUSHBUTTON "Cancel", IDCANCEL, 62, 55, 37, 14,
            WS_CHILD | WS_VISIBLE | WS_TABSTOP
  LTEXT "Progress Bar",
      ID_STATIC, 0, 22, 100, 10
}
```

The header file **prog.h** is shown here.

```
#define IDM_DIALOG  100
#define IDM_HELP    101
#define ID_PROG     102
#define ID_STATIC   103
```

When adding a progress bar, remember it exists to reassure the user that the program is still proceeding normally. Therefore, you will want to increment the bar frequently. Remember, the user will be relying upon its progress as feedback that the program is still running. If you change it too slowly, a nervous user may reset the computer, thinking that the program has crashed!

The next chapter continues to explore the common controls by examining the status bar, the tab control, and the tree view control.

11

Chapter 12

A Last Look at Common Controls

This chapter takes a final look at the Windows 95 common controls. In this chapter we will examine the status window, the tab control, and the tree view control. Remember that Windows 95 includes several additional common controls that you will want to explore on your own.

None of the common controls are supported by Windows 3.1.

Using a Status Window

Frequently an application will need to inform the user about the status of certain program variables, attributes, or parameters. In the past, each program had to define its own way of accomplishing this. However, Windows 95 includes a standard control for this purpose, called the *status window* or *status bar*. A status window is a bar that typically is displayed along the bottom of a window. It is used to display information related to the program.

As you will see, status bars are easy to implement. If you make a status bar a standard feature of each application that you write, you will always provide a consistent interface for status information.

Creating a Status Window

To create a status bar, you can use **CreateStatusWindow( )**. Remember, however, that status bars *are* windows. Thus, you can also create a status bar using either **CreateWindow( )** or **CreateWindowEx( )**, specifying the window class **STATUSCLASSNAME**. To illustrate this fact, the status bar example that follows will use **CreateWindow( )**. (Of course, your code can use either method.)

Typically, a status window will be a child window. It is also usually created using the **WS_VISIBLE** style, so that it is automatically displayed. For example, the following code creates a status window:

```
hStatusWnd = CreateWindow(STATUSCLASSNAME,
            "", /* not used */
            WS_CHILD | WS_VISIBLE,
            0, 0, 0, 0, /* size and position ignored */
```

```
                        hwnd, /* handle of parent */
                        NULL,
                        hInst, /* instance handle */
                        NULL
                    );
```

As the comments suggest, a status window ignores the size and position parameters passed to the **CreateWindow( )** function. This is because a status window is automatically sized to fit its parent window.

A status window is generally divided into parts. (However, a single-part status window is perfectly acceptable.) Once the parts have been established, you may write text to each part individually. Each part is referred to by its index. (The first part taking an index value of 0.)

12

Status Window Messages

A status window does not generate messages. However, your program will send the status bar messages using the standard **SendMessage( )** functions. Common status window messages are shown in Table 12-1.

Almost all applications will send **SB_SETPARTS**, which sets the number of parts to the status bar, and **SB_SETTEXT**, which writes text to a specific part of the status window. Here is the general procedure for creating a status bar:

1. Create the status window.
2. Set the number of parts by sending an **SB_SETPARTS** message.
3. Set the text in each part by sending an **SB_SETTEXT** message.

Once a status bar has been initialized, you can update each part as needed by sending an **SB_SETTEXT** message.

Using a Status Bar

The following program uses a status bar to report the settings within a dialog box. The dialog box contains a spin control and two check boxes. In the status bar, the status of each control is updated whenever the control is

Message	Meaning
SB_GETPARTS	Obtains the coordinate of the right edge of each part. Returns the number of parts in the status bar. *wParam* specifies the number of parts in the status window. *lParam* is a pointer to an integer array that will receive the coordinate of the right edge of each part. The array must be at least as large as the number of parts requested.
SB_GETTEXT	Obtains the text from the specified part. The low-order word of the return value contains the number of characters in the text. The high-order word contains a value that describes how the text is displayed. If it is 0, the text appears lower than the window. If it is **SBT_POPOUT**, the text appears higher than the window. If it is **SBT_NOBORDERS**, the text is displayed without a border. *wParam* specifies the index of the desired part. *lParam* points to a character array that will receive the text. (Make sure that this array is large enough to hold the text contained in the part.)
SB_SETPARTS	Specifies the number of parts in a status bar. It returns non-zero if successful and zero on failure. *wParam* specifies the number of parts. *lParam* is a pointer to an array of integers that contains the coordinate of the right edge of each part.
SB_SETTEXT	Outputs text to a part. It returns non-zero if successful and zero on failure. *wParam* specifies the index of the part that will receive the text and how the text will be displayed. Specifically, the index is ORed with a display value. If this value is zero, then the text appears lower than the window (this is the default). If the display value is **SBT_POPOUT**, the text appears higher than the window. If it is **SBT_NOBORDERS**, the text is displayed without a border. If the display value is **SBT_OWNERDRAW**, the parent window displays the text. *lParam* is a pointer to the string to be displayed.

Commonly
Used Status
Bar Messages
Table 12-1.

changed. The status bar program is shown here. Sample output from the program is shown in Figure 12-1.

```c
/* Demonstrate a status bar. */

#include <windows.h>
#include <commctrl.h>
#include <stdio.h>
#include "status.h"

#define NUMPARTS 3

LRESULT CALLBACK WindowFunc(HWND, UINT, WPARAM, LPARAM);
BOOL CALLBACK DialogFunc(HWND, UINT, WPARAM, LPARAM);
void InitStatus(HWND hwnd);

char szWinName[] = "MyWin"; /* name of window class */

HINSTANCE hInst;
HWND hwnd;
HWND hStatusWnd;

int parts[NUMPARTS];

int WINAPI WinMain(HINSTANCE hThisInst, HINSTANCE hPrevInst,
                   LPSTR lpszArgs, int nWinMode)
{
  MSG msg;
  WNDCLASS wcl;
  HANDLE hAccel;

  /* Define a window class. */
  wcl.hInstance = hThisInst; /* handle to this instance */
  wcl.lpszClassName = szWinName; /* window class name */
  wcl.lpfnWndProc = WindowFunc; /* window function */
  wcl.style = 0; /* default style */

  wcl.hIcon = LoadIcon(NULL, IDI_APPLICATION);
  wcl.hCursor = LoadCursor(NULL, IDC_ARROW);

  /* specify name of menu resource */
  wcl.lpszMenuName = "MYMENU"; /* main menu */

  wcl.cbClsExtra = 0; /* no extra */
  wcl.cbWndExtra = 0; /* information needed */

  /* Make the window white. */
  wcl.hbrBackground = GetStockObject(WHITE_BRUSH);
```

```
  /* Register the window class. */
  if(!RegisterClass(&wcl)) return 0;

/* Now that a window class has been registered, a window
    can be created. */
  hwnd = CreateWindow(
    szWinName, /* name of window class */
    "Using a Status Bar", /* title */
    WS_OVERLAPPEDWINDOW, /* window style - normal */
    CW_USEDEFAULT, /* X coordinate - let Windows decide */
    CW_USEDEFAULT, /* Y coordinate - let Windows decide */
    CW_USEDEFAULT, /* width - let Windows decide */
    CW_USEDEFAULT, /* height - let Windows decide */
    HWND_DESKTOP, /* no parent window */
    NULL, /* no menu */
    hThisInst, /* handle of this instance of the program */
    NULL /* no additional arguments */
  );

  InitCommonControls();

  hInst = hThisInst; /* save the current instance handle */

  /* load accelerators */
  hAccel = LoadAccelerators(hThisInst, "MYMENU");

  /* Display the window. */
  ShowWindow(hwnd, nWinMode);
  UpdateWindow(hwnd);

  /* Create the message loop. */
  while(GetMessage(&msg, NULL, 0, 0))
  {
    if(!TranslateAccelerator(hwnd, hAccel, &msg)) {
      TranslateMessage(&msg); /* allow use of keyboard */
      DispatchMessage(&msg); /* return control to Windows */
    }
  }
  return msg.wParam;
}


/* This function is called by Windows 95 and is passed
    messages from the message queue.
*/
LRESULT CALLBACK WindowFunc(HWND hwnd, UINT message,
                                WPARAM wParam, LPARAM lParam)
{
```

```
      switch(message) {
        case WM_COMMAND:
          switch(LOWORD(wParam)) {
            case IDM_DIALOG:
              DialogBox(hInst, "MYDB", hwnd, DialogFunc);
              break;
            case IDM_HELP:
              MessageBox(hwnd, "Help", "Help", MB_OK);
              break;
          }
          break;
        case WM_DESTROY: /* terminate the program */
          PostQuitMessage(0);
          break;
        default:
          /* Let Windows 95 process any messages not specified in
             the preceding switch statement. */
          return DefWindowProc(hwnd, message, wParam, lParam);
      }
      return 0;
}


/* A simple dialog function. */
BOOL CALLBACK DialogFunc(HWND hdwnd, UINT message,
                         WPARAM wParam, LPARAM lParam)
{
  static long udpos = 0;
  static char str[80];
  static HWND hEboxWnd;
  static HWND udWnd;
  static statusCB1, statusCB2;
  int low=0, high=20;

  switch(message) {
    case WM_INITDIALOG:
      InitStatus(hdwnd); /* initialize the status bar */

      hEboxWnd = GetDlgItem(hdwnd, ID_EB1);
      udWnd = CreateUpDownControl(
                  WS_CHILD | WS_BORDER | WS_VISIBLE |
                  UDS_SETBUDDYINT | UDS_ALIGNRIGHT,
                  10, 10, 50, 50,
                  hdwnd,
                  ID_UPDOWN,
                  hInst,
                  hEboxWnd,
                  high, low, high/2);
      return 1;
```

```
        case WM_VSCROLL: /* process up-down control */
          if(udWnd==(HWND)lParam) {
            udpos = GetDlgItemInt(hdwnd, ID_EB1, NULL, 1);
            sprintf(str, "Up-down: %d", udpos);
            SendMessage(hStatusWnd, SB_SETTEXT,
                        (WPARAM) 0, (LPARAM) str);
          }
          return 1;
        case WM_COMMAND:
          switch(LOWORD(wParam)) {
            case ID_CB1: /* process checkbox 1 */
              statusCB1 = SendDlgItemMessage(hdwnd, ID_CB1,
                        BM_GETCHECK, 0, 0);
              if(statusCB1) sprintf(str, "Option 1 ON");
              else sprintf(str, "Option 1 OFF");
              SendMessage(hStatusWnd, SB_SETTEXT,
                        (WPARAM) 1, (LPARAM) str);
              return 1;
            case ID_CB2: /* process checkbox 2 */
              statusCB2 = SendDlgItemMessage(hdwnd, ID_CB2,
                        BM_GETCHECK, 0, 0);
              if(statusCB2) sprintf(str, "Option 2 ON");
              else sprintf(str, "Option 2 OFF");
              SendMessage(hStatusWnd, SB_SETTEXT,
                        (WPARAM) 2, (LPARAM) str);
              return 1;
            case ID_RESET: /* reset options */
              SendMessage(udWnd, UDM_SETPOS, 0, (LPARAM) high /2);
              SendMessage(hStatusWnd, SB_SETTEXT, (WPARAM) 0,
                  (LPARAM) "Up-down: 10");
              SendDlgItemMessage(hdwnd, ID_CB1,
                        BM_SETCHECK, 0, 0);
              SendDlgItemMessage(hdwnd, ID_CB2,
                        BM_SETCHECK, 0, 0);
              SendMessage(hStatusWnd, SB_SETTEXT, (WPARAM) 1,
                  (LPARAM) "Option 1: OFF");
              SendMessage(hStatusWnd, SB_SETTEXT, (WPARAM) 2,
                  (LPARAM) "Option 2: OFF");
              return 1;
            case IDCANCEL:
            case IDOK:
              EndDialog(hdwnd, 0);
              return 1;
          }
        }
      return 0;
    }
```

```
/* Initialize the status bar. */
void InitStatus(HWND hwnd)
{
  RECT WinDim;
  int i;

  GetClientRect(hwnd, &WinDim);

  for(i=1; i<=NUMPARTS; i++)
    parts[i-1] = WinDim.right/NUMPARTS * i;

  /* Create a status bar */
  hStatusWnd = CreateWindow(STATUSCLASSNAME,
               "", /* not used in this example */
               WS_CHILD | WS_VISIBLE,
               0, 0, 0, 0,
               hwnd,
               NULL,
               hInst,
               NULL
        );

  SendMessage(hStatusWnd, SB_SETPARTS,
              (WPARAM) NUMPARTS, (LPARAM) parts);

  SendMessage(hStatusWnd, SB_SETTEXT, (WPARAM) 0,
              (LPARAM) "Up-down: 10");
  SendMessage(hStatusWnd, SB_SETTEXT, (WPARAM) 1,
              (LPARAM) "Option 1: OFF");
  SendMessage(hStatusWnd, SB_SETTEXT, (WPARAM) 2,
              (LPARAM) "Option 2: OFF");
}
```

This program requires the following resource file:

```
#include <windows.h>
#include "status.h"

MYMENU MENU
{
  MENUITEM "&Dialog", IDM_DIALOG
  MENUITEM "&Help", IDM_HELP
}


MYMENU ACCELERATORS
{
  VK_F2, IDM_DIALOG, VIRTKEY
```

```
   VK_F1, IDM_HELP, VIRTKEY
}

MYDB DIALOG 18, 18, 150, 92
CAPTION "Demonstrate a Status Bar"
STYLE DS_MODALFRAME | WS_POPUP | WS_CAPTION | WS_SYSMENU
{
  PUSHBUTTON "Reset", ID_RESET, 92, 34, 37, 14,
             WS_CHILD | WS_VISIBLE | WS_TABSTOP
  PUSHBUTTON "OK", IDOK, 92, 53, 37, 14,
             WS_CHILD | WS_VISIBLE | WS_TABSTOP
  EDITTEXT ID_EB1, 10, 10, 30, 12, ES_LEFT | WS_CHILD |
           WS_VISIBLE | WS_BORDER
  AUTOCHECKBOX "Option 1", ID_CB1, 10, 40, 48, 12
  AUTOCHECKBOX "Option 2", ID_CB2, 10, 60, 48, 12
}
```

The header file **status.h** is shown here:

```
#define IDM_DIALOG   100
#define IDM_HELP     101
#define ID_UPDOWN    102
#define ID_EB1       103
#define ID_CB1       104
#define ID_CB2       105
#define ID_RESET     106
```

Inside the program, the function **InitStatus( )** creates and initializes the status window. First, the status bar is divided into three equal parts. The

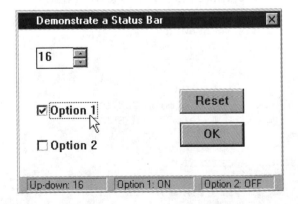

Sample output from the status bar program
Figure 12-1.

division of the status bar is aided by the **GetClientRect( )** API function. This function obtains the current size of the client area of the specified window. It has the following prototype:

BOOL GetClientRect(HWND *hwnd*, LPRECT *lpRect*);

Here, *hwnd* is the handle of the window in question and *lpRect* is a pointer to the **RECT** structure that receives the dimensions of the window's client area.

Since there are three parts to the status bar, the width of the dialog box (as obtained by **GetClientRect( )**) is divided into three parts, which become the end points for the status bar parts and are put into the **parts** array. Remember, the end point of each part—not the width of each part—must be passed to the status window. Once the parts have been set, the initial text in each part is displayed.

Within **DialogFunc( )**, the text within each part of the status bar is updated each time a control is changed. This is accomplished by sending an **SB_SETTEXT** message to the part associated with the control that has changed its state.

Here is one other point about status windows: If the parent window is resized, it will receive a **WM_SIZE** message. To allow the child status window to be resized at the same time, you must pass the **WM_SIZE** message along to the status window using the **SendMessage( )** function. For example, to allow the status window in the preceding example to be automatically resized when the size of its parent dialog box is changed, add the following case code to **DialogFunc( )**. (Of course, the dialog box must be created with the **WS_SIZEBOX** style also included.)

12

```
case WM_SIZE:
  SendMessage(hStatusWnd, WM_SIZE, wParam, lParam);
  break;
```

You might want to try adding this on your own. However, remember that this method will not cause the parts themselves to be resized. It is just that the bar will be lengthened to fill the window. To change the size of the parts, you need to send another **SB_SETPARTS** message, specifying the new part sizes.

Introducing Tab Controls

One of the more visually interesting common controls is the tab control. A tab control emulates the tabs on a set of file folders. Each time a tab is selected, its associated folder comes to the surface. While tab controls are easy to use, they are a bit complicated to program for. In this section, tab control basics are introduced. In the next section, additional tab control features are discussed.

Creating a Tab Control

To create a tab control, you use either **CreateWindow( )** or **CreateWindowEx( )**, specifying the window class **WC_TABCONTROL**. Typically, a tab control will be a child window. It is also usually created using the **WS_VISIBLE** style, so that it is automatically displayed. For example, the following creates a tab control:

```
hTabWnd = CreateWindow(
            WC_TABCONTROL,
            "",
            WS_VISIBLE ¦ WS_TABSTOP ¦ WS_CHILD,
            0, 0, 100, 100,
            hwnd, /* handle of parent */
            NULL,
            hInst, /* instance handle */
            NULL
          );
```

Once created, a tab control can be sent messages by your application or it can generate messages when it is accessed.

Tab items are defined by a **TC_ITEM** structure, which is shown here:

```
typedef struct _TC_ITEM
{
  UINT mask;
  UINT lpReserved1;
  UINT lpReserved2;
  LPSTR pszText;
  int cchTextMax;
  int iImage;
  LPARAM lParam;
} TC_ITEM;
```

In this structure, the value contained in **mask** determines whether the **pszText**, **iImage**, or **lParam** members of the structure contain valid data when the structure receives data from the tab control. **mask** can contain one or more of the following values:

Value in mask	Meaning
TCIF_ALL	**pszText**, **iImage**, and **lParam** contain data.
TCIF_IMAGE	**iImage** contains data.
TCIF_PARAM	**lParam** contains data.
TCIF_TEXT	**pszText** contains data.

When a tab is being set, **pszText** points to the string that will be displayed within the tab. When information about a tab is being obtained, **pszText** must point to an array that will receive the text. In this case, the value of **cchTextMax** specifies the size of the array pointed to by **pszText**.

If there is an image list associated with the tab control, then **iImage** will contain the index of the image associated with the specified tab. If there is no image list associated with the tab control, **iImage** should be –1.

lParam contains application-defined data.

Sending Tab Control Messages

You can send a tab control several different types of messages using the **SendMessage( )** function. Several commonly used tab control messages are shown in Table 12-2. However, since tab control messages are sent frequently, special macros were created that simplify sending them. Tab control macros corresponding to the messages in Table 12-2 are shown here. In all cases, *hTabWnd* is the handle of the tab control.

```
VOID TabCtrl_AdjustRect(HWND hTabWnd, BOOL operation, LPRECT lpRect);
BOOL TabCtrl_DeleteAllItems(HWND hTabWnd);
BOOL TabCtrl_DeleteItem(HWND hTabWnd, int index);
int TabCtrl_GetCurSel(HWND hTabWnd);
BOOL TabCtrl_GetItem(HWND hTabWnd, int index, LPTC_ITEM item);
int TabCtrl_GetItemCount(HWND hTabWnd);
int TabCtrl_InsertItem(HWND hTabWnd, int index, CONST LPTC_ITEM item);
int TabCtrl_SetCurSel(HWND hTabWnd, int index);
BOOL TabCtrl_SetItem(HWND hTabWnd, int index, LPTC_ITEM item);
```

12

In general, the macros are easier to use than the equivalent **SendMessage( )** call.

Message	Meaning
TCM_ADJUSTRECT	Translates between the dimensions of the tab control's display area and its window. *wParam* specifies the operation. If it is non-zero, then the window rectangle is obtained. If it is zero, then the display area is obtained. *lParam* points to a RECT structure that contains the coordinates of the region to be translated. On return, this structure will contain the translated coordinates.
TCM_DELETEALLITEMS	Deletes all tabs in the control. Returns non-zero if successful and zero on failure. *wParam* is 0. *lParam* is 0.
TCM_DELETEITEM	Deletes a specified tab. Returns non-zero if successful and zero on failure. *wParam* specifies the index of the tab to remove. *lParam* is 0.
TCM_GETCURSEL	Returns the index of the currently selected tab. It returns −1 if no tab is selected. *wParam* is 0. *lParam* is 0.
TCM_GETITEMCOUNT	Returns the number of tabs. *wParam* is 0. *lParam* is 0.

Commonly
Used Tab
Control
Messages
Table 12-2.

Message	Meaning
TCM_GETITEM	Obtains information about the specified tab. Returns non-zero if successful and zero on failure. *wParam* specifies the index of the tab. *lParam* is a pointer to a TC_ITEM structure that receives the information about the item.
TCM_INSERTITEM	Creates (i.e., inserts) a new tab. Returns non-zero if successful and zero on failure. *wParam* specifies the index of the tab. *lParam* is a pointer to a TC_ITEM structure that describes the tab.
TCM_SETCURSEL	Selects a tab. Returns the index of the previously selected tab. It returns –1 if no tab was previously selected. *wParam* specifies the index of the tab being selected. *lParam* is zero.
TCM_SETITEM	Sets information about the specified tab. Returns non-zero if successful and zero on failure. *wParam* specifies the index of the tab. *lParam* is a pointer to a TC_ITEM structure that contains the information about the item.

12

Commonly
Used Tab
Control
Messages
(*continued*)
Table 12-2.

When a tab control is created, it has no tabs. Therefore, your program will always send at least one **TCM_INSERTITEM** message to it. Although neither of the examples in this chapter requires its use, one message that your real-world applications will probably use is **TCM_ADJUSTRECT**. This message is used to obtain the dimensions of the display area of a tab control. Remember, when you create a tab control, its window contains the tabs themselves as well as the area in which you will display information or pop up a dialog box. The display area is the part of a tab control window that excludes the tabs. (That is, the display area is the part of the tab control window that you may use to display other items.) Since it is the display area that will contain the information associated with the tab, you will usually need to know its dimensions.

Tab Notification Messages

When a tab control is accessed by the user, a **WM_NOTIFY** message is generated. Tab controls can generate two selection-change notification codes: **TCN_SELCHANGE** and **TCN_SELCHANGING**. **TCN_SELCHANGING** is sent when a tab selection is about to change. **TCN_SELCHANGE** is sent after a new tab is selected.

When a **WM_NOTIFY** message is received, *lParam* will point to an **NMHDR** structure (discussed in Chapter 10). The notification code will be contained in the **code** field of the **NMHDR** structure. The handle of the tab control that generates the message is found in the **hwndFrom** field.

A Simple Tab Demonstration Program

The following short program demonstrates the tab control. It creates a tab control and then creates three tabs, labeled One, Two, and Three. Each time a new tab is selected, a message is displayed reporting this fact. Sample output is shown in Figure 12-2.

```
/* Demonstrate a tab control. */

#include <windows.h>
#include <commctrl.h>
#include <stdio.h>

LRESULT CALLBACK WindowFunc(HWND, UINT, WPARAM, LPARAM);

char szWinName[] = "MyWin"; /* name of window class */

HINSTANCE hInst;
HWND hwnd;
HWND hTabWnd;

int WINAPI WinMain(HINSTANCE hThisInst, HINSTANCE hPrevInst,
                   LPSTR lpszArgs, int nWinMode)
{
```

```
TC_ITEM tci;
MSG msg;
WNDCLASS wcl;
RECT WinDim;

/* Define a window class. */
wcl.hInstance = hThisInst; /* handle to this instance */
wcl.lpszClassName = szWinName; /* window class name */
wcl.lpfnWndProc = WindowFunc; /* window function */
wcl.style = 0; /* default style */

wcl.hIcon = LoadIcon(NULL, IDI_APPLICATION);
wcl.hCursor = LoadCursor(NULL, IDC_ARROW);
wcl.lpszMenuName = NULL; /* no menu */

wcl.cbClsExtra = 0; /* no extra */
wcl.cbWndExtra = 0; /* information needed */

/* Make the window white. */
wcl.hbrBackground = GetStockObject(WHITE_BRUSH);

/* Register the window class. */
if(!RegisterClass(&wcl)) return 0;

/* Now that a window class has been registered, a window
   can be created. */
hwnd = CreateWindow(
  szWinName, /* name of window class */
  "Using a Tab Control", /* title */
  WS_OVERLAPPEDWINDOW, /* window style - normal */
  CW_USEDEFAULT, /* X coordinate - let Windows decide */
  CW_USEDEFAULT, /* Y coordinate - let Windows decide */
  CW_USEDEFAULT, /* width - let Windows decide */
  CW_USEDEFAULT, /* height - let Windows decide */
  HWND_DESKTOP, /* no parent window */
  NULL, /* no menu */
  hThisInst, /* handle of this instance of the program */
  NULL /* no additional arguments */
);

InitCommonControls();

hInst = hThisInst; /* save the current instance handle */

GetClientRect(hwnd, &WinDim);  /* get size of parent window */

/* create a tab control */
hTabWnd = CreateWindow(
```

```
                    WC_TABCONTROL,
                    "",
                    WS_VISIBLE | WS_TABSTOP | WS_CHILD,
                    0, 0, WinDim.right, WinDim.bottom,
                    hwnd,
                    NULL,
                    hInst,
                    NULL
              );

  tci.mask = TCIF_TEXT;

  tci.iImage = -1;

  tci.pszText = "One";
  TabCtrl_InsertItem(hTabWnd, 0, &tci);

  tci.pszText = "Two";
  TabCtrl_InsertItem(hTabWnd, 1, &tci);

  tci.pszText = "Three";
  TabCtrl_InsertItem(hTabWnd, 2, &tci);

  /* Display the window. */
  ShowWindow(hwnd, nWinMode);
  UpdateWindow(hwnd);

  /* Create the message loop. */
  while(GetMessage(&msg, NULL, 0, 0))
  {
    TranslateMessage(&msg); /* allow use of keyboard */
    DispatchMessage(&msg); /* return control to Windows */
  }
  return msg.wParam;
}

/* This function is called by Windows 95 and is passed
   messages from the message queue.
*/
LRESULT CALLBACK WindowFunc(HWND hwnd, UINT message,
                            WPARAM wParam, LPARAM lParam)
{
  NMHDR *nmptr;
  int tabnumber;
  HDC hdc;
  char str[80];
```

```
switch(message) {
  case WM_NOTIFY: /* process a tab change */
    nmptr = (LPNMHDR) lParam;
    if(nmptr->code == TCN_SELCHANGE) {
      tabnumber = TabCtrl_GetCurSel((HWND)nmptr->hwndFrom);
      hdc = GetDC(hTabWnd);
      sprintf(str, "Changed to Tab %d", tabnumber+1);
      SetBkColor(hdc, RGB(200, 200, 200));
      TextOut(hdc, 40, 100, str, strlen(str));
      ReleaseDC(hTabWnd, hdc);
    }
    break;
  case WM_DESTROY: /* terminate the program */
    PostQuitMessage(0);
    break;
  default:
    /* Let Windows 95 process any messages not specified in
       the preceding switch statement. */
    return DefWindowProc(hwnd, message, wParam, lParam);
  }
  return 0;
}
```

12

In the program, just before the tab control is created, a call is made to
GetClientRect( ) to obtain the size of the main window. When the tab
control is created, it is sized to fill the entire client area of its parent window.
While this is arbitrary, it is not uncommon. After the tab control has been
created, three tabs are created.

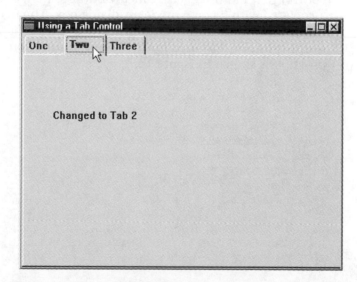

Sample output
from the first
tab control
program
Figure 12-2.

Inside **WindowFunc( )**, each time a **WM_NOTIFY** message contains the
TCN_SELCHANGE code, a message is displayed within the tab control
display area, indicating that the selection has changed to the specified tab.

Using Tab Controls

While tab controls are quite easy to create, they are a bit tricky to use,
because each tab typically has a dialog box associated with it. Each time a
new tab is selected, the currently displayed dialog box must be removed and
the new dialog box displayed. Also, in general, you will want to fit each
dialog box to the display area of the tab control. There are many other subtle
issues associated with tab controls and their associated dialog boxes that
simply are beyond the scope of this book. However, in this section you will
learn the general method of applying a tab control to your application. Once
you understand the basics, you will be able to add other features to your tab
controls on your own.

The fact that a new tab may be selected at any time implies that modeless
(rather than modal) dialog boxes must be used. As you should recall, a
modeless dialog box allows other parts of your application to be activated
without first deactivating the dialog box. (This differs from modal dialog
boxes, which must be closed by the user before other parts of the program
can be used.) Typically, when a new tab is selected, your application will
close the currently displayed dialog box and then activate the next one.
Because a dialog box may be closed at any time, your program must take
appropriate action (such as saving its settings) before displaying the new box.

To taste the flavor of using a tab control, the following program creates a tab
control that has three tabs, called Options, Pitch, and Page Size. Each tab is
associated with its own modeless dialog box. The first dialog box is the one
created for the status bar example earlier in this chapter. The other two are
simply placeholders used for the sake of illustration. Sample output from this
program is shown in Figure 12-3.

```
/* Demonstrate a tab control. */

#include <windows.h>
#include <commctrl.h>
#include <stdio.h>
#include "tab.h"

#define NUMPARTS 3

LRESULT CALLBACK WindowFunc(HWND, UINT, WPARAM, LPARAM);
BOOL CALLBACK DialogFunc1(HWND, UINT, WPARAM, LPARAM);
BOOL CALLBACK DialogFunc2(HWND, UINT, WPARAM, LPARAM);
```

```
BOOL CALLBACK DialogFunc3(HWND, UINT, WPARAM, LPARAM);
void InitStatus(HWND hwnd);

char szWinName[] = "MyWin"; /* name of window class */

HINSTANCE hInst;
HWND hwnd;
HWND hStatusWnd;
HWND hTabWnd;

int parts[NUMPARTS];

HWND hDlg = (HWND) NULL;

int WINAPI WinMain(HINSTANCE hThisInst, HINSTANCE hPrevInst,
                   LPSTR lpszArgs, int nWinMode)
{
  TC_ITEM tci;
  MSG msg;
  WNDCLASS wcl;

  /* Define a window class. */
  wcl.hInstance = hThisInst; /* handle to this instance */
  wcl.lpszClassName = szWinName; /* window class name */
  wcl.lpfnWndProc = WindowFunc; /* window function */
  wcl.style = 0; /* default style */

  wcl.hIcon = LoadIcon(NULL, IDI_APPLICATION);
  wcl.hCursor = LoadCursor(NULL, IDC_ARROW);
  wcl.lpszMenuName = NULL; /* no menu */

  wcl.cbClsExtra = 0; /* no extra */
  wcl.cbWndExtra = 0; /* information needed */

  /* Make the window white. */
  wcl.hbrBackground = GetStockObject(WHITE_BRUSH);

  /* Register the window class. */
  if(!RegisterClass(&wcl)) return 0;

  /* Now that a window class has been registered, a window
     can be created. */
  hwnd = CreateWindow(
    szWinName, /* name of window class */
    "Using a Tab Control", /* title */
    WS_OVERLAPPEDWINDOW, /* window style - normal */
    CW_USEDEFAULT, /* X coordinate - let Windows decide */
    CW_USEDEFAULT, /* Y coordinate - let Windows decide */
```

```
       CW_USEDEFAULT, /* width - let Windows decide */
       CW_USEDEFAULT, /* height - let Windows decide */
       HWND_DESKTOP, /* no parent window */
       NULL, /* no menu */
       hThisInst, /* handle of this instance of the program */
       NULL /* no additional arguments */
   );

   InitCommonControls();

   hInst = hThisInst; /* save the current instance handle */

   hTabWnd = CreateWindow(
             WC_TABCONTROL,
             "",
             WS_VISIBLE | WS_TABSTOP | WS_CHILD,
             20, 20, 325, 250,
             hwnd,
             NULL,
             hInst,
             NULL
           );

   tci.mask = TCIF_TEXT;

   tci.iImage = -1;

   tci.pszText = "Options";
   TabCtrl_InsertItem(hTabWnd, 0, &tci);

   tci.pszText = "Pitch";
   TabCtrl_InsertItem(hTabWnd, 1, &tci);

   tci.pszText = "Page Size";
   TabCtrl_InsertItem(hTabWnd, 2, &tci);

   hDlg = CreateDialog(hInst, "MYDB1", hTabWnd, DialogFunc1);

   /* Display the window. */
   ShowWindow(hwnd, nWinMode);
   UpdateWindow(hwnd);

   /* Create the message loop. */
   while(GetMessage(&msg, NULL, 0, 0))
   {
     if(!IsDialogMessage(hDlg, &msg)) {
       TranslateMessage(&msg); /* allow use of keyboard */
```

12

```
          DispatchMessage(&msg); /* return control to Windows */
      }
    }
  return msg.wParam;
}

/* This function is called by Windows 95 and is passed
   messages from the message queue.
*/
LRESULT CALLBACK WindowFunc(HWND hwnd, UINT message,
                              WPARAM wParam, LPARAM lParam)
{
  NMHDR *nmptr;
  int tabnumber = 0;

  switch(message) {
    case WM_NOTIFY:
      nmptr = (LPNMHDR) lParam;
      if(nmptr->code == TCN_SELCHANGE) {
        if(hDlg) DestroyWindow(hDlg);
        tabnumber = TabCtrl_GetCurSel((HWND)nmptr->hwndFrom);
        switch(tabnumber) {
          case 0:
            hDlg = CreateDialog(hInst, "MYDB1",
                         hTabWnd, DialogFunc1);
            break;
          case 1:
            hDlg = CreateDialog(hInst, "MYDB2",
                         hTabWnd, DialogFunc2);
            break;
          case 2:
            hDlg = CreateDialog(hInst, "MYDB3",
                         hTabWnd, DialogFunc3);
            break;
        }
      }
      break;
    case WM_DESTROY: /* terminate the program */
      if(hDlg) DestroyWindow(hDlg);
      PostQuitMessage(0);
      break;
    default:
      /* Let Windows 95 process any messages not specified in
         the preceding switch statement. */
      return DefWindowProc(hwnd, message, wParam, lParam);
  }
  return 0;
}
```

```
/* First dialog function. */
BOOL CALLBACK DialogFunc1(HWND hdwnd, UINT message,
                          WPARAM wParam, LPARAM lParam)
{
  static long udpos = 0;
  static char str[80];
  static HWND hEboxWnd;
  static HWND udWnd;
  static statusCB1, statusCB2;
  int low=0, high=20;

  switch(message) {
    case WM_INITDIALOG:
      InitStatus(hdwnd);

      hEboxWnd = GetDlgItem(hdwnd, ID_EB1);
      udWnd = CreateUpDownControl(
                  WS_CHILD | WS_BORDER | WS_VISIBLE |
                  UDS_SETBUDDYINT | UDS_ALIGNRIGHT,
                  10, 10, 50, 50,
                  hdwnd,
                  ID_UPDOWN,
                  hInst,
                  hEboxWnd,
                  high, low, high/2);

      return 1;
    case WM_VSCROLL: /* process up/down control */
      if(udWnd==(HWND)lParam) {
        udpos = GetDlgItemInt(hdwnd, ID_EB1, NULL, 1);
        sprintf(str, "Up-down: %d", udpos);
        SendMessage(hStatusWnd, SB_SETTEXT,
                    (WPARAM) 0, (LPARAM) str);
      }
      return 1;
    case WM_COMMAND:
      switch(LOWORD(wParam)) {
        case ID_CB1: /* process check box 1 */
          statusCB1 = SendDlgItemMessage(hdwnd, ID_CB1,
                      BM_GETCHECK, 0, 0);
          if(statusCB1) sprintf(str, "Option 1: ON");
          else sprintf(str, "Option 1: OFF");
          SendMessage(hStatusWnd, SB_SETTEXT,
                      (WPARAM) 1, (LPARAM) str);

          return 1;
        case ID_CB2: /* process check box 2 */
          statusCB2 = SendDlgItemMessage(hdwnd, ID_CB2,
```

```
                              BM_GETCHECK, 0, 0);
             if(statusCB2) sprintf(str, "Option 2: ON");
             else sprintf(str, "Option 2: OFF");
             SendMessage(hStatusWnd, SB_SETTEXT,
                          (WPARAM) 2, (LPARAM) str);
             return 1;
         case ID_RESET: /* reset options */
             SendMessage(udWnd, UDM_SETPOS, 0, (LPARAM) high /2);
             SendMessage(hStatusWnd, SB_SETTEXT, (WPARAM) 0,
                 (LPARAM) "Up-down: 10");
             SendDlgItemMessage(hdwnd, ID_CB1,
                          BM_SETCHECK, 0, 0);
             SendDlgItemMessage(hdwnd, ID_CB2,
                          BM_SETCHECK, 0, 0);
             SendMessage(hStatusWnd, SB_SETTEXT, (WPARAM) 1,
                 (LPARAM) "Option 1: OFF");
             SendMessage(hStatusWnd, SB_SETTEXT, (WPARAM) 2,
                 (LPARAM) "Option 2: OFF");
             return 1;
         case IDCANCEL:
         case IDOK:
             PostQuitMessage(0);
             return 1;
       }
   }
   return 0;
}


/* Second dialog function. This is just a placeholder. */
BOOL CALLBACK DialogFunc2(HWND hdwnd, UINT message,
                            WPARAM wParam, LPARAM lParam)
{
   switch(message) {
     case WM_COMMAND:
       switch(LOWORD(wParam)) {
         case IDOK:
           PostQuitMessage(0);
           return 1;
       }
   }
   return 0;
}


/* Third dialog function. This is just a placeholder. */
BOOL CALLBACK DialogFunc3(HWND hdwnd, UINT message,
                            WPARAM wParam, LPARAM lParam)
{
   switch(message) {
```

12

```
   case WM_COMMAND:
     switch(LOWORD(wParam)) {
       case IDOK:
         PostQuitMessage(0);
         return 1;
     }
 }
 return 0;
}

/* Initialize the status bar. */
void InitStatus(HWND hwnd)
{
  RECT WinDim;
  int I;

  GetClientRect(hwnd, &WinDim);

  for(i=1; i<=NUMPARTS; i++)
    parts[i-1] = WinDim.right/NUMPARTS * i;

  /* Create a status bar */
  hStatusWnd = CreateWindow(STATUSCLASSNAME,
              "", /* not used in this example */
              WS_CHILD | WS_VISIBLE,
              0, 0, 0, 0,
              hwnd,
              NULL,
              hInst,
              NULL
      );

  SendMessage(hStatusWnd, SB_SETPARTS,
              (WPARAM) NUMPARTS, (LPARAM) parts);

  SendMessage(hStatusWnd, SB_SETTEXT, (WPARAM) 0,
              (LPARAM) "Up-down: 10");
  SendMessage(hStatusWnd, SB_SETTEXT, (WPARAM) 1,
              (LPARAM) "Option 1: OFF");
  SendMessage(hStatusWnd, SB_SETTEXT, (WPARAM) 2,
              (LPARAM) "Option 2: OFF");
}
```

This program requires the following resource file:

```
#include <windows.h>
#include "tab.h"
```

```
MYDB1 DIALOG 2, 16, 158, 106
STYLE WS_CHILD | WS_VISIBLE | WS_BORDER
{
  PUSHBUTTON "Reset", ID_RESET, 92, 34, 37, 14,
             WS_CHILD | WS_VISIBLE | WS_TABSTOP
  PUSHBUTTON "OK", IDOK, 92, 53, 37, 14,
             WS_CHILD | WS_VISIBLE | WS_TABSTOP
  EDITTEXT ID_EB1, 10, 10, 30, 12, ES_LEFT | WS_CHILD |
           WS_VISIBLE | WS_BORDER
  AUTOCHECKBOX "Option 1", ID_CB1, 10, 40, 48, 12
  AUTOCHECKBOX "Option 2", ID_CB2, 10, 60, 48, 12
}

MYDB2 DIALOG 2, 16, 158, 106
STYLE WS_CHILD | WS_VISIBLE | WS_BORDER
{
  PUSHBUTTON "OK", IDOK, 92, 53, 37, 14,
             WS_CHILD | WS_VISIBLE | WS_TABSTOP
  LTEXT "Choose Pitch", 1, 10, 10, 60, 12
  AUTORADIOBUTTON "High Pitch", ID_RB1, 10, 40, 48, 12
  AUTORADIOBUTTON "Medium Pitch", ID_RB2, 10, 60, 52, 12
  AUTORADIOBUTTON "Low Pitch", ID_RB2, 10, 80, 48, 12
}

MYDB3 DIALOG  2, 16, 158, 106
STYLE WS_CHILD | WS_VISIBLE | WS_BORDER
{
  PUSHBUTTON "OK", IDOK, 92, 53, 37, 14,
             WS_CHILD | WS_VISIBLE | WS_TABSTOP
  LTEXT "Choose  Page Size", 2, 10, 10, 70, 12
  AUTORADIOBUTTON "Small", ID_RB3, 10, 40, 48, 12
  AUTORADIOBUTTON "Medium", ID_RB4, 10, 60, 48, 12
  AUTORADIOBUTTON "Large", ID_RB5, 10, 80, 48, 12
}
```

12

The header file **tab.h** is shown here:

```
#define IDM_DIALOG   100
#define IDM_HELP     101
#define ID_UPDOWN    102
#define ID_EB1       103
#define ID_CB1       104
#define ID_CB2       105
#define ID_RESET     106
#define ID_RB1       107
#define ID_RB2       108
#define ID_RB3       109
```

```
#define ID_RB4      110
#define ID_RB5      111
```

The interesting portion of this program occurs inside the **WM_NOTIFY** case
of **WindowFunc( )**, which is shown again here for your convenience.

```
case WM_NOTIFY:
  nmptr = (LPNMHDR) lParam;
  if(nmptr->code == TCN_SELCHANGE) {
    if(hDlg) DestroyWindow(hDlg);
    tabnumber = TabCtrl_GetCurSel((HWND)nmptr->hwndFrom);
    switch(tabnumber) {
      case 0:
        hDlg = CreateDialog(hInst, "MYDB1",
                    hTabWnd, DialogFunc1);
        break;
      case 1:
        hDlg = CreateDialog(hInst, "MYDB2",
                    hTabWnd, DialogFunc2);
        break;
      case 2:
        hDlg = CreateDialog(hInst, "MYDB3",
                    hTabWnd, DialogFunc3);
        break;
    }
  }
  break;
```

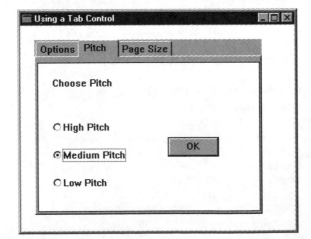

Sample output
from the
second tab
control
program
Figure 12-3.

Each time a new tab is selected, two events occur. First, the dialog box associated with the currently selected tab is removed by calling **DestroyWindow( )**. (As you should recall, to close a modeless dialog box, you must call **DestroyWindow( )** rather than **EndDialog( )**, which is used for modal dialog boxes.) Next, the current tab selection is obtained and its dialog box is created using **CreateDialog( )**. (Remember, **CreateDialog( )** creates modeless dialog boxes.)

Before moving on, you should experiment with this program. Try making changes to the dialog boxes or to the tab control. Also, tab controls may also have tooltips associated with them. As a challenge, you might want to try adding tooltips to the preceding example.

Tree View Controls

12

The last control that we will look at is the tree view control. Tree view controls are used to display information using a tree structure. For example, the file list used by Windows 95's Explorer is an example of a tree view control. Because trees imply a hierarchy, tree view controls should only be used to display hierarchical information. Tree view controls are very powerful and support a large number of different options. In fact, one could easily write a book about tree view controls alone! For this reason, this section only discusses tree view fundamentals. However, once you understand the basics, you will be able to easily incorporate the other tree view features on your own.

Create a Tree View Control

A tree view control is a window that is created using either **CreateWindow( )** or **CreateWindowEx( )** and that specifies the **WC_TREEVIEW** class. Typically, a tree view control will be a child window. It is also usually created using the **WS_VISIBLE** style, so that it is automatically displayed. **WS_TABSTOP** is also commonly included. Tree views also allow additional tree-related styles to be specified when they are created, including:

Style	Meaning
TVS_HASLINES	Lines link branches in the tree.
TVS_LINESATROOT	Lines link root to the branches.
TVS_HASBUTTONS	Expand/collapse buttons are included to the left of each branch.

Including the **TVS_HASLINES** and **TVS_LINESATROOT** styles causes lines to be drawn to each item in the tree. This gives the tree view control its tree-like look. Including **TVS_HASBUTTONS** causes the standard expand/collapse buttons to be added. These buttons contain a **+** if the branch may be expanded at least one more level and a **–** if the branch is fully expanded. You may also click on these buttons to expand or collapse a branch. Typically, all three of these styles are included when a tree view control is created. For example, the following code creates a standard tree view window:

```
hTreeWndCtrl = CreateWindow(
            WC_TREEVIEW,
            "",
            WS_VISIBLE | WS_TABSTOP | WS_CHILD |
            TVS_HASLINES | TVS_HASBUTTONS |
            TVS_LINESATROOT,
            0, 0, 100, 100,
            hwnd, /* handle of parent */
            NULL,
            hInst, /* instance handle */
            NULL
        );
```

When the tree view control is first created, it is empty. You must add each item in the tree, as described in the next section.

Sending Tree View Messages

Tree view controls respond to several messages. Several commonly used tree view control messages are shown in Table 12-3. Since tree view control messages are used so frequently, special macros were created for this purpose. Tree view control macros corresponding to the messages in Table 12-3 are shown here. In all cases, *hTreeWnd* is the handle of the tab control.

BOOL TreeView_DeleteItem(HWND *hTreeWnd*, HTREEITEM *hItem*)
BOOL TreeView_Expand(HWND *hTreeWnd*, HTREEITEM *hItem*, UINT *action*)
BOOL TreeView_GetItem(HWND *hTreeWnd*, LPTV_ITEM *hItem*)
HTREEVIEW TreeView_InsertItem(HWND *hTreeWnd*, LPTV_INSERTSTRUCT *item*)
BOOL TreeView_Select(HWND *hTreeWnd*, HTREEITEM *hItem*, UINT *action*)

The only messages used by the example in this chapter are **TVM_INSERTITEM** and **TVM_EXPAND**. However, your application will probably use others.

12

Message	Meaning
TVM_DELETEITEM	Deletes an item from the tree list. Returns non-zero if successful and zero on failure. *wParam* is 0. *lParam* specifies the handle of the item to delete.
TVM_EXPAND	Expands or collapses the tree list one level. Returns non-zero if successful and zero on failure. *wParam* specifies the operation. It must be either **TVE_COLLAPSE** (collapses tree), **TVE_COLLAPSERESET** (collapses tree and deletes child items), **TVE_EXPAND** (expands a tree), or **TVE_TOGGLE** (toggles state). *lParam* specifies the handle of the parent of the branch.
TVM_GETITEM	Obtains an item's attributes. Returns non-zero if successful and zero on failure. *wParam* is 0. *lParam* specifies a pointer to a **TV_ITEM** structure that receives information about the item.
TVM_INSERTITEM	Inserts an item into the tree. Returns a handle to the item being inserted or NULL on failure. *wParam* is 0. *lParam* specifies a pointer to a **TV_INSERTSTRUCT** that contains information about the item.
TVM_SELECTITEM	Selects a tree view item. Returns non-zero if successful and zero on failure. *wParam* specifies the specific action. If it is **TVGN_CARET**, the item is selected. If it is **TVGN_DROPHILITE**, the item is highlighted for a drag-and-drop operation. If it is **TVGN_FIRSTVISIBLE**, the tree view is scrolled so that the specified item is the first visible item. *lParam* specifies the handle of the item.

Commonly
Used Tree
View Control
Messages
Table 12-3.

When an item is inserted, the item's information is contained in a
TV_INSERTSTRUCT structure, which is shown here:

```
typedef struct _TV_INSERTSTRUCT {
  HTREEITEM hParent;
  HTREEITEM hInsertAfter;
  TV_ITEM item;
} TV_INSERTSTRUCT;
```

Here, **hParent** is the handle to the parent of the item. If the item has no
parent, then this field should contain **TVI_ROOT**. The value in
hInsertAfter determines how the new item will be inserted into the tree. If
it contains the handle of an item, the new item will be inserted after that
item. Otherwise, **hInsertAfter** can be one of the following values:

Value in hInsertAfter	Meaning
TVI_FIRST	Inserts new item at beginning of list
TVI_LAST	Inserts new item at end of list
TVI_SORT	Inserts new item in alphabetical order

The contents of **item** describe the item. This is a **TV_ITEM** structure, which
is shown here:

```
typedef struct _TV_ITEM {
  UINT mask;
  HTREEITEM hItem;
  UINT state;
  UINT stateMask;
  LPSTR pszText;
  int cchTextMax;
  int iImage;
  int iSelectedImage;
  int cChildren;
  LPARAM lParam;
} TV_ITEM;
```

Here, the values in **mask** determine which of the other members of
TV_ITEM contain valid data when this structure receives information from
the tree view control. The values that it may contain are shown here:

Value in mask	Meaning
TVIF_HANDLE	**hItem** contains data.
TVIF_STATE	**state** and **stateMask** contain data.
TVIF_TEXT	**pszText** and **cchTextMax** contain data.
TVIF_IMAGE	**iImage** contains data.
TVIF_SELECTEDIMAGE	**iSelectedImage** contains data.
TVIF_CHILDREN	**cChildren** contains data.
TVIF_LPARAM	**lParam** contains data.

The **state** member contains the state of the tree view control. Here are some common tree state values:

12

State	Meaning
TVIS_DISABLED	Item is disabled.
TVIS_DROPHILITED	Item is highlighted as the target of drag-and-drop operation.
TVIS_EXPANDED	Branch descending from item is fully expanded. (Applies to parent items only.)
TVIS_EXPANDEDONCE	Branch descending from item is expanded one level (or more). (Applies to parent items only.)
TVIS_FOCUSED	Item has input focus.
TVIS_SELECTED	Item is selected.

stateMask determines which tab state to set or obtain. It will also be one or more of the preceding values.

When an item is being inserted into the tree, **pszText** points to the string that will be displayed in the tree. When information about an item is being obtained, **pszText** must point to an array that will receive its text. In this case, the value of **cchTextMax** specifies the size of the array pointed to by **pszText**. Otherwise, **cchTextMax** is ignored.

If there is an image list associated with the tab control, then **iImage** will contain the index of the image associated with the specified tab. If there is no image list associated with the tab control, **iImage** should be –1. **iSelectedImage** contains the selected icon within the list, if such an image exists.

When information about an item is being obtained, **cChildren** will indicate the number of children associated with the specified item.

lParam contains application-defined data.

Tree View Notification Messages

When a tree view control is accessed, it generates a **WM_NOTIFY** message. There are several notification messages associated with tree view controls. Commonly used ones are shown here:

Notification Message	Meaning
TVN_DELETEITEM	An item has been deleted.
TVN_ITEMEXPANDING	A branch is about to expand or collapse.
TVN_ITEMEXPANDED	A branch has expanded or collapsed.
TVN_SELCHANGING	A new item is about to be selected.
TVN_SELCHANGED	A new item has been selected.

For these notification messages, when the **WM_NOTIFY** message is received, *lParam* will point to a **NM_TREEVIEW** structure. The **NM_TREEVIEW** structure is shown here:

```
typedef struct _NM_TREEVIEW {
  NMHDR hdr;
  UINT action;
  TV_ITEM itemOld;
  TV_ITEM itemNew;
  POINT ptDrag;
} NM_TREEVIEW;
```

The first field in **NM_TREEVIEW** is the standard **NMHDR** structure. The notification code will be contained in the **code** field of the **NMHDR** structure. The handle of the tree control that generates the message is found in the **hwndFrom** field of **NMHDR**.

action contains notification-specific information. The structures **itemOld** and **itemNew** contain information about the previously selected item (if applicable) and the newly selected item (if applicable). The location of the mouse at the time the message was generated is contained in **ptDrag**.

For **TVN_SELCHANGING** and **TVN_SELCHANGED**, **itemOld** describes the previously selected item and **itemNew** describes the newly selected item. For **TVN_ITEMEXPANDING** and **TVN_ITEMEXPANDED**, **itemNew** describes the item that is the parent of the branch that is expanding. For **TVN_DELETEITEM**, **itemOld** describes the item that was deleted.

A Tree View Demonstration Program

The following program demonstrates a tree view control. It creates a tree view control and then inserts five items into it. The program also includes a menu that can expand one branch, expand the entire tree, or collapse a branch. Each time a new tree view item is selected, the selection is displayed in the program's window. Sample output from the program is shown in Figure 12-4.

```c
/* Demonstrate a tree control. */

#include <windows.h>
#include <commctrl.h>
#include <string.h>
#include "tree.h"

#define NUM 5

LRESULT CALLBACK WindowFunc(HWND, UINT, WPARAM, LPARAM);
BOOL CALLBACK DialogFunc(HWND, UINT, WPARAM, LPARAM);
void InitTree(void);
void report(HDC hdc, char *s);

char szWinName[] = "MyWin"; /* name of window class */

HINSTANCE hInst;
HWND hwnd;
HWND hTreeWndCtrl;
HWND hTreeWnd[NUM];
HWND hTreeCurrent;

int WINAPI WinMain(HINSTANCE hThisInst, HINSTANCE hPrevInst,
                   LPSTR lpszArgs, int nWinMode)
{
  MSG msg;
  WNDCLASS wcl;
  HANDLE hAccel;
  RECT WinDim;

  /* Define a window class. */
  wcl.hInstance = hThisInst; /* handle to this instance */
  wcl.lpszClassName = szWinName; /* window class name */
  wcl.lpfnWndProc = WindowFunc; /* window function */
  wcl.style = 0; /* default style */

  wcl.hIcon = LoadIcon(NULL, IDI_APPLICATION);
```

12

```
wcl.hCursor = LoadCursor(NULL, IDC_ARROW);
wcl.lpszMenuName = "MYMENU"; /* no menu */

wcl.cbClsExtra = 0; /* no extra */
wcl.cbWndExtra = 0; /* information needed */

/* Make the window white. */
wcl.hbrBackground = GetStockObject(WHITE_BRUSH);

/* Register the window class. */
if(!RegisterClass(&wcl)) return 0;

/* Now that a window class has been registered, a window
   can be created. */
hwnd = CreateWindow(
  szWinName, /* name of window class */
  "Using a Tree Control", /* title */
  WS_OVERLAPPEDWINDOW, /* window style - normal */
  CW_USEDEFAULT, /* X coordinate - let Windows decide */
  CW_USEDEFAULT, /* Y coordinate - let Windows decide */
  CW_USEDEFAULT, /* width - let Windows decide */
  CW_USEDEFAULT, /* height - let Windows decide */
  HWND_DESKTOP, /* no parent window */
  NULL, /* no menu */
  hThisInst, /* handle of this instance of the program */
  NULL /* no additional arguments */
);

InitCommonControls();

hInst = hThisInst; /* save the current instance handle */

GetClientRect(hwnd, &WinDim);  /* get size of parent window */

/* create a tree view */
hTreeWndCtrl = CreateWindow(
                WC_TREEVIEW,
                "",
                WS_VISIBLE | WS_TABSTOP | WS_CHILD |
                TVS_HASLINES | TVS_HASBUTTONS |
                TVS_LINESATROOT,
                0, 0, 100, 100,
                hwnd,
                NULL,
                hInst,
                NULL
            );
```

```
      InitTree();

      /* load accelerators */
      hAccel = LoadAccelerators(hThisInst, "MYMENU");

      /* Display the window. */
      ShowWindow(hwnd, nWinMode);
      UpdateWindow(hwnd);

      /* Create the message loop. */
      while(GetMessage(&msg, NULL, 0, 0))
      {
        if(!TranslateAccelerator(hwnd, hAccel, &msg)) {
          TranslateMessage(&msg); /* allow use of keyboard */
          DispatchMessage(&msg); /* return control to Windows */
        }
      }
      return msg.wParam;
}


/* This function is called by Windows 95 and is passed
   messages from the message queue.
*/
LRESULT CALLBACK WindowFunc(HWND hwnd, UINT message,
                            WPARAM wParam, LPARAM lParam)
{
  HDC hdc;
  static char selection[80] = "";
  NMHDR *nmptr;
  PAINTSTRUCT paintstruct;
  int i;

  switch(message) {
    case WM_COMMAND:
      switch(LOWORD(wParam)) {
        case IDM_EXPAND:
          TreeView_Expand(hTreeWndCtrl, hTreeCurrent, TVE_EXPAND);
          break;
        case IDM_EXPANDALL:
          for(i=0; i<NUM; i++)
            TreeView_Expand(hTreeWndCtrl, hTreeWnd[i], TVE_EXPAND);
          break;
        case IDM_COLLAPSE:
          TreeView_Expand(hTreeWndCtrl, hTreeCurrent, TVE_COLLAPSE);
          break;
        case IDM_HELP:
          MessageBox(hwnd, "Help", "Help", MB_OK);
```

12

```
          break;
      }
      break;
  case WM_NOTIFY:
    nmptr = (LPNMHDR) lParam;
    if(nmptr->code == TVN_SELCHANGED) {
      InvalidateRect(hwnd, NULL, 1);
      if(((LPNM_TREEVIEW)nmptr)->itemNew.hItem == hTreeWnd[0])
        strcpy(selection, "One.");
      else if(((LPNM_TREEVIEW)nmptr)->itemNew.hItem == hTreeWnd[1])
        strcpy(selection, "Two.");
      if(((LPNM_TREEVIEW)nmptr)->itemNew.hItem == hTreeWnd[2])
        strcpy(selection, "Three.");
      if(((LPNM_TREEVIEW)nmptr)->itemNew.hItem == hTreeWnd[3])
        strcpy(selection, "Four.");
      if(((LPNM_TREEVIEW)nmptr)->itemNew.hItem == hTreeWnd[4])
        strcpy(selection, "Five.");

      hTreeCurrent = ((LPNM_TREEVIEW)nmptr)->itemNew.hItem;
    }
    break;
  case WM_PAINT:
    hdc = BeginPaint(hwnd, &paintstruct);
    report(hdc, selection);
    EndPaint(hwnd, &paintstruct);
    break;
  case WM_DESTROY: /* terminate the program */
    PostQuitMessage(0);
    break;
  default:
    /* Let Windows 95 process any messages not specified in
       the preceding switch statement. */
    return DefWindowProc(hwnd, message, wParam, lParam);
  }
  return 0;
}

/* Report Selection */
void report(HDC hdc, char *s)
{
  char str[80];

  if(*s) {
    strcpy(str, "Selection is ");
    strcat(str, s);
  }
  else strcpy(str, "No selection has been made.");
```

```
      TextOut(hdc, 0, 200, str, strlen(str));
  }

  /* Initialize the tree list. */
  void InitTree(void)
  {
    TV_INSERTSTRUCT tvs;
    TV_ITEM tvi;

    tvs.hInsertAfter = TVI_LAST; /* make tree in order given */
    tvi.mask = TVIF_TEXT;

    tvi.pszText = "One";
    tvs.hParent = TVI_ROOT;
    tvs.item = tvi;
    hTreeWnd[0] = TreeView_InsertItem(hTreeWndCtrl, &tvs);
    hTreeCurrent = hTreeWnd[0];

    tvi.pszText = "Two";
    tvs.hParent = hTreeWnd[0];
    tvs.item = tvi;
    hTreeWnd[1] = TreeView_InsertItem(hTreeWndCtrl, &tvs);

    tvi.pszText = "Three";
    tvs.item = tvi;
    tvs.hParent = hTreeWnd[1];
    hTreeWnd[2] = TreeView_InsertItem(hTreeWndCtrl, &tvs);

    tvi.pszText = "Four";
    tvs.item = tvi;
    tvs.hParent = hTreeWnd[2];
    hTreeWnd[3] = TreeView_InsertItem(hTreeWndCtrl, &tvs);

    tvi.pszText = "Five";
    tvs.item = tvi;
    tvs.hParent = hTreeWnd[2];
    hTreeWnd[4] = TreeView_InsertItem(hTreeWndCtrl, &tvs);
  }
```

12

The program requires the following resource file:

```
#include <windows.h>
#include "tree.h"

MYMENU MENU
{
  MENUITEM "&Expand One", IDM_EXPAND
  MENUITEM "Expand &All", IDM_EXPANDALL
```

```
MENUITEM "&Collapse", IDM_COLLAPSE
MENUITEM "&Help", IDM_HELP
}
```

The **tree.h** header file is shown here:

```
#define IDM_EXPAND     100
#define IDM_EXPANDALL  101
#define IDM_COLLAPSE   102
#define IDM_HELP       103
```

In the program, the function **InitTree( )** initializes the tree view control. Notice that the handle of each item is stored in the **hTreeWnd** array. These handles are used to identify items when they are selected in the tree list. **hTreeCurrent** identifies the currently selected item. This handle is used when the user expands or collapses a branch using the menu.

Inside **WindowFunc( )**, each time a new item is selected, a **WM_NOTIFY** message is received and processed. The value of **itemNew** is checked against the list of item handles stored in the **hTreeWnd** array. When the matching handle is found, the new selection is reported.

While this example illustrates the most important and fundamental aspects of tree view controls, it just scratches the surface of their power. For

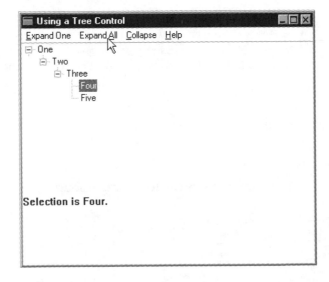

Sample output
from the tree
view program
Figure 12-4.

example, using a tree view, you can drag and drop an item from one tree to another. This and other features are things that you will want to explore on your own.

In the next chapter, we will examine a special subsystem within Windows 95 that supports the console-based interface.

12

Chapter 13

Working with Consoles

While Windows is an excellent operating system for most types of programs, it has had one traditional failing: it has been cumbersome to use for writing character mode programs. A *character mode* program is one that uses mainly the ASCII character set and assumes a character-based device, such as an 80-character by 25-line display system. That is, a character mode application is the type that is commonly written for DOS. Frankly, while Windows was optimized for graphics, menus, dialog boxes, and common controls, it was difficult to write character-based programs for. However, as you will see in this chapter, Windows 95 changes this.

In order to provide better support for character mode programs, Windows 95 provides several new API functions (through the Win32 library) that support the console-style interface. These API functions are collectively called *console functions*. By including support for consoles, Windows 95 makes it easier for a character mode program to coexist with Windows programs. For example, it is now possible to write character mode programs that:

♦ Respond to Windows-style mouse events

♦ Run in their own console session

♦ Have access to the (relevant) API functions

♦ Use pipes and I/O redirection

♦ Allow Windows-based control over keyboard activity, if desired

While graphical programs will always be the most popular type written for Windows 95, the support of consoles is the final brick in the wall that completes the Windows environment. Often you'll need a program that is short, requires little user interaction, and must be written quickly. For example, short file utility programs fall into this category. However, the overhead of implementing these types of programs as full-blown Windows applications is difficult to justify. With Windows 95, these types of programs can now be created as console programs. As such, they will use the simple character mode interface, yet still be fully integrated into the Windows 95 environment. (Remember, DOS programs that are run under Windows are not fully integrated within Windows, and the "marriage" between DOS-style programs and Windows was never a happy one.)

This chapter describes how to write a character mode program and demonstrates several of the console-based API functions.

Character Mode Theory

Character mode programs resemble traditional, non-windowed programs that you almost certainly have written. That is, in a character mode program no window is created. Also, there is no window function. Further, a character mode program begins with a call to **main( )**, not **WinMain( )**. In fact, there will generally not be a function called **WinMain( )** in your program. (If there is, it is simply treated as another function with no special meaning.) For the most part, character mode programs do not use most of the Windows features discussed in the first 12 chapters of this book.

Given the preceding paragraph, you might be wondering two things. First, what general support does Windows 95 give to a character mode program? Second, since a character mode program is not a Windows program in the usual sense, why not just write a DOS-style program instead? The answers are interrelated. First, as mentioned earlier, Windows 95 supplies a number of API functions that allow your character mode program to fully integrate into the Windows 95 environment. For example, mouse support is under the control of Windows 95 even when you are using a character mode program. Second, a character mode program has access to API functions that a DOS-style program doesn't.

If you execute a character mode program from the command prompt, it will inherit that console session. However, as you will soon see, it is possible for each character mode program to allocate its own console. In fact, allocating a console is recommended. A character mode program can also control several attributes of its console that are generally beyond the control of a DOS-style program, for example.

All consoles maintain a cursor that marks the place at which the next output to the console will begin. The cursor is automatically updated after each output operation. It is also possible to set the cursor location within a console to any (legal) location you desire.

13

Allocating a Console

In Windows terminology, a *console* is the interface used by your character mode programs. It contains both an input and an output buffer. The output buffers are also called *screen buffers*. Each character mode program that you write will operate through a console. In Windows 95, there can be several active consoles, each running its own character mode program.

By default, a character mode program either inherits the current console or is given a console if none exists when it is run. However, a better approach is for a character mode program to acquire its own console. The reason for this is simple: Any changes to that console affect only that console and do not affect the inherited console. Therefore, for the cleanest approach to implementing a character mode program, such a program must create its own console. To do this, use the API function **AllocConsole( )**, whose prototype is shown here:

    BOOL AllocConsole(void);

This function acquires a new console session for the program that calls it. The function returns non-zero if successful and zero otherwise. An allocated console is freed automatically when the program terminates.

Once a console has been allocated, it creates a window that behaves more or less like any other window. It includes a title, a control menu, minimize and maximize boxes, and, if needed, scroll bars.

If the character mode program was executed from within a console session, then before a new console can be allocated, the old one inherited by the program must be freed, using **FreeConsole( )**. Its prototype is shown here:

BOOL FreeConsole(void);

The function returns non-zero if successful and zero otherwise.

When creating your character mode application, the best approach is to execute this sequence as the first actions taken by **main( )**.

```
FreeConsole();
AllocConsole()
```

Even if no parent console was previously in effect, no harm is done by calling **FreeConsole( )** and, in any case, a new console is allocated.

A console allocated by your program is automatically freed when your program stops running (unless the console is in use by another task, of course). Your program can also free the console explicitly by calling **FreeConsole( )**.

Giving a Title to a Console

You can give a console window a title using the **SetConsoleTitle( )** API function, shown here:

BOOL SetConsoleTitle(LPTSTR *lpszTitle*);

Here, the string pointed to by *lpszTitle* becomes the title of the console window. The function returns non-zero if successful and zero otherwise.

Acquiring Handles to Standard Input and Output

Many of the console-based API functions require a standard handle to perform I/O. The standard handles are linked to standard input, standard output, and standard error. By default, these handles are linked to the keyboard and the screen. (However, they may be redirected.) For example, when you write to a console, you will write to standard output. Handles to console input and output are of type **HANDLE**.

To acquire a standard handle, use the **GetStdHandle( )** function, whose prototype is shown here:

HANDLE GetStdHandle(DWORD *dwStdDev*);

Here, *dwStdDev* must be one of these macros: **STD_INPUT_HANDLE**, **STD_OUTPUT_HANDLE**, or **STD_ERROR_HANDLE**, which correspond to standard input, standard output, and standard error, respectively. The function returns a handle to the device. On failure, **INVALID_HANDLE_VALUE** is returned.

Outputting Text to the Console

One way to output text to the console is to use the **WriteConsole( )** API function, whose prototype is shown here:

BOOL WriteConsole(HANDLE *hConOut*, CONST VOID **lpString*,
                DWORD *dwLen*, LPDWORD *lpdwNumWritten*,
                LPVOID *lpNotUsed*);

Here, *hConOut* is the handle of console output, generally obtained through a call to **GetStdHandle( )**. *lpString* points to the string that is to be output. The number of characters in *lpString* to output is passed in *dwLen,* and the actual number of characters written is returned in the long integer pointed to by *lpdwNumWritten*. *lpNotUsed* is reserved for future use.

The string is output using the current text and background colors. The output begins at the current cursor location, and the cursor location is automatically updated.

The function returns non-zero if successful and zero otherwise.

It is important to understand that **WriteConsole( )** does not provide any formatting capabilities. This means that you will still need to use a function like **sprintf( )** to first construct the string that you want to output if you want to use **WriteConsole( )** to output formatted data.

Inputting from the Console

To input information entered at the keyboard, use the **ReadConsole( )** function, shown here:

BOOL ReadConsole(HANDLE *hConIn*, LPVOID *lpBuf*,
                DWORD *dwLen*, LPDWORD *lpdwNumRead*,
                LPVOID *lpNotUsed*);

13

Here, *hConIn* is the handle linked to console input. The character array that will receive the characters typed by the user is pointed to by *lpBuf*. (This string is *not* automatically null-terminated.) The function will read up to *dwLen* characters or until ENTER is pressed. The number of characters actually read is returned in the long integer pointed to by *lpdwNumRead*. The *lpNotUsed* parameter is reserved for future use.

The function returns non-zero if successful and zero otherwise.

The exact operation of **ReadConsole( )** is determined by the current console mode. (The console mode can be set using **SetConsoleMode( )**.)

Setting the Cursor Position

To position the cursor, use the **SetConsoleCursorPosition( )** function. Its prototype is shown here:

    BOOL SetConsoleCursorPosition(HANDLE *hConOut*, COORD *XY*);

Here, *hConOut* is the output handle of the console and *XY* is a **COORD** structure that contains the coordinates of the desired cursor location. **COORD** is defined like this:

```
typedef struct _COORD {
  SHORT X;
  SHORT Y;
} COORD;
```

The function returns non-zero if successful and zero on failure.

Setting Text and Background Colors

When using a console, by default text is white and the background is black. You can change this, if you want, by using **SetConsoleTextAttribute( )**, whose prototype is shown here:

    BOOL SetConsoleTextAttribute(HANDLE *hConOut*, WORD *color*);

Here, *hConOut* is the handle linked to console output and *color* is the value that determines the text and background colors. The value of *color* is constructed by ORing together two or more of the following macros, which are defined in **wincon.h**. (**wincon.h** is automatically included when you include **windows.h**.)

Macro	Meaning
FOREGROUND_BLUE	Text includes blue.
FOREGROUND_RED	Text includes red.
FOREGROUND_GREEN	Text includes green.
FOREGROUND_INTENSITY	Text is shown in high intensity.
BACKGROUND_BLUE	Background includes blue.
BACKGROUND_RED	Background includes red.
BACKGROUND_GREEN	Background includes green.
BACKGROUND_INTENSITY	Background is shown in high intensity.

The actual color will be a combination of the color components you specify. To create white, combine all three colors. For black, specify no color.

Consoles Versus the C/C++ Standard I/O Functions

13

Once you have obtained a console, it is permissible (indeed, completely valid) to use the C/C++ standard I/O functions and operators with it. However, using the console API functions just described does give your application more control over the console in many situations. Also, when monitoring console events, only the API functions allow full integration with Windows 95. For example, mouse events are not accessible using the standard C/C++ I/O systems. They are accessible, however, by using the console API functions (as you will soon see).

For the example that follows, the standard C/C++ I/O functions are used only to illustrate their validity.

A Console Demonstration Program

The operation of the console functions just described is demonstrated by the following program. Its operation should be clear.

```
/* Demonstrate Consoles */

#include <windows.h>
#include <string.h>
#include <stdio.h>

main()
{
  HANDLE hStdin, hStdout;
```

```c
char str[255] = "This is an example of output to a console.";
DWORD result;
COORD coord;
int x=0, y=0;
int i;

/* free old console and start fresh with new one */
FreeConsole();
AllocConsole();

/* give console window a title */
SetConsoleTitle("Console Demonstration");

/* get standard handles */
hStdin = GetStdHandle(STD_INPUT_HANDLE);
hStdout = GetStdHandle(STD_OUTPUT_HANDLE);

WriteConsole(hStdout, str, strlen(str), &result, NULL);

/* demonstrate cursor positioning */
for(x=0, y=1; y<10; x+=5, y++) {
  coord.X = x;
  coord.Y = y;
  sprintf(str, "At location %d %d", x, y);
  SetConsoleCursorPosition(hStdout, coord);
  WriteConsole(hStdout, str, strlen(str), &result, NULL);
}

/* change the colors */
coord.X = 0;
coord.Y = 12;
strcpy(str, "This is in blue on green background.");
SetConsoleCursorPosition(hStdout, coord);
SetConsoleTextAttribute(hStdout,
                  FOREGROUND_BLUE | BACKGROUND_GREEN);
WriteConsole(hStdout, str, strlen(str), &result, NULL);

coord.X = 0;
coord.Y = 14;
strcpy(str, "Enter a string: ");
SetConsoleCursorPosition(hStdout, coord);
WriteConsole(hStdout, str, strlen(str), &result, NULL);

/* read input */
ReadConsole(hStdin, str, 80, &result, NULL);
```

```
str[result] = '\0'; /* null terminate */
/* display ASCII code of each character in str */
for(i=0; str[i]; i++) printf("%d ", str[i]);
/* now, display as string */
WriteConsole(hStdout, str, strlen(str), &result, NULL);

/* can use printf(), gets(), etc. */
printf("This is a test.  Enter another string:");
gets(str);
printf("%s\n", str);
printf("Press ENTER: ");

getchar(); /* wait for keypress */

return 0;
}
```

To compile a console program, you may need to use a different set of
compiler and linker commands than you have been using to compile
Windows-style programs. You will need to check your compiler's user
manual for instructions.

13

Sample output from this program is shown in Figure 13-1. Notice that when
a string is input, the carriage return/linefeed sequence is automatically
appended. (These are shown as decimal values 13, 10 when the string is
displayed by its ASCII values.)

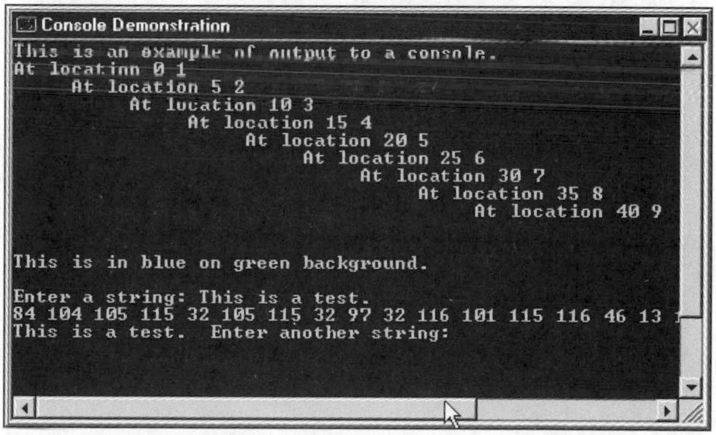

Sample output
from the
console
demonstration
program
Figure 13-1.

Managing the Mouse

One of the main advantages of using Windows 95 consoles over simply letting DOS-style programs execute in a window is that a console gives you access to the mouse. To obtain mouse events (and other information) when using a console, you must use an API console input function called **ReadConsoleInput( )**, whose prototype is shown here:

BOOL ReadConsoleInput(HANDLE *hConIn*, PINPUT_RECORD *pBuf*,
                        DWORD *dwNum*, LPDWORD *lpdwNumRead*);

Here, *hConIn* is the handle of the console you want information about. The parameter *pBuf* is a pointer to a structure of type **INPUT_RECORD**, which will receive the information regarding the requested input event or events. The number of event records to input is specified in *dwNum,* and the amount actually returned by the function will be pointed to by *lpdwNumRead*. The function returns non-zero if successful or zero otherwise.

The **ReadConsoleInput( )** function removes information about one or more input events from the console's input buffer. Each time you strike a key or use the mouse, an input event is generated and the information associated with this event is stored in an **INPUT_RECORD** structure. (Certain other input events may also occur, but these are the only ones of interest to us in this chapter.) The **ReadConsoleInput( )** function reads one or more of these events and makes the input event information available to your program.

Each event record is returned in a structure of type **INPUT_RECORD**, which is shown here:

```
typedef struct _INPUT_RECORD {
  WORD EventType;
  union {
    KEY_EVENT_RECORD KeyEvent;
    MOUSE_EVENT_RECORD MouseEvent;
    WINDOW_BUFFER_SIZE_RECORD WindowBufferSizeEvent;
    MENU_EVENT_RECORD MenuEvent;
    FOCUS_EVENT_RECORD FocusEvent;
  } Event;
} INPUT_RECORD;
```

The contents of **EventType** determine what type of event has occurred. It can be one of the macros in the following list.

Macro	Event
KEY_EVENT	Keypress
MOUSE_EVENT	Mouse action
WINDOW_BUFFER_SIZE_EVENT	Window resized
FOCUS_EVENT	Used by Windows 95
MENU_EVENT	Used by Windows 95

Only mouse and keyboard events are examined here. Briefly, focus and menu events are for the internal use of Windows 95 only. A resize event may be of interest to your program in some situations. In this case, **WindowBufferSizeEvent** contains a **COORD** structure that holds the dimensions of the console window.

Each time a mouse event occurs, the **EventType** field contains **MOUSE_EVENT** and the **Event** union contains a **MOUSE_EVENT_RECORD** structure that describes the mouse event. This structure is shown here:

```
typedef struct _MOUSE_EVENT_RECORD {
  COORD dwMousePosition;
  DWORD dwButtonState;
  DWORD dwControlKeyState;
  DWORD dwEventFlags;
} MOUSE_EVENT_RECORD;
```

The **dwMousePosition** field contains the coordinates of the mouse when the event took place. Since a console is a text-based device, the coordinates are in terms of characters, not pixels.

dwButtonState describes the state of the mouse buttons when the event was generated. If bit one is on, then the left mouse button is pressed. If bit two is on, then the right mouse button is pressed. If bit three is on, the middle button (if it exists) is pressed. More than one bit will be set when more than one button is pressed at the same time.

The **dwControlKeyState** field contains the state of the various control keys when the event occurred. It may contain one or more of the following macros:

SHIFT_PRESSED
RIGHT_CTRL_PRESSED
LEFT_CTRL_PRESSED
RIGHT_ALT_PRESSED
LEFT_ALT_PRESSED
ENHANCED_KEY

13

CAPSLOCK_ON
NUMLOCK_ON
SCROLLLOCK_ON

An enhanced key is one of those added to the standard keyboard by the IBM enhanced keyboard. (For example, the extra arrow keys are enhanced keys.)

dwEventFlags contains either **MOUSE_MOVED** (the mouse has moved) or **DOUBLE_CLICK** (a mouse button has been double-clicked).

Demonstrating the Console Mouse

The following program illustrates how to manage mouse events when using a console.

```c
/* Managing the mouse from a Console. */

#include <windows.h>
#include <string.h>
#include <stdio.h>

main()
{
  HANDLE hStdin, hStdout;
  char str[80] = "Press a key to stop.";
  DWORD result;
  COORD coord;
  int x=0, y=0;
  INPUT_RECORD inBuf;

  /* free old console and start fresh with new one */
  FreeConsole();
  AllocConsole();

  /* give console window a title */
  SetConsoleTitle("Mouse with Console Demonstration");

  /* get standard handles */
  hStdin = GetStdHandle(STD_INPUT_HANDLE);
  hStdout = GetStdHandle(STD_OUTPUT_HANDLE);

  WriteConsole(hStdout, str, strlen(str), &result, NULL);

  /* show mouse events until a key is pressed */
  do {
    ReadConsoleInput(hStdin, &inBuf, 1, &result);
    /* if mouse event occurs, report it */
```

```
       if(inBuf.EventType==MOUSE_EVENT) {
         sprintf(str, "Button state: %lu, X,Y: %3lu,%3lu\n",
                 inBuf.Event.MouseEvent.dwButtonState,
                 inBuf.Event.MouseEvent.dwMousePosition.X,
                 inBuf.Event.MouseEvent.dwMousePosition.Y);
         coord.X = 0;
         coord.Y = 1;
         SetConsoleCursorPosition(hStdout, coord);
         WriteConsole(hStdout, str, strlen(str), &result, NULL);

         /* if a double-click occurs, report it */
         if(inBuf.Event.MouseEvent.dwEventFlags==DOUBLE_CLICK) {
           sprintf(str, "Double click\a");
           coord.X = inBuf.Event.MouseEvent.dwMousePosition.X;
           coord.Y = inBuf.Event.MouseEvent.dwMousePosition.Y;
           SetConsoleCursorPosition(hStdout, coord);
           WriteConsole(hStdout, str, strlen(str), &result, NULL);
           Sleep(600); /* wait */
           SetConsoleCursorPosition(hStdout, coord);
           strcpy(str, "                 "); /* erase message */
           WriteConsole(hStdout, str, strlen(str), &result, NULL);

         }
       }
     } while(inBuf.EventType!=KEY_EVENT);

   return 0;
}
```

13

This program displays the current location of the mouse when it is within the console window as well as the state of the mouse buttons, and it reports when the mouse is double-clicked. The program continues to execute until a key event is generated when you press a key.

The API function **Sleep( )** is used to provide a short delay before the **Double Click** message is erased. This function takes as its argument a value that specifies the number of milliseconds to suspend the execution of the program.

Responding to Keyboard Events

As you know from your previous programming experience, it is quite common for text-based programs to need to respond to keypresses in a more subtle fashion than by simply inputting the keystroke. For example, sometimes your program will need to know if a control key is pressed, or the state of the SHIFT key. Sometimes it is useful to know if a keystroke has been automatically repeated by the user's holding the key down. Also, some applications make use of the *scan code* that corresponds to the key. When you press a key, a scan code (sometimes called a position code) is generated that corresponds to the key's position on the keyboard, which is then translated into an ASCII character. Whatever the need, Windows 95 gives character mode, console-based applications access to all the information associated with a keyboard event. Like mouse events, keyboard events are obtained by calling **ReadConsoleInput( )**, described earlier.

Each time a key is pressed, a keyboard event is generated. When this event is obtained using **ReadConsoleInput( )**, the **EventType** field of the **INPUT_RECORD** structure contains the **KEY_EVENT** value. When this is the case, the **Event** union holds a **KEY_EVENT_RECORD** structure, which describes the event. This structure is shown here:

```
typedef struct _KEY_EVENT_RECORD {
  BOOL bKeyDown;
  WORD wRepeatCount;
  WORD wVirtualKeyCode;
  WORD wVirtualScanCode;
  union {
    WCHAR UnicodeChar;
    CHAR AsciiChar;
  } uChar;
  DWORD dwControlKeyState;
} KEY_EVENT_RECORD;
```

If **bKeyDown** is non-zero, then a key was being pressed when the key event was generated. If it is zero, the key was being released.

When a key is held down and autorepeat takes over, the number of times the keystroke is generated is returned in **wRepeatCount**.

The virtual key code, which is a device-independent key code, is returned in **wVirtualKeyCode**.

The scan (position) code of the key is returned in **wVirtualScanCode**.

The union **uChar** contains the ASCII code of the key being pressed. (It may also contain a wide (16-bit) character for languages that have large character sets.)

The state of the control keys (and other keys) is returned in **dwControlKeyState**. The values are the same as those described for mouse events.

A Sample Key Event Program

The following program demonstrates keyboard events. This program reports each character typed and the state of the various control keys when one is pressed. It continues to execute until you click the left mouse button.

```
/* Managing the keyboard from a Console. */

#include <windows.h>
#include <string.h>
#include <stdio.h>

main()
{
  HANDLE hStdin, hStdout;
  char str[255] = "Press the left mouse button to stop.";
  DWORD result;
  COORD coord;
  int x=0, y=0;
  int i;
  int done = 0;
  INPUT_RECORD inBuf;

  /* free old console and start fresh with new one */
  FreeConsole();
  AllocConsole();

  /* give console window a title */
  SetConsoleTitle("Keyboard Demonstration");

  /* get standard handles */
  hStdin = GetStdHandle(STD_INPUT_HANDLE);
  hStdout = GetStdHandle(STD_OUTPUT_HANDLE);

  WriteConsole(hStdout, str, strlen(str), &result, NULL);

  /* Show keyboard events until left
     mouse button is pressed. */
  do {
    ReadConsoleInput(hStdin, &inBuf, 1, &result);
    /* if key is pressed, report it */
    if(inBuf.EventType==KEY_EVENT) {
      sprintf(str, "Key pressed is: %c\n",
              inBuf.Event.KeyEvent.uChar);
      coord.X = 0;
      coord.Y = 1;
      SetConsoleCursorPosition(hStdout, coord);
      WriteConsole(hStdout, str, strlen(str), &result, NULL);

      /* if a control, alt, etc. key is pressed, report it */
      if(inBuf.Event.KeyEvent.dwControlKeyState &&
         inBuf.Event.KeyEvent.bKeyDown) {
        coord.X = 0;
        coord.Y = 10;
```

13

```
    *str = '\0';
    if(inBuf.Event.KeyEvent.dwControlKeyState
      & RIGHT_ALT_PRESSED)
        strcat(str, "Right alt Key is pressed. ");
    if(inBuf.Event.KeyEvent.dwControlKeyState
      & LEFT_ALT_PRESSED)
        strcat(str, "Left alt Key is pressed. ");
    if(inBuf.Event.KeyEvent.dwControlKeyState
      & RIGHT_CTRL_PRESSED)
        strcat(str, "Right control Key is pressed. ");
    if(inBuf.Event.KeyEvent.dwControlKeyState
      & LEFT_CTRL_PRESSED)
        strcat(str, "Left control Key is pressed. ");
    if(inBuf.Event.KeyEvent.dwControlKeyState
      & SHIFT_PRESSED)
        strcat(str, "Shift key is pressed. ");
    if(inBuf.Event.KeyEvent.dwControlKeyState
      & NUMLOCK_ON)
        strcat(str, "Num lock key is on. ");
    if(inBuf.Event.KeyEvent.dwControlKeyState
      & SCROLLLOCK_ON)
        strcat(str, "Scroll lock key is on. ");
    if(inBuf.Event.KeyEvent.dwControlKeyState
      & CAPSLOCK_ON)
        strcat(str, "Caps lock key is on. ");
    if(inBuf.Event.KeyEvent.dwControlKeyState
      & ENHANCED_KEY)
        strcat(str, "Enhanced key is pressed. ");

    SetConsoleCursorPosition(hStdout, coord);
    strcat(str, "\a");
    WriteConsole(hStdout, str, strlen(str), &result, NULL);
    SetConsoleCursorPosition(hStdout, coord);

    /* wait, then erase the message */
    Sleep(1000);
    coord.X = 0;
    coord.Y = 10;
    i = strlen(str);
    for(*str='\0'; i; i--) strcat(str, " ");
    WriteConsole(hStdout, str, strlen(str), &result, NULL);
    }
  }
  if(inBuf.EventType==MOUSE_EVENT)
    if(inBuf.Event.MouseEvent.dwButtonState==1) done = 1;

} while(!done);

return 0;
}
```

As this chapter has shown, creating character mode programs using Windows 95 is quite easy. Therefore, even though Windows 95 can execute DOS programs, you should always use a Windows 95 console and employ its character mode functions when creating new character mode applications.

In the next chapter, the Windows 95 multitasking system is examined.

13

Chapter 14

Multitasking Processes and Threads

This chapter discusses how you can use multitasking within your Windows 95 programs. As such, it covers two important and interrelated Windows 95 topics: processes and threads. The main emphasis is on threads.

As mentioned in Chapter 1, Windows 95 supports two forms of multitasking. The first type is *process-based*. This is the type of multiprocessing that Windows has supported from its inception. A process is essentially a program that is executing. In process-based multitasking, two or more processes can execute concurrently. The second type of multitasking is *thread-based*. Thread-based multitasking is new to Windows 95. A thread is a path (or *thread*) of execution within a process. In Windows 95, every process has at least one thread, but it may have two or more. Thread-based multitasking allows two or more parts of a single program to execute concurrently. This added multitasking dimension allows you to write extremely efficient programs, because as the programmer you can define the separate threads of execution and thus manage the way that your program executes.

The inclusion of thread-based multitasking has increased the need for a special type of multitasking feature called *synchronization*, which allows the execution of threads (and processes) to be coordinated in certain well-defined ways. Windows 95 has added a complete subsystem devoted to synchronization.

This chapter begins by exploring process-based multitasking and then concentrates on thread-based multitasking. It ends with an overview of thread and process synchronization.

 Windows 3.1 supports only process-based multitasking, not thread-based multitasking. As such, all of the material in this chapter relating to threads is specific to Windows 95. Also, Windows 95's approach to process-based multitasking is substantially enhanced from the Windows 3.1 approach.

Creating a Separate Task

Process-based multitasking is by far the simplest type of multitasking in which your program can engage. In this type of multitasking, one program simply starts the execution of another and then more or less ignores it. In Windows 95, it is possible for one process to start the execution of another using the **CreateProcess( )** API function, whose prototype is shown here:

BOOL CreateProcess(LPCSTR *lpszName*, LPCSTR *lpszComLine*,
                LPSECURITY_ATTRIBUTES *lpProcAttr*,
                LPSECURITY_ATTRIBUTES *lpThreadAttr*,
                BOOL *InheritAttr*, DWORD *How*,
                LPVOID *lpEnv*, LPSTR *lpszDir*,
                LPSTARTUPINFO *lpStartInfo*,
                LPPROCESS_INFORMATION *lpPInfo*);

Don't let the rather long parameter list worry you. As you will soon see, it is possible for most of these parameters to default.

The name of the program to execute, which may include a full path, is specified in the string pointed to by *lpszName*. Any command-line parameters required by the program are specified in the string pointed to by *lpszComLine*. However, if you specify *lpszName* as NULL, then the first token in the string pointed to by *lpszComLine* will be used as the program name. Thus, typically, *lpszName* is specified as NULL and the program name and any required parameters are specified in the string pointed to by *lpszComLine*.

The *lpProcAttr* and *lpThreadAttr* parameters are used to specify any security attributes related to the process being created. These may be specified as NULL, in which case no security attributes are used. Since the security system is not supported by Windows 95, no security attributes will be used when creating processes or threads in this chapter. (However, be aware that you may specify security attributes for the new process if your target operating system—such as Windows NT—allows it.)

If *InheritAttr* is **TRUE** (non-zero), handles in use by the creating process are inherited by the new process. If this parameter is **FALSE** (zero), then handles are not inherited. (**TRUE** and **FALSE** are macros defined by Windows 95 when you include **windows.h**.)

By default, the new process is run "normally." However, the *How* parameter can be used to specify certain additional attributes that affect how the new process will be created. If it is zero, then the defaults apply. The examples in this chapter simply use the defaults supplied by Windows 95, so this parameter is set to zero.

The *lpEnv* parameter points to a buffer that contains the new process's environmental parameters. If this parameter is NULL, then the new process inherits the creating process's environment.

The current drive and directory of the new process can be specified in the string pointed to by *lpszDir*. If this parameter is NULL, then the current drive and directory of the creating process is used.

The parameter *lpStartInfo* is a pointer to a **STARTUPINFO** structure that contains information that determines how the main window of the new process will look. **STARTUPINFO** is defined as shown here:

```
typedef struct _STARTUPINFO {
  DWORD cb; /* size of STARTUPINFO */
  LPSTR lpReserved; /* must be NULL */
  LPSTR lpDesktop; /* name of desktop */
  LPSTR lpTitle; /* title of console (consoles only) */
  DWORD dwX; /* upper-left corner of */
  DWORD dwY; /* new window */
  DWORD dwXSize; /* size of new window */
  DWORD dwYSize; /* size of new window */
  DWORD dwXCountChars; /* console buffer size */
  DWORD dwYCountChars; /* console buffer size */
  DWORD dwFillAttribute; /* initial text color */
  DWORD dwFlags; /* determines which fields are active */
  WORD wShowWindow; /* how window is shown */
  WORD cbReserved2; /* must be 0 */
  LPBYTE lpReserved2; /* must be NULL */
  HANDLE hStdInput; /* standard handles */
  HANDLE hStdOutput;
  HANDLE hStdError;
} STARTUPINFO;
```

14

As this structure suggests, Windows 95 gives you more control over how a process will be created than you will normally ever want! Generally, you will want to use the standard defaults that Windows 95 supplies. In fact, the fields **dwX**, **dwY**, **dwXSize**, **dwYSize**, **dwXCountChars**, **dwYCountChars**, **dwFillAttribute**, and **wShowWindow** are ignored unless they have been enabled by including the proper value as part of the **dwFlags** field. The values for **dwFlags** are shown here:

Macro	Enabled Fields
STARTF_USESHOWWINDOW	**dwShowWindow**
STARTF_USESIZE	**dwXSize** and **dwYSize**
STARTF_USEPOSITION	**dwX** and **dwY**
STARTF_USECOUNTCHARS	**dwXCountChars** and **dwYCountChars**
STARTF_USEFILLATTRIBUTE	**dwFillAttribute**
STARTF_USESTDHANDLES	**hStdInput**, **hStdOutput**

dwFlags may also include one or more of these values:

Macro	Meaning
STARTF_FORCEONFEEDBACK	Feedback cursor is on
STARTF_FORCEOFFFEEDBACK	Feedback cursor is off
STARTF_SCREENSAVER	Process is a screen-saver

Generally, you will not need to use most of the fields in **STARTUPINFO** and you can allow most to be ignored. However, you must specify **cb**, which contains the size of the structure, and several other fields must be set to NULL. For the purposes of this chapter, the new process information specified in the **STARTUPINFO** structure will be set as shown here:

```
STARTUPINFO startin;
/* ... */
/* Start a new process */
startin.cb = sizeof(STARTUPINFO);
startin.lpReserved = NULL;
startin.lpDesktop = NULL;
startin.lpTitle = NULL;
startin.dwFlags = STARTF_USESHOWWINDOW;
startin.cbReserved2 = 0;
startin.lpReserved2 = NULL;
startin.wShowWindow = SW_SHOWMINIMIZED;
```

Here, the process will be started as a minimized window because **dwFlags** is set to **STARTF_USESHOWWINDOW**, which allows the **sShowWindow** field to be used. (By default, the new process's window is shown in a size deemed appropriate by Windows 95.)

The final parameter to **CreateProcess( )** is *lpPInfo*, which is a pointer to a structure of type **PROCESS_INFORMATION**, shown here:

```
typedef struct _PROCESS_INFORMATION {
  HANDLE hProcess; /* handle to new process */
  HANDLE hThread; /* handle to main thread */
  DWORD dwProcessId; /* ID of new process */
  DWORD dwThreadId; /* ID of new thread */
} PROCESS_INFORMATION;
```

Handles to the new process and the main thread of that process are passed back to the creating process in **hProcess** and **hThread**. The new process and thread IDs are returned in **dwProcessId** and **dwThreadId**. Your program can make use of this information or choose to ignore it.

CreateProcess( ) returns non-zero if successful and zero otherwise.

Once created, the new process is largely independent from the creating process. It is possible for the parent process to terminate the child, however. To do so, use the **TerminateProcess( )** API function, shown here:

> BOOL TerminateProcess(HANDLE *hProcess*, UINT *status*);

Here, *hProcess* is the handle to the child process, obtained from the **hProcess** field of *lpPInfo* when the process is created. The value of *status* becomes the exit code of the terminated process. The function returns non-zero if successful and zero on failure.

To start a new process when using Windows 3.1, you must use the WinExec( ) function. Windows 95 still includes this function for compatibility, but describes it as obsolete. When porting code, you should convert WinExec( ) calls to CreateProcess( ).

A Sample Multiprocess Program

The following program demonstrates creating and terminating processes. The program allows you to create up to five child processes. You may also terminate the processes in the reverse order in which they are created. Each time you create a new process, the program **TEST.EXE** is executed, but you can change it to any other Windows 95 program you like. Also, make sure that **TEST.EXE** is in your current working directory.

14

Note: This program, and the others in this chapter, use a virtual window to hold and restore output to the physical window. This procedure was discussed in Chapter 8.

```c
/* Demonstrates process-based multitasking. */

#include <windows.h>
#include <string.h>
#include <stdio.h>
#include "proc.h"

#define PROCMAX 5 /* max. of five processes */

LRESULT CALLBACK WindowFunc(HWND, UINT, WPARAM, LPARAM);

char szWinName[] = "MyWin"; /* name of window class */

char str[255]; /* holds output strings */

int X=0, Y=0; /* current output location */
int maxX, maxY; /* screen dimensions */

int procnum = 0; /* number of active processes */

HDC memdc;
HBITMAP hbit;
HBRUSH hbrush;

PROCESS_INFORMATION pinfo[PROCMAX];

int WINAPI WinMain(HINSTANCE hThisInst, HINSTANCE hPrevInst,
                   LPSTR lpszArgs, int nWinMode)
{
  HWND hwnd;
  MSG msg;
  WNDCLASS wcl;
  HANDLE hAccel;

  /* Define a window class. */
  wcl.hInstance = hThisInst; /* handle to this instance */
  wcl.lpszClassName = szWinName; /* window class name */
  wcl.lpfnWndProc = WindowFunc; /* window function */
  wcl.style = 0; /* default style */

  wcl.hIcon = LoadIcon(NULL, IDI_APPLICATION); /* icon style */
  wcl.hCursor = LoadCursor(NULL, IDC_ARROW); /* cursor style */
```

```
      /* specify name of menu resource */
      wcl.lpszMenuName = "MYMENU"; /* main menu */

      wcl.cbClsExtra = 0; /* no extra */
      wcl.cbWndExtra = 0; /* information needed */

      /* Make the window white. */
      wcl.hbrBackground = GetStockObject(WHITE_BRUSH);

      /* Register the window class. */
      if(!RegisterClass (&wcl)) return 0;

      /* Now that a window class has been registered, a window
         can be created. */
      hwnd = CreateWindow(
        szWinName, /* name of window class */
        "Demonstrate Processes", /* title */
        WS_OVERLAPPEDWINDOW, /* window style - normal */
        CW_USEDEFAULT, /* X coordinate - let Windows decide */
        CW_USEDEFAULT, /* Y coordinate - let Windows decide */
        CW_USEDEFAULT, /* width - let Windows decide */
        CW_USEDEFAULT, /* height - let Windows decide */
        HWND_DESKTOP, /* no parent window */
        NULL, /* no menu */
        hThisInst, /* handle of this instance of the program */
        NULL /* no additional arguments */
      );

      /* load accelerators */
      hAccel = LoadAccelerators(hThisInst, "MYMENU");

      /* Display the window. */
      ShowWindow(hwnd, nWinMode);
      UpdateWindow(hwnd);

      /* Create the message loop. */
      while(GetMessage(&msg, NULL, 0, 0))
      {
        if(!TranslateAccelerator(hwnd, hAccel, &msg)) {
          TranslateMessage(&msg); /* allow use of keyboard */
          DispatchMessage(&msg); /* return control to Windows */
        }
      }
      return msg.wParam;
}

/* This function is called by Windows 95 and is passed
```

14

```
   messages from the message queue.
*/
LRESULT CALLBACK WindowFunc(HWND hwnd, UINT message,
                            WPARAM wParam,
                            LPARAM lParam)
{
  HDC hdc;
  PAINTSTRUCT paintstruct;
  TEXTMETRIC tm;
  STARTUPINFO startin;

  switch(message) {
    case WM_CREATE:
      /* get screen coordinates */
      maxX = GetSystemMetrics(SM_CXSCREEN);
      maxY = GetSystemMetrics(SM_CYSCREEN);

      /* make a compatible memory image device */
      hdc = GetDC(hwnd);
      memdc = CreateCompatibleDC(hdc);
      hbit = CreateCompatibleBitmap(hdc, maxX, maxY);
      SelectObject(memdc, hbit);
      hbrush = GetStockObject(WHITE_BRUSH);
      SelectObject(memdc, hbrush);
      PatBlt(memdc, 0, 0, maxX, maxY, PATCOPY);
      ReleaseDC(hwnd, hdc);
      break;
    case WM_COMMAND:
      switch(LOWORD(wParam)) {
        case ID_PROCESS:
          if(procnum==PROCMAX) {
            MessageBox(hwnd, "Can't Create", "Error", MB_OK);
            break; /* no more than PROCMAX */
          }

          /* get text metrics */
          GetTextMetrics(memdc, &tm);

          sprintf(str, "Execute Process %d.", procnum);
          TextOut(memdc, X, Y, str, strlen(str));
          Y = Y + tm.tmHeight + tm.tmExternalLeading;
          InvalidateRect(hwnd, NULL, 1);

          /* Start a new process */
          startin.cb = sizeof(STARTUPINFO);
          startin.lpReserved = NULL;
          startin.lpDesktop = NULL;
          startin.lpTitle = NULL;
```

```
                  startin.dwFlags = STARTF_USESHOWWINDOW;
                  startin.cbReserved2 = 0;
                  startin.lpReserved2 = NULL;
                  startin.wShowWindow = SW_SHOWMINIMIZED;

                  CreateProcess(NULL, "test.exe",
                             NULL, NULL, FALSE, 0,
                             NULL, NULL, &startin, &pinfo[procnum]);
                procnum++;
                break;
              case ID_KILLPROC:
                if(procnum) procnum--;
                else {
                  MessageBox(hwnd, "No process to terminate.",
                                   "Error", MB_OK);
                  break;
                }

                /* get text metrics */
                GetTextMetrics(memdc, &tm);

                TerminateProcess(pinfo[procnum].hProcess, 0);
                sprintf(str, "Terminate Process %d.", procnum);
                TextOut(memdc, X, Y, str, strlen(str));
                Y = Y + tm.tmHeight + tm.tmExternalLeading;
                InvalidateRect(hwnd, NULL, 1);
                break;
              case ID_HELP:
                MessageBox(hwnd, "F2: Start Process\nF3: Kill Process",
                             "Help", MB_OK);
                break;
          }
          break;
      case WM_PAINT: /* process a repaint request */
        hdc = BeginPaint(hwnd, &paintstruct); /* get DC */

        /* now, copy memory image onto screen */
        BitBlt(hdc, 0, 0, maxX, maxY, memdc, 0, 0, SRCCOPY);
        EndPaint(hwnd, &paintstruct); /* release DC */
        break;
      case WM_DESTROY: /* terminate the program */
        DeleteDC(memdc); /* delete the memory device */
        PostQuitMessage(0);
        break;
      default:
        /* Let Windows 95 process any messages not specified in
         the preceding switch statement. */
        return DefWindowProc(hwnd, message, wParam, lParam);
```

14

```
  }
  return 0;
}
```

Before you can compile this program, you will need to create the header file
proc.h, shown here. (The **ID_THREAD** value will be used by later
examples.)

```
#define ID_PROCESS  100
#define ID_KILLPROC 101
#define ID_THREAD   102
#define ID_HELP     103
```

You will also need to create this resource file:

```
#include "proc.h"
#include <windows.h>

MYMENU MENU
{
  POPUP "&Processes" {
    MENUITEM "&Execute Process", ID_PROCESS
    MENUITEM "&Kill Process", ID_KILLPROC
  }
  MENUITEM "&Help", ID_HELP
}

MYMENU ACCELERATORS
{
  VK_F2, ID_PROCESS, VIRTKEY
  VK_F3, ID_KILLPROC, VIRTKEY
  VK_F1, ID_HELP, VIRTKEY
}
```

Sample output is shown in Figure 14-1.

Creating Multithreaded Programs

While multiprocess programming using Windows 95 is more flexible and
contains more programmer-controlled features than Windows 3.1, it does
not represent any major advance. However, Windows 95's support for
multithreaded programs does! Multithreaded multitasking adds a new
dimension to your programming, because it lets you, the programmer,
more fully control how pieces of your program execute. This allows you
to implement more efficient programs. For example, you could assign one
thread of a program the job of sorting a file, another thread the job of

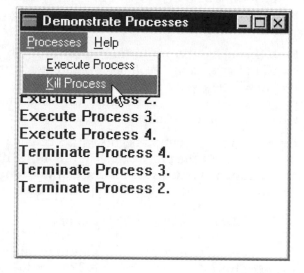

Sample output
from the
process
demonstration
program
Figure 14-1.

gathering information from some remote source, and another thread the
task of performing user input. Because of multithreaded multitasking, each
thread could execute concurrently and no CPU time is wasted.

It is important to understand that all processes have at least one thread of
execution. For the sake of discussion, this is called the *main thread*. However,
it is possible to create more than one thread of execution within the same
process. In general, once a new thread is created, it also begins execution.
Thus, each process starts with one thread of execution and may create one or
more additional threads. In this way, thread-based multitasking is supported.

In this section you will learn how to create a multithreaded program.

Creating a Thread

To create a thread, use the API function **CreateThread( )**. Its prototype is
shown here:

```
HANDLE CreateThread(LPSECURITY_ATTRIBUTES lpAttr,
                    DWORD dwStack,
                    LPTHREAD_START_ROUTINE lpFunc,
                    LPVOID lpParam,
                    DWORD dwFlags,
                    LPDWORD lpdwID);
```

14

Here, *lpAttr* is a pointer to a set of security attributes pertaining to the thread. However, if *lpAttr* is NULL, as should be the case for Windows 95, then no security is used.

Each thread has its own stack. You can specify the size of the new thread's stack, in bytes, using the *dwStack* parameter. If this value is 0, then the thread will be given a stack that is the same size as the main thread of the process that creates it. In this case, the stack will be expanded, if necessary. (Specifying 0 is the common approach taken to thread stack size.)

Each thread of execution begins with a call to a function, called the *thread function*, within the process. Execution of the thread continues until the thread function returns. The address of this function (the entry point to the thread) is specified in *lpFunc*. All thread functions must have this prototype:

DWORD *threadfunc*(LPVOID *param*);

Any argument that you need to pass to the new thread is specified in **CreateThread( )**'s *lpParam*. This 32-bit value is received by the thread's entry function in its parameter. This parameter may be used for any purpose.

The *dwFlags* parameter determines the execution state of the thread. If it is 0, the thread begins execution immediately. If it is **CREATE_SUSPEND**, the thread is created in a suspended state, awaiting execution. (It may be started using a call to **ResumeThread( )**.) The identifier associated with a thread is returned in the double word pointed to by *lpdwID*.

The function returns a handle to the thread if successful or zero if a failure occurs.

Terminating a Thread

As stated, a thread of execution terminates when its entry function returns. The process may also terminate the thread manually, using **TerminateThread( )**, whose prototype is shown here:

BOOL TerminateThread(HANDLE *hThread*, DWORD *dwStatus*);

Here, *hThread* is the handle of the thread to be terminated and *dwStatus* is the termination status. The function returns non-zero if successful and zero otherwise.

When a thread is terminated using **TerminateThread( )**, it is stopped immediately and does not perform any special clean-up activities. Also, **TerminateThread( )** may stop a thread during an important operation. For these reasons, it is usually best (and easiest) to let a thread terminate normally when its entry function returns. This is the approach used by the example programs in this chapter.

A Short Multithreaded Example

The following program creates a thread each time the Execute Thread menu option is selected. The thread beeps 10 times and displays the number of each beep along with its thread ID on the screen. Another thread can be started before the first is finished.

The computer's beep is sounded using the **MessageBeep( )** API function. When called with a parameter of –1, it produces the standard beep.

```
/* A very simple multithreaded program. */

#define PROCMAX 5 /* maximum number of processes */

#include <windows.h>
#include <string.h>
#include <stdio.h>
#include "proc.h"

LRESULT CALLBACK WindowFunc(HWND, UINT, WPARAM, LPARAM);
DWORD MyThread(LPVOID param);

char szWinName[] = "MyWin"; /* name of window class */

char str[255]; /* holds output strings */

int X=0, Y=0; /* current output location */
int maxX, maxY; /* screen dimensions */

int procnum = 0; /* number of active processes */

DWORD Tid; /* thread ID */

HDC memdc;
HBITMAP hbit;
HBRUSH hbrush;

PROCESS_INFORMATION pinfo[PROCMAX];

int WINAPI WinMain(HINSTANCE hThisInst, HINSTANCE hPrevInst,
                   LPSTR lpszArgs, int nWinMode)
{
  HWND hwnd;
  MSG msg;
```

14

```
  WNDCLASS wcl;
  HANDLE hAccel;

  /* Define a window class. */
  wcl.hInstance = hThisInst; /* handle to this instance */
  wcl.lpszClassName = szWinName; /* window class name */
  wcl.lpfnWndProc = WindowFunc; /* window function */
  wcl.style = 0; /* default style */

  wcl.hIcon = LoadIcon(NULL, IDI_APPLICATION); /* icon style */
  wcl.hCursor = LoadCursor(NULL, IDC_ARROW); /* cursor style */

  /* specify name of menu resource */
  wcl.lpszMenuName = "MYMENU"; /* main menu */

  wcl.cbClsExtra = 0; /* no extra */
  wcl.cbWndExtra = 0; /* information needed */

  /* Make the window white. */
  wcl.hbrBackground = GetStockObject(WHITE_BRUSH);

  /* Register the window class. */
  if(!RegisterClass (&wcl)) return 0;

  /* Now that a window class has been registered, a window
     can be created. */
  hwnd = CreateWindow(
    szWinName, /* name of window class */
    "Demonstrate Threads and Processes", /* title */
    WS_OVERLAPPEDWINDOW, /* window style - normal */
    CW_USEDEFAULT, /* X coordinate - let Windows decide */
    CW_USEDEFAULT, /* Y coordinate - let Windows decide */
    CW_USEDEFAULT, /* width - let Windows decide */
    CW_USEDEFAULT, /* height - let Windows decide */
    HWND_DESKTOP, /* no parent window */
    NULL, /* no menu */
    hThisInst, /* handle of this instance of the program */
    NULL /* no additional arguments */
  );

  /* load accelerators */
  hAccel = LoadAccelerators(hThisInst, "MYMENU");

  /* Display the window. */
  ShowWindow(hwnd, nWinMode);
  UpdateWindow(hwnd);

  /* Create the message loop. */
```

```
      while(GetMessage(&msg, NULL, 0, 0))
      {
        if(!TranslateAccelerator(hwnd, hAccel, &msg)) {
          TranslateMessage(&msg); /* allow use of keyboard */
          DispatchMessage(&msg); /* return control to Windows */
        }
      }
      return msg.wParam;
}


/* This function is called by Windows 95 and is passed
   messages from the message queue.
*/
LRESULT CALLBACK WindowFunc(HWND hwnd, UINT message,
                            WPARAM wParam,
                            LPARAM lParam)
{
  HDC hdc;
  PAINTSTRUCT paintstruct;
  TEXTMETRIC tm;
  STARTUPINFO startin;

  switch(message) {
    case WM_CREATE:
      /* get screen coordinates */
      maxX = GetSystemMetrics(SM_CXSCREEN);
      maxY = GetSystemMetrics(SM_CYSCREEN);

      /* make a compatible memory image device */
      hdc = GetDC(hwnd);
      memdc = CreateCompatibleDC(hdc);
      hbit = CreateCompatibleBitmap(hdc, maxX, maxY);
      SelectObject(memdc, hbit);
      hbrush = GetStockObject(WHITE_BRUSH);
      SelectObject(memdc, hbrush);
      PatBlt(memdc, 0, 0, maxX, maxY, PATCOPY);
      ReleaseDC(hwnd, hdc);
      break;
    case WM_COMMAND:
      switch(LOWORD(wParam)) {
        case ID_PROCESS:
          if(procnum==PROCMAX) {
            MessageBox(hwnd, "Can't Create", "Error", MB_OK);
            break; /* no more than PROCMAX */
          }

          /* get text metrics */
          GetTextMetrics(memdc, &tm);
```

```
      sprintf(str, "Execute Process %d.", procnum);
      TextOut(memdc, X, Y, str, strlen(str));
      Y = Y + tm.tmHeight + tm.tmExternalLeading;
      InvalidateRect(hwnd, NULL, 1);

      /* Start a new process */
      startin.cb = sizeof(STARTUPINFO);
      startin.lpReserved = NULL;
      startin.lpDesktop = NULL;
      startin.lpTitle = NULL;
      startin.dwFlags = STARTF_USESHOWWINDOW;
      startin.cbReserved2 = 0;
      startin.lpReserved2 = NULL;
      startin.wShowWindow = SW_SHOWMINIMIZED;

      CreateProcess(NULL, "test.exe",
                    NULL, NULL, FALSE, 0,
                    NULL, NULL, &startin, &pinfo[procnum]);
      procnum++;
      break;
    case ID_KILLPROC:
      if(procnum) procnum--;
      else {
        MessageBox(hwnd, "No process to terminate.",
                         "Error", MB_OK);

        break;
      }

      /* get text metrics */
      GetTextMetrics(memdc, &tm);

      TerminateProcess(pinfo[procnum].hProcess, 0);
      sprintf(str, "Terminate Process %d.", procnum);
      TextOut(memdc, X, Y, str, strlen(str));
      Y = Y + tm.tmHeight + tm.tmExternalLeading;
      InvalidateRect(hwnd, NULL, 1);
      break;
    case ID_THREAD:
      CreateThread(NULL, 0, (LPTHREAD_START_ROUTINE)MyThread,
                   (LPVOID) NULL, 0, &Tid);
      InvalidateRect(hwnd, NULL, 1);
      break;
    case ID_HELP:
      MessageBox(hwnd,
                 "F2: Start Process\nF3: Kill Process\n"
                 "F4: Start Thread",
                 "Help", MB_OK);
```

```
          break;
        }
        break;
      case WM_PAINT: /* process a repaint request */
        hdc = BeginPaint(hwnd, &paintstruct); /* get DC */

        /* now, copy memory image onto screen */
        BitBlt(hdc, 0, 0, maxX, maxY, memdc, 0, 0, SRCCOPY);
        EndPaint(hwnd, &paintstruct); /* release DC */
        break;
      case WM_LBUTTONDOWN: /* process left button */
        X = LOWORD(lParam); /* set X,Y to */
        Y = HIWORD(lParam); /* mouse location */
        break;
      case WM_DESTROY: /* terminate the program */
        DeleteDC(memdc); /* delete the memory device */
        PostQuitMessage(0);
        break;
      default:
        /* Let Windows 95 process any messages not specified in
        the preceding switch statement. */
        return DefWindowProc(hwnd, message, wParam, lParam);
    }
    return 0;
}

/* A thread of execution within the process. */
DWORD MyThread(LPVOID param)
{
  int i;
  DWORD curTid = Tid;
  TEXTMETRIC tm;

  /* get text metrics */
  GetTextMetrics(memdc, &tm);

  for(i=0; i<10; i++) {
    Sleep(500);
    sprintf(str, "Thread ID #%lu, beep #%d",
            curTid, i);
    TextOut(memdc, X, Y, str, strlen(str));
    Y = Y + tm.tmHeight + tm.tmExternalLeading;
    InvalidateRect((HWND) param, NULL, 1);
    MessageBeep(-1);
  }
  return 0;
}
```

14

The program above uses the same **proc.h** file as the previous example, but you will need to enter this resource file:

```
#include "proc.h"
#include <windows.h>

MYMENU MENU
{
  POPUP "&Processes" {
    MENUITEM "&Execute Process", ID_PROCESS
    MENUITEM "&Kill Process", ID_KILLPROC
    MENUITEM "Execute &Thread", ID_THREAD
  }

  MENUITEM "&Help", ID_HELP
}

MYMENU ACCELERATORS
{
  VK_F2, ID_PROCESS, VIRTKEY
  VK_F3, ID_KILLPROC, VIRTKEY
  VK_F4, ID_THREAD, VIRTKEY
  VK_F1, ID_HELP, VIRTKEY
}
```

Sample output from the program is shown in Figure 14-2.

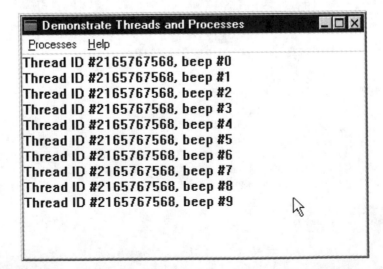

Sample output from the multithreaded program
Figure 14-2.

Using Multiple Threads

A program can have, within reason, as many threads of execution as the system will support. For example, this version of the preceding program starts two threads each time the Execute Thread menu option is selected. Sample output from this program is shown in Figure 14-3.

```
/* Another multithreaded program. */

#define PROCMAX 5 /* maximum number of processes */

#include <windows.h>
#include <string.h>
#include <stdio.h>
#include "proc.h"

LRESULT CALLBACK WindowFunc(HWND, UINT, WPARAM, LPARAM);
DWORD MyThread1(LPVOID param);
DWORD MyThread2(LPVOID param);

char szWinName[] = "MyWin"; /* name of window class */

char str[255]; /* holds output strings */

int X=0, Y=0; /* current output location */
int maxX, maxY; /* screen dimensions */

int procnum = 0; /* number of active processes */

DWORD Tid1, Tid2; /* thread IDs */

HDC memdc;
HBITMAP hbit;
HBRUSH hbrush;

PROCESS_INFORMATION pinfo[PROCMAX];

int WINAPI WinMain(HINSTANCE hThisInst, HINSTANCE hPrevInst,
                   LPSTR lpszArgs, int nWinMode)
{
  HWND hwnd;
  MSG msg;
  WNDCLASS wcl;
  HANDLE hAccel;

  /* Define a window class. */
  wcl.hInstance = hThisInst; /* handle to this instance */
```

14

```
wcl.lpszClassName = szWinName; /* window class name */
wcl.lpfnWndProc = WindowFunc; /* window function */
wcl.style = 0; /* default style */

wcl.hIcon = LoadIcon(NULL, IDI_APPLICATION); /* icon style */
wcl.hCursor = LoadCursor(NULL, IDC_ARROW); /* cursor style */

/* specify name of menu resource */
wcl.lpszMenuName = "MYMENU"; /* main menu */

wcl.cbClsExtra = 0; /* no extra */
wcl.cbWndExtra = 0; /* information needed */

/* Make the window white. */
wcl.hbrBackground = GetStockObject(WHITE_BRUSH);

/* Register the window class. */
if(!RegisterClass (&wcl)) return 0;

/* Now that a window class has been registered, a window
   can be created. */
hwnd = CreateWindow(
  szWinName, /* name of window class */
  "Demonstrate Threads and Processes", /* title */
  WS_OVERLAPPEDWINDOW, /* window style - normal */
  CW_USEDEFAULT, /* X coordinate - let Windows decide */
  CW_USEDEFAULT, /* Y coordinate - let Windows decide */
  CW_USEDEFAULT, /* width - let Windows decide */
  CW_USEDEFAULT, /* height - let Windows decide */
  HWND_DESKTOP, /* no parent window */
  NULL, /* no menu */
  hThisInst, /* handle of this instance of the program */
  NULL /* no additional arguments */
);

/* load accelerators */
hAccel = LoadAccelerators(hThisInst, "MYMENU");

/* Display the window. */
ShowWindow(hwnd, nWinMode);
UpdateWindow(hwnd);

/* Create the message loop. */
while(GetMessage(&msg, NULL, 0, 0))
{
  if(!TranslateAccelerator(hwnd, hAccel, &msg)) {
    TranslateMessage(&msg); /* allow use of keyboard */
    DispatchMessage(&msg); /* return control to Windows */
```

```
        }
      }
    return msg.wParam;
}

/* This function is called by Windows 95 and is passed
   messages from the message queue.
*/
LRESULT CALLBACK WindowFunc(HWND hwnd, UINT message,
                            WPARAM wParam,
                            LPARAM lParam)
{
  HDC hdc;
  PAINTSTRUCT paintstruct;
  TEXTMETRIC tm;
  STARTUPINFO startin;

  switch(message) {
    case WM_CREATE:
      /* get screen coordinates */
      maxX = GetSystemMetrics(SM_CXSCREEN);
      maxY = GetSystemMetrics(SM_CYSCREEN);

      /* make a compatible memory image device */
      hdc = GetDC(hwnd);
      memdc = CreateCompatibleDC(hdc);
      hbit = CreateCompatibleBitmap(hdc, maxX, maxY);
      SelectObject(memdc, hbit);
      hbrush = GetStockObject(WHITE_BRUSH);
      SelectObject(memdc, hbrush);
      PatBlt(memdc, 0, 0, maxX, maxY, PATCOPY);
      ReleaseDC(hwnd, hdc);
      break;
    case WM_COMMAND:
      switch(LOWORD(wParam)) {
        case ID_PROCESS:
          if(procnum==PROCMAX) {
            MessageBox(hwnd, "Can't Create", "Error", MB_OK);
            break; /* no more than PROCMAX */
          }

          /* get text metrics */
          GetTextMetrics(memdc, &tm);

          sprintf(str, "Execute Process %d.", procnum);
          TextOut(memdc, X, Y, str, strlen(str));
          Y = Y + tm.tmHeight + tm.tmExternalLeading;
          InvalidateRect(hwnd, NULL, 1);
```

```
      /* Start a new process */
      startin.cb = sizeof(STARTUPINFO);
      startin.lpReserved = NULL;
      startin.lpDesktop = NULL;
      startin.lpTitle = NULL;
      startin.dwFlags = STARTF_USESHOWWINDOW;
      startin.cbReserved2 = 0;
      startin.lpReserved2 = NULL;
      startin.wShowWindow = SW_SHOWMINIMIZED;

      CreateProcess(NULL, "test.exe",
                    NULL, NULL, FALSE, 0,
                    NULL, NULL, &startin, &pinfo[procnum]);
      procnum++;
      break;
    case ID_KILLPROC:
      if(procnum) procnum--;
      else {
        MessageBox(hwnd, "No process to terminate.",
                   "Error", MB_OK);
        break;
      }

      /* get text metrics */
      GetTextMetrics(memdc, &tm);

      TerminateProcess(pinfo[procnum].hProcess, 0);
      sprintf(str, "Terminate Process %d.", procnum);
      TextOut(memdc, X, Y, str, strlen(str));
      Y = Y + tm.tmHeight + tm.tmExternalLeading;
      InvalidateRect(hwnd, NULL, 1);
      break;
    case ID_THREAD:
      CreateThread(NULL, 0, (LPTHREAD_START_ROUTINE)MyThread1,
                   (LPVOID) hwnd, 0, &Tid1);
      CreateThread(NULL, 0, (LPTHREAD_START_ROUTINE)MyThread2,
                   (LPVOID) hwnd, 0, &Tid2);

      break;
    case ID_HELP:
      MessageBox(hwnd,
                 "F2: Start Process\nF4: Kill Process\n"
                 "F4: Start Thread",
                 "Help", MB_OK);
      break;
  }
  break;
case WM_PAINT: /* process a repaint request */
```

```
        hdc = BeginPaint(hwnd, &paintstruct); /* get DC */

        /* now, copy memory image onto screen */
        BitBlt(hdc, 0, 0, maxX, maxY, memdc, 0, 0, SRCCOPY);
        EndPaint(hwnd, &paintstruct); /* release DC */
        break;
    case WM_LBUTTONDOWN: /* process left button */
        X = LOWORD(lParam); /* set X,Y to */
        Y = HIWORD(lParam); /* mouse location */
        break;
    case WM_DESTROY: /* terminate the program */
        DeleteDC(memdc); /* delete the memory device */
        PostQuitMessage(0);
        break;
    default:
        /* Let Windows 95 process any messages not specified in
        the preceding switch statement. */
        return DefWindowProc(hwnd, message, wParam, lParam);
    }
    return 0;
}

/* First thread of execution. */
DWORD MyThread1(LPVOID param)
{
    int i;
    DWORD curTid = Tid1;
    TEXTMETRIC tm;

    /* get text metrics */
    GetTextMetrics(memdc, &tm);

    for(i=0; i<10; i++) {
        Sleep(500);
        sprintf(str, "Thread ID #%lu, beep #%d",
                curTid, i);
        TextOut(memdc, X, Y, str, strlen(str));
        Y = Y + tm.tmHeight + tm.tmExternalLeading;
        InvalidateRect((HWND) param, NULL, 1);
        MessageBeep(-1);
    }
    return 0;
}

/* Second thread of execution. */
DWORD MyThread2(LPVOID param)
```

14

```
{
  int i;
  DWORD curTid = Tid2;
  TEXTMETRIC tm;

  /* get text metrics */
  GetTextMetrics(memdc, &tm);

  for(i=0; i<10; i++) {
    Sleep(200);
    sprintf(str, "Thread 2");
    TextOut(memdc, X, Y, str, strlen(str));
    Y = Y + tm.tmHeight + tm.tmExternalLeading;
    InvalidateRect((HWND) param, NULL, 1);
  }
  return 0;
}
```

As this program illustrates, when using multiple threads, you define a thread function for each thread and then start each thread separately. All the threads in the process will then execute concurrently. The concurrent execution of the threads is evidenced by the jumbled output produced by the program when they are executed.

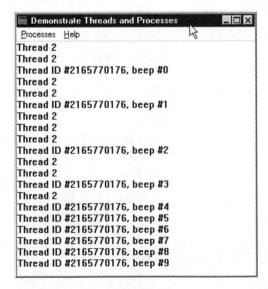

Sample output from the second multithreaded program

Figure 14-3.

Synchronization

When using multiple threads or processes, it is sometimes necessary to synchronize the activities of two or more. The most common reason for this is when two or more threads need access to a shared resource that may be used by only one thread at a time. For example, when one thread is writing to a file, a second thread must be prevented from doing so at the same time. The mechanism that prevents this is called *serialization*. Another reason for synchronization is when one thread is waiting for an event that is caused by another thread. In this case, there must be some means by which the first thread is held in a suspended state until the event has occurred; then the waiting thread must resume execution.

There are two general states that a task may be in. First, it may be *executing*. (or ready to execute as soon as it obtains its time slice). Second, a task may be *blocked*, awaiting some resource or event, in which case its execution is *suspended* until the needed resource is available or the event occurs.

If you are not familiar with the need for synchronization and the serialization problem or its most common solution, the semaphore, the next section discusses it. (If this is familiar territory for you, skip ahead.)

Understanding the Serialization Problem

Windows 95 must provide special services that allow access to a shared resource to be serialized, because without help from the operating system, there is no way for one process or thread to know that it has sole access to a resource. To understand this, imagine that you are writing programs for a multitasking operating system that does not provide any serialization support. Furthermore, imagine that you have two concurrently executing processes, A and B, both of which, from time to time, require access to some resource R (such as a disk file) that must only be accessed by one task at a time.

As a means of preventing one program from accessing R while the other is using it, you try the following solution. First you establish a variable called **flag**, which can be accessed by both programs. Your programs initialize **flag** to 0. Next, before using each piece of code that accesses R, you wait for the flag to be cleared, then set the flag, access R, and finally clear the flag. That is, before either program accesses R, it executes this piece of code:

```
while(flag) ; /* wait for flag to be cleared */
flag = 1; /* set flag */

/* ... access resource R ... */

flag = 0; /* clear the flag */
```

14

The idea behind this code is that neither process will access R if **flag** is set. Conceptually, this approach is in the spirit of the correct solution. However, in actual fact it leaves much to be desired for one simple reason: it won't always work! Let's see why.

Using the code just given, it is possible for both processes to access R at the same time. The **while** loop is, in essence, performing repeated load and compare instructions on **flag**; in other words, it is testing the flag's value. When the flag is cleared, the next line of code sets the flag's value. The trouble is that it is possible for these two operations to be performed in two different time slices. Between the two time slices, the value of **flag** might have been accessed by a different process, thus allowing R to be used by both processes at the same time. To understand this, imagine that process A enters the **while** loop and finds that **flag** is 0, which is the green light to access R. However, before it can set **flag** to 1, its time slice expires and process B resumes execution. If B executes its **while**, it too will find that **flag** is not set and assume that it is safe to access R. However, when A resumes it will also begin accessing R. The crux of the problem is that the testing and setting of **flag** do not comprise one uninterruptible operation. Rather, as just illustrated, they can be separated by a time slice. No matter how you try, there is no way, using only application-level code, that you can absolutely guarantee that one and only one process will access R at any given time.

The solution to the serialization problem is as elegant as it is simple. The operating system (in this case Windows 95) provides a routine that, in one uninterrupted operation, tests and, if possible, sets a flag. In the language of operating systems engineers, this is called a *test and set* operation. For historical reasons, the flags used to control serialization and provide synchronization between processes (and threads) are called *semaphores*. The core Windows 95 functions that support semaphores are discussed in the next section.

Windows 95 Synchronization Objects

Windows 95 supports four types of synchronization objects. All are based, in one way or another, on the concept of the semaphore. The first type is the classic semaphore. A semaphore can be used to allow a limited number of processes or threads access to a resource. When using a semaphore, the resource can be either completely serialized, in which case one and only one thread or process can access it at a time, or the semaphore can be used to allow no more than a small number of processes or threads access at any one time. Semaphores are implemented using a counter that is decremented when a task is granted the semaphore and incremented when the task releases it.

The second synchronization object is the *mutex* semaphore. A mutex semaphore is used to serialize a resource so that one and only one thread or process can access it at any time. In essence, a mutex semaphore is a special-case version of a standard semaphore.

The third synchronization object is the *event object*. It can be used to block access to a resource until some other thread or process signals that it may be used. (That is, an event object signals that a specified event has occurred.)

Finally, you can prevent a section of code from being used by more than one thread at a time by making it into a *critical section* using a critical section object. Once a critical section is entered by one thread, no other thread may use it until the first thread has left the critical section. (Critical sections only apply to threads within a process.)

With the exception of critical sections, the other synchronization objects can be used to serialize threads within a process or to serialize processes themselves. In fact, semaphores are a common means of interprocess communication.

This chapter describes how to create and use a semaphore and an event object. After you understand these two synchronization objects, the other two will be easy for you to explore on your own.

Using a Semaphore to Synchronize Threads

14

Before you can use a semaphore, you must create one using **CreateSemaphore( )**, whose prototype is shown here:

```
HANDLE CreateSemaphore(LPSECURITY_ATTRIBUTES lpAttr,
                       LONG InitialCount,
                       LONG MaxCount,
                       LPSTR lpszName);
```

Here, *lpAttr* is a pointer to the security attributes, or NULL if no security attributes are used (as is the case for Windows 95).

A semaphore can allow one or more tasks access to an object. The number of tasks allowed to simultaneously access an object is determined by the value of *MaxCount*. If this value is 1, then the semaphore acts much like a mutex semaphore, allowing one and only one thread or process to gain access to the resource at any one time.

Semaphores use a counter to keep track of how many tasks have currently been granted access. If the count is 0, then no further access can be granted until a task releases the semaphore. The initial count of the semaphore is specified in *InitialCount*. If this value is 0, then initially all objects waiting on the semaphore will be blocked until the semaphore is released elsewhere by your program. Typically, this value is set initially to 1 or more, indicating that the semaphore can be granted to at least one task. In any event, *InitialCount* must be non-negative and less than or equal to the value specified in *MaxCount*.

lpszName points to a string that becomes the name of the semaphore object. Semaphores are global objects that may be used by other processes. As such, when two processes each open a semaphore using the same name, both are referring to the same semaphore. In this way, two processes can be synchronized. The name may also be NULL, in which case the semaphore is localized to one process.

The **CreateSemaphore( )** function returns a handle to the semaphore if successful or NULL on failure.

Once you have created a semaphore, you use it by calling two related functions: **WaitForSingleObject( )** and **ReleaseSemaphore( )**. The prototypes for these functions are shown here:

DWORD WaitForSingleObject(HANDLE *hObject*, DWORD *dwHowLong*);

BOOL ReleaseSemaphore(HANDLE *hSema*, LONG *Count*,
                  LPLONG *lpPrevCount*);

WaitForSingleObject( ) waits on a semaphore (or other type of object). Here, *hObject* is the handle to the semaphore created earlier. The *dwHowLong* parameter specifies, in milliseconds, how long the calling routine will wait. Once that time has elapsed, a time-out error will be returned. To wait indefinitely, use the value **INFINITE**. The function returns **WAIT_OBJECT_0** when successful (that is, when access is granted). It returns **WAIT_TIMEOUT** when a specified time-out is reached. Each time **WaitForSingleObject( )** succeeds, the counter associated with the semaphore is decremented.

ReleaseSemaphore( ) releases the semaphore and allows another thread to use it. Here, *hSema* is the handle to the semaphore. *Count* determines what value will be added to the semaphore counter. Typically, this value is 1. The *lpPrevCount* parameter points to a variable that will contain the previous semaphore count. If you don't need this count, pass NULL for this parameter. The function returns non-zero if successful and zero on failure.

The following program demonstrates how to use a semaphore. It reworks the previous program so that the two threads will not execute concurrently. That is, it forces the threads to be serialized. Notice that the semaphore handle is a global variable that is created when the window is first created.

This allows it to be used by all threads (including the main thread) in the program.

```
/* A multithreaded program that illustrates synchronization
   using a standard semaphore. */

#define PROCMAX 5 /* maximum number of processes */

#include <windows.h>
#include <string.h>
#include <stdio.h>
#include "proc.h"

LRESULT CALLBACK WindowFunc(HWND, UINT, WPARAM, LPARAM);
DWORD MyThread1(LPVOID param);
DWORD MyThread2(LPVOID param);

char szWinName[] = "MyWin"; /* name of window class */

char str[255]; /* holds output strings */

int X-0, Y=0; /* current output location */
int maxX, maxY; /* screen dimensions */

int procnum = 0;

DWORD Tid1, Tid2; /* thread IDs */

HDC memdc;
HBITMAP hbit;
HBRUSH hbrush;

PROCESS_INFORMATION pinfo[PROCMAX];

HANDLE hSema; /* handle to semaphore */

TEXTMETRIC tm;

int WINAPI WinMain(HINSTANCE hThisInst, HINSTANCE hPrevInst,
                   LPSTR lpszArgs, int nWinMode)
{
  HWND hwnd;
  MSG msg;
  WNDCLASS wcl;
  HANDLE hAccel;

  /* Define a window class. */
  wcl.hInstance = hThisInst; /* handle to this instance */
```

14

```
wcl.lpszClassName = szWinName; /* window class name */
wcl.lpfnWndProc = WindowFunc; /* window function */
wcl.style = 0; /* default style */

wcl.hIcon = LoadIcon(NULL, IDI_APPLICATION); /* icon style */
wcl.hCursor = LoadCursor(NULL, IDC_ARROW); /* cursor style */

/* specify name of menu resource */
wcl.lpszMenuName = "MYMENU"; /* main menu */

wcl.cbClsExtra = 0; /* no extra */
wcl.cbWndExtra = 0; /* information needed */

/* Make the window white. */
wcl.hbrBackground = GetStockObject(WHITE_BRUSH);

/* Register the window class. */
if(!RegisterClass (&wcl)) return 0;

/* Now that a window class has been registered, a window
   can be created. */
hwnd = CreateWindow(
  szWinName, /* name of window class */
  "Demonstrate Semaphores and Synchronization", /* title */
  WS_OVERLAPPEDWINDOW, /* window style - normal */
  CW_USEDEFAULT, /* X coordinate - let Windows decide */
  CW_USEDEFAULT, /* Y coordinate - let Windows decide */
  CW_USEDEFAULT, /* width - let Windows decide */
  CW_USEDEFAULT, /* height - let Windows decide */
  HWND_DESKTOP, /* no parent window */
  NULL, /* no menu */
  hThisInst, /* handle of this instance of the program */
  NULL /* no additional arguments */
);

/* load accelerators */
hAccel = LoadAccelerators(hThisInst, "MYMENU");

/* Display the window. */
ShowWindow(hwnd, nWinMode);
UpdateWindow(hwnd);

/* Create the message loop. */
while(GetMessage(&msg, NULL, 0, 0))
{
  if(!TranslateAccelerator(hwnd, hAccel, &msg)) {
    TranslateMessage(&msg); /* allow use of keyboard */
    DispatchMessage(&msg); /* return control to Windows */
```

```
      }
    }
    return msg.wParam;
}

/* This function is called by Windows 95 and is passed
   messages from the message queue.
*/
LRESULT CALLBACK WindowFunc(HWND hwnd, UINT message,
                           WPARAM wParam,
                           LPARAM lParam)
{
  HDC hdc;
  PAINTSTRUCT paintstruct;
  STARTUPINFO startin;

  switch(message) {
    case WM_CREATE:
      hSema = CreateSemaphore(NULL, 1, 1, "mysem");

      /* get screen coordinates */
      maxX = GetSystemMetrics(SM_CXSCREEN);
      maxY = GetSystemMetrics(SM_CYSCREEN);

      /* make a compatible memory image device */
      hdc = GetDC(hwnd);
      memdc = CreateCompatibleDC(hdc);
      hbit = CreateCompatibleBitmap(hdc, maxX, maxY);
      SelectObject(memdc, hbit);
      hbrush = GetStockObject(WHITE_BRUSH);
      SelectObject(memdc, hbrush);
      PatBlt(memdc, 0, 0, maxX, maxY, PATCOPY);
      ReleaseDC(hwnd, hdc);
      break;
    case WM_COMMAND:
      switch(LOWORD(wParam)) {
        case ID_PROCESS:
          if(procnum==PROCMAX) {
            MessageBox(hwnd, "Can't Create", "Error", MB_OK);
            break; /* no more than PROCMAX */
          }

          /* get text metrics */
          GetTextMetrics(memdc, &tm);

          sprintf(str, "Execute Process %d.", procnum);
          TextOut(memdc, X, Y, str, strlen(str));
          Y = Y + tm.tmHeight + tm.tmExternalLeading;
```

14

```
      InvalidateRect(hwnd, NULL, 1);

      /* Start a new process */
      startin.cb = sizeof(STARTUPINFO);
      startin.lpReserved = NULL;
      startin.lpDesktop = NULL;
      startin.lpTitle = NULL;
      startin.dwFlags = STARTF_USESHOWWINDOW;
      startin.cbReserved2 = 0;
      startin.lpReserved2 = NULL;
      startin.wShowWindow = SW_SHOWMINIMIZED;

      CreateProcess(NULL, "test.exe",
                    NULL, NULL, FALSE, 0,
                    NULL, NULL, &startin, &pinfo[procnum]);
      procnum++;
      break;
    case ID_KILLPROC:
      if(procnum) procnum--;
      else {
        MessageBox(hwnd, "No process to terminate.",
                         "Error", MB_OK);
        break;
      }

      /* get text metrics */
      GetTextMetrics(memdc, &tm);

      TerminateProcess(pinfo[procnum].hProcess, 0);
      sprintf(str, "Terminate Process %d.", procnum);
      TextOut(memdc, X, Y, str, strlen(str));
      Y = Y + tm.tmHeight + tm.tmExternalLeading;
      InvalidateRect(hwnd, NULL, 1);
      break;
    case ID_THREAD:
      CreateThread(NULL, 0, (LPTHREAD_START_ROUTINE)MyThread1,
                   (LPVOID) hwnd, 0, &Tid1);
      CreateThread(NULL, 0, (LPTHREAD_START_ROUTINE)MyThread2,
                   (LPVOID) hwnd, 0, &Tid2);
      break;
    case ID_HELP:
      MessageBox(hwnd, "F2: Start Process\nF3: Start Thread",
                 "Help", MB_OK);
      break;
  }
  break;
```

```
        case WM_PAINT: /* process a repaint request */
          hdc = BeginPaint(hwnd, &paintstruct); /* get DC */

          /* now, copy memory image onto screen */
          BitBlt(hdc, 0, 0, maxX, maxY, memdc, 0, 0, SRCCOPY);
          EndPaint(hwnd, &paintstruct); /* release DC */
          break;
        case WM_LBUTTONDOWN: /* process left button */
          X = LOWORD(lParam); /* set X,Y to */
          Y = HIWORD(lParam); /* mouse location */
          break;
        case WM_DESTROY: /* terminate the program */
          DeleteDC(memdc); /* delete the memory device */
          PostQuitMessage(0);
          break;
        default:
          /* Let Windows 95 process any messages not specified in
          the preceding switch statement. */
          return DefWindowProc(hwnd, message, wParam, lParam);
    }
    return 0;
}

/* First thread of execution. */
DWORD MyThread1(LPVOID param)
{
    int i;
    DWORD curTid = Tid1;

    /* get text metrics */
    GetTextMetrics(memdc, &tm);

    /* wait for access to be granted */
    if(WaitForSingleObject(hSema, 10000)==WAIT_TIMEOUT) {
        MessageBox((HWND)param, "Time Out Thread 1",
                   "Semaphore Error", MB_OK);
        return 0;
    }

    for(i=0; i<10; i++) {
        Sleep(500);
        sprintf(str, "Thread 1, ID #%lu, beep #%d",
                curTid, i);
        TextOut(memdc, X, Y, str, strlen(str));
        Y = Y + tm.tmHeight + tm.tmExternalLeading;
        InvalidateRect((HWND) param, NULL, 1);
        MessageBeep(-1);
    }
```

14

```
    ReleaseSemaphore(hSema, 1, NULL);
    return 0;
}

/* Second thread of execution. */
DWORD MyThread2(LPVOID param)
{
  int i;
  DWORD curTid = Tid2;

  /* get text metrics */
  GetTextMetrics(memdc, &tm);

  /* wait for access to be granted */
  if(WaitForSingleObject(hSema, 10000)==WAIT_TIMEOUT) {
    MessageBox((HWND)param, "Time Out Thread 2",
               "Semaphore Error", MB_OK);
    return 0;
  }

  for(i=0; i<10; i++) {
    Sleep(200);
    sprintf(str, "Thread 2");
    TextOut(memdc, X, Y, str, strlen(str));
    Y = Y + tm.tmHeight + tm.tmExternalLeading;
    InvalidateRect((HWND) param, NULL, 1);
  }
  ReleaseSemaphore(hSema, 1, NULL);
  return 0;
}
```

Using an Event Object

As explained earlier, an event object is used to notify one thread or process
when an event has occurred. To create an event object, use the
CreateEvent( ) API function shown here:

> HANDLE CreateEvent(LPSECURITY_ATTRIBUTES *lpAttr*,
>   BOOL *Manual*, BOOL *Initial*,
>   LPSTR *lpszName*);

Here, *lpAttr* is a pointer to security attributes. If NULL, then no security
attributes are used, which is the case for Windows 95. The value of *Manual*
determines how the event object will be affected after the event has
occurred. If *Manual* is **TRUE** (non-zero), then the event object is reset only
by a call to the **ResetEvent( )** function. Otherwise, the event object is reset
automatically after a blocked thread is granted access. The value of *Initial*

specifies the initial state of the object. If it is **TRUE**, the event object is set (the event is signaled). If it is **FALSE**, the event object is cleared (the event is not signaled).

lpszName points to a string that becomes the name of the event object. Event objects are global objects that may be used by other processes. As such, when two processes each open an event object using the same name, both are referring to the same object. In this way, two processes can be synchronized. The name may also be NULL, in which case the object is localized to one process.

CreateEvent( ) returns a handle to the event object if successful and NULL otherwise.

Once an event object has been created, the thread (or process) that is waiting for the event to occur simply calls **WaitForSingleObject( )**, using the handle of the event object as the first parameter. This causes execution of that thread or process to be suspended until the event occurs.

To signal that an event has occurred, use the **SetEvent( )** function, shown here:

> BOOL SetEvent(HANDLE *hEventObject*);

Here, *hEventObject* is the handle of a previously created event object. When this function is called, the first thread or process waiting for the event will return from **WaitForSingleObject( )** and begin execution.

14

To see how an event object operates, modify the preceding program as follows. First, declare a global handle called **hEvent**. Next, add the following line inside the **WM_CREATE** case statement:

```
hEvent = CreateEvent(NULL, FALSE, FALSE, "myevent");
```

Then change **MyThread1( )** and **MyThread2( )** as shown here:

```
/* First thread of execution. */
DWORD MyThread1(LPVOID param)
{
  int i;
  DWORD curTid = Tid1;

  /* get text metrics */
  GetTextMetrics(memdc, &tm);

  /* wait for event */
  if(WaitForSingleObject(hEvent, 10000)==WAIT_TIMEOUT) {
```

```
        MessageBox((HWND)param, "Time Out Thread 1",
                "Event Error", MB_OK);
        return 0;
    }

  for(i=0; i<10; i++) {
    Sleep(500);
    sprintf(str, "Thread ID #%lu, beep #%d",
            curTid, i);
    TextOut(memdc, X, Y, str, strlen(str));
    Y = Y + tm.tmHeight + tm.tmExternalLeading;
    InvalidateRect((HWND) param, NULL, 1);
    MessageBeep(-1);
  }
  return 0;
}

/* Second thread of execution. */
DWORD MyThread2(LPVOID param)
{
  int i;
  DWORD curTid = Tid2;

  /* get text metrics */
  GetTextMetrics(memdc, &tm);

  for(i=0; i<10; i++) {
    Sleep(200);
    sprintf(str, "Thread 2");
    TextOut(memdc, X, Y, str, strlen(str));
    Y = Y + tm.tmHeight + tm.tmExternalLeading;
    InvalidateRect((HWND) param, NULL, 1);
  }

  /* send event notification */
  SetEvent(hEvent);
  return 0;
}
```

Now when the program executes, **MyThread1( )** is blocked until
MyThread2( ) completes and signals that it is done.

Things to Try

This chapter really just scratches the surface of Windows 95's multitasking
and synchronization subsystems and abilities. Some areas that you will want
to explore on your own include setting and changing a thread's or process's

scheduling priority. A task's priority partially determines how much CPU time it is given. Another thing to try is using a semaphore (or other synchronization objects) as a means of communicating between two processes.

In the next chapter, three subsystems of the API are explored.

14

Chapter

15

Exploring the API: The Clipboard, Carets, and Dropped Files

In the preceding chapters, those aspects of Windows 95 common to most programs have been discussed. However, Windows 95 contains many more features and functions you can use. In fact, the Win32 application program interface (API) contains several hundred functions, and this book only scratches the surface of what you have available. Any real-world application will undoubtedly use several more of the API functions.

The sheer size of the API makes it intimidating. However, what makes the API manageable is the fact that it is a collection of subsystems. Once you understand the purpose and general operation of a subsystem, it is usually quite easy to use. You have already used pieces of several subsystems in the previous chapters. For example, you have used the window subsystem to create a window, the dialog box subsystem to support dialog boxes, and the mouse subsystem to manage the mouse. Several of the more common Windows 95 subsystems are briefly described in Table 15-1.

Subsystem Name	Purpose
Accelerators	Manages accelerator keys
Atoms	Creates and manages atoms (unique integer values)
Bitmaps	Manages bitmapped resources
Carets	Manages carets (text cursors)
Communications	Supports asynchronous communication
Consoles	Supports consoles
Clipboard	Manages the clipboard
Clipping regions	Manages clipping regions
Controls	Controls
Curve drawing	Draws arcs
Device contexts	Creates and manages device contexts
Dialog boxes	Creates and manages dialog boxes
Drag-drop files	Supports drag-drop file functions
Drawing tools	Creates and manages drawing tools, such as brushes and pens
DDE	Support for dynamic data exchange
File I/O	File I/O
Fonts	Creates and manages text fonts
GDI objects	Obtains, selects, or deletes objects
Icons	Creates, loads, and manages icons
Keyboard	Manages the keyboard
Line-drawing	Draws lines
Mapping	Manages window mapping modes and coordinate translations
MDI	Supports the multi-document interface
Menus	Manages menus
Messages	Manages the Windows 95 message system
Metafiles	Support for metafiles
Mouse	Manages the mouse
OLE	Object linking and embedding
Painting and drawing	Supports the filling of regions, the display of text, and responses to the WM_PAINT message
Palette	Manages the color palette

Common
Windows 95
Subsystems
Table 15-1.

Subsystem Name	Purpose
Paths	Supports complex graphics output
Pipe	Supports pipes
Printing	Manages printed output
Processes and threads	Manages multitasking
Rectangles	Manages rectangular regions
Scrolling	Manages scroll bars
Sound	Generates sound
Strings	Supports string resources
Text output	Outputs text to a window
Time and timers	Manages system time and timers
Version control	Version management
Windows	Creates and manages windows

Common
Windows 95
Subsystems
(*continued*)
Table 15-1.

Some of the API subsystems are quite small. For example, the dropped file system contains only 4 functions. A few are very complex. For example, the OLE (object linking and embedding) subsystem is composed of over 100 functions and is itself almost like an operating system within an operating system. However, most of the API subsystems contain around 20 to 30 functions and are easy to understand and to use.

It is, of course, far beyond the scope of this book to describe each of the Windows 95 subsystems. (A complete subsystem-by-subsystem description of the entire Win32 API can be found in Volumes 2 and 3 of the *Osborne Windows Programming Series* by Schildt, Pappas, and Murray (Berkeley, CA: Osborne/McGraw-Hill, 1994).) However, to illustrate how the subsystems simplify Windows programming and make the API more accessible, three will be briefly examined in this chapter: the clipboard, carets, and dropped-file functions.

15

Using the Clipboard

In Windows, the clipboard has two main functions. First, it serves as short-term storage for some item of data. For example, when you move a block of text using a text editor, you temporarily copy the text to the clipboard and then copy it from the clipboard to its new location in your document. The second function of the clipboard is to perform the simplest form of interprocess communication available to a Windows program. In this capacity, it is one of the most popular ways that users exchange data between different programs. Fortunately, the clipboard is managed in the same way whether it is used for short-term storage or for sharing data between programs.

The clipboard is a region of global memory that is shared by all processes running in the system. Your program may interact with the clipboard by writing data to it or reading data from it—or both. Further, one program may write data to the clipboard and another program may read that data. Both of these situations are illustrated by the example program shown later in this section.

The Clipboard Subsystem

The clipboard is managed by a subsystem of the API that contains 16 functions. The clipboard functions and their purposes are shown in Table 15-2.

Even though the clipboard subsystem defines several functions, you will not usually need to use them all. In fact, of these functions, we will only be using **OpenClipboard( )**, **EmptyClipboard( )**, **SetClipboardData( )**, **GetClipboardData( )**, and **CloseClipboard( )** in the example program. As you will see when you explore other API subsystems, it is common for a subsystem to contain several functions that apply only to special situations. Usually your application will need to make use of only those functions that apply to the subsystem's most common usage. For example, in the case of the clipboard subsystem, it is possible for a program to monitor the clipboard. A program that does this is called a *clipboard viewer*. As you can see, several of the functions shown in Table 15-2 support the creation and management of a clipboard viewer. However, if your application does not use a clipboard viewer, none of these functions apply. The key point to understand is that each API subsystem gives you all the functions you will need to fully utilize the feature of Windows that it supports. Your program, however, need only use those functions that it requires.

The clipboard is one of the easier Windows features to support in your programs because it involves only two basic operations: putting data into the clipboard and getting data from the clipboard. The following sections describe how these operations are accomplished.

Function	Purpose
ChangeClipboardChain	Removes a window from the list of clipboard viewers
CloseClipboard	Terminates access to the clipboard
CountClipboardFormats	Obtains the number of different data formats currently in the clipboard
EmptyClipboard	Clears the clipboard
EnumClipboardFormats	Enumerates the currently available clipboard formats
GetClipboardData	Returns a handle to the clipboard data
GetClipboardFormatName	Obtains the name of a custom format
GetClipboardOwner	Returns the handle of the window that currently owns the clipboard
GetClipboardViewer	Obtains the handle of the first clipboard viewer
GetOpenClipboardWindow	Returns the handle of the window that currently has the clipboard open
GetPriorityClipboardFormat	Gets best format for data
IsClipboardFormatAvailable	Determines if a data format is available
OpenClipboard	Opens the clipboard
RegisterClipboardFormat	Registers a custom clipboard data format
SetClipboardData	Puts data into the clipboard
SetClipboardViewer	Inserts a clipboard viewer into the list of viewers

The Clipboard
Functions
Table 15-2.

15

Putting Data into the Clipboard

The general procedure for putting data into the clipboard is as follows:

1. Allocate a block of global memory large enough to hold the data that you want to put into the clipboard.
2. Copy your data into the global memory.

3. Open the clipboard.
4. Clear any preexisting clipboard contents.
5. Set the clipboard's data to your allocated memory.
6. Close the clipboard.

The following code fragment implements these steps:

```
/* obtain global memory */
hGout  = GlobalAlloc(GHND | DMEM_DDESHARE,
                     (DWORD) 100);
p   = GlobalLock(hGout);

/* copy data into global memory */

GlobalUnlock(hGout);
if(OpenClipboard(hwnd)) {
  EmptyClipboard();
  SetClipboardData(CF_TEXT, hGout);
  CloseClipboard();
}
```

Here, **hGout** is a handle to global memory and **p** is a pointer. Let's examine this fragment in detail. In the first line, global memory is allocated using **GlobalAlloc( )**, which has this prototype:

HGLOBAL GlobalAlloc(UINT *How*, DWORD *dwSize*);

GlobalAlloc( ) allocates memory from the global heap and returns a handle to it. It returns NULL if the memory cannot be allocated. The number of bytes to allocate is passed in *dwSize*. If this amount of memory is unavailable, then the function fails. Precisely how memory is allocated from the global heap is determined by the value of *How*, which must be a valid combination of the values described in Table 15-3.

The memory allocated by **GlobalAlloc( )** becomes a global memory object. When allocating memory for the clipboard, memory must be moveable and shareable.

As stated, **GlobalAlloc( )** returns a handle, *not* a pointer to the allocated memory. To obtain a pointer to the memory allocated by **GlobalAlloc( )**, you must call **GlobalLock( )**. Its prototype is shown here:

LPVOID GlobalLock(HGLOBAL *hObj*);

GlobalLock( ) locks the object specified by the handle passed in *hObj*. A locked object cannot be moved or discarded. **GlobalLock( )** returns the

Macro	Effect
GHND	Memory is moveable and initialized to zero.
GMEM_DDESHARE	Memory is used for DDE, OLE, or clipboard operations.
GMEM_DISCARDABLE	Memory is discardable.
GMEM_FIXED	Memory is not moveable.
GMEM_LOWER	Memory is not bank switched. (This value is ignored because it is obsolete.)
GMEM_MOVEABLE	Memory is moveable.
GMEM_NOCOMPACT	Memory may not be compacted or removed.
GMEM_NODISCARD	Memory may not be discarded.
GMEM_NOTIFY	A notification function is called when the memory is discarded. (Obsolete.)
GMEM_NOT_BANKED	Memory is not bank switched. (This value is ignored because it is obsolete.)
GMEM_SHARE	Same as GMEM_DDESHARE.
GMEM_ZEROINIT	Memory is initialized to zero.
GPTR	Memory is not moveable and is initialized to zero.

Memory
Allocation
Macros and
Their Effects
Table 15-3.

address of the start of the object if successful and NULL on failure. A global memory object must be locked before it can be used by your program. Thus, **GlobalLock( )** is the way that your program obtains a pointer to a global memory object. Locking the memory also prevents another process from accessing it while it is in use by your program.

After you have obtained a pointer to the global memory, you must then copy whatever information you want to put into the clipboard into that memory via the pointer. Once you have copied the data, you may unlock the memory by calling **GlobalUnlock( )**, whose prototype is shown here:

    BOOL GlobalUnlock(HGLOBAL *hObj*);

GlobalUnlock( ) returns zero if successful and non-zero otherwise. The handle of the memory to unlock is passed in *hObj*.

After your data has been copied into global memory, you must next open the clipboard by calling **OpenClipboard( )**, whose prototype is shown here:

BOOL OpenClipboard(HWND *hWnd*);

OpenClipboard( ) grants the calling application access to the clipboard (that is, the clipboard is opened). When an application opens the clipboard, other applications may not use it. The function returns non-zero if the clipboard may be opened and zero if access is denied. The handle of the window opening the clipboard is passed in *hWnd*.

Once the clipboard has been successfully opened, your application must first clear any preexisting clipboard contents by calling **EmptyClipboard( )**. Its prototype is shown here:

BOOL EmptyClipboard(void);

EmptyClipboard( ) destroys any preexisting data in the clipboard, frees all preexisting data handles, and assigns the clipboard to the calling process. The clipboard must be open before **EmptyClipboard( )** is called. The function returns non-zero if successful and zero otherwise.

To put data into the clipboard, the clipboard must be set to point to the memory that contains your data by calling **SetClipboardData( )**, whose prototype is shown here:

HANDLE SetClipboardData(UINT *Format*, HANDLE *hData*);

SetClipboardData( ) sets the region of memory that contains the data used by the clipboard. It returns a handle to the data if successful and NULL if an error occurs. The handle to the region of memory is passed in *hData*, which must be a handle to a global data object.

The format of the data is specified in *Format*. The value of *Format* may be either a custom format or one of the built-in formats described in Table 15-4.

For **CF_TEXT**, **CF_OEMTEXT**, and **CF_UNICODETEXT** formats, the text is null-terminated and lines end with carriage-return/linefeed sequences. Formats in the range **CF_PRIVATEFIRST** through **CF_PRIVATELAST** are reserved for private clipboard formats. Formats in the range **CF_GDIOBJFIRST** through **CF_GDIOBJLAST** are reserved for custom GDI object formats.

After the data has been set, your program should immediately relinquish control of the clipboard by calling **CloseClipboard( )**, shown here:

BOOL CloseClipboard(void);

This function returns non-zero if successful and zero on failure.

Format	Format Type
CF_BITMAP	Bitmap
CF_DIB	Bitmap plus BITMAPINFO header
CF_DIF	Data interchange format
CF_DSPBITMAP	Private bitmap
CF_DSPENHMETAFILE	Enhanced private metafile
CF_DSPMETAFILEPICT	Private metafile
CF_DSPTEXT	Private text
CF_ENHMETAFILE	Enhanced metafile
CF_METAFILEPICT	METAFILEPICT-style metafile
CF_OEMTEXT	OEM text
CF_OWNERDISPLAY	Private format defined by owner
CF_PALETTE	Color palette
CF_PENDATA	Format for pen-based computing extensions
CF_RIFF	Resource interchange file format
CF_SYLK	Symbolic link
CF_TEXT	Text
CF_TIFF	Tag image file format
CF_WAVE	Sound resource WAVE file
CF_UNICODETEXT	Text in UNICODE

Commonly Used Built-in Clipboard Formats
Table 15-4.

Reading Data from the Clipboard

15

To read data from the clipboard, follow this general procedure:

1. Open the clipboard.
2. Obtain a pointer to the clipboard's data.
3. Copy the data from the clipboard.
4. Close the clipboard.

The following fragment implements these steps:

```
if(OpenClipboard(hwnd)) {
  hGin = GetClipboardData(CF_TEXT);
  p = GlobalLock(hGin);
```

```
/* copy data from the clipboard */

GlobalUnlock(hGin);
CloseClipboard();
}
```

Before the clipboard data can be accessed, it must be opened. Next, a handle to the global memory associated with the clipboard is obtained using a call to **GetClipboardData( )**. Its prototype is shown here:

HANDLE GetClipboardData(UINT *Format*);

GetClipboardData( ) returns a handle to the global data object that contains information in the specified format. The format of the data is passed in *Format*. If no such data is found, then the function returns NULL. In this fragment, the data format is **CF_TEXT**. To convert the handle returned by **GetClipboardData( )** into a pointer, use **GlobalLock( )** (described earlier).

Next, your program must copy the data from the clipboard's memory. Since the handle returned by **GetClipboardData( )** is to a region of memory that is controlled by the clipboard, your program should copy information from this region at once, prior to returning control back to Windows. The reason is easy to understand: once control returns to Windows, the clipboard may be overwritten with new information.

A Clipboard Demonstration Program

The following program demonstrates clipboard access. It allows you to write data to the clipboard and to read data from it. As the program is written, it only works with text data. However, you might find it interesting to try expanding the program to accept other data formats. Sample output from the program is shown in Figure 15-1. The program loads the clipboard when the menu option Clipboard Output is selected. It gets input from the clipboard when Clipboard Input is chosen. You can also load the clipboard with text from another program (such as a text editor) and then input it by choosing Clipboard Input.

```
/* Demonstrate the clipboard. */

#include <windows.h>
#include <string.h>
#include "clip.h"

#define MAXSIZE 100
```

```
LRESULT CALLBACK WindowFunc(HWND, UINT, WPARAM, LPARAM);

char szWinName[] = "MyWin"; /* name of window class */

HGLOBAL hGout, hGin;
char text[] = "This is sample clipboard text.";

int WINAPI WinMain(HINSTANCE hThisInst, HINSTANCE hPrevInst,
                   LPSTR lpszArgs, int nWinMode)
{
  HWND hwnd;
  MSG msg;
  WNDCLASS wcl;
  HACCEL hAccel;

  /* Define a window class. */
  wcl.hInstance = hThisInst; /* handle to this instance */
  wcl.lpszClassName = szWinName; /* window class name */
  wcl.lpfnWndProc = WindowFunc; /* window function */
  wcl.style = 0; /* default style */

  wcl.hIcon = LoadIcon(NULL, IDI_APPLICATION); /* icon style */
  wcl.hCursor = LoadCursor(NULL, IDC_ARROW); /* cursor style */

  /* specify name of menu resource */
  wcl.lpszMenuName = "MYMENU"; /* main menu */

  wcl.cbClsExtra = 0; /* no extra */
  wcl.cbWndExtra = 0; /* information needed */

  /* Make the window white. */
  wcl.hbrBackground = GetStockObject(WHITE_BRUSH);

  /* Register the window class. */
  if(!RegisterClass (&wcl)) return 0;

  /* Now that a window class has been registered, a window
     can be created. */
  hwnd = CreateWindow(
    szWinName, /* name of window class */
    "Using the Clipboard", /* title */
    WS_OVERLAPPEDWINDOW, /* window style - normal */
    CW_USEDEFAULT, /* X coordinate - let Windows decide */
    CW_USEDEFAULT, /* Y coordinate - let Windows decide */
    CW_USEDEFAULT, /* width - let Windows decide */
    CW_USEDEFAULT, /* height - let Windows decide */
    HWND_DESKTOP, /* no parent window */
```

15

```
    NULL, /* no menu */
    hThisInst, /* handle of this instance of the program */
    NULL /* no additional arguments */
  );

  /* load the keyboard accelerators */
  hAccel = LoadAccelerators(hThisInst, "MYMENU");

  /* Display the window. */
  ShowWindow(hwnd, nWinMode);
  UpdateWindow(hwnd);

  /* Create the message loop. */
  while(GetMessage(&msg, NULL, 0, 0))
  {
    if(!TranslateAccelerator(hwnd, hAccel, &msg)) {
      TranslateMessage(&msg); /* allow use of keyboard */
      DispatchMessage(&msg); /* return control to Windows */
    }
  }
  return msg.wParam;
}

/* This function is called by Windows 95 and is passed
   messages from the message queue.
*/
LRESULT CALLBACK WindowFunc(HWND hwnd, UINT message,
                            WPARAM wParam, LPARAM lParam)
{
  int i;
  char *p;
  char str[255];

  switch (message) {
    case WM_COMMAND:
      switch(LOWORD(wParam)) {
        case ID_OUTTOCLIP:
          hGout = GlobalAlloc(GHND | GMEM_DDESHARE,
                              (DWORD) MAXSIZE);
          p = GlobalLock(hGout);
          strcpy(p, text); /* copy text to global memory */
          GlobalUnlock(hGout);
          if(OpenClipboard(hwnd)) {
            EmptyClipboard();
            SetClipboardData(CF_TEXT, hGout);
            CloseClipboard();
            MessageBox(hwnd, text, "Output to Clipboard", MB_OK);
          }
```

```
            break;
         case ID_READFROMCLIP:
            if(OpenClipboard(hwnd)) {
               hGin = GetClipboardData(CF_TEXT);
               p = GlobalLock(hGin);

               /* copy text from global memory */
               for(i=0; i<MAXSIZE; i++) str[i] = *p++;
               *p = '\0'; /* null-terminate */

               GlobalUnlock(hGin);
               CloseClipboard();
               MessageBox(hwnd, str, "Input from Clipboard", MB_OK);
            }
            break;
      }
      break;
    case WM_DESTROY: /* terminate the program */
      PostQuitMessage(0);
      break;
    /* Let Windows 95 process any messages not specified in
       the preceding cases. */
    default:
      return(DefWindowProc(hwnd, message, wParam, lParam));
  }
  return 0;
}
```

This program requires the following resource file:

```
#include <windows.h>
#include "clip.h"

MYMENU MENU
{
  POPUP "Option"
  {
    MENUITEM "Clipboard Output", ID_OUTTOCLIP
    MENUITEM "Clipboard Input", ID_READFROMCLIP
  }
}


MYMENU ACCELERATORS
{
  VK_F1, ID_OUTTOCLIP, VIRTKEY
  VK_F2, ID_READFROMCLIP, VIRTKEY
}
```

15

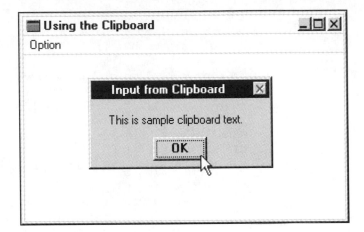

Sample output
from the
clipboard
program
Figure 15-1.

The header file **clip.h** is shown here:

```
#define ID_OUTTOCLIP      101
#define ID_READFROMCLIP   102
```

Using Text Cursors

Unlike the clipboard, which is one of the most commonly used API
subsystems, the subsystem that supports text cursors is one of the most
overlooked. In the language of Windows, a text cursor is called a *caret*.
(Technically, a caret is a non-mouse cursor. But this almost always means a
text cursor.) Carets are typically used to indicate where the next keystroke
will be echoed when keyboard input is taking place. Creating a caret is one
way to display a cursor in the client area of a window. There is only one
caret in the system. That is, carets are system-wide resources. Thus, changes
you make to the caret may affect other programs.

The general procedure for using a caret is as follows: Your program should
create a caret when one of its windows gains input focus and destroy it
before losing input focus. A window gains input focus when you click the
mouse on a window or when you select a window using keyboard
commands. When input focus is gained, a **WM_SETFOCUS** message is
received. When input focus is lost (i.e., when another window gains input
focus), your program will receive a **WM_KILLFOCUS** message.

The functions that comprise the caret subsystem are shown in Table 15-5. Of
these functions, the sample program shown later in this section uses
CreateCaret( ), **DestroyCaret( )**, **SetCaretPos( )**, and **ShowCaret( )**.

Function	Purpose
CreateCaret	Creates a caret
DestroyCaret	Destroys a caret
GetCaretBlinkTime	Obtains the rate at which the caret blinks
GetCaretPos	Obtains the location of the caret
HideCaret	Hides the caret (i.e., the caret is removed from the window)
SetCaretBlinkTime	Sets the rate at which the caret blinks
SetCaretPos	Moves the caret to the specified location
ShowCaret	Displays the caret

The Caret
Subsystem
Functions
Table 15-5.

Creating a Caret

A caret is created using the **CreateCaret( )** function, shown here:

```
BOOL CreateCaret(HWND hWnd, HBITMAP hbm,
                 int nWidth, int nHeight);
```

CreateCaret( ) acquires control of the caret for a window and determines its shape. The window is specified by *hWnd*. The dimensions of the caret are specified by *nWidth* and *nHeight*. These values may be defaulted by setting them equal to NULL. **CreateCaret( )** returns non-zero if successful and zero on failure.

The caret may be either a bitmapped image or a block cursor. For a block cursor, the width and height determines its shape and extents. In this case, *hbm* must be either NULL or 1. If *hbm* is NULL, then the caret is shown normally. If *hbm* is 1, then the caret is shown in low intensity. To use a bitmap as the caret, pass its handle in *hbm*. In this case, the *nWidth* and *nHeight* parameters are not relevant.

Showing and Hiding a Caret

By default, carets are hidden (that is, not displayed). They may be displayed by calling **ShowCaret( )**. The prototype for **ShowCaret( )** is shown here:

```
BOOL ShowCaret(HWND hWnd);
```

The handle of the window that owns the caret is specified in *hWnd*. The caret is shown at the current caret location. The function returns non-zero if successful and zero on failure.

15

Carets can be hidden (removed from view) using **HideCaret( )**. Its prototype is shown here:

    BOOL HideCaret(HWND *hWnd*);

hWnd is the handle of the window that owns the caret. **HideCaret( )** returns non-zero if successful and zero on failure.

To return a hidden caret to view, call **ShowCaret( )**. Calls to **HideCaret( )** are cumulative and must be undone with an equal number of calls to **ShowCaret( )**. For example, calling **HideCaret( )** five times implies that your program must call **ShowCaret( )** five times in order to return the caret to the screen.

Setting a Caret's Position

A caret may be positioned at a specific location in a window by calling **SetCaretPos( )**, shown here:

    BOOL SetCaretPos(int *nX*, int *nY*);

SetCaretPos( ) positions the caret at the location specified by *nX,nY*. Your program must be the focus of input before calling this function. The function returns non-zero if successful and zero on failure.

Destroying a Caret

Before your program loses input focus, you must destroy the caret by calling **DestroyCaret( )**. Its prototype is shown here:

    BOOL DestroyCaret(void);

This function returns non-zero if successful and zero on failure.

DestroyCaret( ) destroys the caret owned by the program that calls it. Destroying the caret removes it from the screen.

A Short Caret Demonstration Program

The following program demonstrates carets. It creates a box-shaped caret when input focus is gained. Each time the left mouse button is pressed, the caret moves to the location of the mouse. When the right mouse button is pressed, the size of the caret is increased. Sample output is shown in Figure 15-2.

```
/* Caret demonstration program. */

#include <windows.h>

LRESULT CALLBACK WindowFunc(HWND, UINT, WPARAM, LPARAM);

char szWinName[] = "MyWin"; /* name of window class */

int WINAPI WinMain(HINSTANCE hThisInst, HINSTANCE hPrevInst,
                   LPSTR lpszArgs, int nWinMode)
{
  HWND hwnd;
  MSG msg;
  WNDCLASS wcl;

  /* Define a window class. */
  wcl.hInstance = hThisInst; /* handle to this instance */
  wcl.lpszClassName = szWinName; /* window class name */
  wcl.lpfnWndProc = WindowFunc; /* window function */
  wcl.style = 0; /* default style */

  wcl.hIcon = LoadIcon(NULL, IDI_APPLICATION); /* icon style */
  wcl.hCursor = LoadCursor(NULL, IDC_ARROW); /* cursor style */
  wcl.lpszMenuName = NULL; /* no main menu */

  wcl.cbClsExtra = 0; /* no extra */
  wcl.cbWndExtra = 0; /* information needed */

  /* Make the window white. */
  wcl.hbrBackground = GetStockObject(WHITE_BRUSH);

  /* Register the window class. */
  if(!RegisterClass (&wcl)) return 0;

  /* Now that a window class has been registered, a window
     can be created. */
  hwnd = CreateWindow(
    szWinName, /* name of window class */
    "Demonstrate Carets", /* title */
    WS_OVERLAPPEDWINDOW, /* window style - normal */
    CW_USEDEFAULT, /* X coordinate - let Windows decide */
    CW_USEDEFAULT, /* Y coordinate - let Windows decide */
    CW_USEDEFAULT, /* width - let Windows decide */
    CW_USEDEFAULT, /* height - let Windows decide */
    HWND_DESKTOP, /* no parent window */
    NULL, /* no menu */
    hThisInst, /* handle of this instance of the program */
    NULL /* no additional arguments */
```

15

```
    );

    /* Display the window. */
    ShowWindow(hwnd, nWinMode);
    UpdateWindow(hwnd);

    /* Create the message loop. */
    while(GetMessage(&msg, NULL, 0, 0))
    {
      TranslateMessage(&msg); /* allow use of keyboard */
      DispatchMessage(&msg); /* return control to Windows */
    }
    return msg.wParam;
}

/* This function is called by Windows 95 and is passed
   messages from the message queue.
*/
LRESULT CALLBACK WindowFunc(HWND hwnd, UINT message,
                            WPARAM wParam, LPARAM lParam)
{
  static int CaretX=0, CaretY=0;
  static int width=1, height=1;

  switch (message) {
    case WM_LBUTTONDOWN: /* left button moves caret */
      CaretX = LOWORD(lParam);
      CaretY = HIWORD(lParam);
      SetCaretPos(CaretX, CaretY);
      break;
    case WM_RBUTTONDOWN: /* Right button changes caret */
      DestroyCaret();
      width += 2;  height += 2;
      CreateCaret(hwnd, NULL, width, height);
      ShowCaret(hwnd);
      break;
    case WM_SETFOCUS: /* create caret when focus is acquired */
      CreateCaret(hwnd, NULL, width, height);
      SetCaretPos(CaretX, CaretY);
      ShowCaret(hwnd);
      break;
    case WM_KILLFOCUS: /* destroy before losing focus */
      DestroyCaret();
      break;
    case WM_DESTROY: /* terminate the program */
      DestroyCaret();
      PostQuitMessage(0);
      break;
```

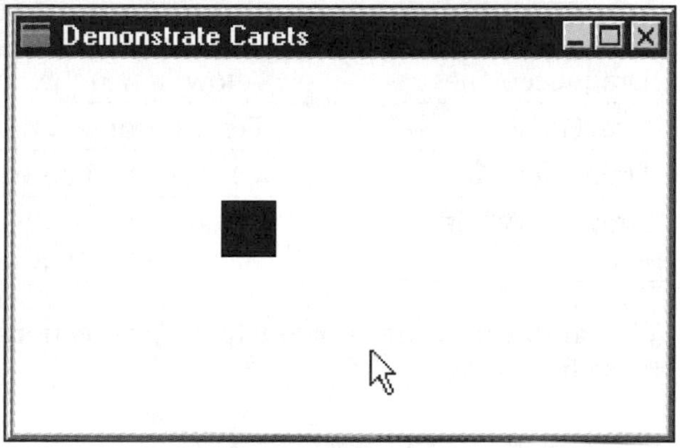

Sample output
from the caret
demonstration
program
Figure 15-2.

```
    /* Let Windows 95 process any messages not specified in
        the preceding cases. */
    default:
        return(DefWindowProc(hwnd, message, wParam, lParam));
    }
    return 0;
}
```

Drag-Drop Files

The last API subsystem that we will examine supports drag-drop files. Using
this subsystem, you can drag a file from the Explorer (or its predecessor, the
File Manager) to your application. When you do this, your application will
receive the file's name (including its path). What your application does with
this information is completely up to you. For example, if your application is
a text editor, by using the drag-drop file functions, you could allow the user
to drag a file from the Explorer to the text editor. The dropped file could
then be edited.

Note: You must include the header file **shellapi.h** to use the
dropped functions.

The functions that comprise the drag-drop file subsystem are shown here:

Function	Purpose
DragAcceptFiles	Allows a window to accept dropped files
DragFinish	Frees a dropped file handle
DragQueryFile	Obtains the name of a dropped file
DragQueryPoint	Obtains the coordinates within the window at which point the file is dropped

The sample program shown later in this section uses all four of these functions.

Accepting Dropped Files

In order for your application to accept dropped files, it must first call
DragAcceptFiles( ), whose prototype is shown here:

     void DragAcceptFiles(HWND *hWnd*, BOOL *Status*);

The handle to the window that will accept a dropped file is passed in *hWnd*.
If *Status* is non-zero, then the window will accept dropped files. This will
cause the window to receive a **WM_DROPFILES** message when a file is
dropped into the window. If *Status* is zero, then the window will not accept
dropped files.

Obtaining the Name of a Dropped File

When a file is dropped into a window, a **WM_DROPFILES** message is
received. To obtain the name of the file, call **DragQueryFile( )**, shown here:

     UINT DragQueryFile(HDROP *hDragDrop*, UINT *Index*,
                 LPSTR *lpszFilename*, UINT *Size*);

The handle of the dropped file is passed in *hDragDrop*. This handle is
acquired from *wParam* when a **WM_DROPFILES** message is received. Since
several files can be dropped in a group, the index of the desired file is passed
in *Index*. File indexes begin with zero. If this parameter is –1, then the
function returns the total number of dropped files.

The filename is copied in the character array pointed to by *lpszFilename*. The
number of characters copied is returned. (If this parameter is NULL, then the
length of the filename is returned.) The size of this array is passed in *Size*.

Obtaining the Location of a Dropped File

The location within a window at which point a file is dropped can be obtained using **DragQueryPoint( )**, whose prototype is shown here:

   BOOL DragQueryPoint(HDROP *hDragDrop*, LPPOINT *lpPoint*);

If the file is dropped within the client area of the window, the function returns non-zero. If the file is dropped outside the client area, zero is returned.

The handle of the dropped file is passed in *hDragDrop*. This handle is obtained from *wParam* when a **WM_DROPFILES** message is received. On return, the location at which the file is dropped is contained in the **POINT** structure pointed to by *lpPoint*. **POINT** is defined like this:

```
typedef struct tagPOINT
{
  LONG x;
  LONG y;
} POINT;
```

Freeing a Dropped File Handle

To free a dropped file handle, call **DragFinish( )**, whose prototype is shown here:

   void DragFinish(HDROP *hDragDrop*);

The handle specified in *hDragDrop* is obtained from *wParam* when a **WM_DROPFILES** message is received.

15

A Sample Drag-Drop File Program

The following program accepts dropped files. It displays the name of the file and the location at which it was dropped. To try the program, drag a file from the Explorer. Sample output is shown in Figure 15-3.

```
/*
  Demonstrate drag-drop file functions.

  To use: Execute this program.  Then, using the Explorer,
          drag a file from the file list to the window created
          by this program and drop it there. This program will
```

```
           then report the name of the file you dropped and the
           location at which it was dropped.
*/

#include <windows.h>
#include <shellapi.h>
#include <stdio.h>
#include <string.h>

LRESULT CALLBACK WindowFunc(HWND, UINT, WPARAM, LPARAM);

char szWinName[] = "MyWin"; /* name of window class */

int WINAPI WinMain(HINSTANCE hThisInst, HINSTANCE hPrevInst,
                   LPSTR lpszArgs, int nWinMode)
{
  HWND hwnd;
  MSG msg;
  WNDCLASS wcl;

  /* Define a window class. */
  wcl.hInstance = hThisInst; /* handle to this instance */
  wcl.lpszClassName = szWinName; /* window class name */
  wcl.lpfnWndProc = WindowFunc; /* window function */
  wcl.style = 0; /* default style */

  wcl.hIcon = LoadIcon(NULL, IDI_APPLICATION); /* icon style */
  wcl.hCursor = LoadCursor(NULL, IDC_ARROW); /* cursor style */
  wcl.lpszMenuName = NULL; /* no main menu */

  wcl.cbClsExtra = 0; /* no extra */
  wcl.cbWndExtra = 0; /* information needed */

  /* Make the window white. */
  wcl.hbrBackground = GetStockObject(WHITE_BRUSH);

  /* Register the window class. */
  if(!RegisterClass (&wcl)) return 0;

  /* Now that a window class has been registered, a window
     can be created. */
  hwnd = CreateWindow(
    szWinName, /* name of window class */
    "Demonstrate Drag-Drop File Functions", /* title */
    WS_OVERLAPPEDWINDOW, /* window style - normal */
    CW_USEDEFAULT, /* X coordinate - let Windows decide */
```

```
       CW_USEDEFAULT, /* Y coordinate - let Windows decide */
       CW_USEDEFAULT, /* width - let Windows decide */
       CW_USEDEFAULT, /* height - let Windows decide */
       HWND_DESKTOP, /* no parent window */
       NULL, /* no menu */
       hThisInst, /* handle of this instance of the program */
       NULL /* no additional arguments */
     );

     /* Display the window. */
     ShowWindow(hwnd, nWinMode);
     UpdateWindow(hwnd);

     /* Create the message loop. */
     while(GetMessage(&msg, NULL, 0, 0))
     {
       TranslateMessage(&msg); /* allow use of keyboard */
       DispatchMessage(&msg); /* return control to Windows */
     }
     return msg.wParam;
}


/* This function is called by Windows 95 and is passed
   messages from the message queue.
*/
LRESULT CALLBACK WindowFunc(HWND hwnd, UINT message,
                            WPARAM wParam, LPARAM lParam)
{
  POINT pt;
  char str[255];
  char fname[255];

  switch (message) {
    case WM_CREATE:
      /* enable dropped file messages */
      DragAcceptFiles(hwnd, 1);
      break;
    case WM_DROPFILES: /* process dropped file messages */
      DragQueryFile((HDROP) wParam, 0, fname, sizeof(fname));
      DragQueryPoint((HDROP) wParam, &pt);
      sprintf(str, " dropped at %d %d", pt.x, pt.y);
      strcat(fname, str);
      MessageBox(hwnd, fname,
                 "Filename and Location of Drop", MB_OK);
      DragFinish((HDROP) wParam);
      break;
```

15

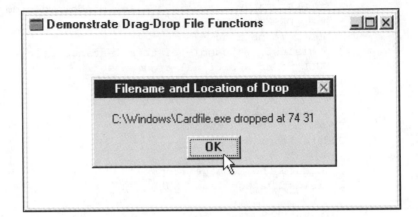

Sample output
from the
dropped file
program
Figure 15-3.

```
case WM_DESTROY: /* terminate the program */
  PostQuitMessage(0);
  break;

/* Let Windows 95 process any messages not specified in
   the preceding cases. */
default:
  return(DefWindowProc(hwnd, message, wParam, lParam));
}
return 0;
}
```

Final Thoughts

You have come a long way in your study of Windows 95 since the first
chapter. Keep in mind that this book only discusses a fraction of the total
API functions available for you to use. If you are going to be doing serious
programming in Windows 95, you must have an API function reference, and you
must take some time to study it. If you are coming from a DOS environment,
remember that Windows in general, and Windows 95 specifically, are
exponentially more complex. Becoming an excellent Windows programmer
requires significant dedication, but the rewards are worth it.

Appendix A

Resource Language Quick Reference

Several resource language statements are discussed in this book. However, the Windows resource script language contains several additional commands. This appendix lists and presents an overview of the most commonly used resource commands along with their most frequently used options. This appendix is intended only as a supplement to the material in the book proper. If you will be doing extensive work with resource files, you will need to have on hand a resource file reference manual.

Keep in mind that new resource commands and options are added when enhancements to Windows occur. You should check the resource guide that comes with your Windows-compatible compiler for current details regarding resource files. Table A-1 shows a list of the resource language statements and gives a brief description of each.

Note: This appendix is adapted (and used by permission) from *The Osborne Windows Programming Series, Volume 1,* by Schildt, Pappas, and Murray (Berkeley, CA: Osborne/McGraw-Hill, 1994).

Resource Statements	Purpose
ACCELERATORS	Defines keys that allow quick selection of menu items.
AUTO3STATE	Creates a three-state automatic check box.
AUTOCHECKBOX	Creates an automatic check box.
AUTORADIOBUTTON	Creates an automatic radio button.
BITMAP	Allows a bitmapped image to be loaded by the application.
CAPTION	Specifies the title for a dialog box.
CHARACTERISTICS	Contains developer-specified information.
CHECKBOX	Creates a check box.
CLASS	Defines the dialog box.
COMBOBOX	Creates a combination box.
CONTROL	Defines a control.
CTEXT	Creates a centered text control.
CURSOR	Allows a bitmapped cursor image to be loaded.
DEFPUSHBUTTON	Creates a default push button.
DIALOG	Defines a dialog box.
DIALOGEX	Creates an extended-style dialog box.
EDITTEXT	Creates an edit control.
EXSTYLE	Specifies extended dialog box styles.
FONT	Defines the font used for drawing text within the dialog box. It can also be used to specify a file containing a new font resource.
GROUPBOX	Creates a group box (that is, two or more controls grouped together).
ICON	Creates an icon control that displays an icon within a dialog box. It can also be used to specify a file containing a bitmapped icon resource.
LISTBOX	Creates a rectangular area that contains a list of strings to be selected by the user.
LTEXT	Creates a left-justified text control.
MENU	Defines a menu resource within a dialog box. It can also be used to specify a menu resource for the application itself.

Resource Statements

Table A-1.

Resource Statements	Purpose
MENUEX	Specifies an extended-style menu resource.
MENUITEM	Defines a menu item. Menu items are usually listed when the menu pops up.
MESSAGETABLE	Creates a message table resource.
POPUP	Defines a popup menu.
PUSHBOX	A type of push button.
PUSHBUTTON	Creates a push button.
RADIOBUTTON	Creates a radio button.
RCDATA	Defines a raw data resource, such as a bitmap defined by an array of integer numbers.
RTEXT	Creates a right-justified text control.
SCROLLBAR	Creates a scroll bar.
STATE3	Creates a three-state check box.
STRINGTABLE	Defines null-terminated ASCII string resources.
STYLE	Defines the style of a dialog box. The style can be a popup or child window.
User-Defined	Allows the definition of a custom resource.
VERSION	Specifies developer-defined version information.
VERSIONINFO	Creates a version information resource.

Resource
Statements
(*continued*)
Table A-1.

In the following sections, an overview of each resource statement is presented.

Note: In addition to the resource commands, a resource file may also contain C/C++–style preprocessor directives.

ACCELERATORS

This statement defines accelerator keys. An accelerator (or "hot key") is a technique for speeding up a menu selection. Accelerator key messages are processed with the **TranslateAccelerator( )** function into **WM_COMMAND** or **WM_SYSCOMMAND** Windows messages.

Syntax and Example
The syntax statement for **ACCELERATORS** is

```
table_name ACCELERATORS
{
```

A

    event, idvalue [, *type*][*options*]
}

An example of the **ACCELERATORS** statement is shown in the following fragment:

```
BackGndColors ACCELERATORS
{
  VK_F1,   IDM_BLACK,   VIRTKEY
  VK_F2,   IDM_WHITE,   VIRTKEY
             .
             .
             .
  VK_F12, IDM_LTGRAY, VIRTKEY
}
```

Parameters and Values

table_name is the name or integer ID value for the resource. *event* identifies the key to be used as an accelerator. The key can be a character key identified with the ASCII character in double quotes (such as "a") or a numeric value for the character, in which case the *type* is **ASCII**. A caret (^) character indicates the use of the control character. A virtual-key character can be identified in the same manner, but here the *type* parameter must be **VIRTKEY**. The *idvalue* is an identification value associated with the key. The *options* can be **NOINVERT**, **ALT**, **SHIFT**, or **CONTROL**. **NOINVERT** keeps a top-level menu item from being highlighted when the accelerator is used. **ALT**, **SHIFT**, and **CONTROL** activate a virtual key accelerator only when the corresponding **ALT**, **SHIFT**, or **CONTROL** key is also down.

AUTO3STATE

This statement creates an automatic three-state (checked, unchecked, or grayed) check box. It is otherwise similar to **AUTOCHECKBOX**, described next.

AUTOCHECKBOX

This statement defines an automatic check box control. Check boxes are small, rectangular controls with text next to them. An automatic check box is automatically checked when it is selected.

Syntax and Example

The syntax statement for **AUTOCHECKBOX** is

    AUTOCHECKBOX *cb_text, id, x, y, width, height* [, *style*]

An example of the **AUTOCHECKBOX** statement is

```
AUTOCHECKBOX "Option 1", 6, 15, 15, 35, 15
```

Parameters

cb_text is a string that is displayed to the right of the check box. The *id* parameter is an integer value associated with the check box. The *x* and *y* parameters are the coordinates for the left-top side of the control relative to the left-top side of the dialog box. The *width* and *height* parameters determine the size of the control. *style* can be any combination of button class styles combined with the bitwise OR operator. The default is **BS_AUTOCHECKBOX ¦ WS_TABSTOP**. See the various style tables under the **CONTROL** and **STYLE** statements.

AUTORADIOBUTTON

This statement defines an automatic radio button. This control is displayed as a small circle with a text description. When selected, the circle is highlighted and a message is sent to the parent. When next selected, the circle is returned to its normal appearance. The buttons in a set of **AUTORADIOBUTTON**s are automatically mutually exclusive.

Syntax and Example

The syntax statement for **AUTORADIOBUTTON** is

AUTORADIOBUTTON *rb_text, id, x, y, width, height* [*, style*]

An example of the **AUTORADIOBUTTON** statement is

```
AUTORADIOBUTTON "Duplex", ID_BOLD, 20, 20, 60, 70
```

Parameters

rb_text is a string that is displayed alongside the button. The *id* parameter is a unique integer value assigned to the resource. The *x* and *y* parameters are the coordinates for the left-top side of the control relative to the origin of the dialog box. The *width* and *height* parameters determine the size of the control. The *style* can be any combination of **BUTTON** class styles along with any of the following: **WS_DISABLED**, **WS_GROUP**, and **WS_TABSTOP**. The default is **BS_AUTORADIOBUTTON** and **WS_TABSTOP**. See the various style tables under the **CONTROL** and **STYLE** statements.

A

BITMAP

This statement defines a bitmap resource for use directly in an application, a menu, or a dialog box.

Syntax and Example

The syntax statement for **BITMAP** is

> *id_name* BITMAP [*loading*][*memory*] *filename*

An example of the **BITMAP** statement can be as simple as

```
mybitmap BITMAP mybitmap.bmp
```

Parameters

The *id_name* parameter is a unique ID name or integer value assigned to the resource. The *loading* option determines when the resource is actually loaded. **PRELOAD** loads the resource when the application is started. **LOADONCALL** loads the resource when needed. The *memory* option determines whether the resource remains **FIXED** in memory, is **MOVEABLE** (the default), or is **DISCARDABLE** when not needed. The *filename* can be any valid filename pointing to a file containing a bitmap resource.

CAPTION

This statement produces a title for the optional caption bar of the dialog box.

Syntax and Example

The syntax statement for **CAPTION** is

> CAPTION *text*

An example of the **CAPTION** statement is

```
CAPTION "Enter All Data"
```

Parameters

text is a normal ASCII string contained between double quotes.

CHARACTERISTICS

This statement is used to embed developer-defined information.

Syntax and Example

The syntax statement for **CHARACTERISTICS** is

> CHARACTERISTICS *value*

An example of the **CHARACTERISTICS** statement is

```
CHARACTERISTICS 99
```

Parameters

value is a double-word value.

CHARACTERISTICS may be used when specifying accelerators, dialog boxes, menus, string tables, and the **RCDATA** statement.

CHECKBOX

This statement defines a dialog check box control. Check boxes are small, rectangular controls with text next to them.

Syntax and Example

The syntax statement for **CHECKBOX** is

CHECKBOX *cb_text, id, x, y, width, height* [, *style*]

An example of the **CHECKBOX** statement is

```
CHECKBOX "Underscore", 6, 15, 15, 35, 15
```

Parameters

cb_text is a string that is displayed to the right of the check box. The *id* parameter is an integer value associated with the check box. The *x* and *y* parameters are the coordinates for the left-top side of the control relative to the left-top side of the dialog box. The *width* and *height* parameters determine the size of the control. *style* can be any combination of button class styles combined with the bitwise OR operator. The default is **BS_CHECKBOX | WS_TABSTOP**. See the various style tables under the **CONTROL** and **STYLE** statements.

CLASS

This statement defines a dialog box class. By default, a normal dialog box is created.

Syntax and Example

The syntax statement for **CLASS** is

CLASS *class_type*

A

An example of the **CLASS** statement is

```
CLASS "first_class"
```

Parameters

The *class_type* is represented by an integer or an ASCII string in double quotes. This class must be identified by the **cdWndExtra** member of the **WNDCLASS** and **WNDCLASSEX** structures and set equal to **DLGWINDOWEXTRA**. The **DefDlgProc( )** function is used to guarantee that all messages are processed.

COMBOBOX

This statement defines a combination box control. A combo box is an edit box (or static text) together with a list box. The list box can be constantly displayed or expanded by the user. If a static text box is used, it always contains the list box selection. An edit box allows the user to enter the selection. The list box then reflects, by highlighting, the entered selection.

Syntax and Example

The syntax statement for **COMBOBOX** is

COMBOBOX *id, x, y, width, height* [, *style*]

An example of the **COMBOBOX** statement is

```
COMBOBOX CB_ID, 15, 20, 100, 100, WS_VSCROLL
```

Parameters

The *id* parameter is an integer value associated with the combo box. The *x* and *y* parameters are the coordinates for the left-top side of the control relative to the left-top side of the dialog box. The *width* and *height* parameters determine the size of the control. The *style* can be any combination of **COMBOBOX** class styles combined with the bitwise OR operator. The default is **CBS_SIMPLE ¦ WS_TABSTOP**. See the various style tables under the **CONTROL** and **STYLE** statements.

CONTROL

This statement defines a control.

Syntax and Example

The syntax statement for **CONTROL** is

CONTROL *c_text*, *id*, *class*, *style*, *x*, *y*, *width*, *height*

An example using the **CONTROL** statement is

```
CONTROL "&Color", ID_COLOR, COMBOBOX, CBS_AUTOHSCROLL,
        10, 10, 100, 120
```

Parameters

c_text is a string that is associated with the control. The *id* parameter is an integer value associated with the control.

The *class* parameter gives the class type and can be one of the following values:

BUTTON
COMBOBOX
EDIT
LISTBOX
SCROLLBAR
STATIC

The class *style* can be a combination of styles bitwise ORed together. See Tables A-2 through A-7 for a list of commonly used class styles.

The *x* and *y* parameters are the coordinates for the left-top side of the control relative to the left-top side of the parent window. The *width* and *height* parameters determine the size of the control.

CTEXT

The **CTEXT** statement, exclusive to dialog boxes, produces a rectangular control with centered text. Word wrapping occurs when string length exceeds the line length.

Syntax and Example

The syntax statement for **CTEXT** is

CTEXT *c_text*, *id*, *x*, *y*, *width*, *height* [, *style*]

An example of the **CTEXT** statement is

```
CTEXT "Wild Colors", ID_WCOLORS, 20, 20, 150, 150
```

A

Style	Purpose
BS_3STATE	Creates a three-state button.
BS_AUTO3STATE	Creates an automatic three-state button.
BS_AUTOCHECKBOX	Creates an automatic check box.
BS_AUTORADIOBUTTON	Creates an automatic radio button.
BS_BITMAP	Button contains a bitmap.
BS_BOTTOM	Displays text on bottom of button.
BS_CENTER	Displays text in center of button.
BS_CHECKBOX	Creates a check box.
BS_DEFPUSHBUTTON	Creates a default push button.
BS_GROUPBOX	Creates a group box.
BS_ICON	Button contains an icon.
BS_LEFT	Left justifies text.
BS_LEFTTEXT	Places text to the left side of the control. (This style is obsolete for Windows 95. Use **BS_RIGHTBUTTON**, instead.)
BS_MULTILINE	Displays multiple lines of text.
BS_NOTIFY	Parent window receives notification messages in addition to standard button messages.
BS_OWNERDRAW	Creates an owner-drawn button.
BS_PUSHBUTTON	Creates a push button.
BS_PUSHLIKE	Button is raised when not pushed, depressed when pushed.
BS_RADIOBUTTON	Creates a radio button.
BS_RIGHT	Right justifies text.
BS_RIGHTBUTTON	Displays text to the left of a check box or radio button. (By default, text is displayed on the right.)
BS_TEXT	Button displays text.
BS_TOP	Displays text at top of button.
BS_VCENTER	Vertically centers text.

BUTTON
Class Styles
Table A-2.

Parameters

c_text specifies the text to be displayed. The *id* parameter is an integer value associated with the centered text. The *x* and *y* parameters are the coordinates for the left-top side of the control relative to the origin of the dialog box. The *width* and *height* parameters determine the size of the control. The *style* can be any combination of **SS_CENTER**, **WS_TABSTOP**, and **WS_GROUP** bitwise ORed together. The default is **CS_CENTER ¦ WS_GROUP**. See the various style tables under the **CONTROL** and **STYLE** statements.

Style	Purpose
CBS_AUTOHSCROLL	Scrolls text in an edit control to the right, automatically. Otherwise, the text string is confined to the size of the edit control.
CBS_DISABLENOSCROLL	Displays an inactive (i.e., grayed) scroll bar when the list box does not contain enough items to warrant a scroll.
CBS_DROPDOWN	Creates a drop-down list box.
CBS_DROPDOWNLIST	Creates a static text box that displays the current selection in a list box.
CBS_HASSTRINGS	Indicates that the owner-drawn combo box contains strings.
CBS_LOWERCASE	Displays all text in lowercase.
CBS_NOINTEGRALHEIGHT	Does not allow Windows to resize the combo box.
CBS_OEMCONVERT	Converts text from ANSI characters to OEM-defined characters and vice versa.
CBS_OWNERDRAWFIXED	Fixed-size, owner-drawn box.
CBS_OWNERDRAWVARIABLE	Variable-size, owner-drawn box.
CBS_SIMPLE	Standard list box.
CBS_SORT	Sorts list box strings automatically.
CBS_UPPERCASE	All text is displayed in uppercase.

COMBOBOX
Class Styles
Table A-3.

Style	Purpose
ES_AUTOHSCROLL	Automatically scrolls right.
ES_AUTOVSCROLL	Automatically scrolls up.
ES_CENTER	Centers text.
ES_LEFT	Left justifies text.
ES_LOWERCASE	Changes all text to lowercase as it is entered.
ES_MULTILINE	Creates a multiline edit control.
ES_NOHIDESEL	Prevents hiding the selection when focus is lost.
ES_NUMBER	Only digits may be entered into edit box.
ES_OEMCONVERT	Automatic conversion from ANSI to OEM character set and vice versa.
ES_PASSWORD	Conceals user-entered text. Used to input passwords.
ES_READONLY	Edit box does not allow editing.
ES_RIGHT	Right justifies text.
ES_UPPERCASE	Converts all text to uppercase as it is entered.
ES_WANTRETURN	Inserts a carriage return when ENTER is pushed. Otherwise, a default push button may be selected. Only affects multiline controls.

EDIT Class
Styles
Table A-4.

A

Style	Purpose
LBS_DISABLENOSCROLL	Displays an inactive vertical scroll bar control when the list box can hold all items (that is, when no scroll bar is needed). Without this option, no scroll bar is shown unless there are items to scroll.
LBS_EXTENDEDSEL	Permits multiple list box items to be selected.
LBS_HASSTRINGS	Indicates that an owner-drawn list box contains strings.
LBS_MULTICOLUMN	Specifies a multicolumn list box that can be scrolled horizontally.
LBS_MULTIPLESEL	Strings are selected or deselected by single or double clicks with the mouse.
LBS_NOINTEGRALHEIGHT	Does not allow Windows to resize the list box from original specifications.
LBS_NOREDRAW	Does not allow the appearance of a list box to change.
LBS_NOSEL	Items cannot be selected using a list box.
LBS_NOTIFY	When a string is selected, a message is sent to the parent window.
LBS_OWNERDRAWFIXED	Fixed-size, owner-drawn list box.
LBS_OWNERDRAWVARIABLE	Variable-size, owner-drawn list box.
LBS_SORT	List box strings are alphabetically sorted.
LBS_STANDARD	Standard (default) list box.
LBS_USETABSTOPS	Tab characters are accepted.
LBS_WANTKEYBOARDINPUT	Allows WM_VKEYTOITEM and WM_CHARTOITEM messages to be processed when a list box has focus and a key is pressed.

LISTBOX
Class Styles
Table A-5.

CURSOR

This statement defines a mouse cursor.

Syntax and Example
The syntax statement for **CURSOR** is

> *id_name* CURSOR [*loading*][*memory*] *filename*

Style	Purpose
SBS_BOTTOMALIGN	The bottom edge of the scroll bar is aligned with the bottom edge of the window.
SBS_HORZ	Specifies a horizontal scroll bar.
SBS_LEFTALIGN	The left edge of the scroll bar is aligned with the left edge of the window.
SBS_RIGHTALIGN	The right edge of the scroll bar is aligned with the right edge of the window.
SBS_SIZEBOX	Specifies a size box.
SBS_SIZEBOXBOTTOMRIGHTALIGN	Aligns the lower-right corner of the size box with the lower-right corner of the window.
SBS_SIZEBOXTOPLEFTALIGN	Aligns the upper-left corner of the size box with the upper-left corner of the window.
SBS_SIZEGRIP	Size box with raised edge.
SBS_TOPALIGN	Aligns the upper edge of the scroll bar with the upper edge of the window.
SBS_VERT	Specifies a vertical scroll bar.

SCROLLBAR
Class Styles
Table A-6.

Style	Purpose
SS_BITMAP	Control contains a bitmap.
SS_BLACKFRAME	Produces a box drawn with a frame. The frame color is determined by the Windows default color settings and is black for window frames.
SS_BLACKRECT	Produces a rectangle filled with color. The color is black in the default Windows color palette for window frames.
SS_CENTER	Text is centered within the specified rectangle.
SS_CENTERIMAGE	Text or graphics image is centered.
SS_ENHMETAFILE	Metafile image is displayed.
SS_ETCHEDFRAME	Boundaries of the static control are displayed using the **EDGE_ETCHED** style.
SS_ETCHEDHORZ	Top and bottom boundaries are displayed using the **EDGE_ETCHED** style.
SS_ETCHEDVERT	Left and right boundaries are displayed using the **EDGE_ETCHED** style.

STATIC Class
Styles
Table A-7.

A

Style	Purpose
SS_GRAYFRAME	Produces a box drawn with a frame. The frame color is determined by the Windows default color settings and is that of the screen background.
SS_GRAYRECT	Produces a rectangle filled with color. The color is gray in the default Windows color palette for screen backgrounds.
SS_ICON	Specifies an icon. The name used is the name assigned by the ICON resource statement.
SS_LEFT	Specifies a rectangle and then left justifies the given text.
SS_LEFTNOWORDWRAP	Specifies a rectangle and then left justifies the given text. Wrapping does not occur. Words extending beyond the display size are clipped.
SS_NOPREFIX	Ampersand characters (&) are ignored in text strings.
SS_NOTIFY	Parent window receives notification messages.
SS_OWNERDRAW	Owner is responsible for drawing the control.
SS_REALSIZEIMAGE	Icon and bitmap images are not resized.
SS_RIGHT	Specifies a rectangle and then right justifies the given text.
SS_RIGHTJUST	When the static control contains an icon or bitmap, only the left and top boundaries can be resized.
SS_SIMPLE	Creates a rectangle and displays a single line of left-justified string.
SS_SUNKEN	Control appears to be lower than the surface of the screen.
SS_WHITEFRAME	Produces a box drawn with a frame. The frame color is determined by the Windows default color settings and is that of the window's background.
SS_WHITERECT	Produces a rectangle filled with color. The color is white in the default Windows color palette for window backgrounds.

STATIC Class
Styles
(continued)
Table A-7.

An example of the **CURSOR** statement is

```
cursorA CURSOR "c:\\win\\mycur.cur"
```

Parameters

The *id_name* parameter is a unique ID name or integer value assigned to the resource. The *loading* option determines when the resource is actually loaded. **PRELOAD** loads the resource when the application is started. **LOADONCALL** loads the resource when needed. The *memory* option determines whether the resource remains **FIXED** in memory, is **MOVEABLE** (the default), or is **DISCARDABLE** when not needed. The *filename* can be any valid filename pointing to a file containing a cursor resource.

DEFPUSHBUTTON

This statement defines a default push button. A default push button is automatically selected when the dialog box that contains it is first activated. The default push button is a small, rectangular control containing optional text, and is drawn with a bold outline.

Syntax and Example

The syntax statement for **DEFPUSHBUTTON** is

DEFPUSHBUTTON *pb_text, id, x, y, width, height* [, *style*]

An example of the **DEFPUSHBUTTON** statement is

```
DEFPUSHBUTTON "Okay", ID_OK, 20, 20, 35, 35
```

Parameters

pb_text is a string that is displayed inside the push button. The *id* parameter is a unique ID name or integer value assigned to the resource. The *x* and *y* parameters are the coordinates for the left-top side of the control relative to the origin of the dialog box. The *width* and *height* parameters determine the size of the control. *style* can be any combination of **BS_DEFPUSHBUTTON**, **WS_TABSTOP**, **WS_GROUP**, or **WS_DISABLED** bitwise ORed together. The default is **BS_DEFPUSHBUTTON | WS_TABSTOP**. See the various style tables under the **CONTROL** and **STYLE** statements.

A

DIALOG

This statement defines a dialog box.

Syntax and Example

The syntax statement for **DIALOG** is

id_name DIALOG [*loading*][*memory*] *x, y, width, height*

A simple example of the **DIALOG** statement is

```
ShapeDiaBox DIALOG 6, 18, 160, 100
```

Parameters

The *id_name* parameter is a unique ID name or integer value assigned to the resource. The *loading* option determines when the resource is actually loaded. **PRELOAD** loads the resource when the application is started. **LOADONCALL** loads the resource when needed. The *memory* option determines whether the resource remains **FIXED** in memory, is **MOVEABLE** (the default), or is **DISCARDABLE** when not needed. The *x* and *y* parameters are the coordinates for the left-top side of the control. The *width* and *height* parameters determine the size of the control. The *style* can be any combination of styles bitwise ORed together. For example, the following styles are often combined: **DS_MODALFRAME | WS_POPUP | WS_VISIBLE | WS_CAPTION | WS_SYSMENU**. See the various style tables under the **CONTROL** and **STYLE** statements.

DIALOGEX

DIALOGEX is an extended form of the **DIALOG** statement. **DIALOGEX** also supports extended styles for dialog boxes and the controls defined within those boxes.

Syntax

The syntax statement for **DIALOGEX** is

id_name DIALOGEX [*loading*][*memory*] *x, y, width, height*
[, *IDHelp*]

Parameters

The parameters are the same as described for **DIALOG**, with the addition of *IDHelp*. *IDHelp* specifies an optional help identifier related to the dialog box.

DIALOGEX accommodates extended styles using the **EXSTYLE** command. Consult your resource compiler reference manual for further details.

EDITTEXT

This statement defines an edit box.

Syntax and Example

The syntax statement for **EDITTEXT** is

EDITTEXT *id, x, y, width, height* [*, style*]

An example of the **EDITTEXT** statement is

```
EDITTEXT IDD_UPPERX, 97, 28, 32, 12, ES_AUTOHSCROLL
```

Parameters

The *id* parameter is a unique ID name or integer value assigned to the resource. The *x* and *y* parameters are the coordinates for the left-top side of the control relative to the origin of the dialog box. The *width* and *height* parameters determine the size of the control. *style* can be any combination of styles bitwise ORed together. These include **WS_TABSTOP**, **WS_GROUP**, **WS_VSCROLL**, **WS_HSCROLL**, and **WS_DISABLE**. The default style is **ES_LEFT**, **WS_BORDER**, and **WS_TABSTOP**. See the various style tables under the **CONTROL** and **STYLE** statements.

EXSTYLE

This statement specifies extended dialog box style parameters. It is otherwise similar to **STYLE**. A list of the extended style macros can be found in the standard Windows header file **winuser.h**. (They all start with **WS_EX**.) Consult your resource compiler reference manual for further details.

FONT

This statement defines a font resource definition statement or specifies the font used to draw text in a dialog box.

Syntax and Example

The syntax statements for **FONT** are

FONT *point_size, typeface*

id_name FONT [*loading*][*memory*] *filename*

Examples of the **FONT** statement include

```
FONT  10, "Courier New"

myfont FONT PRELOAD MOVEABLE system96.fnt
```

A

Parameters

point_size is the requested point size for the font. The *typeface* choices are defined in **win.ini**. The *id_name* parameter is a unique ID name or integer value assigned to the resource. The *loading* option determines when the resource is actually loaded. **PRELOAD** loads the resource when the application is started. **LOADONCALL** loads the resource when needed. The *memory* option determines whether the resource remains **FIXED** in memory, is **MOVEABLE** (the default), or is **DISCARDABLE** when not needed.

GROUPBOX

This statement defines a group box. A group box control is a rectangle used to contain other controls.

Syntax and Example

The syntax statement for **GROUPBOX** is

    GROUPBOX *gb_text, id, x, y, width, height* [, *style*]

An example of the **GROUPBOX** statement is

```
GROUPBOX "Chart Labels", ID_CHART, 20, 20, 150, 200
```

Parameters

gb_text is a string that is displayed in the upper-left corner of the box. The *id* parameter is a unique ID name or integer value assigned to the resource. The *x* and *y* parameters are the coordinates for the left-top side of the control relative to the origin of the dialog box. The *width* and *height* parameters determine the size of the control. The *style* can be any combination of **BS_GROUPBOX**, **WS_TABSTOP**, or **WS_DISABLED** bitwise ORed together. The default is **BS_GROUPBOX**. See the various style tables under the **CONTROL** and **STYLE** statements.

ICON

This statement defines an icon control or resource.

Syntax and Example

The syntax statements for **ICON** include

    ICON *icon_name, id, x, y* [, *width, height, style*]

    id_name ICON [*loading*][*memory*] *filename*

Examples of the **ICON** control and resource include

```
ICON "graphicon", ID_ICON, 40, 50
```

```
myicon ICON MOVEABLE graph.ico
```

Parameters
In the first form, the *icon_name* parameter specifies the name of the icon. The *id* parameter is a unique ID name or integer value assigned to the resource. The *x* and *y* parameters are the coordinates for the left-top side of the control relative to the origin of the dialog box. The *width* and *height* are ignored and should be 0. The *style* can only be **SS_ICON**.

In the second form, the *id_name* parameter is a unique ID name or integer value assigned to the resource. The *loading* option determines when the resource is actually loaded. **PRELOAD** loads the resource when the application is started. **LOADONCALL** loads the resource when needed. The *memory* option determines whether the resource remains **FIXED** in memory, is **MOVEABLE** (the default), or is **DISCARDABLE** when not needed.

LISTBOX
This statement defines a list box.

Syntax and Example
The syntax statement for **LISTBOX** is

> LISTBOX *id*, *x*, *y*, *width*, *height* [, *style*]

An example of the **LISTBOX** statement is

```
LISTBOX ID_LB, 20, 20, 75, 90
```

Parameters
The *id* parameter is a unique ID name or integer value assigned to the resource. The *x* and *y* parameters are the coordinates for the left-top side of the control relative to the origin of the dialog box. The *width* and *height* parameters determine the size of the control. *style* can be any combination of the list box styles plus **WS_BORDER** and **WS_VSCROLL** bitwise ORed together. The default is **WS_BORDER | LBS_NOTIFY**. See the various style tables under the **CONTROL** and **STYLE** statements.

A

LTEXT

This statement defines a left-justified static text control.

Syntax and Example

The syntax statement for **LTEXT** is

LTEXT *l_text*, *id*, *x*, *y*, *width*, *height* [, *style*]

An example of the **LTEXT** statement is

```
LTEXT "Enter an integer", ID_INT, 20, 30, 80, 90
```

Parameters

l_text specifies the text to be displayed. The *id* parameter is a unique ID name or integer value assigned to the resource. The *x* and *y* parameters are the coordinates for the left-top side of the control relative to the origin of the dialog box. The *width* and *height* parameters determine the size of the control. *style* can be any combination of the following: **SS_LEFT**, **WS_GROUP**, and **WS_TABSTOP**. The default is **SS_LEFT ¦ WS_GROUP**. See the various style tables under the **CONTROL** and **STYLE** statements.

MENU

This statement specifies a menu for a dialog box or describes the actual contents of a menu.

Syntax and Example

The syntax statements for **MENU** are

MENU *menu_name*

id_menu MENU [*loading*][*memory*]

Examples of the **MENU** statement are

```
MENU   filemenu

AboutMenu MENU
{
  POPUP "Integer-Input"
  {
    MENUITEM "About Box...", IDM_ABOUT
  }
}
```

Parameters

The *menu_name* parameter is the name assigned to the menu or an integer value. *id_menu* is a menu identifier composed of a string of characters or an integer value. The *loading* option determines when the resource is actually loaded. **PRELOAD** loads the resource when the application is started. **LOADONCALL** loads the resource when needed. The *memory* option determines whether the resource remains **FIXED** in memory, is **MOVEABLE** (the default), or is **DISCARDABLE** when not needed.

MENUEX

MENUEX is an extended form of **MENU**. It is similar to **MENU**, but it lets you specify help identifiers for popup menus. You may also associate an identifier with a popup menu. Consult your resource compiler reference manual for additional details.

MENUITEM

This statement defines an option or choice for use in a menu.

Syntax and Example

The syntax statement for **MENUITEM** is

> MENUITEM *menu_text, result* [, *option_list*]

An example of the **MENUITEM** statement is

```
AboutMenu MENU
{
  POPUP "Integer-Input"
  {
    MENUITEM "About Box...", IDM_ABOUT
  }
}
```

A

Parameters

The *menu_text* parameter specifies the name of the menu item. The ampersand (&) character can precede a character in the text string. The effect will be that the character is underlined and the item can be selected by typing that character. You may include a tab by using **\t** or cause the text to be right-aligned by preceding it with a **\a**. The *result* parameter is an integer returned to the owner window when the menu item is selected.

option_list specifies the appearance of the menu. A **CHECKED** option places a check mark next to the menu item. A **GRAYED** option draws the menu item in a gray or light color. The **HELP** option is used to identify a help menu item. The **INACTIVE** option displays the item, but does not allow selection. The **MENUBARBREAK** option separates menu items with a vertical column. The **MENUBREAK** option places the menu item on a new line. When **MENUBREAK** is used for popup menu items, a new column is created without a vertical dividing line.

POPUP

This statement creates a popup menu.

Syntax and Example

The syntax statement for **POPUP** is

    POPUP *pu_text* [, *option_list*]

An example of the **POPUP** statement is

```
AboutMenu MENU
{
  POPUP "Integer-Input"
  {
    MENUITEM "About Box...", IDM_ABOUT
  }
}
```

Parameters

The *pu_text* string specifies the name of the menu. This is a simple string contained between double quotes. *option_list* specifies the appearance of the menu item. A **CHECKED** option places a check mark next to the menu item. A **GRAYED** option draws the menu item in a gray or light color. The **HELP** option is used to identify a help menu item. The **INACTIVE** option displays the item, but does not allow selection. The **MENUBARBREAK** option separates menu items with a vertical column. The **MENUBREAK** option places the menu item on a new line. When **MENUBREAK** is used for popup menu items, a new column is created without a vertical dividing line.

PUSHBOX and PUSHBUTTON

These statements define a push-button control. A push button is a rounded rectangle containing text that, when selected, generates a message. A push box is like a push button except that no "button" is shown—only the text is displayed.

Syntax and Example

The syntax statements for **PUSHBUTTON** and **PUSHBOX** are

PUSHBUTTON *pb_text, id, x, y, width, height* [, *style*]

PUSHBOX *pb_text, id, x, y, width, height* [, *style*]

An example of the **PUSHBUTTON** statement is

```
PUSHBUTTON "OK", ID_OK, 20, 20, 40, 40
```

Parameters

The *pb_text* string specifies the text inside the push button. The *id* parameter is a unique ID name or integer value assigned to the resource. The *x* and *y* parameters are the coordinates for the left-top side of the control relative to the origin of the dialog box. The *width* and *height* parameters determine the size of the control. *style* can be any combination of **BS_PUSHBUTTON** and any of the following: **WS_DISABLED**, **WS_GROUP**, and **WS_TABSTOP**. The default combination is **BS_PUSHBUTTON** and **WS_TABSTOP**. (A push box uses the **BS_PUSHBOX** style.) See the various style tables under the **CONTROL** and **STYLE** statements.

RADIOBUTTON

This statement defines a radio button . This control is drawn with a small circle and descriptive text. Radio buttons are mutually exclusive.

Syntax and Example

The syntax statement for **RADIOBUTTON** is

RADIOBUTTON *rb_text, id, x, y, width, height* [, *style*]

An example of the **RADIOBUTTON** statement is

```
RADIOBUTTON "Bold", ID_BOLD, 20, 20, 60 70
```

A

Parameters

The *rb_text* string specifies the text associated with the radio button. The *id* parameter is a unique ID name or integer value assigned to the resource. The *x* and *y* parameters are the coordinates for the left-top side of the control relative to the origin of the dialog box. The *width* and *height* parameters determine the size of the control. *style* can be any combination of **BUTTON** class styles along with any of the following: **WS_DISABLED**, **WS_GROUP**, and **WS_TABSTOP**. The default combination is **BS_RADIOBUTTON** and **WS_TABSTOP**. See the various style tables under the **CONTROL** and **STYLE** statements.

RCDATA

This statement creates a raw data resource.

Syntax and Example

The syntax for the **RCDATA** statement is

> *id_name* RCDATA [*loading*][*memory*]

An example of the **RCDATA** statement is

```
new_data RCDATA
{
  0x03b5,  /* hex number */
  "value", /* string */
  768      /* integer */
}
```

Parameters

id_name is a raw resource identifier composed of a string of characters or an integer value. The *loading* option determines when the resource is actually loaded. **PRELOAD** loads the resource when the application is started. **LOADONCALL** loads the resource when needed. The *memory* option determines whether the resource remains **FIXED** in memory, is **MOVEABLE** (the default), or is **DISCARDABLE** when not needed.

RTEXT

This statement defines an **RTEXT** control for dialog boxes. Text is displayed, right-justified, in the rectangular area.

Syntax and Example

The syntax statement for **RTEXT** is

RTEXT *r_text, id, x, y, width, height* [, *style*]

An example of the **RTEXT** statement is

```
RTEXT "Enter a string", ID_STR, 25, 35, 85, 95
```

Parameters

The *r_text* string specifies the text to be displayed. The *id* parameter is a unique ID name or integer value assigned to the resource. The *x* and *y* parameters are the coordinates for the left-top side of the control relative to the origin of the dialog box. The *width* and *height* parameters determine the size of the control. *style* can be any combination of the following: **SS_RIGHT**, **WS_GROUP**, and **WS_TABSTOP**. The default is **SS_RIGHT** **WS_GROUP**. See the various style tables under the **CONTROL** and **STYLE** statements.

SCROLLBAR

This statement defines a scroll bar. Scroll bars are used to scroll the window horizontally or vertically. Scroll bars are manually managed resources.

Syntax and Example

The syntax statement for **SCROLLBAR** is

SCROLLBAR *id, x, y, width, height* [, *style*]

An example of the **SCROLLBAR** statement is

```
SCROLLBAR ID_SCROLL, 100, 200, 20, 200
```

A

Parameters

The *id* parameter is a unique ID name or integer value assigned to the resource. The *x* and *y* parameters are the coordinates for the left-top side of the control relative to the origin of the dialog box. The *width* and *height* parameters determine the size of the control. *style* can include any combination of the following: **WS_DISABLED**, **WS_GROUP**, and **WS_TABSTOP**. The default is **SBS_HORZ**. See the various style tables under the **CONTROL** and **STYLE** statements.

STATE3

This statement produces a three-state (checked, unchecked, or grayed) check box. It is syntactically similar to **CHECKBOX**. Refer to **CHECKBOX** for details.

STRINGTABLE

This statement defines string resources. These null-terminated strings are typically loaded by an application as needed.

Syntax and Example

The syntax statement for **STRINGTABLE** is

STRINGTABLE [*loading*][*memory*]

An example of the **STRINGTABLE** statement is

```
STRINGTABLE   PRELOAD MOVEABLE
{
  IDS_MESS1,    "Warning!"
  IDS_MESS2,    "Safe!"
  IDS_MESS3,    "End Operation"
}
```

Parameters

The *loading* option determines when the resource is actually loaded. **PRELOAD** loads the resource when the application is started. **LOADONCALL** loads the resource when needed. The *memory* option determines whether the resource remains **FIXED** in memory, is **MOVEABLE** (the default), or is **DISCARDABLE** when not needed.

STYLE

This statement defines either a popup or child window style for a dialog box.

Syntax

The syntax statement for **STYLE** is

STYLE *style*

Parameters

The default style for a dialog box is **WS_POPUP**, **WS_BORDER**, and **WS_SYSMENU**, but values from Table A-8 can also be selected.

Style	Purpose
DS_LOCALEDIT	Data segment memory will be used by edit controls used in dialog boxes. (Obsolete for Windows 95.)
DS_MODALFRAME	Draws a dialog box with a modal frame.
DS_NOIDLEMSG	Eliminates the WM_ENTERIDLE message normally sent to the dialog box owner when the dialog box is displayed.
DS_SYSMODAL	Draws a system-modal dialog box.
WS_BORDER	Draws a window with a border.
WS_CAPTION	Draws a window with a caption if a title bar is present.
WS_CHILD	Draws a child window instead of a popup window.
WS_CHILDWINDOW	Draws a child window with the WS_CHILD style.
WS_CLIPCHILDREN	Will not permit drawing in the child window when drawing in the parent.
WS_CLIPSIBLINGS	When one child window is repainted, other child windows are not affected.
WS_DISABLED	Creates a disabled window.
WS_DLGFRAME	Draws a window with a modal dialog box frame. (No title is present.)
WS_GROUP	Specifies the first control in a group of controls.
WS_HSCROLL	Window includes a horizontal scroll bar.
WS_ICONIC	Initially draws a window in its minimized form.
WS_MAXIMIZED	Initially draws a window in its maximized form.
WS_MAXIMIZEBOX	Window includes a maximize box in the upper-right corner.
WS_MINIMIZE	Initially draws a window in its minimized form.
WS_MINIMIZEBOX	Window includes a minimize box in the upper-right corner.
WS_OVERLAPPED	Draws an overlapped window with a border and caption.
WS_OVERLAPPED WINDOW	Draws an overlapped window with the following styles combined: WS_OVERLAPPED WS_SYSMENU WS_CAPTION WS_THICKFRAME WS_MINIMIZEBOX WS_MAXIMIZEBOX

Commonly
Used Style
Values
Table A-8.

A

Style	Purpose
WS_POPUP	Creates a popup window instead of a child window.
WS_POPUPWINDOW	Creates a popup window with the following styles combined: WS_BORDER WS_POPUP WS_SYSMENU
WS_SIZEBOX	Window includes a size box in the upper-right corner.
WS_SYSMENU	Window includes a system menu box in the upper-left corner.
WS_TABSTOP	Specifies controls that can be selected with the TAB key.
WS_THICKFRAME	Draws a window with a thick frame. Thick frames are used to size windows.
WS_VISIBLE	Draws a visible window.

Commonly
Used Style
Values
(continued)
Table A-8.

User-Defined

This statement defines user-defined resources. User-defined statements contain application-specific data and can be in any format, even raw data.

Syntax and Example
The syntax statement for user-defined resources is

id_name id_type [*loading*][*memory*] *filename*

An example of the user-defined resource is

```
ID_UDR   MYRES
{
  0x03b5      /* hex number */
  "value"     /* string */
  768         /* integer */
}
```

Parameters
The *id_name* parameter is a resource name or integer identification number. *id_type* specifies the resource type. (Integer values used for this *id_type* must be greater than 255.) The *loading* option determines when the resource is actually loaded. **PRELOAD** loads the resource when the application is

started. **LOADONCALL** loads the resource when needed. The *memory* option determines whether the resource remains **FIXED** in memory, is **MOVEABLE** (the default), or is **DISCARDABLE** when not needed.

VERSION

This statement is used by developers to embed version information about a resource.

Syntax
The syntax statement for **VERSION** is

VERSION *value*

Parameters
value is a developer-defined, double-word value.

VERSION may be used when specifying accelerators, dialog boxes, menus, string tables, and the **RCDATA** statement.

VERSIONINFO

This statement defines a version information resource. Its use will generally be defined by the project leader or chief architect of an application. It is most often used to provide information to program installation utilities. As such, this command is not used in day-to-day programming.

A

Appendix B

A Few Words About OLE 2

Windows 95 provides support for one very important API subsystem: OLE 2. OLE stands for *object linking and embedding*. In the broadest sense, OLE is a form of interprocess communication. Specifically, it allows one application to link or embed information created by another application. When this is done, a *compound document* is created. While OLE version 1.0 was devised in 1991, it was seldom used. However, with the advent of OLE 2, the number of OLE-compatible applications is expected to increase substantially.

The most important thing you need to understand about OLE 2 is that it is more than just an improved version of OLE 1. OLE version 1 was designed specifically to support the linking and embedding of objects; OLE 2 is designed to support the creation of extensible applications. While part of the extensibility of an application is linking and embedding, OLE 2 goes far beyond these two operations.

OLE 2 is a very large, complex subsystem. It uses an object-oriented approach to interprocess communication. Also, it innovates a new method by which one process accesses another. To program for OLE 2 requires substantial programming expertise and experience, and a complete description of OLE 2 would require a very large book. Even a brief technical overview runs several hundred pages. For these reasons, a discussion of OLE 2 is not included in this book. However, since OLE 2 is likely to become an important part of the Windows 95 programming environment, the brief discussion in this appendix will give you a handle on this important but difficult topic.

Note: This appendix is designed only to provide you with a "jump start" to OLE 2 programming. To program using OLE 2, you will need to invest substantial time and effort. You will also need to have available to you a set of OLE 2 reference guides.

What Is Linking and Embedding?

Since linking and embedding are at the core of OLE 2, it is important that you understand what these two terms mean.

A compound document may include two types of objects: *linked* and *embedded*. When an object is linked, the compound document contains a reference (i.e., *link*) to the object, but the object itself is not actually stored in the document. When an object is embedded, the object itself becomes part of the compound document. Each method has advantages and disadvantages.

The main advantage of object linking is that the linked object may be changed by another application (generally the one that created it), and these changes will automatically be reflected in your compound document. Put differently, a linked object always ensures that your document will contain the latest version of the object. A secondary advantage is that the size of the compound document will be smaller than it would be if the object were embedded, because only a link to the object (not the object itself) is contained in the document. The principal disadvantage of object linking is that the object is not fixed in your compound document. For example, if you inadvertently change a linked object, it will also be changed within any document to which it is linked.

The advantage of embedded objects is that they are contained within the compound document. Thus, if your document contains only embedded objects, it can be transmitted to another computer and still contain all of its information. The disadvantage of embedded objects is that the size of the compound document will be larger, because it actually contains the object.

The Component Object Model

OLE 2 is based on the *component object model*. This model defines the way OLE 2–compatible applications interact with each other. Specifically, it defines (among other things) interfaces, memory management, interprocess communication, and dynamic loading of a required object. However, the single most important thing that you need to understand about OLE 2 (and its most fundamental design attribute) is that it uses standard interfaces that all OLE 2 applications must have. It is through these interfaces that one application communicates with another.

In OLE 2 there are two types of applications: *containers* and *servers*. In the simplest sense, a container is an application that requires data, and a server is an application that supplies data. A container is a compound document. Another term for container is *client*; another term for server is *object*. The way that a container and server communicate is through the interfaces defined by the component object model.

OLE 2 Interfaces

All OLE 2–compatible applications maintain an interface that every other OLE 2–compatible application may use to establish communication. While there are several interfaces defined by OLE 2, all OLE 2–compatible programs will have the one called **IUnknown**. Using the functionality provided in **IUnknown**, one application can find out what other interfaces are available in another application. While the technical details are far beyond the scope of this appendix, it is important that you understand in general what an OLE 2 interface is and how one program accesses another through it.

Each interface consists of a table of function pointers. These pointers point to the functions that comprise the interface. When a container seeks communication with a server, it obtains a pointer to the server's interface table. The container may then access the functions provided by the server through the function pointer table.

Since OLE 2 defines many types of interfaces, you might be wondering how a client application knows what interfaces are available in the server. The

B

answer is **QueryInterface( )**, a function provided by the **IUnknown** interface. Using **QueryInterface( )**, one application can find out what other interfaces are available in another application and obtain a pointer to them.

OLE Automation

Another aspect of OLE 2 is called OLE automation. Using OLE automation, it is possible for one application to access, control, and manipulate another application's objects. OLE automation is designed to allow the creation of sophisticated system-wide tools that have access to the functionality of the various applications contained within the system. OLE automation is at the frontier of Windows programming.

Is OLE 2 the Future of Windows?

Although OLE was initially designed only to support object linking and embedding, OLE 2 has dramatically expanded its role. The interface model defined by OLE 2 has applications far beyond linking and embedding. Also, OLE automation opens the way to an entirely new class of application programs. Most importantly, the concepts in OLE 2 present an alternative, object-oriented way to view the entire Windows environment. Although it will be a few years before the effects of OLE 2 are known, it is safe to say that OLE 2 will be an important part of Windows programming well into the next century.

Index

C

T

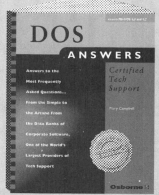
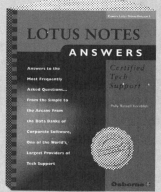
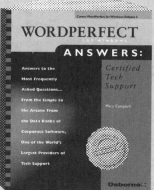

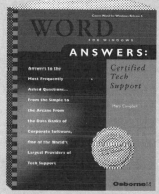
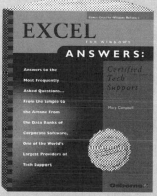

Revolutionary Information on the Information REVOLUTION

Alluring opportunities abound for the global investor. But avoiding investment land mines can be tricky business. The first release in the Business Week Library of Computing lets you master all the winning strategies. Everything is here—from analyzing and selecting the best companies, to tax planning, using investment software tools, and more. Disks include MetaStock, Windows On WallStreet, and Telescan, the leading investment analysis software.

The Business Week Guide to Global Investments Using Electronic Tools
by Robert Schwabach
Includes Three 3.5-Inch Disks
$39.95 U.S.A. ISBN: 0-07-882055-3

The Business Week Guide to Multimedia Presentations Create Dynamic Presentations That Inspire
by Robert Lindstrom
Includes One CD-ROM
$39.95 U.S.A.
ISBN: 0-07-882057-X

The Internet Yellow Pages
by Harley Hahn and Rick Stout
$27.95 U.S.A.
ISBN: 0-07-882023-5

BYTE's Mac Programmer's Cookbook
by Rob Terrell
Includes
One 3.5-Inch Disk
$29.95 U.S.A.
ISBN: 0-07-882062-6

Multimedia: Making It Work, Second Edition
by Tay Vaughan
Includes
One CD-ROM
$34.95 U.S.A.
ISBN: 0-07-882035-9

Learn From The CLASSICS

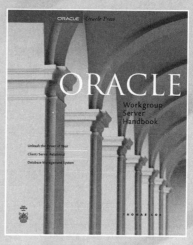

ORACLE DBA HANDBOOK

by Kevin Loney
Every DBA can learn to manage a networked Oracle database efficiently and effectively with this comprehensive guide. Oracle Magazine columnist Kevin Loney covers everything a DBA needs to manage Oracle, from architecture to layout considerations to supporting packages. A command reference and configuration guidelines are included as well as scripts and tips. The **Oracle DBA Handbook** is the ideal support and resource for all new and existing DBAs.

Price: $34.95
Available September 1994
ISBN: 0-07-881182-1
Pages: 608, paperback

TUNING ORACLE

by Michael J. Corey, Michael Abbey, and Daniel J. Dechichio, Jr.
Learn to customize Oracle for optimal performance and productivity with this focused guide. Michael Corey, president of the International Oracle Users Group, and Michael Abbey and Daniel Dechichio, recognized Oracle experts, teach strategies and systems to help administrators avoid problems, increase database speed, and ensure overall security. For a powerful and versatile database, **Tuning Oracle** is your ultimate resource for making Oracle reach its full potential.

Price: $29.95 U.S.A.
Available November, 1994
ISBN: 0-07-881181-3
Pages: 544, paperback

ORACLE WORKGROUP SERVER HANDBOOK

by Thomas B. Cox
Take full advantage of the power and flexibility of the new Oracle Workgroup Server with this comprehensive handbook. Thomas Cox helps users master the intricacies of this relational database management system, including creating a database, developing queries, and using SQL as well as explaining and defining declarations, referential integrity, and more. Perfect for both users and administrators, the **Oracle Workgroup Server Handbook** is the one authoriative book.

Price: $34.95
Available October 1994
ISBN: 0-07-881186-4
Pages: 448, paperback

 **Oracle Press**

Driving Your Information Systems for Optimal Performance

BC640SL

LOTUS NOTES

ANSWERS:

Certified Tech Support

Polly Kornblith

From the Data
Banks of Corporate
Software, One of
the World's Largest
Providers of
Tech Support,
Answers to the Most
Frequently Asked
Questions... From
the Simple to
the Arcane.

Osborne

Lotus Notes Answers: Certified Tech Support
by Polly Russell Kornblith
$16.95 U.S.A.
ISBN: 0-07-882055-3

Think Fast
PASSING
LANE AHEAD

What's the quickest route to tech support? Osborne's new Certified Tech Support series. Developed in conjunction with Corporate Software Inc., one of the largest providers of tech support fielding more than 200,000 calls a month, Osborne delivers the most authoritative question and answer books available anywhere. Speed up your computing and stay in the lead with answers to the most frequently asked end-user questions—from the simple to the arcane. And watch for more books in the series.

YELLOW PAGES

The Internet Yellow Pages
by Harley Hahn
and Rick Stout
$27.95 U.S.A.
ISBN: 0-07-882023-5

Sound Blaster: The Official Book, Second Edition
by Peter M. Ridge,
David Golden, Ivan Luk,
Scott Sindorf, and
Richard Heimlich
Includes One 3.5-Inch Disk
$34.95 U.S.A.
ISBN: 0-07-882000-6

Osborne Windows Programming Series
by Herbert Schildt,
Chris H. Pappas, and
William H. Murray, III
Vol. I - Programming Fundamentals
$39.95 U.S.A.
ISBN: 0-07-881990-3
Vol. 2 - General Purpose API Functions
$49.95 U.S.A.
ISBN: 0-07-881991-1
Vol. 3 - Special Purpose API Functions
$49.95 U.S.A.
ISBN: 0-07-881992-X

The Microsoft Access Handbook
by Mary Campbell
$27.95 U.S.A.
ISBN: 0-07-882014-6

BC640SL

ORDER BOOKS DIRECTLY FROM OSBORNE/McGRAW-HILL

For a complete catalog of Osborne's books, call 510-549-6600 or write to us at 2600 Tenth Street, Berkeley, CA 94710

☎ **Call Toll-Free:** *1-800-822-8158*
24 hours a day, 7 days a week in U.S. and Canada

✉ **Mail this order form to:**
McGraw-Hill, Inc.
Customer Service Dept.
P.O. Box 547
Blacklick, OH 43004

🖨 **Fax this order form to:**
1-614-759-3644

💻 **EMAIL**
7007.1531@COMPUSERVE.COM
COMPUSERVE GO MH

Ship to:

Name _____

Company _____

Address _____

City / State / Zip _____

Daytime Telephone: _____
(We'll contact you if there's a question about your order.)

ISBN #	BOOK TITLE	Quantity	Price	Total
0-07-88				
0-07-88				
0-07-88				
0-07-88				
0-07-88				
0-07088				
0-07-88				
0-07-88				
0-07-88				
0-07-88				
0-07-88				
0-07-88				
0-07-88				
0-07-88				

Shipping & Handling Charge from Chart Below

Subtotal

Please Add Applicable State & Local Sales Tax

TOTAL

Shipping & Handling Charges

Order Amount	U.S.	Outside U.S.
Less than $15	$3.50	$5.50
$15.00 - $24.99	$4.00	$6.00
$25.00 - $49.99	$5.00	$7.00
$50.00 - $74.99	$6.00	$8.00
$75.00 - and up	$7.00	$9.00

Occasionally we allow other selected companies to use our mailing list. If you would prefer that we not include you in these extra mailings, please check here: ☐

METHOD OF PAYMENT

☐ Check or money order enclosed (payable to Osborne/McGraw-Hill)

☐ AMERICAN EXPRESS   ☐ DISCOVER   ☐ MasterCard   ☐ VISA

Account No. ☐☐☐☐☐☐☐☐☐☐☐☐☐☐☐

Expiration Date _____

Signature _____

In a hurry? Call 1-800-822-8158 anytime, day or night, or visit your local bookstore.

Thank you for your order   Code BC640SL